Alien Intrusion

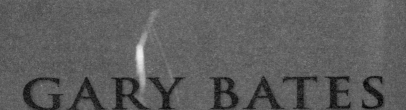

GARY BATES

Master
Books

First printing: December 2004
Second printing: February 2005

ISBN: 0-89051-435-6
Library of Congress Number: 2004118184

All Scripture is from the New International Version of the Bible unless specified otherwise.

Printed in the United States of America

Please visit our website for other great titles:
www.masterbooks.net

For information regarding author interviews,
please contact the publicity department at (870) 438-5288.

Dedicated to
my father and mother
for a lifetime of love and support

ACKNOWLEDGMENTS

Grateful thanks go to Frances, my wife and life partner who critiqued the first drafts. To my longsuffering family who probably thought I really had been abducted by aliens during the long hours I disappeared in front of my home computer — I love you guys. To Dr. Carl Wieland, thank you for your faith, friendship, encouragement, editing, and continual sharpening. To co-editor Mike Matthews, what can I say except, "You're a legend, mate!" I am indebted to many reviewers, editors, helpers, and guidance counselors, at various stages of production. They are: Brendon O'Loughlin, Steve Cardno, Kym Holwerda, Dr. Jonathan Sarfati, Philip Bell, Dr. John Hartnett, and Alex Williams. Thanks also to Ronald Story and Joe Jordan for your assistance.

CONTENTS

Why Would a Cosmologist Care about UFOs?

By Dr. John G. Hartnett

Dr. Hartnett received his Ph.D. in physics, with distinction, from the University of Western Australia, where he currently teaches and is a research fellow. At the time of writing, he is a collaborator in developing ultra-precise technology for atomic clocks that will be used on board the International Space Station. His other research includes ultra–low-noise radar; tests of fundamental theories of physics, such as general relativity; and measurement of drift in fundamental constants and their cosmological implications. He has published more than 40 papers in scientific journals and holds two patents.

First of all, I love a good mystery.

Second, science does not have all the answers.

Even though I am a cosmologist at a leading university in Australia, and I do extensive research on fundamental theories of physics and measurement of the time dependence of so-called "constants," I know that there are many mysteries which cannot be solved with simple experiments.

UFOs are one of the biggest mysteries of our time — indeed, of all time — attracting literally millions of believers (and quite a few skeptics). "What are UFOs?" is a question virtually everyone has asked at one time or another. Many have already made up their minds on the subject. However, rather than dismiss the whole debate out of hand, any open-minded person should at least weigh *all* the evidence before reaching a conclusion. Why reject the possibility of UFOs, unless you have some preconceived notion that you're afraid to see threatened?

The study of UFOs offers a wealth of valuable lessons — far beyond telling us whether aliens really crashed at Roswell. The study of this one wildly popular topic unveils many broader truths about human nature, life, and the supernatural. Besides, Gary's book is fun to read, and it touches on all sorts of related popular topics — science fiction, famous films, government cover-ups, hoaxes, serious research, and even the most ancient and increasingly popular "source" about alien invaders, the Hebrew Scriptures, popularized by Erich von Däniken's *Chariots of the Gods,* among others.

The study of extraterrestrial life also raises the question, "How did our universe come to be?" That's the question that I'm spending my life studying. (Scientists who study the origin, history, and structure of the universe [*cosmos*] are called cosmologists.) Nearly all modern cosmologists believe that everything was kick-started by a big bang about 15 billion years ago, and all the life in the universe evolved through natural processes. But I've discovered that such known "facts" — just like the study of UFOs — are not always as clear-cut as we've been led to believe, and "where we came from" directly relates to the subject of aliens and UFOs investigated in this captivating book.

Nearly 100 years since Einstein's theories were published, the origin and structure of the universe still eludes cosmologists. New cosmological theories are rife today, more than ever before. In fact, they are getting more "exotic" all the time, creating some bizarre paradoxes, opening the door to all sorts of different beliefs.

You may have heard a host of different explanations for UFOs, but Gary's book provides some eye-opening research that forces the reader to rethink his assumptions about what is true. The book was extremely interesting and profitable for me, and I trust that you'll find the book just as intriguing (and entertaining). Whether or not you agree with Gary's conclusions, you'll never see the topic in the same light again.

Be prepared to have your own assumptions about this world — and the cosmos — challenged. What we "see" is not always as it seems!

Why Write Yet Another Book on UFOs?

So much has already been written and claimed about the "UFO phenomenon." Where do they come from; what is their purpose; can they tell us where *we* came from? With so many claimed visitations and experiences, one would think that all the questions would have been answered by now. However, the questions show no sign of abating. Quite the opposite.

The growing popularity of UFOs may surprise you, if you have never bothered to take a deeper look. Is it possible that UFOs don't gain as much publicity as they used to, because the idea that "aliens are with us" has become more mainstream? Just ask a few teenagers, and several of them will tell you that they believe aliens exist and may have been humankind's original creators.

As a young person, my own love of science fiction and alien worlds shaped my view of my place in the universe. Looking back, I can now see that the things I believed to be true were so because I *desired* them to be true. However, even then, I wrestled with the true nature of aliens and the apparent contradictions of the UFO phenomenon. Today, I have become aware that this "wrestling with the contradictions" is common among other serious researchers and ordinary people alike.

I have written this book out of a genuine desire to understand the truth about this phenomenon, and I have tried to assess the evidence as objectively as possible. Although at times I may disagree with other researchers, I have a great respect and compassion for the people who have been caught up in alien phenomena, sometimes with very distressing consequences, as you will see. After all, how would you deal with someone who genuinely believes that they are regularly visited by aliens, and who now claims to be on a mission of peace for them? Or the person whose self-esteem and character has been forever altered as a result of the belief that they underwent brutal medical examinations aboard a spaceship? Then there are the reports of millions of ordinary people who have allegedly seen UFOs in the sky, performing aerial acrobatics that defy logic.

I trust that, after you examine the best evidence available on the major incidents and key issues related to UFOs, you will reach a confident and satisfying conclusion.

Chapter One

The Invasion Gets Underway

A modern phenomenon

The Martians are coming! On a nationally syndicated radio show, a reporter from Intercontinental Radio News interrupts the scheduled broadcast to report that astronomers have detected enormous blue flames shooting up from the surface of Mars.

Once again, the reporter interjects to advise that a small meteor has impacted on a farm near Grover's Mill, New Jersey. The radio show then cuts to live, on-site reporter Carl Phillips, who comments that this is a very strange meteor indeed. The top is screwing off! What is happening — could this be a spaceship? The shock and horror of this unbelievable situation is conveyed in Phillips's almost hysterical tone:

> A humped shape is rising out of the pit. I can make out a small beam of light against a mirror. What's that? There's a jet of flame springing from the mirror, and it leaps right at the advancing men. It strikes them head on! Good Lord, they're turning into flame! Now the whole field's caught fire. The woods . . . the barns . . . the gas tanks of automobiles . . . it's spreading everywhere. It's coming this way. About 20 yards to my right. . . .

A short silence. Then an announcer resumes:

> Ladies and gentlemen, I have just been handed a message that came in from Grover's Mill by telephone. Just one moment please. At least 40 people, including six state troopers, lie dead in a field east of the village of Grover's Mill, their bodies burned and distorted beyond all possible recognition.

The creature — a Martian — simply slips back into his machine, and reappears controlling a huge three-legged vehicle armed with a death ray, which effortlessly disposes of 7,000 armed soldiers.

The Secretary of the Interior then addresses the nation:

> Citizens of the nation. I shall not try to conceal the gravity of the situation that confronts the country, nor the concern of your government in protecting the lives and property of its people. . . . We must continue the performance of our duties, each and every one of us, so that we may confront this destructive adversary with a nation united, courageous, and consecrated to the preservation of human supremacy on this earth.[1]

The government was powerless. Or at least that's what millions of Americans believed — but it was a hoax. The date was October 30, 1938.

Panic

This event is now bookmarked in the pages of modern history, and is still talked about today. At the time, mass hysteria ensued all over the country. People fled their homes and took up arms to defend themselves. Thousands called the police, and even the National Guard was mobilized. The switchboard of the *New York Times* was jammed. One caller asked, "What time will it be the end of the world?"[2]

Yet all of this was triggered by a fictional radio show. Note — *radio*. Listeners did not have the modern-day

Photo courtesy of Library of Congress

Orson Welles

visual "benefits" of Hollywood special effects. Their imaginations sufficed. It was simply a play being broadcast by the world-renowned actor Orson Welles. His troupe aired a weekly show known as "The Mercury Theater," but on this particular week, and in honor of Halloween, they decided to reproduce a real-time version of science fiction novelist H.G. Wells's *War of the Worlds* — about a Martian invasion of the earth. The play was meant to resemble an authentic news broadcast, and although an announcement explained this at the beginning of the show, the next disclaimer was not made for another 40 minutes.

What prompted such a reaction? After all, it's not as if the country was awash with UFO sightings, like today. There were no rocket ships, and jet aircraft had not been invented yet. What could inspire people to so easily believe in an invasion from Mars? Many years before, amateur astronomer Percival Lowell claimed, in his book *Mars and Its Canals,* that ancient civilizations had created canals on Mars. Since the publication of that book, many people had begun to ponder the question of life on Mars.

A sighting at San Francisco, California, Oct. 10, 1956

In spite of the complete absence of hard evidence to support the notion that beings might exist on other planets, people readily believed. They also presumed that this alien race had advanced technologies. In effect, the modern phenomenon of UFOs (unidentified flying objects) had landed! The alien invasion had begun — at least in the minds of the masses.

The power to influence

The broadcast took place at a time when global tensions were escalating. The prospect of another world war was looming, and it was commonplace for radio shows to be interrupted with news of Nazi Germany's latest threats. The modern technological age had also arrived, with its potential for mass destruction, as the world first witnessed during the unparalleled slaughter of the Great War. But more importantly, mass media had arrived. One broadcast could reach a whole nation and convince the population of something that was not real. Some years later, the *War of the Worlds* was also broadcast in Santiago, Chile, in 1944 and Quito, Ecuador, in 1949, creating similar widespread panic. It seems that the general public, now becoming reliant on mass media, could be fooled time and time again.

Dorothy Thompson, in the *New York Tribune,* writes:

> All unwittingly, Mr. Orson Welles and "The Mercury Theater of the Air" have made one of the most fascinating and important demonstrations of all time. They have proved that a few effective voices, accompanied by sound effects, can convince masses of people of a totally unrealistic, completely fantastic proposition as to create a nationwide panic. They have demonstrated more potently than any argument, demonstrated beyond a question of a doubt, the appalling dangers and enormous effectiveness of popular and theatrical demagoguery. . . .[3]

Orson Welles had gained more publicity than he could have purchased for millions of dollars. Even today, the mere mention of his name evokes memories of one of the most notorious media stunts the world has seen. He had demonstrated how the media could alter public perception with little effort.

Today, many media-savvy UFO cults realize that the quickest way to catch the public's attention is to make some way-out speculative claim about being whisked away in a flying saucer and meeting Jesus on another planet. Blend science fiction and belief (in the guise of religion) and you will get noticed. Ronald Story, editor of *The Mammoth Encyclopedia of Extraterrestrial Encounters*, observes:

> . . . science fiction has become our myth, and science has become our religion. Due mainly to media influences and a hideously complicated world, most people are finding it increasingly difficult to distinguish fantasy from reality.[4]

The Raelians, for example, is a UFO cult that was little known a few years ago but now claims to have over 55,000 devotees. In early 2003, they claimed to have successfully delivered the world's first human-cloned baby via Clonaid, a company founded by the sect's leader, Claude Vorilhon — a.k.a. Rael. The Raelians claim that extraterrestrials created human beings through cloning when they arrived on the earth 25,000 years ago in flying saucers. After throwing in human cloning (a controversial subject in its own right), the Raelians have succeeded in widely promoting their brand of extraterrestrial religion. When discussing the so-called achievements of Clonaid's head scientist, Brigitte Boisselier, Rael reportedly said:

> If it's not true, she's also making history with one of the biggest hoaxes in history, so in both ways it's wonderful. Because thanks to what she is doing now, the whole world knows about the Raelian movement. I am very happy with that.[5]

It was estimated that the Raelian sect received over $500 million worth of media coverage around the world. Rael adds, "This event saved me 20 years of work."[6]

And as we shall see, we now live in an age where, more than ever before, UFO/extraterrestrial beliefs are no longer the specialty of science fiction writers. They have become mainstream.

The events of 1938 all occurred before the advent of modern special effects and technology that nowadays blend science fiction imagery into reality. These have given a major impetus to the modern upsurge of belief in UFOs and extraterrestrial life. The most popular entertainment genre in the world today is science fiction. It has become a modern obsession, and as Dorothy Thompson already noted, the media can influence the mindset of the masses and at the same time cater to the hunger for such wizardry.

All this may seem to dismiss the whole "alien phenomenon" as the over-active imagination of science fiction buffs and money-seeking, religious UFO "nut cases." But although the influence of science fiction is clear, it is not the sole reason for increased belief in alien visitations. There are millions of people who, like me, love science fiction. Many of its devotees have vastly different world views — some believe in UFOs and some don't.

But the UFO interest does appear to be satisfying more than just idle curiosity for the mysterious, or hunger for intrigue. There are deeper philosophical questions, like the meaning of our existence, for which most people want answers. And although most don't realize it, their interest is born out of a religious need or desire. In the German magazine *Focus,* sociologist Gerald Eberlein is quoted as saying:

> . . . research has shown that people who are not affiliated with any church, but who claim they are religious are

particularly susceptible to the possible existence of extraterrestrials. For them, UFOlogy [the study of UFOs] is a substitute religion.[7]

This religious longing also suggests one reason that the modern
UFO movement is entwined with traditional religious beliefs and, as
we shall see, particularly Christianity and the Bible. Ronald Story put
forward this cogent reason for the rapid acceptance of UFO beliefs:
people have always been influenced by authority figures, he says; in earlier times the clergy's opinions held sway, influencing the way in which
people sought to satisfy their spiritual needs. He writes:

> Unlike earlier times, today we look to science for answers
> for most of our questions about life in the universe. The world
> has become more materialistic than spiritualistic, and so our
> spiritual needs go largely unmet.[8]

*Are we really alone? What is the meaning of our existence? Can ET
help us?* We shall attempt to answer these questions in this book as we
examine the best evidence at our disposal.

Let the fun begin!

Not many years ago, to claim you had seen a UFO would have
caused your friends to look at you strangely. Now, almost every day,
somewhere in the world there are reports of UFOs. The majority, it is
claimed, can be explained away as merely natural phenomena (swamp
gas, the planet Venus, etc.). However, there is a stubborn residue of
cases (usually between 2 and 5 percent) that are not easily explained. It
should be pointed out that the lack of a natural explanation does not
mean that one may not eventually arise, if we had access to all of the
facts. And just because the sightings cannot be explained as naturally
occurring phenomena, it does not necessarily follow that they are of
alien spaceships.

Nonetheless, people seem *eager* to believe that aliens exist, despite
the lack of hard evidence and the huge number of proven frauds and
hoaxes. Numerous polls (Gallup, Roper, PBS/Nova) claim, for example, that up to 20 million Americans have seen a UFO. And shocking-
ly, over 4 million even claim to have been physically abducted by aliens
(we will discuss the evidence for these claims later, as with all the other
questions raised in the early chapters of this book). But as we shall see,

there are bizarre aspects to many such "alien encounter" experiences, which defy naturalistic explanations. Much serious scientific research has been undertaken to explain this phenomenon.

Can such a large percentage of the population all be given to "flights of fancy" or be delusional? Most of us would tend to think, "There are too many reports for something *not* to be going on," and that it's a case of "Where there's smoke, there's fire." A closer look will reveal that there is indeed something going on.

Back in 1947, a Gallup poll suggested that the majority of Americans did not think UFOs were alien craft. William Alnor, in his book *UFOs in the New Age,* quotes research that suggested most people thought ". . . they were illusions, hoaxes, secret weapons, or phenomena that could not be explained."[9]

That was also the year that, in the opinion of skeptics and UFOlogists alike, the modern UFO era began. People's perceptions were altered by a rash of sightings that ignited modern UFOlogy.

In June of that year, Seattle businessman Kenneth Arnold was piloting his private plane over the Cascade Mountains, Washington, when he saw something unusual. The next day, the *East Oregonian* (Oregon) newspaper reportedly carried this story:

> He said he sighted nine saucer-like aircraft flying in formation at 3 p.m. yesterday, extremely bright — as if they were nickel plated — and flying at an immense rate of speed. He estimated they were at an altitude between 9,500 and 10,000 feet and clocked them from Mt. Rainier to Mt. Adams, arriving at the amazing speed of about 1,200 miles an hour. "It seemed impossible," he said, "but there it is — I must believe my eyes."[10]

He described the craft as "saucer-like" because he claimed that they moved like "saucers that skipped across the water," giving rise to the term "flying saucers." This captured the public imagination. By the end of 1947, more than 850 sightings were reported in the media. Can we explain this surge as people now scanning the skies in anticipation of a sighting, or was there a genuine escalation in UFO activity? Approximately 150 of these sightings later made their way into the files of the U.S. military's infamous Project Blue Book.[11] This was also the year of the legendary "Roswell incident," when an alleged alien craft crash-landed in New Mexico and the U.S. Air Force supposedly retrieved alien bodies from the wreckage (this incident is discussed in depth later in this book). Shortly after this rash of sightings, the U.S. government responded by assembling an investigation team to uncover the truth about UFOs. Originally designed to appease the public's increasing fascination, the official investigations into the UFO phenomenon, code named Projects Sign and Grudge, and subsequently Project Blue Book, ran for over 20 years. (Project Blue Book ended in 1969, with a report card proclaiming, "There is nothing to declare.")

Some "high fliers" get "visited"

If the majority didn't "believe" at the beginning of 1947, the situation is vastly different today. Some outspoken and very high-profile people claim to have had a UFO experience. (The expression UFO, technically meaning an "unidentified flying object," has become a more generic term to describe the entire modern phenomenon incorporating UFOs, extraterrestrial visitations, abductions, etc.) Those who have experienced a UFO consistently report believing that aliens must be visiting us from another world or even another dimension. In other words, though they may have been tentative about the possibility of UFOs before the incident (as opposed to UFO skeptics who say it cannot happen), they often become convinced that it is *definitely* happening. Rather than believing there might still be a rational explanation for the UFO, the person generally finds the event so real that it transforms their perception of the world they are living in. For most people, it becomes a profound, reality-altering experience.

Opinion polls which imply high numbers of sightings and visitations only serve to reinforce the "aliens are visiting us" notion. "Way out" claims make news, which in turn encourages more believers, who in turn now look for experiences. The prevalence of these reports encourages rumors of conspiracies and cover-ups by governments, the argument being, "It's happened to so many people — the government must know something!" A 1996 Gallup poll claimed that over 70 percent of the population believed that the government knew more about UFOs than it was letting on. This is a very popular theme in movies such as *Independence Day* and the *Men in Black* series.

For example, the international news service CNN claimed that a former aide of former U.S. President Bill Clinton was petitioning the current U.S. government to declassify its secret records about UFOs and other related incidents. The one-time aide, John Podesta, said that the information would:

. . . provide scientists with data that will assist in determining the real nature of this phenomenon.[12]

CNN went on to say:

Despite earning little credence, cases of strange aerial phenomena that defy explanation abound — whether witnessed by thousands of Arizona residents, commercial airline pilots, or a U.S. president.[13]

The U.S. president to whom they were referring was none other than Jimmy Carter. He became the world's highest-profile UFO believer when in 1976, during a presidential election campaign, he publicly spoke about his own UFO experiences that occurred back in 1969. He was reported as saying:

It was the darndest thing I've ever seen. It was big, it changed colors, and it was about the size of the moon. We watched it for ten minutes, but none of us could figure out what it was. One thing's for sure, I'll never make fun of people who say they've seen unidentified flying objects in the sky. If I become president, I'll make every piece of information this country has about UFO sightings available to the public and the scientists. I am convinced that UFOs exist because I've seen one. . . .[14]

Note how his experience changed him. He became a vocal advocate of solving the mystery — it was a real and mysterious event for him. Should people have been concerned, though? A potential future president of the most powerful nation on Earth believes that there is "more than meets the eye" with regard to UFOs. Moreover, he is subtly implying that the government of the day

Photo courtesy of Library of Congress

President Jimmy Carter

is keeping secret its information regarding UFOs. Did such a "wacky" statement jeopardize his presidential election chances? Apparently not — he was subsequently elected. This demonstrates how widespread such beliefs had become. His statement was no longer regarded as "extreme." By now, most people believed that there was a mystery to be solved, and many believed that he was going to solve it for them. His credibility over the years has not diminished as a result, either. He has been a nominee for the prestigious international Nobel Peace Prize on several occasions, and won the award in 2002 due to his "statesmanship" in world affairs.

So what information did Carter manage to unearth for the general public during his term? None, it would appear, because he did not raise the matter again in public. But a failure to uncover evidence only seems to foster the appetite of UFO enthusiasts. Many believe that Carter simply succumbed to internal pressures and became complicit in UFO cover-ups, or that he was kept from the truth by the same government agencies that allegedly "hid the truth on Blue Book."

This is a popular theme in UFOlogy, and was used to great effect in the blockbuster film *Independence Day*. In this movie, Earth was undergoing a global invasion from hostile aliens. After a presidential aide admitted that the president had not been told anything about previous alien visitations (such things were on a need-to-know basis), the president demanded the full story and was subsequently flown to a top-secret base known as Area 51, 90 miles north of Las Vegas, Nevada. This military establishment had supposedly been conducting investigations and experiments around the alien craft and corpses that were recovered from the infamous Roswell crash of 1947 (as we shall discuss later, there really was an incident at Roswell).

Carter's UFO claims caused alarm among Christians of the day, too, because their traditional world view was under siege. If Carter (who claimed to be a "born-again" Christian) believed that the UFO he saw was piloted by aliens, then such comments appeared to contradict the view of many fundamentalist Christians who believe that the Bible does not allow for the creation of "ETs" on other planets. Many Christians view the Bible as the inerrant revelation of a Creator God. Some UFO buffs, atheists, and others claim that the Bible is "past its shelf life" because "aliens are real." Others even claim that the Bible is, in fact, a record of alien visitations to the earth. Whatever the view, the Bible seems to play an important part in UFO beliefs, and, as we shall see, it is often alluded to by our alleged extraterrestrial visitors. Fascinating! Did Carter abandon his belief in the Bible as a result of the sighting, or had he now accepted that UFOs had to "fit into the Bible" somewhere?

The Extraterrestrial Hypothesis (ETH)

Today, a new, "modern" religion has grown around UFO beliefs. There are literally hundreds of UFO organizations and, collectively, tens of thousands of books, websites, and movies that have dealt with the subject. There are also thousands of individuals (contactees) and religious cults who claim to be regularly visited by, or are receiving messages from, friendly aliens. UFOlogist J. Richard Greenwell describes this as follows:

> The most popular and appealing notion about UFOs is the extraterrestrial hypothesis (ETH),[15] the idea that intelligent beings from other planets are visiting Earth. To some it is more than a hypothesis and can best be described as a belief.[16]

A very common thread wound through such beliefs is that our ET "space brothers" are more highly evolved, both physically and spiritually, than human beings, and that they are here to "help us" and oversee our own "evolution." This claim is a quantum leap from merely seeing unexplainable lights in the sky. Countless people have been led to reject conventional spiritual beliefs or at least reinterpret them (like Carter, perhaps) in light of the "weight of UFO evidence." One of the most famous UFO researchers of all time, Jacques Vallée, wrote that society itself is being transformed by these beliefs:

> Belief in the reality of UFOs is spreading rapidly at all levels of society throughout the world. Books and periodicals appear at an ever-increasing rate. Documentaries and major films are being made now by young people of the UFO generation (young men and women who were born just after World War II and who grew up with flying saucer stories) who have moved into influential positions in the media. . . . Many of the themes of yesterday's counter-culture can be traced back to the "messages from space" coming from UFO contactees of the forties and fifties.[17]

Vallée wrote these words back in 1979, two years after *Star Wars* and *Close Encounters of the Third Kind* blazed across our movie screens, catapulting the UFO phenomenon to even greater heights, and on a scale that shows no sign of abating.

An astronaut speaks out

Skeptics often comment that the majority of UFO sightings are reported by amateurs — i.e., laypeople who wouldn't know a weather balloon from a satellite. This may be true, but it cannot account for sightings by people who should know. Take, for example, former U.S. Air Force pilot and NASA (National Aeronautics and Space Administration) astronaut Gordon Cooper, who was reported to have seen a UFO during a space flight. This incident occurred in 1963. America's

Photo courtesy of NASA

Gordon Cooper

NBC News reported that, during his final orbit of the earth on his Mercury mission, he saw a greenish-glowing object ahead of his capsule, approaching him. It is claimed that when he reported the incident, the tracking station at Muchea, just north of Perth, Western Australia, also confirmed the sighting on their radar. Much has been made of this incident, and UFOlogists are keen to seize upon the report as "proof" by an independent, unbiased, and reliable witness (due to his profile and military standing). It is easy to find dozens of websites supporting this claim (see later chapters for a deeper look at Cooper's UFO).

The reality is, though, that Cooper was not really unbiased by that time; he was already a believer in the ETH. In subsequent interviews, he claimed that he first saw UFOs in the early 1950s, and that he even saw one land at Edwards Air Force Base in 1957.[18] This "prebelief" seems to be a common factor with many people who claim to have seen a UFO or who have had an abduction experience. Whatever really occurred during that famous Mercury space flight, there is no doubt that Cooper was by that time an avid UFOlogist. He even addressed the United Nations (U.N.) on the subject. In July 1978, ETH enthusiast and then prime minister of Grenada, Sir Eric Gairy, was petitioning the U.N. to create a special group for the purpose of investigating UFOs. He believed that America was keeping quiet despite knowing the "truth" about them. Gordon Cooper supported this idea, and during a lengthy speech, he was quoted as saying:

> I believe that these extraterrestrial vehicles and their crews are visiting the planet from other planets that are a little more technically advanced than we are on earth. I feel that we need to have a top-level coordinated program to scientifically collect and analyze data from all over the earth concerning any type of encounter and to determine how best to interfere with these visitors in a friendly fashion. . . .[19]

Other UFOlogists attending Cooper's address included Dr. J. Allen Hynek, by now one of the best-known and most respected UFO investigators in the world. A former skeptic who once dismissed sightings as being made up by "kooks and crackpots," Hynek formed the Center for UFO Studies (CUFOS) along with a young Jacques Vallée (mentioned earlier). Originally, Hynek worked as a consultant astronomer on Project Blue Book, and also invented the term "close encounters" as part of his Hynek Classification System.[20] A "close encounter of the third kind" refers to a UFO with visible occupants, and this was also the title of Steven Spielberg's hugely successful 1977 movie, and it is generally believed that the character of French expert Claude Lacombe was based on Jacques Vallée. Hynek also served as the film's technical advisor, and appeared briefly in the movie in a small cameo role. The "element of truth" — just enough to inspire all sorts of theories — captivated moviegoers, just as it has with *Independence Day* and its allusions to Roswell and secret government installations.

Close Encounters of the Third Kind [1977] — *CE-III*

Steven Spielberg made the "big time" with the hugely successful shark attack movie *Jaws* (1975). *CE-III* was the director's follow-up movie, and his previous success ensured that he had more money this time for special effects. Following hot on the heels of the first *Star Wars* epic, it became one of the most successful sci-fi movies of the post–*Star Wars* era — it is regarded as a classic by some. After this movie, there was a flood of copycat genre movies trying to cash in on the phenomenal success of *Star Wars* and *CE-III*. In a coincidence of timing, there was also renewed interest in UFOs. Britain was undergoing its largest UFO frenzy since the summer of 1952.[21]

The story was based on the book *The UFO Experience* (1972), by Dr. J. Allen Hynek. The movie starts with the mysterious reappearance of previously lost WWII fighters still in pristine condition (and in the middle of a desert), and a scene where air traffic controllers are receiving reports from jet airliners who are being forced to share their airspace with UFOs. The central character is electrical engineer Roy Neary, who, after a midnight emergency service call, encounters a UFO on a lonely dark road. His experience is unnerving, to say the least. His pickup is bathed in brilliant light and the electrical systems go haywire. After this "close encounter of the second kind" *(CE-II)*, Neary pursues the rapidly moving lights of the UFO, takes a bend in the road at high speed, and almost knocks over a child. Others on the road, including the child's mother, are similarly obsessed with the lights in the sky. Neary discovers that she and others have also had a close encounter.

The movie reveals that the aliens have telepathically implanted images into the contactees' minds, which lead them to near madness as they try to unravel the "mystery inside their heads." The young child is abducted later in the movie in a terrifying scene where his mother is powerless to prevent the abduction.

The movie's climax takes place at Devil's Tower in Wyoming (which was the image planted in his head) where Neary discovers that the government has established a base and landing strip in anticipation of a friendly rendezvous with the aliens, once again built on conspiracy notions that the government is not telling the truth.

The visual effects were stunning for their day. The pilots of the aforementioned WWII planes step off the alien mothership, not having aged at all in some 40 years. The young boy who was previously abducted is released as well. The movie depicts Spielberg's (a UFO enthusiast in his own right) vision of what extraterrestrials look like.

This created an interesting phenomenon after the movie's release. Prior to *CE-III*, reports of alleged aliens with long, thin necks were non-existent. After the film, they became common. Before the film, alien eyes were reported as being human-like with a pupil and iris with white surrounds. Afterward, they were black, slanted, and much larger — an image that endures today. [22]

However, despite the involvement of heavyweights like Hynek and others, the U.N. was not convinced. This may have had something to do with Cooper's alliance with Gairy, who was a corrupt and brutal despot in his own country. Strange bedfellows indeed!

One of the 20th century's most enduring heroes was also a "believer." General Douglas MacArthur, who valiantly led the Allied forces in the Pacific region during World War II, was reported in the *New York Times* in 1955 as saying:

> Because of the developments of science, all the countries on earth will have to unite to survive and to make a common front against attack by people from other planets. The politics of the future will be cosmic, or interplanetary. [23]

Another credible witness, whose beliefs had a major impact, is former Marine Corps Major Donald Keyhoe. In the late 1940s, he was one of the first to allege that the U.S. Air Force was withholding information about UFOs. Keyhoe even claimed to possess many files and photographs of UFO sightings by pilots — his contemporaries in the military establishment. His book, *The Flying Saucers Are Real* (1950), set off a firestorm of controversy all over the world. An online promotion of his book aptly states:

> Virtually single-handedly Major Keyhoe prompted a quantum shift in our collective consciousness when he successfully shifted the credibility issue from UFO witnesses to the U.S. government and military. [24]

Although meant as an advertisement, it accurately describes how the burden of proof shifted, once again adding to the conspiracy theories that abound. The absence of proof is not an obstacle, it seems. All you need is a "credible" witness who has had an experience, and then you dare someone else — like the government — to "prove it *didn't* happen." Unfortunately, this sort of mindset permeates UFOlogy culture, making it very difficult to get a "straight story." With so many hoaxers, too, seeking their five minutes of fame, it is a taxing task to wade through the information, the more so because the reports are based on experience rather than physical evidence. A typical comment is that "UFOs must be real because of the weight of evidence." But it is not any "weight" of empirical evidence, rather a proliferation of "let me tell you what I saw" experiences. This does not deny that these experiences may have actually occurred, but we've all heard "fishing stories" of how a six-inch minnow became a three-foot "whopper" in the retelling. Add to this normal human failing a "potentially spectacular" UFO claim, with eager media and UFOlogists beating down your door, and often the truth is lost along the way — either in the recounting by the witness or in the telling of the tale by the media. This gives you some idea of how difficult the process of determining the truth can be. But, nonetheless, we shall try to determine the true nature of the phenomenon.

Unlike mere hearsay, many experiences (and, in particular, abduction encounters) are sometimes recalled during hypnosis, adding weight to the idea that there was no deliberate fabrication. Abduction experiences are a complex topic, which have a complete chapter devoted to them.

Some sightings have stood the test of time due to multiple witnesses observing the event. One such sighting occurred in July 19, 1952, when several fast-moving objects "buzzed" the White House

UFOs buzzing the Capitol dome, Washington, DC

— home of the U.S. president in America's capital. These objects were seen on three separate radar installations, including Washington's National Airport and Andrews Air Force Base. There were similar occurrences a week later, resulting in the dispatch of F-94 interceptor jets. A subsequent press conference resulted in the largest attendance of the media since World War II, and a Disney video called *Alien Encounters* even has footage of the incident, with the narrator stating:

> This is not swamp gas. It is not a flock of birds. This is an actual spacecraft piloted by alien intelligence — one sighting from tens of thousands made over the last 50 years on virtually every continent on the globe.[25]

Of course, there is no way to substantiate the fantastic claims about the "alien pilots." But Disney is correct on one thing — there are countless sightings all over the world, and we have only mentioned a fraction of the famous people who claim to have seen a UFO.

Surely NASA would know?

On sheer size alone, NASA (America's National Aeronautics and Space Administration) is the world's premier space exploration agency. In the Cold War climate of the 1960s and 1970s, the United States (through NASA) and the Soviet Union engaged in the "space race." These countries spurred each other on in a game of one-upmanship to show off the success of their respective countries' political ideologies.

Such was the pace of technology that, just 12 years after the Soviets launched the first object, *Sputnik* (Russian for "companion" or "satellite"), into space on October 4, 1957, a manned spacecraft landed on the moon and returned its occupants safely to Earth. In most people's eyes, NASA had won the race. But they would never again reach the giddy heights of popularity that they did when astronaut Neil Armstrong first set foot upon the lunar surface during the *Apollo 11* mission on July 20, 1967.

This was one of the most enduring and most watched events in human history, and arguably one of America's finest moments. The political agenda was realized courtesy of NASA and an open checkbook. By the time of the *Apollo 14* and *15* missions, manned visits to the moon were already being regarded as "run of the mill" and something of an anticlimax. Many now started to question the exorbitant cost of the missions, particularly as there was no sign of life on the moon.

With *Apollo 17*, although many more missions had been planned, one of the greatest chapters in mankind's history came to a close. In the 1970s, the oil sheiks had initiated an "energy crisis" and people felt the pain and shock of rising prices. In a knee-jerk reaction, the perceived "fat" of NASA was trimmed. If the public had to watch its pennies, then so should NASA.

With the budget cuts, a reusable vehicle, the space shuttle, was developed. This policy of belt-tightening would continue for many years. Even in the 1990s, NASA's administrator, Daniel S. Goldin, echoed this policy when he initiated his "faster, better, cheaper" program.

However, after an initial flurry of enthusiasm for the shuttle, public interest waned once more. Conducting lab experiments in space is not an attention grabber. Unfortunately, a disaster set back space exploration even more when the shuttle *Challenger* exploded shortly after lift-off, killing all on board, including the first-ever civilian astronaut — teacher Christa McAuliffe. This rekindled the public's attention, but for all the wrong reasons, and the space shuttle program was grounded until answers were forthcoming. Many felt that NASA would be fighting for its very existence as annual budget cuts continued. The space shuttle was also carrying commercial cargo, so "why should the taxpayer's money be used?" NASA appeared to be increasingly irrelevant.

The "savior"

The NASA website says about Goldin, whose tenure ran from 1992 to 2001:

> In naming him one of the 100 most influential men and women in government, the *National Journal* observed that "most space watchers say that Goldin is a brilliant visionary who brought NASA back from the brink of a black hole." Nowhere has Goldin's vision been more evident than in his comprehensive strategy for space exploration. He initiated the Origins Program to understand how the Universe has evolved, to learn how life began on Earth and to see if life exists elsewhere.[26]

Under the auspices of the Origins Program, Goldin had redirected the major focus of NASA into the search for extraterrestrial life. In one respect, this had always been one of the agendas during trips to the moon and in the planning of visits to Mars. A manned mission to

Mars was actually scheduled for the 1980s, but after probes had visited the Martian surface and found it lifeless like the moon, there seemed to be insufficient justification for a visit, particularly in a climate of belt tightening. Because Apollo was cut short, NASA was left without any major projects or real direction.

> Through Goldin's aggressive management reforms, annual budgets were reduced, producing a $40 billion reduction from prior budget plans.[27]

Goldin had become NASA's savior. Through a clever perceived change of policy, the public thought that NASA was now interested in looking for alien life. In a climate where science fiction "rules," the government agency had become relevant again — more than relevant, as it was now transforming the public imagination rather than lagging behind it.

The power of the idea of "alien" life was substantially demonstrated when in 1996 media reports proclaimed, "Conclusive evidence for Martian life."[28] NASA's trump card was not ET in the flesh, but came from a little piece of rock found in the Antarctic (discussed in detail later in this book), which reportedly contained fossilized bacteria from Mars. Its discovery had suddenly ignited interest in the activities of NASA once again. Front pages of newspapers all over the world shouted, "Evidence of Life on Mars!" The implication was obvious: "There is life elsewhere in the universe." The event even sparked a presidential announcement, Bill Clinton declaring:

> If this discovery is confirmed, it would surely be one of the most stunning insights into our universe that science has discovered.[29]

This was tremendous publicity for NASA, and just at a time when the U.S. Congress was discussing funding cuts once again. NASA had apparently realized that the U.S. Congress does not fund unpopular projects. Shrewdly, it seems, they had learned to play the political game and had jumped on the ET bandwagon. The Martian rock made number one on the hit parade, with commentators noting:

> If asked what was the hot media topic of 1996, many would reply, "The sensational claim that scientists have discovered life from Mars."[30]

In what was either a fortunate coincidence in timing or a brilliantly orchestrated ploy, the Mars rock announcement came hot on the heels of the number-one box-office movie, *Independence Day.*

Independence Day [1996]

Approaching the Fourth of July, as America prepares to celebrate its Independence Day, the earth is visited by enormous flying saucers that take up residence over the major cities of the world. Initially, there is no hint of their intentions until a computer expert, working for a television network, tries to find out what is disrupting the TV station's signal. He discovers that the alien craft are utilizing our own satellites, and have synchronized a countdown in partnership with their moon-sized mother ship in orbit above the upper atmosphere. It is a countdown to the annihilation of the human race.

On this discovery, America's war-hero president escapes the destruction of Washington, D.C. in the nick of time. The image of the White House being destroyed by an enormous heat ray is a disturbing yet enduring one. The special effects are breathtakingly powerful, as this destruction is repeated in all the major cities of the world. Earth's defenses, even nuclear missiles, are powerless to stop the aliens.

It is then revealed (even the president didn't know) that the military had captured an alien craft and several bodies at Roswell in 1947 (implying that the stories are true). On demand, the president is whisked to the top-secret installation at Area 51. When a live alien is recovered by the movie's air force pilot hero, the alien awakes and telepathically (a common theme in UFO beliefs) reveals to the president that the human race is being exterminated because the aliens require the earth's natural resources.

The captured "Roswell ship" has reactivated due to the appearance of the mother ship, and our resident computer genius devises a way to fly it to the mother ship and upload a computer virus that will deactivate the force fields around all the extraterrestrial spacecraft. The "virus" concept is highly reminiscent of the 1953 feature film *The War of the Worlds*, which was based on the H.G. Wells novel of the same name. In the movie, a biological virus, like the common cold, kills the aliens, whose immune systems have no defense against the illness.

In the movie's final scenes, the Americans deactivate the shields and relay the good news to their fellow men all over the world. No longer are there political boundaries or ideological differences, as mankind is united in a common cause to repel the alien invaders. In a Churchillian speech, the president announces that the Fourth of July, Independence Day, now belongs to the whole earth and to every nation, not just America. The effort is successful, and alien ships are brought down all over the world.

This was a hugely popular movie that set box office records for opening-day attendance all over the world, mostly due to the trailer images of well-known icons, such as the White House, being destroyed.

The Roswell-type conspiracy theories about government "cover-ups," which formed the basis of this movie, also inspired a generation of TV series such as *Dark Skies*, *Roswell*, and *The X Files*.

Many observers now felt that the time was right for a manned mission to Mars. Claims of water on Mars, as well as the interest generated by the Martian rock, indicated that the public mood was ready. During the *Mars Pathfinder* mission in 1997, live photographs of the Martian surface were beamed back to Earth and posted on the NASA website, which recorded over three quarters of a billion "hits" — a barometer of public interest. The news broadcaster CNN also helped the ETH/alien agenda, as its cameras kept intermittently flashing to Roswell to cover another event — the 50th anniversary of the "Roswell incident" of 1947. Tens of thousands of UFO enthusiasts descended on the town. Among the activities was a flying saucer soapbox derby.[31]

The dream appeared to come closer in 2003, when President George W. Bush was expected to announce plans for a manned mission to Mars under the mission name *Prometheus*, during his annual State of the Union address on January 28, 2003. This mission included the Nuclear Space Initiative — to develop the first nuclear-powered spacecraft that could reach Mars in as little as two months. U.S. public interest shifted to an impending war with Iraq, however, so the president delayed the announcement.[32] NASA's plans were disrupted once again, on February 1, 2003, when the space shuttle *Columbia* disintegrated upon re-entry, killing all seven occupants. The specter of more budget cuts hung over the space agency.

But NASA's prospects did not turn out to be so grim, and this perceived negative event was used to ask for an increase in funding to develop better and safer space vehicles. Early in 2004, President Bush announced that NASA was going to receive a massive boost to its budget as part of U.S. plans to have a permanently manned base on the moon, which, in turn, would serve as a steppingstone for manned flights to Mars. It suggests that the allure of finding ET life can overcome even the most difficult of situations. The "glory days" may be returning for NASA.

NASA and the "meaning of life"

It is clear how the drama has unfolded for NASA. From the brink of becoming an "also ran" government agency, they have cleverly used popular culture to market their own "extraterrestrial searches" in spite of recent disasters. This, in turn, helps to engender belief in alien life, making the idea stronger than ever. The direction was established back on January 17, 1996, in a speech to the American Astronomical Society, when NASA's Goldin listed the goals of his administration. He said:

> The fourth goal is to search for Earth-like planets that may be habitable or inhabited through direct detection and spectroscopic measurement.[33]

One certainly gains the impression that they are looking for, and perhaps expecting to find, alien civilizations (note the use of the word "inhabited"). The public imagination can literally run wild with such provocative announcements, spelling out the message: "If we meet them and they are more advanced, more evolved, and more ancient, then perhaps they can provide humanity with the answers it's looking for. Perhaps those receiving religious messages from our extraterrestrial 'space brothers' are onto something. There might be something out there after all."

Although this fueling of the imagination is partly based on science fantasy rather than fact, the potential to solve such "mysteries" is a mouth-watering proposition to the public, and NASA certainly does not openly negate such ideas. They actually seem to be propagating quasi-religious notions of their own. Their Origins website states:

> NASA's Origins Program seeks to answer two enduring human questions that we once considered around ancient

campfires, yet still keep alive in today's classrooms: *"Where do we come from? Are we alone?"* [emphasis in original][34]

This is reminiscent of the "deeper philosophical questions" that we suggested earlier, and once again demonstrates one of the reasons for the popularity of the whole extraterrestrial hypothesis — mankind is looking for meaning, and science is our society's god. The idea that there is something bigger than ourselves is driving exploration of space in search of a rendezvous with aliens who will be able to answer our questions for us. Human beings are enamored with mystery.

Astrobiology

The story goes that in 1998 an unknown NASA official coined a new marketing term to replace the uninteresting moniker "planetary sciences." The new term "astrobiology" emerged. The following is a quote from NASA's Origins website:

> Astrobiology is the study of life in the universe. It's a new field of research that covers the origin, evolution, distribution, and destiny of life — wherever it might exist.[35]

Note that this is "the study of life wherever it might exist." Bruce Runnegar, head of the NASA Astrobiology Institute (NAI) simplifies the real motivation behind the name change:

> It's a mission that the taxpayers can understand and support. . . . Everybody wants to know where we came from and whether or not we are alone in the universe.[36]

Once again this is a populist approach that fuels the fires of imagination — and brings in the funding. The NASA website goes on to state that astrobiology draws upon a wide-ranging field of sciences, such as biology, chemistry, and geology, and that universities are now starting to add "this exciting new field as a degree in which people can major."[37] Astrobiology is all-encompassing, in that it not only includes the study of life on Earth, but beyond it as well. But it includes another more well-defined field that is supposed to study *actual* life beyond the earth. It is a specialist field called exobiology.

The notion that "objective" scientists are specializing in this area gives the impression that something must exist. But one may logically ask — how can you actually study something that, to date, has not been observed to exist? One could be cynical and suggest that an exo-biologist is drawing his wages under false pretences.

The implications of NASA's "little lump of Martian rock" — the so-called evidence of extraterrestrial life — have been far-reaching. Even many years after the event, Carol Cleland, from the philosophy department at the University of Colorado, said:

> The claims are still as controversial as when they first came out, but it made people realize how easy it could be for life to be happening elsewhere. . . . That, more than anything else, was the birth of astrobiology as a serious subject.[38]

Using a popular scientist and his religious agenda

Avowed atheist and science fiction writer, the late Dr. Carl Sagan, endorsed the idea of life on other worlds as far back as 1966. In 1998, NASA formed an Astrobiology Institute shortly after the discovery of the hotly disputed Martian rock. The focus of NASA in the immediate future will be the search for more extrasolar planets (i.e., planets outside of our own solar system — discussed in a later chapter). Along with the Mars rock, these "hot topics" have catapulted the field of astrobiology to the forefront of modern space exploration.

Photo courtesy of NASA

Carl Sagan

Sagan was convinced of the existence of extraterrestrial life, despite being an ETH skeptic (the ETH specifically suggests that ETs are visiting our planet). He has played a leading role in convincing the public about the existence of life in space. As a best-selling author, he has won a Pulitzer Prize, and his book *Cosmos* became the largest-selling science book ever published in the English language. An award-winning television series of the same name followed, and was seen by an estimated 500 million people.[39] At the beginning of the series, Sagan proclaims *his* vision of the universe, with an inspiring image of surf crashing in the background, while he intones:

The cosmos is all that is or ever was or ever will be.[40]

This statement displays Sagan's atheistic and materialist beliefs — he did not believe that a Creator, such as the Judeo-Christian God of the Bible, was responsible for the creation of the cosmos.

Sagan played a leading role in NASA's space program, as a consultant and advisor, from its inception. He briefed all Apollo astronauts before their lunar flights, and was a leading experimenter on the *Mariner, Viking, Voyager*, and *Galileo* planetary expeditions.[41] His influence in guiding and forming NASA's vision is well known, and as an atheist he believed that evolution (the idea that life developed via chance random processes over millions of years) was fact.

In his powerful and distinctly anti-Christian science fiction movie *Contact* (based on his earlier novel — he was co-producer and co-writer of the movie), the question of whether there are any other life forms in the universe was asked three times, to which the reply was, "If there isn't, it would be an awful waste of space."

Aliens and the evolution connection

For scientific reasons we shall discuss later, Sagan did not, and NASA does not, believe that aliens are visiting the earth in spaceships or that they have yet communicated or made contact with us in any way (ETH). Yet on the basis of their well-advertised efforts to look for extraterrestrial life, it would be easy to conclude otherwise.

In the series *Cosmos*, Sagan reflects on mankind's insignificance in the universe and compares us to "a mote of dust that floats in the morning sky."[42] NASA clearly does believe, as Sagan did, that life exists elsewhere in this enormous universe. This is derived from their view that the big bang and evolution are the mechanisms of creation. Simply put: *if evolution occurred on the earth, it must have occurred elsewhere in this enormous universe* (remember Sagan's comments about the universe being a waste of space if there wasn't other life?).

Sagan's popularity, his influence in NASA, and countless honorary degrees (as well as his earned doctorate) not only made him a leading light and spokesperson on the science of space, but gave his own religious ideas on origins unprecedented respectability (it is a "faith" position because it deals with unobservable past events). Although he may have been a believer in ET life, his materialistic (as in "matter is all there is") view of origins caused him to be a leading skeptic against anything supernatural. This would have put him at odds with many UFOlogists and cultists, who believe that some UFO sightings, abductions, and visitations are of a supernatural and religious nature. However, many others believe that ancient religious writings, including the Bible, are recollections of a primitive culture that mistook their experiences of alien encounters as visitations by gods (or even demons).

Many cults also believe that the purpose of these ancient alien visits was to oversee human evolution. Most UFOlogists regard the modern human race as a more enlightened species that should reject the "primitive" religious notions of our ancestors. Many claim that the increased number of sightings, visitations, and abductions today is because the "space brothers" have come to help us ascend to our next stage of enlightenment, or "spiritual" evolution.

Although the skeptic/Sagan view and the UFO cultic view are in opposition to each other with regard to the spiritual dimension of extraterrestrial life, they do, in fact, both have a religious view of the universe — it forms a part of their deepest beliefs about reality. Their ideas have not been substantiated by science "fact." The common denominator of both camps is the belief that evolution has occurred for countless eons on the earth and all over the universe. This point cannot be emphasized strongly enough — it is the basis for virtually all belief in alien life, whatever form one thinks that life may take. This idea of "cosmos-wide evolution" has important implications for our study, as we shall see.

Contrary to what most people think, belief in evolution is not a prerequisite for doing space science (or any other science). Wernher von Braun, a German rocket scientist engaged by the Nazis during World War II, was described by many as the "father of NASA." Von Braun was passionate about the exploration of space, but for reasons that vastly differ from the current NASA

Wernher von Braun

ones. As a Bible-believing Christian, he expected that space exploration would reveal the glory of God, not little green men. Under his inspiration, the NASA team developed the rockets that put the first Americans in space during the *Mercury, Gemini,* and *Apollo* missions, and the *Saturn V* rockets used during the *Apollo* missions remain the largest launch vehicles ever built. It is worth noting that the technology used in today's space shuttle program is directly due to von Braun's vision and pioneering work. He wrote:

> I find it . . . difficult to understand a scientist who does not acknowledge the presence of a superior rationality behind the existence of the universe.[43]

Many would agree with von Braun, but instead invoke the idea that the universe itself is an evolving, self-perpetuating, self-guiding force that could produce many different life forms in a variety of locations. Author Ann Lamont commented about von Braun, in her book *21 Great Scientists Who Believed the Bible,* that:

> Von Braun was a strong critic of the modern tendency to teach science from an evolutionary standpoint, without examining the creationist alternative as well. He believed that such an approach was unscientific. . . . He believed that the reason "for the amazing string of successes we had with our Apollo flights to the moon . . . was that we tried to never overlook anything. It is in that same sense of scientific honesty that I endorse the presentation of alternative theories for the origin of the universe, life, and man. . . . Manned space flight is an amazing achievement . . . for viewing the awesome reaches of space. An outlook . . . at the vast mysteries of the universe should only confirm our belief in the certainty of its Creator."[44]

There are also many UFO cults (like the Raelians) who believe that life on Earth was "created" by intelligence from elsewhere. For example, they credit the aliens for the creation of the unbelievably complex information written on DNA molecules that are found in all living things on Earth. However, they have only succeeded in shifting the problem of "creation" into outer space, because we would then need to ask — who created the aliens? Or did they evolve? It is this quest for meaning that causes mankind to look to the heavens for answers.

In considering the reasons why man searches the stars, and why some believe in the possibility of extraterrestrial life, it is therefore valid to consider all underlying philosophies, including those of Sagan, Wernher von·Braun, and others like them.

What does NASA really believe?

Without a closer look, NASA appears to have done little to downplay, or even address, the notion of alien-piloted UFOs or abductions. On the surface, this would appear very strange, given the massive number of people who claim to have had UFO experiences around the world. One would think that the ETH is directly related to NASA's field of expertise. However, we have demonstrated that it would not be in their interests to debunk these notions too vigorously, or the public may question their exploration of space. So what is their official position on the subject?

Only one official article could be found on their website directly relating to this matter. It says:

> No branch of the United States Government is currently involved with or responsible for investigations into the possibility of advanced alien civilizations on other planets or for investigating Unidentified Flying Objects (UFOs). The U.S. Air Force (USAF) and NASA have had intermittent, independent investigations of the possibility of alien life on other planets; however, none of these has produced factual evidence that life exists on other planets, nor that UFOs are related to aliens. From 1947 to 1969, the Air Force investigated UFOs; [Blue Book and the Condon Report] then in 1977, NASA was asked to examine the possibility of resuming UFO investigations. After studying all of the facts available, it was determined that nothing would be gained by further investigation, since there was an absence of tangible evidence.[45]

They could perhaps be described as being a little disingenuous on the subject; NASA and its consultants clearly do believe, as Sagan did, that it is highly likely that intelligent life exists on other planets. So what is going on here? On the one hand they use the search for alien life as the justification for their space program, while on the other they admit they have no factual evidence that life exists on other planets.

As an illustration of this seeming insincerity, unmanned space missions *Pioneer 10* and *11* carried small metal plaques, and *Voyagers 1* and *2* carried a kind of time capsule, all designed to communicate a picture of our world to extraterrestrials. On the *Voyagers* (launched in 1977) 12-inch gold-plated copper disks, containing sounds and images of the earth, were attached. Notably, Carl Sagan was the head of a NASA committee involved in selecting the 115 images and sounds that are included on these exclusive phonograph records. Also included were a cartridge and needle, and interestingly a message from then U.S. President, and UFO believer Jimmy Carter. This once again gained tremendous publicity for NASA, but also served a genuine purpose for the ET believers. It was intended that, after the *Voyagers* had completed their initial missions of visiting the planets in our solar system, they would continue outward, beyond our solar system, exploring the galaxy on their way. *Voyager 1* is currently at least twice the distance from Earth that Pluto is (farther than any other man-made object), and is still soaring away at a speed of 38,000 miles per hour (17 kilometers per second). Both craft are still transmitting data to Earth via the Deep Space Network, but they haven't recorded meeting any space travelers so far.[46]

NASA has also used another method of scanning the distant stars and galaxies for alien civilizations, via the once-heavily-funded SETI (Search for Extraterrestrial Intelligence) program (see chapter 2).

Popular culture transformed

Today, society seems thoroughly convinced that extraterrestrial life exists, demonstrated by the fact that universities are offering specialist studies in this area. Yet there are no documented cases of any life on other planets, let alone an extraterrestrial encounter.

Scientists are viewed as rational, objective beings that only deal "with the facts." In this regard, they have become the high priests of our society, being viewed in an almost infallible light. Operational science (the study of how the world works through finding out and applying natural laws) has led to amazing growth in technologies and discoveries. This has promoted science to something approaching an icon of worship. Many look to science for a form of salvation, believing that it will hold the key to solving all of the world's problems. There are many people alive today who once thought that lasers, travel to the moon, and palm computers were sheer science fiction. If such wild fantasies can become scientific fact in one generation, surely the distant future promises almost limitless technological developments. It is not difficult to believe that, if our technology can grow so rapidly, then civilizations elsewhere in the universe, which have been developing for countless millennia, must be unbelievably advanced. This idea is promoted heavily in science fiction and in the media.

It is quite normal for scientists to start with unproven ideas or theories, but most ordinary people don't realize this. Science "facts" are always interpreted within a framework of belief, and scientists often passionately disagree with each other on many basic issues, particularly when it comes to the origin of life. Some ideas are just plain unprovable. This demonstrates that "scientific evidence" does not indisputably prove truth by itself — it is interpreted within a framework of pre-existing beliefs.

This is seen in astrobiology and exobiology. Despite having no proof of any alien life, modern astrobiological evangelists, like Sagan, have already made up their minds that it must exist, based on their ideas about how life must have evolved on Earth (in the unobservable past). Their ideas have strongly influenced the majority of the populace on this planet. But how have their views become so strong and influential? There are two apparent reasons.

First, our lives have been affected and transformed by science. Modern communications, jets, and rockets that can deliver nuclear warheads and destroy cities have "shrunk" our planet. News of conflict on the other side of the world is beamed into our homes in living color. People all across the world watched in horror, experienced in "real time," as the World Trade Center collapsed after the terrorist attacks on September 11, 2001.

The same technology that brings wonder and blessing has also made us feel vulnerable. We have realized that, no matter where we are on this planet, we could be hurt by events elsewhere, such as a nuclear explosion or man-made pollution, which is apparently causing global warming and even holes in our ozone.

The second reason is the influence of the media, which has gained its near-instantaneous ability to broadcast news and events from those selfsame advances in science and technology. Great sway is held over the public imagination by way of the media's promulgation of ideas and philosophies — particularly in relation to science. We have already discussed NASA, an icon of achievement in its own right, whose exploits (and thus ideas) have been heavily covered by the media. Television shows, movies, and other popular media have become such a normal part of our everyday lives that we underestimate their influence upon our thinking.

If popular media are not incredibly influential, why do countless marketing groups spend billions of dollars promoting products? As a reader, could you honestly say that you have never been emotionally affected by any image on your TV screen — never hidden under the pillow at a terrifying moment in a TV drama? Or if you've ever viewed a science fiction movie that had UFO themes, has the thought not crossed your mind that maybe, just maybe, the government really does know more than they are telling us?

No one is immune from the power of images that almost transplant themselves into our minds, aptly demonstrated by the *War of the Worlds* panic. Even Spielberg's *Close Encounters,* although science fiction, led millions to believe that aliens were responsible for many unusual disappearances of people, planes, and other unexplained phenomena. The subtle blend of part reality/part fiction combines to provide a powerful and intoxicating cocktail that spurs our imagination on to "possible" realities.

Many such themes link UFOs with current events. In the Cold War of the 1950s and 1960s, the threat of a nuclear confrontation loomed large on the world stage. All-out nuclear war would have effectively extinguished human life on Earth. Many people thought then that UFOs were the result of secret technologies being developed by the enemy or even their own "team." Many similar conspiracy ideas still abound today. One powerful science fiction movie that captured the mood of the time but also catapulted the concept of visiting alien UFOs into the pubic imagination was the 1950s classic *The Day the Earth Stood Still.*

The Day the Earth Stood Still [1951]

This movie is based on a short story by Harry Bates called "Farewell to the Master." Filmed in black and white, it depicts the arrival of a flying saucer which is greeted by the usual alarmist military response (typical for the Cold War era, anyway). Out steps an enormously powerful eight-foot-tall robot known as Gort. Then an alien ambassador named Klaatu appears requesting that the world's political leaders gather because he has a sobering message to give them. Claiming to be a representative of an intergalactic federation that has been monitoring Earth's activities for many years, his federation is concerned about the escalation of wars on the earth and our nuclear capability. (Lead actor Michael Rennie's "regal" and authoritative English accent adds to the aura of superiority.) His request is denied, and after being wounded by a bullet, he blends into the human world, befriending a young boy and his mother. Klaatu gives the mother instructions for dealing with the robot Gort, should anything happen to him.

Klaatu decides that a demonstration of power is necessary to convince man of the seriousness of his mission. Warning Earth's leaders first, Gort shuts down all sources of power on the earth, except for airplanes, hospitals, and other essential services. Klaatu warns that if the earth does not disarm, Gort will be left behind as an intergalactic policeman, and at the first sign of trouble, it will destroy the earth. It seems that man, portrayed through the eyes of the more advanced aliens, was not even worthy of being allowed to self-destruct — it needed to be done by a superior race. The destructive machines of Klaatu's world were designed for good, not war. The imagery reflects the idealism of American culture, which justified building atomic weapons for good — to overcome the evil of communism.

This movie was quite different for science fiction movies of its time because it portrayed aliens as human-like, although supposedly more advanced in technology. Up until this point, aliens had mainly been portrayed as evil, grotesque-looking creatures with the sole agenda of taking over the earth.

It is difficult for today's generation to understand the fear that pervaded this era and the powerful emotions that this movie evoked. Nations were ready to attack or go to war at a moment's notice, and this state of anxiety was used to brilliant effect, fixing the theme of the movie into peoples' psyche. As mankind was developing more and more fearsome technologies, the movie warned us that self-annihilation was imminent, and that we were an "aggressive, less evolved species" that needed help from our more evolved and benevolent neighbors in space. This was one of the first science fiction movies to promote spiritual themes, a trend that continues today. The movie even showed its lead character, Klaatu (who was actually saving mankind from itself), being resurrected from the dead by his robot Gort, as an allegory of Jesus Christ. When Klaatu goes out among the populace, he chooses the name "Carpenter" (Jesus was a carpenter), and remarks to the woman that "the Almighty Spirit" has the power of life and death, not Klaatu's science. If the Almighty Spirit was the Father, and Klaatu the Son, then Gort is the Holy Spirit. The scriptwriter, North, said of these similarities:

> It was my private little joke. I never discussed this angle with Blaustein [producer] or Wise [director] because I didn't want it expressed. I hoped the Christ comparison would be subliminal.[47]

Joke or not, the religious themes have remained part of the UFO psyche.

The "Force is with us"

For the majority of the 20th century, cowboys and Indians and war movies proved to be the most popular form of adventure movie and entertainment escapism (especially after two world wars had scarred the planet). However, a not-so-subtle change took place in the latter third of the century. Science fiction movies became, and have remained, exceedingly popular. In their early days, many had a horror theme. The quality of some was appalling, lacking any realism — and as we have pointed out, realism, or just a dash of it, is the key to making the subject believable. Although popular, very few of them could be called cinematic giants. Some received critical acclaim for the themes they portrayed, but few achieved both critical and enormous box office success.

Science fiction and modern special effects have no doubt helped the average person understand the enormity and strangeness of the universe. They have shown us incredible new machines and the concept of faster-than-light travel by "warping" or "folding" space. They have opened up strange new worlds and a menagerie of bizarre alien creatures. One movie, however, was to capture the popular imagination as never before, attracting critical acclaim *and* becoming the second-highest-grossing movie of all time. That movie was *Star Wars*.

George Lucas's *Star Wars* (released in 1977) became a cinema classic. It captured the old style of "good guys versus bad guys shoot 'em up" escapism, combined with a stunning display of special effects. However, its greatest attraction is as a story of human nature — how we handle adversity and choose our paths in life. Its focus is the eternal struggle of good versus evil in all of us, and about mankind finding our place in the universe. These spiritual themes were prevalent in the film's portrayal of the "Force" — a mysterious energy that is supposedly present in all living creatures. Its power could be harnessed — for good or for evil. This is a New Age religious theme that suggests "god is in you and in everything else, too." This same impersonal god is the "Force" that supposedly binds all living things together.

Interestingly, this is also the most common theme that the "space brothers" have been telling their earthly followers for many years. Even George Lucas admitted the following:

> I put the Force into the movie in order to try to awaken a certain kind of spirituality in young people. . . . I think there is a God. No question. What that God is or what we know about God, I'm not sure.[48]

He must have succeeded. There is good evidence to suggest that such pop culture has awakened in many young people the question of "How did it all begin?" Informal surveys of high school students show that the majority believe that a god or "force" is responsible for the creation of the universe. Undoubtedly, the portrayal of human frailty, and its religious overtones, helped moviegoers relate to the struggles of the main characters. A popular movie review website had this to say about the original Star Wars:

> Star Wars, George Lucas's stunning sci-fi masterpiece, is arguably one of the most inventive and entertaining films ever made, garnering generations of loyal fans who are forever imprinted with the memory of its characters and dialogue.[49]

The review aptly illustrates that the Star Wars legacy has endured. For the first time, a science fiction movie garnered critical, as well as box office, acclaim and crossed into mainstream popularity, ensuring that millions more would become addicted to "sci-fi." Two more movies in the series followed, forming an initial trilogy, which ended with the Return of the Jedi in 1983. Such was their legacy that in 1999, director George Lucas returned to filming to shoot prequels to the original trilogy, some 16 years after Jedi. In one of the most eagerly awaited events of the last century (yes, it was that big), Star Wars: Episode I — The Phantom Menace was released. It immediately climbed to number four on the all-time box office list.

After the huge success of the original *Star Wars*, a literal flood of similar movies followed. The public could not get enough of sci-fi. Even the crew of the old television series *Star Trek*, no longer in production and doomed to reruns, was called into action once again — but this time on the movie screen for six episodes. Then, due to the success of the movie versions, a new television series appeared called *Star Trek: The Next Generation*. The newer version became the most popular syndicated TV show in history, and it, too, has spawned multiple spin-off series.

E. T. the Extraterrestrial, Alien (four movies), *Cocoon* (two movies), *Contact, Dune, Battlestar Galactica, The Time Machine, The Fifth Element, The X Files, Roswell, Dark Skies* — the list of popular sci-fi movies and TV series is far too long to mention them all. But in gauging the popularity of sci-fi, the most up-to-date information at the time of writing this book shows that four of the five highest-grossing movies of all time are science fiction (although the list continually fluctuates). When analyzing the top-grossing movies, science fiction films regularly feature in the top entries.[50]

The increasing popularity of science fiction and increased sightings of UFOs and alleged visitations seems to go hand in hand in a kind of symbiotic relationship. UFOlogist Thomas Eddie Bullard notes:

> Science fiction has anticipated much UFO lore and UFO lore has found its way into science fiction time and again. The relationship has been a busy two-way street. An examination of the science fiction literature cautions that whatever the nature of UFOs, the beliefs people have and the stories they tell about these objects reflect cultural expectations and concerns as well as objective observation. Reports combine both cultural beliefs and perceptual experience. An intriguing trend toward magic and the supernatural, as opposed to mechanical wonders, has lent a fairy-tale quality to much recent fiction. A similar trend is apparent in UFO reports as abductions and other sightings seem to involve non-physical objects and surrealistic experiences. Perhaps a new mystical consciousness is in the making.[51]

Most think that UFOlogy has its roots in science, and that the study of UFOs will reveal explanations for the origin of life and that mankind will benefit from the technological abilities of supposedly superior alien races. However, regardless of which aspect of the UFO phenomenon we consider — science fiction themes, the prophetic messages of the cults, or the quest for futuristic knowledge to save ourselves — it seems to reflect an underlying desire in man for knowing the meaning of life and bettering our existence. Many of the commentators quoted in this chapter have also noticed this spiritual link. This observation strongly testifies to a universal belief that there is more to life than our meager, pleasure-seeking, short-term existence on this planet. There *is* a spiritual hunger within every human being. Every religion has tried to grapple with the mystery of, and meaning to, man's existence.

Perhaps UFOlogy is set to become the world's fastest-growing and most unifying religion.

In 1960, NASA commissioned a report to determine the effect on society should they discover and release information about the existence of extraterrestrials. It drew a terrifying conclusion:

> While the discovery of intelligent life in other parts of the universe is not likely in the immediate future, it could nevertheless, happen at any time. Discovery of intelligent beings on other planets could lead to an all-out effort by Earth to contact them, or it could send sweeping changes or even the downfall of civilization. . . . societies sure of their place have disintegrated when confronted by a superior society.[52]

Does this mean the government really is hiding the truth? Are UFOs slowly conditioning us, preparing us for change? We shall now delve deeper and uncover the evidence about UFOs and extraterrestrial life, and determine whether mankind can indeed find salvation in the stars.

Endnotes

1 "War of the Worlds Radio Broadcast Causes Panic," <www.history1900s.about.com/library/weekly/aa072701a.htm>, January 21, 2003.

2 "Orson Welles's War of the Worlds," <lamar.colostate.edu/~dvest/346/project/kovacek/kar's%2020web%20Page.htm>, January 15, 2003.

3 "War of the Worlds: How Orson Welles Drew the Nation into a Shared Illusion," <www.transparencynow.com/welles.htm>, January 15, 2003.

4 Ronald D. Story, editor, *The Mammoth Encyclopedia of Extraterrestrial Encounters* (London: Constable & Robinson, 2002), p. 679.

5 As reported in the Pro-Life Infonet newsletter, <www.prolifeinfo.org>, January 23, 2003.

6 Ibid.

7 Erdling Hallo, "Ufologie," *Focus* 45:254.

8 Story, *The Mammoth Encyclopedia of Extraterrestrial Encounters*, p. 679.

9 Douglas Curran, *In Advance of the Landing: Folk Concepts of Outer Space* (New York: Abbeville Press, 1985), p. 13, 1985, cited in William T. Alnor, *UFOs in the New Age* (Grand Rapids, MI: Baker Book House, 1992), p. 73.

10 "Project 1947," <www.project1947.com/fig/1947a.htm>, January 27, 2003.

11 Story, *The Mammoth Encyclopedia of Extraterrestrial Encounters*, p. 679.

12 "Clinton Aide Slams Pentagon's UFO Secrecy," <www.cnn.com/2002/TECH/space/10/22/ufo.records/index.html>, January 22, 2003.

13 Ibid.

14 "Quotes from Prominent People," <www.etcontact.net/Quotes.htm>, January 27, 2003.

15 The "ETH" is a standard term in UFOlogy.

16 Story, *The Mammoth Encyclopedia of Extraterrestrial Encounters*, in an article by Richard J. Greenwell, p. 209.

17 Jacques Vallée, *Messengers of Deception* (Berkeley, CA: And/Or Press, 1979), p. 9, cited in Alnor, *UFOs in the New Age*, p. 72.

18 "Gordon Cooper: No Mercury UFOs," <www.space.com/sciencefiction/phenomena/cooper.html>, January 22, 2003.

19 "UFOs and the United Nations," <www.cyber-north.com/ufo/united.html>, January 27, 2003.

20 "UFO Folklore: Dr. J. Allen Hynek," <www.qtm.net/~geibdan/a1998/dec/hynek.htm>, January 27, 2003.

21 "Screen Memories," <www.hedweb.com/mark.ufofilm.htm>, December 10, 2002.

22 Story, *The Mammoth Encyclopedia of Extraterrestrial Encounters*, in an article by Martin S. Kottmeyer and Ronald D. Story, p. 158.

23 *New York Times*, October 8, 1955, cited in "Quotes from Prominent World Government & Military Officials," <www.etcontact.net/Other/QuotePages/QuotesGovernment.htm>, January 28, 2003.

24 "Learn the Truth about UFOs," <www.ebooks-and-ezines.com/ufos-are-real>, January 27, 2003.

25 Robert Urich, from *Alien Encounters*, by Walt Disney Productions, cited in "Disney and UFOs," <www.qtm.net/~geibdan/disney.html>, January 27, 2003.

26 "Solar System Exploration," <solarsystem.jpl.NASA.gov/features/goldin.html>, January 30, 2003.

27 Ibid.

28 For example, Ivan Noble, " 'Conclusive evidence' for Martian life," <news.bbc.co.uk/1/hi/sci/tech/1190948.stm>, September 16, 2003.

29 *Time*, August 19, 1996, p. 83.

30 "Life on Mars," <www.answersingenesis.org/docs/2461.asp>, February 13, 2003.

31 William T. Alnor, *UFO Cults and the New Millennium* (Grand Rapids, MI: Baker Book House, 1998), p. 76.

32 "White House Go-Ahead On NASA Nuclear Prometheus Project," <www.space.com/businesstechnology/nuclear_power_030117.html>, February 2, 2003.

33 "Dan Goldin's speech to the American Astronomical Society," <origins.jpl.NASA.gov/library/speeches/goldin2.html>, January 28, 2003.

34 "Origins: What Is the Origins Program?" <www.origins.jpl.NASA.gov/whatis/whatis.html>, January 28, 2003.

35 "Astrobiology," <www.origins.jpl.NASA.gov/astrobiology/astrobiology.html>, January 31, 2003.

36 "Astrobiology Isn't a Dirty Word Anymore," <www.the-scientist.com/yr2004/jan/prof2_040119.html>, January 19, 2004.

37 "Astrobiology," <www.origins.jpl.NASA.gov/astrobiology/astrobiology.html>, January 31, 2003

38 "Astrobiology Isn't a Dirty Word Anymore," <www.the-scientist.com/yr2004/jan/prof2_040119.html>, January 19, 2004.

39 "Solar System Exploration," <solarsystem.jpl.NASA.gov/features/sagan.html>, January 31, 2003.

40 Carl Sagan, *Cosmos Video, Episode 1: The Shores of the Cosmic Ocean* (Turner Home Entertainment, 1989), cited in "Contact: A Eulogy to Carl Sagan," <www.probe.org/docs/contact.html>, January 29, 2003.

41 "Solar System Exploration," <solarsystem.jpl.NASA.gov/features/sagan.html>, January 31, 2003.

42 Ibid.

43 Wernher von Braun cited in Ann Lamont, *21 Great Scientists Who*

Believed the Bible (Brisbane, Australia: Answers in Genesis, 1997), p. 250–251.

44 Lamont, *21 Great Scientists Who Believed the Bible*, p. 250–251.

45 "The US Government and Unidentified Flying Objects," <www.hq.NASA. gov/office/pao/facts/HTML/FS-015-HQ.html>, January 31, 2003.

46 "Voyager's Greeting to the Universe," <voyager.jpl.NASA.gov/spacecraft/ goldenrec.html>, January 31, 2003. "Voyager," <voyager.jpl.NASA.gov/ mission/mission.html>, January 31, 2003.

47 Peter Biskind, "Seeing Is Believing." References to Jesus and other spiritual leaders as alien emissaries would later become standard fare in UFO literature. See, for example, R.L. Dione, "God Drives a Flying Saucer" (1973), cited in "Screen Memories," <www.hedweb.com.mark. ufofilm.htm>, December 10, 2002.

48 *Time*, "Star Wars: The Phantom Menace — The Force of Myth or Pop-culture Hype?" <www.atheists.org/flash.line/star1.htm>, February 9, 2003.

49 "Yahoo movies," <movies.yahoo.com/shop?d=hv&cf=info&id=1800121 659&intl=us>, February 9, 2003.

50 "All Time Box Office," <movies.yahoo.com/hv/boxoffice-alltime/rank. html>, September 3, 2002.

51 Story, *The Mammoth Encyclopedia of Extraterrestrial Encounters*, in an article by Thomas E. Bullard, p. 629.

52 Chuck Missler and Mark Eastman, *Alien Encounters* (Indianapolis, IN: Koinonia House, 2003), p. 193.

Chapter Two

The Science of Fiction

A gruesome beginning

We have already seen the strong symbiosis between UFOlogy and science fiction, and sci-fi has successfully predicted many useful technologies, as we will see. However, much of modern science fiction is fantasy-driven and portrays many phenomena or technologies that could never exist. Much of it also contains supernatural concepts that are often presented as some form of quasi-science.[1]

Some would argue that modern science fiction has its roots in the writings of authors such as Edgar Allen Poe and, in particular, Mary Shelley. Shelley was born in 1797, the daughter of journalist William Godwin and feminist author Mary Wollstonecraft.[2] She is best remembered for her novel *Frankenstein,* which has been made into over 50 movies spanning several decades. Although she claimed the idea for *Frankenstein* came to her in a dream, her husband, the poet Percy Bysshe Shelley, attended experiments performed by Luigi Galvani in which he used electricity to make the severed legs of frogs move. Shelley borrowed this concept for her novel, in which electricity brings to life a man-like creature assembled from the body parts of corpses. For its time, the novel portrayed unspeakable ghoulish horror, and it remained controversial for many years. Yet it displays the true characteristics of science fiction in adopting cutting-edge concepts of the day while it stretches the imagination and pushes the boundaries of credibility. This is why science fiction is so captivating. The part-science, part-fiction "blur" creates a mysterious yearning for the story to be somehow true. It has an almost addictive attraction about it.

Some of the most prolific science fiction writers are scientists, but most of them simply have an interest or background in science. It has been said that science fiction writers are also visionaries. In some respects, this also applies to scientists in general, who start with ideas and then set out to investigate them.

Even earlier than Shelley, one of the founding fathers of modern scientific study was also a science fiction writer. His name was Johannes Kepler (1571–1630). A committed Christian, Kepler reasoned that the universe was designed by an intelligent Creator, and therefore was ordered and not chaotic. As an astronomer, he used this belief to study the motion of the planets, and was one of the first to support the Copernican view that the earth and other planets orbited the sun, instead of the other way around. His three laws of planetary motion, particularly the relative motion of the sun and moon, helped us understand the seasons, phases of the moon, tides, eclipses, and so on. His discoveries had enormous implications for our modern world in such areas as agriculture, fishing, and even space exploration. They helped dispel confusion in his day between astrology and astronomy, and laid the foundation for Sir Isaac Newton's later research in the study of gravity.[3]

Few know that Kepler also wrote fiction. Of most interest is his story called *Sominium*, the tale of a man who is flown to the moon by a demon.[4] Kepler based this story on his knowledge of astronomy at the time. But the demonic element came from his Christian beliefs, which included the view that demons are fallen angels under the influence of Satan. Kepler's story highlights that even science fiction stories are predicated on a world view, although Bible-based science fiction is an oddity in a literary genre dominated by evolutionary themes.

The first author to try to incorporate scientific accuracy into his fictional writings was Frenchman Jules Verne. Early in his life, Verne came across the works of Edgar Allen Poe and was captivated by them.

Although impressed at his storytelling ability, Verne was unimpressed by Poe's scientific details. Verne asked:

> Why did not Poe take the trouble to correct his science? His story would have lost nothing and gained much.

Verne, although not a scientist, devoted himself to studying science in order that his novels, which were to achieve lasting worldwide fame, might have a realistic bent. His most well-known books include *Journey to the Center of the Earth* (1866), *From the Earth to the Moon* (1865), *20,000 Leagues Under the Sea* (1869), and *Around the World in 80 Days* (1872).[5]

Verne was a prolific writer and produced at least two books a year for over 40 years. In his heyday, long before the advent of modern communications and media, he achieved global popularity. To this day, he remains one of the most widely read authors of all time.

The power of one

The person whom many regard as the father of modern science fiction is Herbert George Wells (1866–1946) — more popularly known as H.G. Wells. After marrying his cousin Isabel in 1883, he was a teacher and pupil at Midhurst Grammar School, and obtained a scholarship to the Normal School of Science in London. There he studied biology under Thomas H. Huxley, who in his day was the most vocal advocate of Charles Darwin's theory of evolution — so much so that he is known as "Darwin's Bulldog." Wells became bored with his study and left without a degree. But Huxley's influence upon Wells was profound. He became a Fabian socialist (like fellow novelist George Bernard Shaw). These views also led him to reject traditional Victorian morality based upon the tenets of Christianity, and advocate almost complete freedom, particularly with regard to sex. He also abandoned his wife, Isabel, for one of his students, Amy Catherine, whom he married in 1895.

In an era of Christian-based morality, Wells became antiestablishment, and like his mentor Huxley, a passionate advocate of evolution. Wells's beliefs are reflected in many of his science fiction novels, which were social and political parodies of his time. Like Kepler, his world view dominated his fiction.

Arguably, *The War of the Worlds* is his most famous novel. Even back in 1898, his view that alien creatures like Martians could exist was based on his belief in evolution. The opening passage of his book showed subtle condescension toward opposing world views:

> No one would have believed in the last years of the nineteenth century that this world was being watched keenly and closely by intelligences greater than man's and yet as mortal as his own; that as men busied themselves about their various concerns they were scrutinized and studied, perhaps almost as narrowly as a man with a microscope might scrutinize the transient creatures that swarm and multiply in a drop of water. With infinite complacency men went to and fro over this globe about their little affairs, serene in their assurance of their empire over matter. . . . No one gave a thought to the *older worlds* of space as sources of human danger, or thought of them only to dismiss the idea of life upon them as impossible or improbable. It is curious to recall some of the mental habits of those departed days. At most, terrestrial men fancied there might be other men upon Mars, perhaps inferior to themselves and ready to welcome a *missionary enterprise*. Yet across the gulf of space, minds that are to our minds as ours are to those of the beasts that perish, *intellects vast* and cool and unsympathetic, regarded this earth with envious eyes, and slowly and surely drew their plans against us. And early in the twentieth century came the *great disillusionment* [emphases added].[6]

Wells believed in evolution and advanced alien races, and as a result he ridiculed Christian ideals as arrogant by suggesting that they might feel compelled to dispatch missionaries to these "inferior" races.

This famous passage has a prophetic quality about it, too, because it succinctly states part of the extraterrestrial hypothesis (ETH) of today — including the belief that aliens are allegedly carrying out scientific observations on humans. Wells sums up his rejection of the Christian idea that an omnipotent God is the ultimate authority in the universe in his next statement:

> If all the animals and man had been evolved in this ascendant manner, then there had been no first parents, no Eden and no Fall. And if there had been no fall, then the entire historical fabric of Christianity, the story of the first sin and the reason for an atonement, upon which the current teaching

based Christian emotion and morality, collapsed like a house of cards.[7]

In other words, he was saying that the Christian world view, including its morality, is based on a Creator God as described in the Book of Genesis, which also describes the entrance of sin, death, and immorality into our world. If evolution is true, as Wells believed, then this Genesis account is false. So Wells consciously disregarded Christian morality. He was a self-conscious humanist. Humanism, as used by Wells, simply means that man decides truth for himself and that there is no infinitely wise God who knows best and thus sets rules or guidelines for the benefit of humanity. And mankind is thus not the central focus of the universe, as the Bible implies, so one should have no problem in invoking ET races elsewhere in the universe. Moreover, if advanced alien civilizations have survived for millions of years and have advanced to greater technological heights than humankind, then it only reinforces the irrelevance of God. In other words, "The aliens have got on quite well without Him, so who needs Him?" The "no need for a god" idea (at the least, no need for the supreme deity of Judeo-Christian religion) dominates most UFOlogy and science fiction stories.

Another famous Wells story to be turned into a feature film was *The Time Machine*.

The Time Machine, by H.G. Wells (1895)

This classic novel was made into three major feature films — in 1960, 1978, and 2001. The best is probably the 1960s version with the Australian actor Rod Taylor in the lead role. It tells the story of a time traveler who journeys into the future to A.D. 802,701. Here he discovers that man has evolved into two separate species — the Eloi, a weak, small race who live in an Eden-like paradise above the ground, and the bestial ape-like Morlocks, who dwell underground.

The Morlocks routinely capture and eat the fragile Eloi. This was a parody based on Wells's Marxist views of class divisions. The Morlocks represented the workers or a subclass who were driven to long working hours — the underground darkness representing bleak factory-like conditions. The Eloi were representative of the upper class, who had become fat and weak by being reliant on (and exploiting) the working class — that is, until the Morlocks "evolved" into the stronger species.

After returning to his own time, he again ventures further into the future to a period when the earth has stopped rotating. There he encounters crab-like creatures and a winged creature similar to a huge white butterfly that rules the planet. Finally, he travels to the time A.D. 30,000,000 where he finds little life and the earth in its death throes — cooling down. He returns to his normal time, horrified at what he has seen — the same fate that evolutionists today think will eventually befall our planet.[8]

In some of his prognostications, there is no doubt that Wells was a great visionary. He predicted a second world war, the airplane, the tank, the atomic bomb, and even crowded superhighways. Yet many of his predictions did not come to pass. Wells wrote over 100 books, but was pessimistic about the lasting influence of his work — a mistaken prediction in itself.

The Time Machine was one of the first science fiction writings to promote the future evolution of life forms on Earth, different from today's. Applied to outer space, plus or minus a few billion years, modern writers reason that evolution could have produced millions, or even billions, of strange life forms on innumerable planets (see the following two chapters for a closer look at this idea).

A "walking encyclopedia"

Isaac Asimov

One of the most famous science fiction writers to push belief in widespread evolution all over the universe was Isaac Asimov (1920–1992). He was almost unbelievably prolific, with over 500 books to his credit on subjects as diverse as anatomy, physiology, astronomy, the Bible, biology, chemistry, etymology, geography, Greek mythology, history, humor, mathematics, and physics. However, he is best known for his science fiction books[9] — some of which have been described as the greatest science fiction ever written. His most enduring work is *Foundation*, which formed the basis of many other related books. The first three books in the series became known as the *Foundation Trilogy*, which deals with the fall of the "Galactic Empire" and the establishment of a "Foundation" of "Psychohistorians" (supposedly a scientific method of predicting the future).[10] This fascination with the future (as reflected in the paragraph below, excerpted from *Foundation*) has become standard fare in UFO beliefs.

> While no one in power believes that a Galactic civilization that has endured for hundreds of generations could ever fall, they recognize that knowledge is power. If this "Psychohistorian" can help keep them in power, he is worth keeping around. They agree to let Seldon [Hari Seldon], and a number of his colleagues, set up a "Foundation," on a remote planet, to compile an encyclopedia of all of man's knowledge. This, Hari has told them, will lessen the fall and keep those in power safe. In reality, Seldon sets up two Foundations with another purpose. One that only a few know. Hari Seldon plots the paths of the Foundation, from its start to, one thousand years later, its leadership of the galaxy.[11]

A prominent feature of Asimov's writing was robots. His novel *The Positronic Man* was converted into a movie called *The Bicentennial Man*. He often predicted that computers would eventually evolve into sentient beings and be treated as equals with humans.

The inspiration for *Star Trek: The Next Generation*'s Commander Data, an android with a positronic brain and circuitry, was Asimov, and his character indirectly pays homage to him. Wordsmith Michael Quinion notes:

> He is usually credited with inventing the *Three Laws of Robotics* that are supposed to guide the actions of all sentient robots. . . .
>
> He based the word positronic on positron, a subatomic particle similar to an electron, but with a positive charge instead of a negative one. This had been discovered and named by the American physicist Carl Anderson in 1932. It seems that there is no earlier reference to the adjective before Asimov

began to employ it. Indeed, of the four citations for the word *positronic* in the *Oxford English Dictionary*, three are from works by him, which seems a touch excessive. Interestingly, all four of them relate to SF [science fiction] sources. . . .[12]

He adds:

He [Asimov] needed a scientific-sounding term that would suggest the brains of his intelligent creations to be innovative and futuristic, and so he invented the word "positronic" to describe matter that was suitable for the construction of an artificial brain with "enforced calculated neuronic paths." Total nonsense, of course, as Asimov himself was the first to admit.[13]

One would think that the idea of sentient or "self-aware" robots should have great appeal for those endorsing the view that the earth has been visited by intergalactic travelers. One of the great problems for any aliens visiting from distant stars is the insurmountable distances, which would take thousands or millions of years to traverse. In all of the accounts of alien visitations today, few have questioned why advanced alien races have not sent robotic "proxies." All of the contacts thus far are claimed to be with organic alien beings. Even though the robot theme was played to great effect in the classic, and now cult, science fiction movie *The Day the Earth Stood Still,* to date there has been scant mention of robots among the myriad of UFO sightings.

Asimov's "Laws of Robotics" appeared in his novel *I, Robot* (1950), which subsequently became a major 2004 Hollywood movie. These insightful propositions set out his ideas about the required protocols for a sentient robot. They are:

A graphic of the robot "Gort" from *The Day the Earth Stood Still*

1. A robot may not injure a human being, or through inaction, allow a human being to come to harm.

2. A robot must obey the orders given it by human beings except where such orders would conflict with the first law.

3. A robot must protect its own existence as long as such protection does not conflict with the first or second laws.

Although fictional, these ideas were held in high esteem and almost regarded as "truth" in some quarters. For years these laws dominated the behavior of robots in other science fiction stories also, demonstrating how influential and "impactful" science fiction ideas can become. However, in recent years, the idea of non-violent robots seems to have lost its appeal. In *Star Trek,* Data is certainly capable of killing, as are the millions of robot drones in *Star Wars* episodes 1 and 2.

Asimov had an encyclopedic knowledge of "just about everything" and an opinion on just as much. This knowledge and the enormity of Asimov's work (both the range of subjects and the breadth of science contained therein) caused many readers to hold him in awe. Interestingly, having an almost worshipful following seems to be very common for science fiction writers. Asimov, in particular, still has an enormous number of followers, many of whom virtually hang on his every word. He was a futurist, and to some, he became a modern prophet. Many other science fiction writers have been held in similar high regard.

The adulation of many sci-fi writers is probably due to the visionary nature of their work, and the "quest for meaning" we mentioned in the first chapter. Perhaps another reason is that many of their predictions have been correct. Their futuristic visions have an alluring quality of their own, and are regarded as the best hope for a "courageous new world." However, many predictions have not turned out to be true, so logic dictates caution about revering the words of people who make mistakes. Leaders of many UFO cults have been proven wrong time and time again, some followers even being led to death by their self-deluded "messiahs" (see chapter 9 on the UFO cults). But in the UFO cults, and even in evangelical Christian circles today, there is a proliferation of prophets whose predictions often prove to be unreliable. Has the "allure of the future" infiltrated the Christian church? Many of their "prophets" are elevated to an iconic status, a phenomenon that is certainly common to, and prevalent in, many other religions and cults. One only needs to take a look at the predictions of the science fiction-based UFO cults to see this "fascination with the future." Because science fiction often takes on religious proportions and has enormous sway over individuals and society in general, it is worthwhile examining the underlying beliefs of science fiction writers.

The faith of ideas

Like Wells, Asimov was a proud atheist and similarly vocal about his own religious view. Remember that atheism, by definition, is also a religious view. The word "religion" comes from the Latin *religare* (*re*: back, *ligare*: to bind), expressing the idea that one is "bound" to one's beliefs, which guide all of one's actions. Religion can therefore include the belief that there is no supernatural realm.

Asked about the opposing world view that God is Creator, he said:

> In my opinion, the biblical account of the creation of the universe and of the earth and humanity is wrong in almost every respect.[14]

For him, this leaves only one other option — evolution. Understanding how men like Asimov viewed origins is critical to understanding their writings and the ETH in general. It is clear that alien life could have come into existence by only one of two ways — it evolved (natural), or a supreme God or intelligence created it (supernatural). An author's view about the origin of life is foundational to everything else he believes, as will be discussed in the next chapters.

Although he did not believe in a deity/Creator, Asimov was a religious man and had the "faith to prove it," as he proudly proclaimed:

> I have faith and belief myself. I believe that the universe is comprehensible within the bounds of natural law and that the human brain can discover those natural laws and comprehend the universe. I believe that nothing beyond those natural laws is needed. I have no evidence for this. It is simply what I have faith in and what I believe.[15]

He acknowledged that it requires faith when it comes to "believing" how the universe came into existence. Interestingly, even though he opposed the traditional Western Christian world view, he acknowledged the necessary link to spirituality in science fiction when he said,

". . . it is impossible to write science fiction and *really* ignore religion."[16]

Author Michael Brummond has written in detail about the religion in Asimov's writings. He noticed several parallels to Christianity in *Foundation*. In that book, Asimov wrote:

> . . . all this talk of about [sic] the Prophet Hari Seldon and how he appointed the Foundation to carry on his commandments that there might some day be a return of the Earthly paradise: and how anyone who disobeys his commandments will be destroyed for eternity. They believe it.[17]

Brummond says:

> The parallelism to Christianity is apparent: the Prophet Hari Seldon represents Jesus Christ, the Foundation is organized religion, the commandments are similar to those given to Moses in the Old Testament, the Earthly paradise is Heaven, and to be destroyed for eternity is the Christian idea of Hell. . . . Overall, it can be seen that Asimov does use religious themes in his works, and often they resemble Christian motifs. The use of religion is not intended, according to Asimov, to burlesque religion, but to profess his beliefs against the existence of a god, or an afterlife.[18]

Asimov believed that God was a man-made invention. The modern UFO movement, which generally believes that a new age is dawning upon the earth courtesy of our extraterrestrial "space brothers" (as they have been called), parallels these ideas, as we shall see later. As an "expert on everything" Asimov became a sought-after social commentator. He also used his writings to spread his opinions and influence the culture. His science fiction, in particular, inspired many to adopt his evolutionary world view and the notion that civilized alien races could have arisen on other planets.

A vision of future past

In profiling the most influential science fiction writers of our time, no list would be complete without Sir Arthur C. Clarke. Author of more than 60 books, he has won just about every conceivable science fiction award from his peers.

His most remembered work was adapted as a blockbuster film called *2001: A Space Odyssey*. This was inspired by Clarke's short story "The Sentinel." In recognition of his co-authorship of the movie script, he shared an Academy Award nomination with director Stanley Kubrick.

2001: A Space Odyssey (1968)

Released in 1968 (after four years in production), this was the most "realistic" science fiction movie of its time. It is a story about evolution — the dawn of man. The story starts four million years ago. There is a strange shiny monolith on Earth, which seems to inspire the apes to pick up tools or even weapons for the very first time. It then zooms forward to the present time when another monolith is found on the moon, emitting signals to Jupiter.

An expedition travels to Jupiter to solve the mystery. A human-sounding computer, the HAL 9000, controls the spacecraft. In 1968, talking computers were fantastic and futuristic and truly in the realm of science fiction. HAL's single-minded programming decides that humans are a danger to the mission. It disposes of the crew one by one.

The last crew member, Dave, alone in space without the tools he'd fashioned to get there, faces his final challenge. But he escapes HAL's plotting and manages to dismantle him. The isolation of space is not lost on the viewer. A terrifying journey ends in a curiously earthly room. Dave sees himself first as an old man and finally dying, at which moment he sees the monolith. Having reached a point that may be interpreted as death, the pinnacle of evolution, or both, Kubrick baffles us with the star-child, a giant human-embryo-cum-planet, suggesting that man has reached his next stage of evolution — some sort of spiritual enlightenment.[19] It is these final frames that pose the biggest riddle for viewers. One frequently proposed answer is that the evolutionary "circle of life" has concluded and man has fully evolved — or a final stage of evolutionary development is about to occur, represented by the baby and its very large head proportional to its body (portraying the concept that its brain has evolved further). Since the major theme of the movie is to trace human evolution from its ape-like beginning, it is reasonable to conclude that the last frames somehow represent the full evolution of man to a final level of intelligence and/or insight.

When the spaceship approaches its destination — the planet Jupiter — there are some amazing mystical special effects, seemingly meant to symbolize that man has arrived at something like the "Omega point." This is the idea of the man who can be called the father of the modern New Age movement, Catholic priest and evolutionist Teilhard de Chardin. To de Chardin, all of reality was evolution; all of nature was propelled by some mysterious evolutionary force toward an ultimate culmination, which he coined the "Omega point" and mystically connected to notions of the "cosmic Christ." This evolutionary neo-paganism, which owes much to Eastern ideas of Nirvana and the like, is on clear display in this film.[20]

The soundtrack music was dominated by the theme of *Thus Spake Zarathustra*. This piece of music is named after one of the writings of the philosopher Nietzsche, who advocated the Darwin-inspired idea of the "superman," later adopted by Hitler's National Socialists.

This movie had a strange ethereal quality. It evoked the mysterious but did not quite give us the answer to the mysteries it raised — or did it? At the time, space was the "flavor of the month" due to the *Apollo* program, which had its zenith shortly after in 1969 when *Apollo 11* landed on the lunar surface. Moviegoers saw the movie time and again, trying to understand the vision. One website devoted to the riddle of "2001" said:

> Let us try to crack this riddle. We will see, in fact, that "2001" does contain a message about reality — one of ultimate importance for every human being.[21]

Arthur C. Clarke

Clarke is a self-avowed atheist, yet his writings contain supernatural or metaphysical themes. Like the other "most famous" authors I mentioned, his materialistic views dominated his writings. In reality, the movie had overt New Age concepts based in materialism, which has evolutionary philosophy as its "engine room."

But his reputation rested, in large measure, on his ability to make predictions that became science fact. Even Isaac Asimov said about Clarke, "No one has done more than Clarke in the way of enlightened prediction."[22] One of Clarke's most impressive predictions was the development of space stations and satellites that act as transmitters for radio signals. He made this prediction back in 1945, long before the first space launch. Because of this foresight, he is known as the father of modern satellites. In addition to his literary skill, he is a highly respected science commentator. He co-broadcast the *Apollo 11, 12,* and *15* missions for CBS, with anchorman Walter Cronkite and astronaut Walter Schirra. He was also past chairman of the British Interplanetary Society and a member of the International Academy of Astronautics, the Royal Astronomical Society, and many other scientific organizations. Such recognition has given him unprecedented stature among science fiction writers, and similarly he has made an enormous impact on the way society views itself. One biographer of Clarke wrote:

> At the heart of every Arthur C. Clarke novel lies a small puzzle with large ramifications. He is an author who takes an idea and drops it into a quiet pool of thought. There's a splash — that's the intriguing nature of Clarke's scientific genius. . . . He's a science fiction writer whose imaginings reverberate outside the realm of fiction.[23]

At the Wernher von Braun lecture series held at the Smithsonian National Air and Space Museum in 1997, Clarke was the keynote speaker. After viewing pictures from NASA's orbiting *Mars Global Surveyor,* he repeated several times that he was serious in suggesting that the pictures showed dense vegetation on Mars.[24] Clarke is a firm believer in life on Mars, and wishes for a manned flight to the planet. He has always expressed his disappointment that manned missions to the moon ceased. Clarke believes that mankind's future will be in the stars, and that the technology is only a matter of time.

The tyranny of distance

Sharing the podium with Clarke that evening was *Apollo 17* moonwalker Eugene Cernan, who, like Clarke, believes that man will be living on Mars some day. His statements that evening suggested that mankind is on the verge of a new era in space exploration that will overtake our old world very quickly. He remarked that there is little difference between science fiction and science fact, and that

> the only difference is time, a dimension we know so little about. . . . That's science fiction today, but give us time. [25]

Although Cernan was suggesting that, in time, the technology to live on Mars would be developed, time is a problem in more ways than one. If man is going to travel to the planets in our solar system, let alone the galaxies, he needs space vehicles that will get him there very quickly. This is also a necessary requirement if the ETH is to have any validity.

The ability to travel millions of light-years (a light-year is about 5 trillion miles or 8 trillion km) in a matter of hours or days is one of the central concepts in modern science fiction. This differs from most early science fiction stories, which depict the exploration of the earth and its unknown reaches, such as the ocean depths or deep inside the core of our planet. Once these regions became familiar, stories focused on the planets within our solar system. Science *fact* showed these to be apparently inert and lifeless, or even highly toxic and physically violent to life. So now the focus has shifted to distant stars and galaxies. This pattern has also occurred in UFOlogy: in the early days, many of the supposed alien visitors to Earth were said to be from places such as Venus, Mars, and Jupiter, but nowadays they are said to come from distant star systems like Pleiades, Zeta Reticuli, or Sirius.

Alien civilizations are presumed to exist because of the realization that this incomprehensibly large universe contains billions upon billions of stars, and possibly a similar number of planets that could be like our Earth. However, contrary to popular expectation, this same enormity makes alien visitations even less likely.

To understand the scope of this problem, let's take a quick look at the known composition of our universe. The nine planets in our solar system revolve around our sun. The sun is actually a star, similar to others we observe shining in the night sky. It is one of maybe 400 billion such stars in our own galaxy, known as the Milky Way. Then there are possibly billions of galaxies like the Milky Way, each containing billions of stars.

Now let's try to comprehend the size of our universe by taking a journey. We are going to need to travel unbelievably fast — at the speed of light, which, according to Einstein's theory of special relativity, is the maximum speed possible (we shall discuss why in a moment). If it were possible to travel at light speed *(c)*, you would be traveling at the astonishing speed of 186,000 miles (300,000 kilometers) per second. Taking off, you could circle the earth seven times in one second. Leaving our planet, you would pass the moon in two seconds and Mars in just four minutes, and it would take you only five hours to reach Pluto, the farthermost planet in our solar system. (Earth is 93 million miles [148 million km] from the sun and Pluto is around 40 times farther from the sun than we are.)

Now let's leave the solar system and travel into the Milky Way. The next closest star is Proxima Centauri, which is 4.2 light-years away. Traveling at 300,000 km every second, it would take you 4.2 years to get there. To traverse our own galaxy, the Milky Way, it would take you about 100,000 years, but upon leaving the Milky Way, it would now take approximately 2,300,000 years to reach Andromeda, the nearest galaxy like our own. The next closest galaxy after that would take us 20 million years to reach — traveling at the speed of light, remember. Yet, we have only just begun to travel the universe, because there are billions more galaxies to visit.[26] There are so many stars in the universe that a human being could not even live long enough to count them all, if that's all he was doing all the time. The vastness of this universe is almost incomprehensible to man — it is hard to believe it exists — yet it *is* real.

However, a very strange phenomenon occurs during our journey through the galaxy, because if we could travel at the speed of light, we would arrive at our destination without perceiving any passage of time. But an observer on the earth would observe the passage of years (of course, people don't live that long, but this is a hypothetical analogy). In other words, a return trip to Proxima Centauri would take 8.4 years (actually longer because it would be necessary to speed up and slow down) but you would come back younger than people who remained on the earth. You would not have aged, but they would be 8.4 years older. This is a problem often ignored by science fiction stories and movies. As one UFO skeptic argues:

> Einstein theorized that the maximum speed possible would
> be c, that is, the speed of light. This is because as our speed increases, our mass increases until at c, our mass becomes infinite.
> Most people think that because objects become weightless in

space, they would be easy to propel, but this is incorrect. Even in space, the more mass an object has, the more energy you need to propel it. To illustrate, let's say that an astronaut is on a space walk and is going to throw two objects. The first object is a one-pound ball and the second object is a 30,000-pound ball. Neither ball weighs anything because there is virtually no gravity up there. If the astronaut has a good baseball arm, he would be able to throw the small ball very fast. However, he would barely budge the large ball. It would feel like he was pushing against a wall. The only movement taking place (apart from a slight movement of the big ball), would be the astronaut moving backward.

How much energy will it take to propel a spaceship to ultra-high speeds? To keep things easy to visualize, we are going to calculate the energy needed to propel a one-pound object to 50% of the speed of light. The formula to determine this is:

$$\text{Kinetic Energy} = \frac{1}{2}\,(\text{mass})\,(\text{velocity})\,(\text{velocity})$$

To propel an object that weighs one pound to a velocity 50% of the speed of light would require an energy source equal to the energy of 98 Hiroshima-sized atomic bombs. That's a tremendous amount of energy.[27]

To put the energy requirements into perspective, let's consider some interesting facts about NASA's space shuttle — the most excellent space machine available to us today:

- It takes only about eight minutes for the space shuttle to accelerate to a speed of more than 17,000 miles (27,358 kilometers) per hour, the velocity required to enter Earth's orbit (escape velocity to leave our planet is 25,000 mph or 40,000 kph).

- The space shuttle main engine weighs $1/7$ as much as a train engine but delivers as much horsepower as 39 locomotives.

- The turbo pump on the space shuttle's main engine is so powerful it could drain an average family-sized swimming pool in 25 seconds.[28]

- The space shuttle's three main engines and two solid rocket boosters generate some 7.3 million pounds (3.3 million kilograms) of thrust at liftoff. America's first manned launch vehicle, the Redstone rocket, produced 78,000 pounds (35,381 kilograms) of thrust. That's just over 1 percent of the space shuttle's power.

- If their heat energy could be converted to electric power, two boosters firing for two minutes only would produce 2.2 million kilowatt hours of power, enough to supply the entire power demand of 87,000 homes for a full day.

These details highlight that the space shuttle is a staggering piece of technology, which uses enormous amounts of energy. Yet it pales into insignificance compared to the energy requirements needed to propel a spaceship at anywhere near light speed. It would require energy equal to 23 million atomic bombs to propel the space shuttle to 50 percent of the speed of light *(c)*. At 90 percent of *c,* it requires the energy of 73 million atomic bombs, or 351 years of the combined power output of all U.S. energy facilities. Of course, once the spaceship reaches its intended destination, it will need to slow down. To stop the spaceship, it would require the same amount of energy as it took to get it moving. If the spaceship plans on returning back to Earth, it would need energy to speed up and slow down one more time. This means we need four times the original energy requirements listed above.[29]

Quite simply, we do not have energy sources at our disposal that could achieve these goals. At the best speed of the *Apollo* craft, which took three days to get to the moon, it would take 870,000 years to reach Proxima Centauri.[30]

Warp factors

This is a huge problem for the ETH because even at light speed, interstellar journeys would take millions of years. Visiting aliens would have to defy the known laws of physics. But we need not worry — science fiction to the rescue!

Because our solar system is thought to be lifeless, science fiction writers have had to dream up strange new worlds or, as Captain Kirk from the *Star Trek* series said, "To boldly go where no man has gone before."

In bemoaning the physical impossibility of faster-than-light travel, novelist Norman Spinrad was quoted as saying it is:

> . . . a pain in the neck to science fiction writers. The literary necessity for faster-than-light travel is all too obvious. Without it, we could have no stories of galactic empires, not much anthropological science fiction, few pictures of alien cultures or outré [sic] planets, a dearth of first-contact stories — in short, science fiction writers would be pretty much confined to our own solar system. . . . Thus, hyperspace. Or overdrive. Or whatever it takes to get our literary spaceships from star to star in literarily usable time.[31]

Most people are familiar with the expression "warp drive" *(Star Trek)*, and other variations, such as "hyperspace" *(Star Wars)* or "folding space" *(Dune)*. Here we see once again how science fiction has made its way into UFO lore, because faster-than-light travel is obviously presumed by supporters of the ETH (extraterrestrial hypothesis).

To understand the concept of warp travel (much faster than *c*), we need to understand that space, although it is a vacuum, is not empty. It is a medium of some sort (scientists are still debating this). Some, like Einstein, call it the "ether." For example, for the light of a distant star to be able to reach the earth, it must travel through "something" — be transmitted through a medium, if you like. This medium is space, or ether. Although special relativity forbids faster-than-light travel within space-time, physicist Miguel Alcubierre of the University of Wales has theorized that space-time itself (the actual fabric of space) may be able to move faster. By expanding space-time behind the spaceship and forming an opposite contraction in front of it, you are in effect creating a wave or bubble of the space-time itself and riding it. Outside observers see motion faster than at the speed of light.[32] Imagine swimming at a certain speed. Now, catch a wave, and you can travel much faster than your original maximum speed.

The expression "folding space" is best described like this. Imagine traveling from one end of a sheet of paper to the other. If you fold the paper in half so that the two ends meet, you have just shortened the distance or "warped" it. Applied to space travel, you are actually using energy to fold the space-time continuum. At least that's the theory. But to travel faster than light by warping or folding space, you have to invent some unknown exotic matter that could generate sufficient energy to warp space in the first place. The whole process is hypothetical and not (at present) testable.

One proposal for exotic propulsion is a "matter to antimatter" power generator. Antimatter is the opposite of normal matter. That is, the electrons have a positive charge instead of a negative one (and are thus called positrons), and protons become antiprotons because they have a negative charge instead of a positive one. All of this produces an anti-atom.

The website *How Stuff Works* explains antimatter this way:

> When antimatter comes into contact with normal matter, these equal but opposite particles collide to produce an explosion emitting pure radiation, which travels out of the point of the explosion at the speed of light. Both particles that created the explosion are completely annihilated . . . leaving behind other subatomic particles. The explosion that occurs when antimatter and matter interact transfers the entire mass of both objects into energy. Scientists believe that this energy is more powerful than any that can be generated by other propulsion methods.[33]

Sounds simple, but the trouble is we cannot find any antimatter, except for tiny amounts in radioactive decay. According to the big-bang theory of how our universe came into existence, there should be equal amounts of antimatter as well as the normal matter that we actually observe (this is a serious objection to this popular view of the evolution of the universe, by the way). Scientists can make antimatter in the laboratory using particle accelerators and atom-smashing devices, but in a whole year, researchers can only produce enough antimatter to power a normal light bulb for a few seconds.

Another theorized method of folding space is "wormholes." Wormholes are simply shortcuts that fold space (imagine taking a shortcut through the center of a ball rather than traveling along the surface). The trouble is, no one has ever seen one, and there is no reason to believe they exist. Like warp drive, they remain purely science fiction.

Space is full of stuff!

Even if the power problems could be solved, there are other serious hiccups for the viability of faster-than-light travel. Although there is a lot of empty "space" in space, there are also many objects, both large and small.

- **Ultra–high-speed collisions.**

    It is estimated that there are 100,000 dust particles per cubic kilometer of space. At light speed (c=300,000 km per second), an impact with just one of these tiny objects would destroy a spaceship. Even at one-tenth the speed of light, the impact would be equivalent to about 10 tons of TNT.[34] Encountering a larger, say, pea-sized object while flying at just 50 percent of c would produce kinetic energy equal to 2.2 atomic bombs. Damage was caused to the space shuttle *Challenger* when in 1983 it hit a small paint flake with such force that it gouged a small crater in the front window (these windows were designed to be extremely robust).[35] The Hubble Space Telescope already has several holes in its structure after just 12 years circling the earth, traveling at just a fraction of the speeds required for galactic travel.

    Science fiction has invented concepts such as force fields and deflector shields to deal with these problems. Although some electrically charged objects can be deflected using electromagnetic fields, how such concepts could be applied to withstand impacts as large as multiple atomic bombs remains imaginary. This would only increase the energy requirements of the ship, too, because an equally powerful force would have to be generated to deflect such objects.

- **Detecting approaching objects.**

    Traveling at ultra-high speeds makes detecting objects in your path virtually impossible. If you are warping at several times c, then some way of transmitting faster-than-light signals would have to be invented. Faster-than-light particles called "tachyons" have been theorized by many, but as far as we know they do not actually exist. According to Einstein, c is the maximum speed possible in the universe, but it would be impossible for any craft to achieve because it would require infinite energy to attain it. In addition, it would seem impossible to develop technology that could detect a grain of sand, for example, millions of light-years away.

- **Avoiding approaching objects.**

    As a spaceship maneuvers, such as changing course or accelerating, it would exert g forces on its occupants. A g force of 1 is equivalent to the earth's gravity (similar to what you feel when you're going down a steep rollercoaster). At 3 g's, an air force fighter pilot could rupture the blood vessels in his eyes. At 5 g's, the pilot would pass out, and 9 g's would kill the pilot in a matter of seconds. Any further increase would start to tear the plane apart. Changing directions at light speed or above would exert *millions of g's* on the ship and its occupants.[36] Science fiction stories have come up with the idea of "inertial dampers" to stop the crew from flying out of their seats or from being splattered against the walls of the ship. It seems that every science fiction invention created to overcome an obstacle only creates another one.

- **Other problems.**

    Another problem in space is cosmic rays. Prolonged exposure can be fatal, and no one knows whether traveling at light speed or faster would increase the dosage.

    Creating artificial gravity is another brainteaser. To date, no one has conjectured how to overcome this problem. Astronauts on the Russian *Mir* space station adapted to weightlessness in space in a matter of weeks, but recovering back on Earth took them several months or even years. During their time in space, astronauts can suffer severe medical difficulties, such as loss of bone density. This is a serious health risk, and the loss cannot be easily or quickly recovered upon return to Earth. In addition, traveling near the speed of light causes even the relatively harmless low frequency radiation to become deadly to humans. This is because the wavelengths become shortened, and thus, high frequency due to the Doppler effect.[37]

    But in science fiction it is possible to overcome anything. The third of Arthur C. Clarke's *Three Laws* states, "Any sufficiently advanced technology is indistinguishable from magic."[38] Conversely, magic may be indistinguishable from any advanced technology. As Ronald Story said (quoted in chapter 1), ". . . most people are finding it increasingly difficult to distinguish fantasy from reality."

Little green men and SETI

Mankind generally is convinced not only that extraterrestrial life exists elsewhere in the universe, but also that such alien life, including intelligent life, could be abundant. With this in mind, we have begun sending and receiving radio signals in the hope of communicating with an alien race. The first "signal" received from space was a regularly spaced blip that repeated every 1⅓ seconds. Excitedly, many investigators thought this might be a message from some extraterrestrial entity or civilization. Later, astrophysicists realized that the radio waves were emitted by something they called a pulsar.

A pulsar is a very dense star, possibly one that has endured some form of gravitational collapse. It is called a pulsar because it pulses. That is, it rotates so rapidly that it sends out extremely regular pulses of radio waves. Astronomers were so impressed, they called it LGM-1 ("Little Green Men-1"). One of its discoverers, Jocelyn Bell Burnell, said:

> One of the ideas that we entertained was that it might be little green men — a civilization outside in space somewhere trying to communicate with us.[39]

This gives some idea of what they were expecting. As our technology increased, it led to an understanding of the vastness of the universe, and further speculation that there must be millions, or even billions, of other civilizations. If the development of technology is our goal, then science fiction concepts "set the bar" as to what might be achieved. It is the "engine room" that has driven the imagination as to "what might be out there."

The idea that the universe must be teeming with life is already viewed as respectable science. One of the prime movers for this view is Dr. Frank Drake, who, in 1960, while working as a radio astronomer, commenced Project Ozma, which was the first organized search for extraterrestrial intelligent radio signals. He also developed a binary code system to help him decrypt alien communications.

Drake constructed the first interstellar message ever transmitted via radio waves by our planet for the benefit of any extraterrestrial civilizations. This message is known as the "Arecibo Message of November 1974." His messages have also been incorporated on the plaques on the *Pioneer 10* and *11* missions (designed by Drake, Carl Sagan, and his wife, Linda Salzman Sagan), and on the "*Voyager* Record" aboard the *Voyager* spacecraft.[40]

In 1961, he developed a formula for calculating the number of supposed technological civilizations that might exist in our own Milky Way galaxy. This became known as the Drake equation. It has become the most accepted rationale (a seemingly quantifiable hypothesis) for the existence of extraterrestrial life. The equation is expressed as follows:

$$N = R_* \cdot f_p \cdot n_e \cdot f_l \cdot f_i \cdot f_c \cdot L$$

N   *The number of civilizations in the Milky Way Galaxy whose radio emissions are detectable.*

R$_*$ *The rate of formation of suitable stars.*
That is, stars with an adequate "habitable zone."

f$_p$ *The fraction of those stars with planets.*
Although the percentage of sun-like stars with planets is currently unknown, evidence indicates that planetary systems may be common for stars like the sun.

n$_e$ *The number of "Earths" per planetary system.*
How many planets occupy a habitable zone where they would be able to maintain a temperature that would allow liquid water? A planet in the habitable zone could have the basic conditions for life as we know it.

f$_l$ *The fraction of those planets where life develops.*
Although a planet orbits in the habitable zone of a suitable star, other factors are necessary for life to arise. Thus, only a fraction of suitable planets will actually develop life.

f$_i$ *The fraction of life sites where intelligence develops.*
Life on Earth began over 3.5 billion years ago. Intelligence took a long time to develop. On other life-bearing planets it may happen faster, it may take longer, or it may not develop at all.

f$_c$ *The fraction of planets where technology develops.*
The fraction of planets with intelligent life that develop technological civilizations, i.e., technology that releases detectable signs of their existence into space.

L   *The "lifetime" of communicating civilizations.*
The length of time such civilizations release detectable signals into space.[41]

The world's largest and longest-running effort to search for extra-terrestrial life has been carried out by the SETI Institute (Search for

Extraterrestrial Intelligence), where Drake once served as president and chairman of the board. The institute's work is predicated on Frank Drake's equation, yet its own website admits:

> Among the factors considered are the number of sun-like stars in our galaxy, the fraction of habitable planets supporting communicating civilizations, etc. When these various factors are multiplied together one can compute N, the number of transmitting civilizations. Unfortunately, many of the factors are poorly known, so estimates of *N range from one (we are alone in the Galaxy) to thousands or even millions* [emphasis added].[42]

Despite the complex appearance of Drake's equation, this is a frank admission (pardon the pun) which highlights its entirely conjectural nature. The whole hypothesis only makes some sort of vague sense if one believes that evolution is occurring all over the universe. However, the equation itself is a work of fiction. Most factors in the equation are presently non-quantifiable, and to date not even one intelligible transmission has ever been received from space.

The forerunner of SETI was Drake's pioneering work of 1960. His work was continued in the 1970s by Benjamin Zuckerman and Patrick Palmer in a project known as Ozma II. Whereas the original Ozma had the use of a single radio telescope, version II had 384, and scanned over 700 stars compared to the original Ozma's two.[43] Then in 1984, SETI, as we know it today, was formed under the guidance and vision of Tom Pierson and Frank Drake. Up until 1994, SETI was partly funded by NASA, but the program was unpopular with the U.S. Congress, and they cut off funding several times. Until recently, SETI was privately funded by corporations such as Hewlett Packard and individuals like Paul Allen, one of the co-founders of Microsoft. Even UFO enthusiast and famous movie director Steven Spielberg has contributed funds. Allen, a staunch evolutionist and one of SETI's keenest promulgators, has personally donated many millions of dollars, and he even has a telescope array named in his honor. His major interest is Project Phoenix, which is a targeted search as opposed to a general sweep of the sky. SETI says of Phoenix:

> Since 1995, it has been scrutinizing the vicinities of nearby, Sun-like stars, hoping to pick up a signal that would tell

us that we're not alone. . . . Project Phoenix is the name of the SETI Institute's research project to search for extraterrestrial intelligence. The name derives from the mythological Egyptian bird that rose from the ashes of its own demise — in the case of SETI, the ashes of congressional funding cuts.[44]

The silence is deafening

One of the reasons that SETI and Project Phoenix were not the "flavor of the month" for the public purse was their failure to detect anything. SETI's network of radio telescopes can scan 28 million radio frequencies per second, and is estimated to be 100 trillion times more effective than Project Ozma. In addition to SETI's efforts, there have been over 60 other projects spanning more than 40 years. Despite these massive efforts, and billions of dollars of funding, not once have they ever detected ET trying to "phone home"! Another well-known project is SETI@home. This involves using home computer users in a massive computing project that analyzes data gathered by the Arecibo radio telescope.

Like advocates Drake, Sagan, and others, SETI does not subscribe to the ETH and openly says so:

> Many Americans (and quite a few citizens of other countries) are convinced that extraterrestrials may be buzzing the countryside in their spacecraft, or occasionally alighting in the back yard to abduct a few humans for breeding experiments. This would be of enormous interest and importance of course, and (in our opinion) impossible to hide, particularly if it's happening internationally. The presence of aliens on our planet is not something you would want to hide: it would be the biggest science story of all time, and tens of thousands of university researchers would be working away on it. However, despite the popularity of aliens on both silver and phosphor screens and a half-century of UFO sightings, the lack of credible physical evidence has made it difficult for serious scientists to believe that UFOs have anything to do with extraterrestrial visitors.[45]

Frank Drake commented:

> SETI was a four-letter word in NASA. . . . It was not uttered in speeches, or in documents.[46]

This is not what many really want to hear. It might be prudent for SETI to learn a few marketing tips from NASA — and indeed they have — the public's fascination for extraterrestrial life, and also its involvement via the SETI@home project, has proved to be SETI's savior. Incredibly, SETI recently received a boost in funding from an unexpected source — its former critic, NASA. Why did NASA so radically change its policy toward something formerly deemed a waste of money — especially since nothing changed as far as evidence was concerned? The answer seems obvious, even though NASA denies that anything in its approach to space exploration has changed. NASA's *Origins* program has captured public interest and loosened the public purse, and SETI's ET focus certainly does no harm to NASA's stocks. Lamar Smith, a member of the U.S. House of Representatives, confirmed that SETI was more popular than it was given credit for, when he said:

> Funding should match public interest ... and I don't believe it does.[47]

SETI still has many critics, though, and it appears that it cannot please everyone. UFOlogists are annoyed because SETI won't "join the club" and promote the ETH, and some skeptics, such as astrophysicist Frank J. Tipler of Tulane University, have some serious objections to the idea of even funding the search for extraterrestrials. He goes as far as charging SETI advocates with promoting unfalsifiable, and hence pseudoscientific, hypotheses.[48] He was quoted as saying:

> SETI will become a science — and hence be worth doing — only when its proponents tell us exactly what will convince them that it is reasonable to assume we are alone.[49]

What he is really saying is that SETI (like NASA and others) is using science to explore fictional beliefs. Supporters of the ETH believe that absence of evidence is not evidence of absence, and that it will just be a matter of time before we make contact. The search for ETs has truly become "the science of fiction."

Endnotes

1 David J. Laughlin, "Science Fiction: A Biblical Perspective," *TJ* (the in-depth journal of creation) 15(2):81–88, 2001.

2 "Mary Shelley," <www.bbc.co.uk/science/space/scifi/whos_who/mary_shelley.shtml>, February 12, 2003.

3   Ann Lamont, *21 Great Scientists Who Believed the Bible* (Brisbane, Australia: Answers in Genesis, 1997), p. 18–19.

4   "Johannes Kepler," <www.bbc.co.uk/science/space/scifi/whos_who/kepler.shtml>, December 12, 2002.

5   "Jules Verne," <www.bbc.co.uk/science/space/scifi/whos_who/jules_verne.shtml>, December 12, 2002.

6   "The War of the Worlds," <www.fourmilab.ch/etexts/www/warworlds/b1c1.html>, February 15, 2003.

7   H.G. Wells, *The Outline of History — Being a Plain History of Life and Mankind* (London: Cassell & Company Ltd. [fourth revision], Vol. 2, 1925), p. 616, cited in Laughlin, "Science Fiction: A Biblical Perspective," *TJ* 15(2):81–88, 2001.

8   Laughlin, "Science Fiction: A Biblical Perspective."

9   "Religion in Asimov's Writings," <www.angelfire.com/wi/mikebru/Alps.html>, February 12, 2003.

10   "Isaac Asimov's Foundation Series," <www.vavatch.co.uk/books/asimov/index.htm#1>, February 15, 2003.

11   "Foundation (by Lacey)," <www.asimovians.com/bookreviews.php?op=showcontent&id=57>, February 15, 2003.

12   "World Wide Words," <www.quinion.com/words/topicalwords/tw-pos1.htm>, February 15, 2003.

13   Ibid.

14   *Free Inquiry* (Spring 1982), quoted in "Isaac Asimov in Science and the Bible," <www.positiveatheism.org/hist/asimov.htm#REAGANDOCT>, February 17, 2003.

15   Isaac Asimov, *Counting the Eons* (London: Grafton Books), p. 10, cited in "An Atheist Believes," <www.answersingenesis.org/home/area/magazines/docs/v13n2_asimov.asp>, February 12, 2003.

16   Asimov, *Gold* (New York: Harper Collins, 1995), p. 297–302, cited in "Religion in Asimov's Writings," <www.angelfire.com/wi/mikebru/Alps.html>, February 12, 2003.

17   Asimov, *The Foundation Trilogy* (New York: Equinox, 1974), p. 103, cited in "Religion in Asimov's Writings," <www.angelfire.com/wi/mikebru/Alps.html>, February 12, 2003.

18   "Religion in Asimov's Writings," <www.angelfire.com/wi/mikebru/Alps.html>, February 12, 2003.

19 "Lost the Plot: 2001: A Space Odyssey," <www.bbc.co.uk/films/2001/12/07/2001_space_odyessy_lost_the_plot_article.shtml>, February 16, 2003.

20 "2001: A Space Oddity," <www.answersingenesis.org/docs2001/0110mr.asp>, February 12, 2003.

21 "The 2001 Principle," <www.2001principle.net/2002.htm>, February 16, 2003.

22 "Legendary Science Fiction Writer Arthur C. Clarke at 80," <news.bbc.co.uk/1/world/analysis/400081.stm>, February 12, 2003.

23 "Arthur C. Clarke Unauthorized Homepage," <www.lsi.usp.br/~rbianchi/clarke/ACC.Homepage.html>, February 12, 2003.

24 "Discussions from the Wernher von Braun Memorial Lecture Series at the Smithsonian National Air and Space Museum, 6 June 2001," reported in "Arthur C. Clarke Stands by His Belief in Life on Mars," <www.space.com/peopleinterviews/clarke_mars_010601.html>, February 12, 2003.

25 Ibid.

26 John R. Cross, *The Stranger on the Road to Emmaus* (Sanford, FL: GoodSeed International, 1999), p. 16–17.

27 "UFO-3: Ultra High Speeds Are Impossible," <www.biblehelp.org/ufo3.htm>, February 20, 2003.

28 Presume a below-ground pool about 25 feet, or 8 meters, long.

29 "UFO-3: Ultra High Speeds Are Impossible," <www.biblehelp.org/ufo3.htm>, February 20, 2003.

30 Ken Ham and Don Batten, *Is There Intelligent Life in Outer Space?* (Brisbane, Australia: Answers in Genesis, 2002), p. 11.

31 X. Spinrad, "Rubber Sciences," *The Craft of Science Fiction* (New York: Harper & Row, 1976), p. 57 cited in Laughlin, "Science Fiction: A Biblical Perspective," *TJ* 15(2):81–88, 2001.

32 "The Warp Drive: Hyper-Fast Travel within General Relativity," <www.astro.cf.ac.uk/groups/relativity/papers/abstracts/miguel94a.html>, February 20, 2003.

33 "What Is Antimatter?" <science.howstuffworks.com/antimatter1.htm>, February 21, 2003.

34 Ham and Batten, *Is There Intelligent Life in Outer Space?*

35 "UFO-4: High Speed Collisions," <www.biblehelp.org/ufo4.htm>, February 1, 2003.

36 "UFO-8: Unable to Avoid Objects in Its Path," <www.biblehelp.org/ufo8.htm>, February 21, 2003.

37 The Doppler effect can cause the wavelengths of light to move up or down (be redshifted or blueshifted) dependent on the speed and direction of the object. It is the reason for the change of pitch in, for example, the sound of a car's engine as it moves toward you and then away from you. See chapter 3 for more discussion on this.

38 "Arthur C. Clarke's Laws," <www.lsi.usp.br/~rbianchi/clarke/ACC.Laws.html>, February 21, 2003.

39 Ham and Batten, *Is There Intelligent Life in Outer Space?* p. 16.

40 Ronald D. Story, editor, *The Mammoth Encyclopedia of Extraterrestrial Encounters*, "SETI Institute," by Frank Drake (London: Constable & Robinson, 2002), p. 192–193.

41 Ibid.

42 "Frequently Asked Questions," <www.seti.org/about_us/faq.html#anchor300489>, February 22, 2003.

43 Story, *The Mammoth Encyclopedia of Extraterrestrial Encounters*, article by Robert Sheaffer, p. 637–640.

44 "Frequently Asked Questions," <www.seti.org/about_us/faq.html#anchor300489>, February 22, 2003.

45 Ibid.

46 "Search for Life Out There Gains Respect, Bit by Bit," <www.nytimes.com/2003/07/08/science/space/08SETI.html>, July 8, 2003.

47 Ibid.

48 Story, *The Encyclopedia of Extraterrestrial Encounters*, article by Robert Sheaffer, p. 637–640.

49 Ibid.

Chapter Three

Is There Life on Other Planets?

The Fermi paradox

In 1950, Nobel Prize winner and pioneer of atomic energy, Enrico Fermi, while working at Los Alamos nuclear facility in New Mexico, raised this straightforward question:

> Are we the only technologically advanced civilization in the universe, and if we are not, then where are they? Why haven't we seen any traces of extraterrestrial life such as probes or transmissions?

Modern space agencies admit that they have failed — so far — to find even the slightest signs of intelligent extraterrestrial life. *National Geographic* magazine pointed out, in an interview with SETI's senior astronomer, Seth Shostak:

> He and his colleagues have never found proof [that] any-one . . . or anything . . . "up there" is trying to make contact.[1]

This failure presents a real challenge for SETI scientists. If the universe is billions of years older than the earth, then intelligent life would have had plenty of time to evolve elsewhere. So why aren't the airwaves filled with their communications? Shostak suggested an answer:

> The usual assumption is they're some sort of soft, squishy aliens like you see in the movies — just a little more advanced than we so we can find them. But the galaxy [our Milky Way] is two or three times that age [of the earth], so there are going to be some societies out there that are millions of years, maybe more, beyond ours.[2]

Enrico Fermi

In other words, Shostak believes that we may be a primitive culture trying to communicate with older, more advanced civilizations, similar to a jungle tribe that bangs on drums and is listening for return messages from yuppies who communicate with mobile phones. If this is the case, then Shostak believes it should be enough to find even the merest speck of life, past or present, on other planets. He explains:

> If another world — [such as Mars] the next world out from the Sun — is proved to have supported life, *that would imply* that the cosmos is drenched with living things. We could conclude that planets with life are as common as phone poles [emphasis added].[3]

But this suggestion does not satisfy Fermi's original question. Surely intelligent aliens would be curious explorers just like us. In a 15-billion-year-old universe there should have been plenty of time for at least the very first advanced race to send starships to colonize planets. Even if the first colonizing expedition took a million years of travel (assuming several generations of explorers), the new colony, once established, and the original civilization, could then both send out another ship apiece to colonize other planets, doubling the number of new colonies every million years. After 10 million years, there would be 1,024 alien colonies, and after 20 million years, there would be one million. At that rate, in 40 million years, there would be one trillion civilizations. After 15 billion years, the number of alien civilizations in the universe would be tripping over each other — and this overpopulation assumes only one race of intelligent aliens.[4] The problem would be compounded further if two separate races had evolved.

This "lack of ETs" idea has become known as the Fermi paradox — in short, "Where is everybody?" Even SETI enthusiasts admit that the paradox is a difficult one to ignore, because any advanced alien race would surely have developed technology in the electromagnetic spectrum to be able to communicate as effectively as humans have done, and thus, we should be picking up their communications. Nonetheless, it is argued that we are dealing with the unknown, and therefore an unknown set of parameters — "The universe is a big place, so one cannot say for sure!"

Real science we can understand

Despite the space agencies' lack of success in intercepting alien communications or discovering signs of alien life, scientists and UFOlogists alike are keen to keep up the search. What evidence are they looking for, and how can we know when they have found it?

In the following chapters, we shall carefully evaluate the evidence that UFOlogists have already put forward to support the ETH (extraterrestrial hypothesis); that is, the belief that extraterrestrials have been regularly visiting the earth. To look at the evidence fairly and objectively, it is essential first to understand the difference between claims which are scientifically testable and those which (whether true or otherwise) are not, and thus fall into the realm of beliefs held by faith.

We have earlier mentioned that pre-existing beliefs are always involved when people consider evidence; that is, the "facts" are always interpreted within an existing world view or framework of belief. Right at the very core of someone's belief about extraterrestrials is the controversial issue of "origins"; a person will frequently base his ideas about the origin of alien life on his beliefs about how life arose on Earth. For instance, the science fiction writers mentioned in the last chapter (some of whom are self-avowed atheists) all based their writings on their beliefs about origins.

We have already discussed the subjective nature of claims in UFOlogy that are often presented as "evidence." Can we scientifically investigate the claims made by "contactees" and "abductees," who often say they have received messages delivered by our "space brothers"?

Millions of people claim to have seen UFOs or been contacted by aliens — even to the extent of being transported in spaceships with detailed descriptions of machinery. Yet we have never recovered an alien spacecraft or even found undisputed fragments of one. Nor have we captured any alien in the act of abduction. In fact, to date, and to the author's best knowledge, there has not been one single documented encounter of a human with an alien that can be appropriately verified.

In an effort to explain this widespread phenomenon, John Mack, who was a world-famous alien abduction researcher and former professor of psychiatry at Harvard University, said that these claims are stretching our understanding of reality. He observed:

> Other cultures have always known that there were other realities, other beings, other dimensions. There is a world of other dimensions, of other realities that can cross over into our own world.[5]

Is Mack suggesting that so-called aliens may be visitors from another reality, dimension, or even universe? These ideas, sometimes called the Interdimensional Hypothesis (IDH) or the Extradimensional Hypothesis (EDH), gained notoriety as a result of the writings of UFOlogist Jacques Vallée (whose research we shall take a look at later) among others. Whether he is correct or not, his hypothesis appears to be outside of our present scientific ability to test. Unlike IDH and EDH, we can look at the ETH because, for extraterrestrial life forms to really exist, it is fair to assume that they must have a place to live. We can at least use the scientific method to search for their homes.

For example, science shows that the ability to travel at faster-than-light speeds within our universe is a *physical* impossibility (previous chapter), so extraterrestrial visitors must be inhabitants of our solar system or planets of nearby star systems that would not require several "lifetimes" of travel time to reach the earth. By this process we can eliminate all that is *impossible,* leaving us with a list of what is *possible.* However, what if we cannot find any suitable "hard" evidence to verify that the "possible" is "probable" or perhaps "real"? Then the best we can do, as a last resort, is to consider which belief system best fits the circumstantial evidence.

Before we proceed with our investigation of UFOs, we need to understand the limits of science. We can divide scientific procedure into two types commonly in usage today. The first is *operational* or *process science*. This is the science that everyone is familiar with. We enjoy the benefits of operational science every day. Advances in technology have given us modern medicine, electronics, aviation, and engineering; they have even put man on the moon. These discoveries are built upon principles that we can test and use in experiments — *in the present*. For example, you can go to the kitchen and boil water at 100° Celsius (at sea level). Tomorrow you can repeat the same experiment and will get the same results. With operational science, there is little room for speculation or guesswork.

The other type of science is *historical* or *origins science*. This involves working out what happened in the past. Unlike operational science, historical science is severely limited because we cannot experiment on, or test directly, past events. We do not have a time machine, so we cannot repeat or observe events in history. As we have previously mentioned, this problem is at the very core of the whole hypothesis of extraterrestrial life, which assumes that life emerged spontaneously on Earth; therefore it must have emerged spontaneously elsewhere as well. There is no testable, repeatable experiment to show, for instance, whether reptiles changed into birds, or apes into humans, as claimed by evolutionists. Even if one could arrange an experiment to turn a reptile into a bird, this experiment would not prove that the same thing happened "once upon a time."

We do see changes in living things, which are interpreted as supporting the hypothesis of macroevolutionary change. This might be so if these were generally "creative" in the sense of generating new functional genetic information (the evidence to date indicates the opposite) but even then would not prove that it had happened in the past (see next chapter).

The origin of life on Earth is presumed to have occurred only once; so no living person has *ever* seen such a thing. In such historical (or forensic) science, the present-day facts (data) must be interpreted to fill in the gaps about the past. The scientist is forced to make inferences based on assumptions. The further he goes back into the past, the more he is removed from the events, and the more the methods of operational science become invalid. Speculation and pre-existing beliefs play a major role in the interpretation of data. If a scientist is already convinced that evolution is true, he will extrapolate results along that line of thinking (his views are religious because he has a *belief* system about the past). And vice versa for those who are already convinced that evolution is untrue, of course. Experts in historical science have astutely observed:

> The conflicts between "science" and "religion" occur in . . . historical science, not in operational science. Unfortunately, the respect earned by the successes of operational science confounds many into thinking that the conjectural claims arising from origins science carry the same authority.[6]

Atheistic evolutionists generally reject the notion that an outside intelligence created the universe, because this is a religious belief, not science. Instead, they invoke an initial big bang that had no cause. Yet many famous atheistic scientists, such as Sir Fred Hoyle and Sir Francis Crick (whose beliefs are discussed in the next chapter), have no problem with invoking "intelligence," e.g., interfering aliens who supposedly created the first life on Earth. As we shall see, every view about origins, including the claim of materialists (materialism is the belief that matter is all there is) that "no god was necessary," falls outside operational science (we were not there to see or test the events). They are all clearly religious beliefs. So where does "science" begin?

Science and beliefs

Beliefs about the past have nothing to do with the ability of scientists to do good operational science. Many of the founding fathers of operational science were, in fact, motivated by their belief that the universe was made by a rational Creator.[7] Famous names include Robert Boyle, Isaac Newton, Johannes Kepler, John Ambrose Fleming, Lord Kelvin, and Louis Pasteur. They believed that an orderly universe is the hallmark of a designer.

Billions of people around the world still believe in a creation by a divine being, and, amazingly, many thousands of highly qualified scientists also subscribe to this view. This fact may come as a surprise to many, but only because evolution is the prevailing belief and is presumed to be an indisputable fact.

If we are considering "world-shaking" claims that ETs are visiting the earth, surely we should presume nothing! Only by understanding the limits of operational science and by keeping an open mind can we properly investigate the evidence for life on other planets.

The big bang — briefly

It is our intention in the next few chapters to examine, in non-technical layman's terms, the underlying philosophies of historical science — beginning with the big bang (the evolution of the cosmos). This theory claims to account for the creation of matter and subsequently all life forms, including any extraterrestrial ones. According to the big-bang theory, everything came into existence by itself, out of "nothing," about 15 billion years ago. Most people accept this view based on the word of scientists. But few ordinary people have ever examined the details. The story goes like this. In the beginning there was nothing, but apparently a "quantum fluctuation" produced a singularity or "kernel" of energy that, some say, was no bigger than a pinhead — and this "pinhead" contained the entire universe and all the matter in it, including space itself. Scientists don't know what could have triggered such an event — it remains a complete unknown.

Actually, because time itself is said to have been brought into existence at the same moment, and because all the laws of science break down in such a "singularity," we *can't* know — in principle. And of course the alleged event can never be observed or repeated. Thus, by definition, the big-bang origin of the universe (even if it really were to have happened that way) cannot be said to be a scientific fact, but more in the realm of belief.

I recall attending a UFO conference where a seasoned investigator claimed that this was "real" science, which underpinned his belief about UFOs. The big bang had created innumerable planets elsewhere in the universe. He then explained that, since the great cosmic science experiment — namely evolution — had occurred on the earth, it must have occurred elsewhere in the universe.

In an aptly described article called "Guth's Grand Guess," famous cosmologist and father of the inflation model of the big bang Alan Guth admitted, albeit in a tongue-in-cheek fashion:

> The universe burst into something from absolutely nothing — zero, nada. And as it got bigger, it became filled with even more stuff that came from absolutely nowhere.[8]

As the theory goes, the universe, mainly in the form of radiation, spread outward, and temperatures cooled enough for the first atoms to form. After about five billion years, the first stars began to form out of cooling gas clouds. Eventually, other processes gave rise to galaxies, our Milky Way and planets.[9]

Interestingly, many argue that it is implausible to invoke a Creator who created matter from nothing. However, the big-bang theory invokes a similar belief without any basis in observed reality. Both are religious beliefs. This indicates the importance of starting assumptions in any origins theory.

Many cosmologists do not like to refer to the big-bang theory as an explosion of matter, arguing that it is really an *expansion* of space-time and energy.[10] Their reason is that the average person (including most non-specialist scientists) thinks of the entire material of the universe expanding into *pre-existing space*, thus our universe would have an edge and a center (like an expanding balloon). However, the most popular theory among the big-bang experts is that matter and space itself are expanding together, with no edge or center.

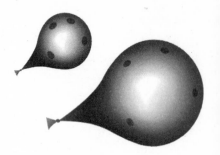

Expanding balloons

The theory is a little convoluted, but try to imagine the universe and its galaxies existing *only on the surface* of a small balloon (i.e., the galaxies are like sequins stuck onto the two-dimensional surface of a balloon). As the balloon expands (in three dimensions), all the galaxies move away from each other in every direction in two dimensions. Imagine you were an ant on the surface of the balloon. No matter how far you kept traveling in any direction, you would never reach the "end" of this two-dimensional "universe" because there is no edge, even though you might eventually end up where you started. Since there is no edge, there is no center to this two-dimensional space, either.

But our normal understanding of three dimensions (height, length, and breadth) is not adequate to explain the big-bang theory. We have to shift our balloon model "up a gear" to include a fourth dimension called "hyperspace."[11] In effect, just as our ant's two-dimensional (2-D) world was wrapped around a 3-D sphere, this 3-D universe of ours is, in big-bang thinking, wrapped around a 4-D hypersphere. So, just as the balloon's surface had no edge or center, neither does this model of our universe. As the 3-D expansion of the balloon causes a 2-D moving apart of the objects on the surface, so a 4-D expansion of our hypersphere causes every object to move away from every other object in 3-D. This is why, say big-bangers, all distant galaxies appear to be moving away from us. If we were out on a distant galaxy, everything would also appear to be moving away from us. If you are having trouble imagining this, don't worry — you're not alone! Experts say, "It's impossible to imagine — you've just got to accept it."

There is a reason for detailing these complexities. Most think that the details about the origin of our universe have been worked out. But it is a non-testable and convoluted theory, and there are some prominent figures in the world of astronomy who reject it. And "just accepting" scientists' conjectures has enormous implications for our study.

The emptiness that is supposed to be inside the balloon is known as hyperspace. This part of the theory allows science fiction writers to imagine traveling through "wormholes," or to conceive of "folding space" so that their imaginary vessels can make shortcuts across hyperspace. But what scientific evidence has led to this idea?

Because the universe gives the appearance that it is (or has been) "stretched" by expansion, the light traveling to Earth from distant galaxies has also been stretched. This causes the wavelength of the actual light to be redshifted, or its wavelengths lengthened (or stretched) toward the red end of the light spectrum. (Conversely, if light wavelengths were contracted/shortened, they would be blueshifted.)

Initial observations from the earth showed that the light from distant galaxies in every direction has been redshifted, interpreted to mean that all galaxies are moving away from the earth. A very normal and reasonable explanation for this would be that our galaxy, the Milky Way (and thus Earth), is somewhere near the center of the universe. (This would be so even if there had never been a primeval "big bang" from some single point.)

We will now see one reason why we stress that philosophical assumptions underlie all origins science. The *prima facie*,[12] obvious, and straightforward interpretation of redshifted light is *unacceptable* because it lends itself to the notion that the earth is in a special place; i.e., it is the result of purpose or design. The famous astronomer Edwin Hubble (after whom the Hubble Space Telescope is named) admitted this:

Such a condition [these red shifts] would imply that we
occupy a unique position in the universe analogous, in a sense,
to the ancient conception of a central earth. The hypothesis
cannot be disproved but it is unwelcome. . . . But the unwelcome supposition of a favored location must be avoided at all
costs. Such a favoured position, of course, is intolerable; moreover, it represents a discrepancy with the theory, because the
theory postulates homogeneity [smoothness or evenness].[13]

Hubble was really saying that, although the evidence suggests we
are somewhere near the center, it was an unacceptable proposition to
him.

George Francis Rayner Ellis is another high-profile cosmologist
who has co-authored papers with big-bang guru and science populist
Stephen Hawking. In a profile in *Scientific American*, he honestly admitted the role of philosophical assumptions:

People need to be aware that there is a range of models
that could explain the observations. . . . For instance, I can
construct you a spherically symmetrical universe with earth at
its center, and you cannot disprove it based on observations.
. . . You can only exclude it on philosophical grounds. In my
view there is absolutely nothing wrong in that. What I want to
bring into the open is the fact that we are using philosophical
criteria [beliefs] in choosing our models. A lot of cosmology
tries to hide that.[14]

The belief in cosmological evolution has spurred the belief that
ETs have filled our universe. Dr. Carl Sagan, although a UFO skeptic, believed that extraterrestrial life had proliferated throughout our
universe. Yet in calculating the odds that life could evolve on just one
planet, he estimated it to be roughly one chance in ten followed by two
billion zeros. This number is so unimaginably large that it would fill
several thousand copies of this book.[15]

In contrast, current astronomical discoveries about redshifts
make sense within the cosmology of the Bible — perhaps the most
widely held alternative explanation for how our universe came to
be. For instance, the Old Testament of the Bible contains 17 separate verses that state, in one form or another, that God "stretched
out" the heavens during His process of creation. Many cosmologists

find this claim unbelievable because they consider the Bible to be just a collection of stories written by "early" men thousands of years ago, who had no knowledge of such things. But many UFO believers think otherwise, deducing that the Bible's scientific insight must have come from an extraterrestrial source with "superior" knowledge of the universe.

The reason that many reject the Bible's cosmology is religious, not scientific. Cosmologists who reject the Bible's viewpoint have already discounted the idea of an intelligence behind the universe, and they have invented other models in an effort to solve the problem of red-shifted starlight without giving Earth "a favored location" or supposing an intelligent Creator. Evolutionary cosmologist P.W. Atkins explains:

> My aim is to argue that the Universe can come into existence without intervention, and that there is no need to invoke the idea of a Supreme Being. . . . Our task should be clear. . . . We have to embark upon the track of the absolute zero of intervention. . . . The only faith we need for the journey is the belief that everything can be understood and, ultimately, there is nothing to explain.[16]

One should take notice of the language here. "My aim . . . our task . . . the only faith." When it comes to origins, many scientists are intent on proving their pre-existing beliefs.

Has the big bang's bubble burst?

The fantastic and ingenious idea of the big bang stretching the universe on a 4-D sphere is an attempt to solve the redshift problem. It provides a naturalistic interpretation for those who reject the supernatural. Unfortunately for them, there are substantial problems with the big-bang idea.

• **Differing models**

There are various models of the big bang, such as the eternally oscillating model (which dispenses with the need to explain the original kernel of energy). Some models have finite universes, and others have infinite universes. Obviously, not every model can be correct. The conflict between theories highlights the conjectural nature of origins science, and big-bang ideology in particular.

• What lit the fuse?

There is no coherent explanation of how the initial primeval ball of pure energy came into existence, or what caused it to expand. What caused a quantum fluctuation in nothingness? What caused the laws of physics that govern the behavior of such fluctuations in the first place? Who knows?

• No antimatter

Our understanding of physics requires an equal production of antimatter for all matter created in the process of converting energy to matter. Yet there is a scarcity of detectable antimatter in the universe. This is a very serious objection to the big-bang hypothesis for which there has been no satisfactory explanation.

• Stars dying

Even though it is argued that there is some evidence of stars forming, it is unlikely that this is the process by which stars came into being in the first place. There is no known mechanism by which stars can form by gravity collapse from a cloud of gas, unless something like an exploding star compresses the gas (it would take a star to make a star). And there is more direct evidence of stars dying, outnumbering any that may be forming. The evidence overall is for a decaying universe, not an evolving one.

• Inadequate gravitational force to form planets

According to the accretion theory, dust particles in clouds (supposedly the remnants of exploding stars) were initially attracted to each other and eventually formed lumps and, subsequently, planets. Although even small particles have a minuscule gravitational attraction, it is too small to allow planets to form in the alleged time frame of the universe.

• The problem of uniform temperatures in background microwave radiation

Low-energy microwave radiation permeates space (only about 3 degrees Kelvin "K", which is minus 270°C — 3 degrees above absolute zero when all atoms effectively stop moving). This radiation is supposedly an afterglow of the energy from the big bang. This claim is really "much ado about nothing." Whatever the temperature of deep space, the evolutionist could always say that this was an afterglow of a big bang. If cosmologists had discovered lower or higher temperatures, they could easily have fiddled with their start-up assumptions to make the evidence fit. Such fudging has been demonstrated.[17] And the statement that the exact temperature was "predicted" by big-bang theory is factually incorrect.[18]

In reality, this background radiation is a serious problem for the big-bang theory. The temperature is apparently even (homogenous) all over the known universe. In the conditions predicted by the big bang, there is not enough time for the heat to have dissipated evenly from one side of the universe to the other, even though infrared radiation travels at light speed.

Cosmologist Robert Oldershaw was quoted in *New Scientist* as saying:

> The Big Bang model has several serious problems. . . . When the original inflation model ran into contradictions, it was replaced by a modification called the "new inflation." Some have even advocated a second inflationary period — "double inflation." . . . Let us consider some of the problems. First, the big bang is treated as an unexplainable event without a cause. Second, the big bang could not explain convincingly how matter got organized into lumps (galaxies and clusters of galaxies). And thirdly, it did not predict that for the universe to be held together in the way it is, more than 90 percent of the universe would have been in the form of some strange unknown dark form of matter. . . . It is astounding that the Big Bang hypothesis is the only cosmological model that physicists have taken seriously.[19]

He goes on to say:

> The first trend is that physicists are increasingly devising mathematically elegant hypotheses, which they say are "compelling" but which nevertheless cannot be verified by experiments or observations. The second trend is that theorists are reluctant to give up their elegant notions, preferring to modify the theory rather than discard it even when observations do not support it. . . . There are many . . . hypotheses of the "new physics" that suffer from a lack of testable predictions. Some that come to mind are the existence of "hidden dimensions,"

"shadow matter," "wormholes" in space-time, and the "many worlds" interpretation of quantum mechanics. . . . We are in serious danger of ending up with elegant theories that have little or nothing to do with how the real world works. . . ."[20]

The evolutionary origin of life in the universe is supposed to have been started by the big bang — an event that most people, including scientists, believe just happened. It is central to the ETH for the evolution of extraterrestrial life to have occurred on other planets. This is why we have spent considerable time on the big bang, demonstrating the philosophical nature of the unverifiable ideas involved.

Noah's flood on Mars?

It seems that mankind has been obsessed with Mars for as long as we have had records. Early last century, an astronomer named Percival Lowell spent 25 years studying the surface of Mars. In 1905, he concluded that water from the icecaps of Mars was flowing down into canals that had been constructed by intelligent beings. He was inspired by Italian astronomer Giovanni Schiaparelli, who in 1877 saw thin, dark lines on the Martian surface. Schiaparelli called these lines *canali*, which, translated, simply means "channels" without implying intelligent construction. Lowell had simply misunderstood the description.[21]

Yet Lowell's mistake influenced many people, including H.G. Wells, whose writings influenced many others, as we have already seen. Before long, most people thought there actually was life on Mars. For example, in the United States, a public symposium was held in 1928 called *Eminent Astronomers Give Their Reasons for Their Belief that Life Exists on the Great Red Planet*[22] — a widely held belief founded on an unproven hypothesis. However, as more powerful telescopes and unmanned craft scoured the surface, it proved to be uninhabited by any alien race. Canyons on Mars suggest that the surface may indeed have been scoured by water at one time.

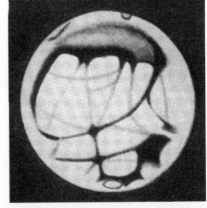

Schiaparelli's Martian canals

The *Valles Marineris* is one such canyon, the walls of which seem to have sedimentary layers (layers of rock deposited by a moving fluid, such as water). The canyon is so large that the earth's Grand Canyon could fit inside it several times over. Writer Robert S. Boyd commented:

> A flood of Biblical proportions — enough to fill the Mediterranean Sea — gushed down from the highlands of Mars, a billion or so years ago, the latest pictures from the Pathfinder confirmed Monday.[23]

Incredibly, many believe that Mars may have been globally covered with water. The observational evidence, including heavily layered canyons and channels, suggests it to be the case. Adding support to this claim, NASA scientists also indicated that some rocks gave the appearance of having been saturated with water at some past stage. Curiously though, these same scientists reject the possibility of a global flood on the earth, where sedimentary layers cover most of the surface, and which is 70 percent covered with water. The quote above is, of course, a reference to Noah's flood, recorded in the Bible.

There are a few who believe that this "Great Flood" on Earth was somehow triggered by advanced aliens overseeing mankind's evolution, cleansing the earth of impure beings. In language reminiscent of the Bible, many of these believers in a past alien flood believe that the Bible foretells a future cleansing by aliens, as well. UFOlogists and UFO cults often refer to biblical texts as proof that the ancient extraterrestrial astronauts have witnessed or overseen the historical events recorded in them.

God drives a flying saucer

Why do our "alien visitors" seem to be obsessed with the Bible more than any other religious book? Religious beliefs aside, the Bible is regarded by many scholars as the most accurate ancient book in the world, so it would make sense for UFOs to be "in it" if they are real. Many writers have taken up the cause of uncovering UFOs in the Bible. A practicing Catholic teacher and scientist by the name of R.L. Dione suggested that UFOs are God's messengers (angels) and are the ones responsible for prophecies, the content of the Bible, and the miracles recorded in it. This is a popular view held by many prominent "movers and shakers" in the UFO movement. Even Jesus supposedly had energy channeled to Him by ET craft that enabled Him to perform His miracles. Dione's book *God Drives a Flying Saucer* claimed to prove that God was not supernatural but a supertechnological being who created man in His own image. He wrote:

> Flying saucers are not only real, but closely associated with the Christian religion. . . .[24]

And that:

> . . . God, while humanoid, is nevertheless immortal through technology. . . . All of these conclusions will be documented, explained, and proved in the pages that follow.[25]

Traditional Christianity still flourishes, so it is fair to say that Dione's "proof" was not as earthshattering as he claimed. His scientific conclusions were based on interpretations. He operated in the realm of historical science. UFO researchers Clifford Wilson and John Weldon stated that Dione's views were based on his presuppositions — his belief that science and technology can explain everything. Dione also claimed that heaven was merely a supertechnological society. But where is this heaven? Where did God — this super ET — come from? How did He come into being? Because many discount a supernatural explanation for any aspect of reality, they hold out hope that perhaps ancient and advanced extraterrestrials could hold the key to our past, present, and future.

Writing in *Science,* author James Mullaney muses:

> Can it be that an eventual understanding of the UFO mystery will bring us into closer touch with reality and the universe itself?[26]

The Red Planet — the best hope for ET life

Now we shall look at the evidence for life in our own solar system — a bit closer to home. In the early days of the UFO "explosion" (1950s–1970s), speculation was rife that aliens were visiting us from planets within our own solar system. For example, famous "contactees" such as George Adamski, Frank Stranges, and Howard Mengler stated that ETs lived on planets such as Venus and Jupiter. Police patrolman and alleged abductee Herbert Schirmer claimed that his visitors, although from another galaxy, had bases on most of the local planets.

But Mars has always held a special fascination, and with continued interest in water on the surface, Mars has become a "hot prospect" for extraterrestrial life once again. Recent reports suggest that huge volumes of water exist just below the Martian surface. NASA's *Odyssey* instruments had been trained on the Martian surface for nearly a year before Bill Friedman, one of the project's scientists, declared:

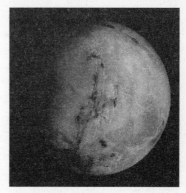

Mars

> In fact, there's enough water to cover the entire planet to a depth of at least five inches [12 cm], and we've only analyzed the top few feet of soil.[27]

Many others believe that further discoveries will reveal even greater quantities of water, a cause for celebration because, supposedly, "where there is water there will be life." One of Australia's most prominent scientists, Professor Paul Davies, exclaimed:

> I believe not only that Mars has harboured life, but it may actually be the cradle of life. . . . We don't know where life began, but a kilometre or two below the surface of Mars seems a good place.[28]

Water would explain many of the seemingly water-made geological formations seen on the surface. A Martian exploration craft called *Beagle 2* (named after the ship that took naturalist Charles Darwin around the world), and two NASA vehicles (*Spirit* and *Opportunity*) were sent to Mars to examine the soil, looking for water and also any signs of life, past or present.

Sadly, and after much hype, the European Space Agency's *Beagle 2* went AWOL[29] on Mars and remains "lost in space."

However, after several weeks of transmissions from their Martian rovers, on March 2, 2004, NASA scientists announced that at least one part of Mars appeared to have a persistently wet environment that may have been hospitable to life.[30] But any basic understanding of chemistry will tell you that life does not spontaneously arise just because of the presence of water.

There is more to the Mars life hypothesis than a simple obsession with water. Billion-dollar budgets in the name of science have a religious significance — they offer the answer to the question of origins, and thus, something about the meaning and purpose of life.

A real visitor from outer space?

Belief that life existed, or still exists, on Mars was seemingly vindicated some years before the most recent landings, courtesy of NASA's "Martian Rock," alluded to in chapter 1. To date, it is the "greatest" single piece of evidence for life on Mars.

In August of 1996, headlines screamed the biggest news story of the year: "Life on Mars." A 4.2-lb. (1.9-kg) lump of basalt rock that was originally discovered in Antarctica in 1984 was reported to have arrived on the earth between 11,000 and 13,000 years ago. At the time, many scientists maintained that it contained fossilized microbial life — bacteria — from Mars. Technically known as ALH84001 (Alan Hills 84001), this potato-sized rock purportedly made its way to the earth after being ejected from the Martian surface as a result of an asteroid or comet impact, or possibly even a volcanic eruption. In considering these spectacular claims, one should realistically consider the incredible odds of there being an impact in just the right location that was capable of generating sufficient force to escape the Martian gravity. Volcanoes, for example, simply do not eject objects at this speed. Although Mars has less gravity than Earth, this would require an escape velocity of 18,360 km per hour (5.1 km per second, or 5 times the speed of a rifle bullet). Scientists then postulate an even more unlikely scenario in which ALH84001 supposedly took up orbit around the sun for an indeterminate period, until it eventually encountered the earth.[31]

One of the strongest reasons given for the rock's origin on Mars is the composition of gases trapped inside its pores. It is supposed to resemble the chemical composition of samples taken from the Mars *Viking Lander*. However, its mineral composition differs from 11 other meteorites that are supposed to be Martian.

Physical chemist Dr. Jonathan Sarfati has commented on another popular piece of evidence:

> The rock contains a mineral called magnetite, also called lodestone (which was used in the first compasses), as well as another mineral similar to "fool's gold." These minerals can be

Photo courtesy of NASA

Model of *Viking Lander*

formed by living organisms or by processes having nothing to do with life. It is the occurrence of these minerals together which suggests (to some) that they were formed by living cells. But the researchers haven't ruled out all possible non-living processes.[32]

The rock also contains molecules known as PAHs or polycyclic aromatic hydrocarbons, which are known to be common in many asteroids, adding weight to the theory that the rock came from space. However, they are also found in common soot or diesel exhaust, and these fossil fuels have an Earth-bound biological origin.

The rock also has microscopic, fossilized worm-like whiskers that are supposed to have been once-living organisms. Sarfati comments again:

> A huge problem with the alleged fossil bacteria is their tiny size — many times smaller than all known free-living bacteria. . . . Most people don't know that another team which analyzed the *same rock* found that it *lacked* a key sign of biological activity. The leader, Jim Papike, director of the Institute of Meteoritics at the University of New Mexico, said: "When we looked at the ratio [of two types of sulfur], there was no evidence that it was in a ratio for life forms." In fact, he said that the ratio pointed in the opposite direction [emphasis in original].

These "whiskers" are composed of carbonate materials similar to limestone or marble. Back in 1996, Sarfati suggested that the globules could have been formed by processes completely unconnected with life, and that they showed evidence of rapid heating. Then in 2002, a rock in the Auckland Domain Museum was discovered to contain "life crystals" similar to ALH84001. The only problem for NASA and its pro-Martian life advocates was that this new rock was known to have come from a volcanic eruption in New Zealand in the mid–19th century. The conclusion from this newly discovered rock was that it had been ejected in a hot state and rapidly cooled in icy conditions. This process produced fossil whiskers that look identical to those in the Martian meteorite.[33] Perhaps Sarfati was right all along.

The evidences for the "Martian rock" are anything but conclusive. Yet they have apparently added up to be the most convincing evidence for extraterrestrial life ever seen. But even Professor Colin Pillinger, lead scientist on *Beagle 2*, admitted:

> This doesn't actually prove that the evidence in the meteorite is for life on Mars. We cannot say absolutely, hand on heart, that this is something which happened on Mars until we find organic matter in a genuine Martian sample. We have to go to Mars and if there is doubt we will have to bring samples back. If there is still doubt, we will have to send a person there to carry out the experiments in situ.[34]

One may well ask how this really came to be such an earth-shattering discovery. Sarfati again comments on the whole affair:

> It was certainly a coincidence that the first "life from Mars" fanfare in 1996 came just as the U.S. Congress was proposing to cut NASA's funding, although they had collected ALH84001 back in 1984. The noted astronomer Sir Fred Hoyle argued that it was perhaps a publicity stunt to gain more government money: "Considering NASA is absolutely avid to get funding from Congress, one has to be a bit suspicious." It is certainly a coincidence now that the announcement comes just before the new U.S. President is about to announce his budget. To be fair to the researchers in both cases, they presented actual scientific data, although the *interpretation* of the data is dubious.[35]

The "life on Mars" juggernaut showed no signs of slowing down. Speculation was rife everywhere. Even Dan Goldin, chief administrator of NASA, was forced to concede:

> I want everyone to understand that we are not talking about little green men here . . . exciting, even compelling, but not conclusive.[36]

Nonetheless, in the minds of the masses, this was the first step — the first proof — that there was life on other planets. Although the media would have us believe that the issue is beyond doubt, it is clear that this "proof" of Martian ET life (supposedly 3.6 billion years old) is in fact highly controversial among the scientific community. The excitement about the rock and the rovers has no doubt expedited NASA's future manned expeditions to Mars.

The "face" on Mars

In July 1976, NASA's *Viking 1* was photographing the Martian surface for suitable locations for planned future landings. When the photos were released to the public, one in particular captured the attention of the world's media. It resembled a humanoid face complete with headdress. Speculation grew that this 1.2-mile-wide x 1.6-mile-long (1.9 km x 2.6 km) structure could be an ancient monument, perhaps a testimony to a past civilization.[37] In the same region on Mars, known as Cydonia, there also appeared to be objects that resembled the ruins of other man-made structures, such as pyramids. Could these actually be the "calling cards" of extraterrestrial visitors to our solar system? Did an ancient civilization once inhabit the planet? Before these questions were even answered, scientists and UFOlogists alike were speculating on what may have wiped out the population!

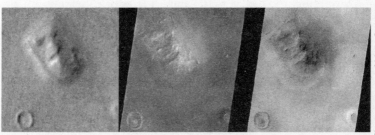

Photo courtesy of Malin Space Science Systems/NASA

The "face" on Mars, with the light at different angles

The person most responsible for promoting the "face on Mars" theory was speaker and writer Richard C. Hoagland. In his popular 1987 book *The Monuments of Mars: A City on the Edge of Forever,* he captivated public attention with the idea that these Martian artifacts were evidences of a fortress, an artificial cliff, a five-sided pyramid, and a collection of other structures dubbed the "City Square."

Hoagland himself was also promoted as somewhat of a science expert and a consultant in the fields of astronomy, planetarium curating, and space-program education. Apparently, at the age of 19 he became the curator of the Museum of Science in Springfield, Massachusetts. He also appeared on many television specials as the resident science specialist, including NBC's special on the *Surveyor 1* moon landing. In 1968, he was asked to become a consultant to CBS News and served as a science advisor to Walter Cronkite.

However, Gary Posner, contributor to *The Encyclopedia of Extraterrestrial Encounters* (EEE), reports that NASA had little or no interest in Hoagland's speculations, and did not intend to explore the region of Cydonia any further. The EEE report also describes Hoagland as self-educated, and indicated that in NASA's view he lacked any credibility at all.[38]

Then in 1998, the *Mars Global Surveyor* specifically photographed more images of "the face" at a much greater resolution than before. To silence criticism, NASA revealed the face to be nothing more than a natural feature. When the sun shines at a relatively low angle, shadows accentuate certain features, making the landscape face-like. Posner comments:

> With the benefit of 20/20 hindsight, has Hoagland now abandoned his "City"? Oddly, a visit to his Web site (<www.enterprisemission.com>) reveals just the opposite.[39]

Once more, the media were willing partners in "talking up" the extraterrestrial hypothesis, and the public was led astray yet again. Even today, theories about the Mars face are as popular as ever with many famous UFOlogists, despite the lack of credible evidence.

Our local patch — the solar system

Reports of UFO sightings early in the 20th century gave way to alleged contacts and then abductions and messages from space. As we mentioned earlier, many of the early "space brothers" claimed (and some still do) to be from the planets in our solar system, such as Mercury, Venus, Saturn, Jupiter and its moons, and even Pluto. But is this possible?

There are nine planets in our solar system all revolving around the sun. However, *Viking 1* and *2* and subsequent probes to Mars have shown no evidence of alien races or any signs of life. The two unmanned *Voyager* craft, despite carrying messages into space, have never had a "close encounter," although they have taken thousands of pictures of Jupiter, Saturn, and Uranus. Other probes have visited the other planets, and they have revealed nothing but harsh, unlivable conditions in our neighborhood.

The closest planet to the sun is Mercury. It is also the second-smallest planet (about half the size of Earth) after Pluto, which is the smallest and farthermost planet from the sun. A Mercurian year is only 88 days, the time it takes to orbit the sun. Its orbit is highly elliptical, which causes radical shifts in temperature on its surface. Facing the sun, its temperature can be as high as 700°F (371°C). On the dark side of the planet, it can plummet to as low as -300°F (-149°C).

Venus is no more hospitable. An early contactee, a preacher-cum-author named Frank Stranges, claimed a meeting in 1959 — in the Pentagon no less — with a Venusian who went by the name of Val Thor. He apparently claimed that his mission was "to help mankind return to the Lord" (Jesus of the Bible).[40] Stranges made this claim before research found the planet to have surface temperatures of 900°F (480°C), hot enough to melt lead! When confronted with the evidence of inhospitable conditions on Venus, Stranges said it wasn't a problem because they were living below the surface anyway! But any inhabitant would be choked by the carbon dioxide atmosphere, and scalded by noxious clouds of sulfuric acid vapor. Violent storms rage in the atmosphere continually.

Mars has no oxygen in the atmosphere, and evening temperatures plummet to -100°F (-38°C). Next is Jupiter, a gas giant with no solid surface, although it might have a solid core. It is the largest planet in our solar system — about the size of 318 Earths. Radiation and magnetic storms bombard the planet.[41] Gravity on Jupiter is about 2.5 times the earth's; a 176-lb. (80-kg) person would weigh 440 lb. (200 kg) and would have some difficulty moving around.

The farther out we travel — to Saturn, Uranus, Neptune, and Pluto — the more we discover only freezing temperatures and poisonous atmospheres. The physical extremes are beyond our imagining. Everywhere in our solar system we find environments non-conducive to life — everywhere except the earth, that is. This brings into even sharper focus the question of where the aliens might be coming from.

Recent probes continue to discover even more moons surrounding some of the outer giants like Saturn, but from what has been discovered thus far, our opinions about finding extraterrestrial life on these planets or their moons is unlikely to change. Is it just a coincidence that nowadays most "visitors" seem to come from farther away, elsewhere in the galaxy where we cannot test their claims? The early beliefs about ET life in our neighborhood have proven to be false and inaccurate, so it's prudent to be cautious before accepting even more wild and speculative claims.

The search for extrasolar planets

The search for life has now stretched beyond our solar system. Early in the last century, astronomer Edwin Hubble discovered that the small nebulae in the sky were, in fact, neighboring islands of stars — galaxies outside of our own that contained hundreds of billions of stars. Frank Drake's equation has prompted NASA, SETI, and many others to begin carefully observing individual stars for signs of accompanying planets. This has become known as the search for extrasolar planets.

The first discovery of an extrasolar planet orbiting a star similar to our sun came in 1995, when Michael Mayor and Didier Queloz of Geneva announced that they had found a rapidly orbiting mass close to star 51 Pegasi. The discovery sparked great excitement. Calculations for the size of the planet ranged from half the mass of Jupiter to more than twice its mass.[42] Given the enormous size of Jupiter to start with, that's a pretty generous range of estimates, and when it comes to habitable planets, size does matter.

It will prove difficult to find extrasolar planets capable of sustaining life. Because they are so distant, extrasolar planets are generally too small to be directly observed by present methods; that is, astronomers do not actually see the planets because their reflected light is so weak, being overpowered by their nearby sun. Planets are presumed to exist because their mass affects the stars they orbit. For example, Jupiter causes a slight "wobble" in our own sun, as it pulls the sun off center.[43]

As the star wobbles from the gravitation of a planet, the frequency of the starlight we observe from it can shift up and down (the redshift and blueshift we discussed earlier). This is known as the Doppler effect.

A similar thing happens with sound waves. You may have noticed how an approaching police siren seems to change sound when it suddenly passes you and begins moving away.

Another planet-hunting method is the *transit method*. This is used to detect a planet passing between its star and our earth. The orbiting mass causes a minute drop in the intensity of light from the star. We can observe a similar effect when Mercury or Venus passes between our sun and the earth.

You may have noticed that I am a little cautious in celebrating these supposedly irrefutable evidences of extrasolar planets. For a planet's sun to be affected, its mass must be of a size similar to Jupiter. Some are even calculated to be 200 times that size. For this reason, there is considerable debate as to whether they are actually planets at all. It is reasoned that, due to their enormous mass, they are more likely to be small suns, such as brown dwarf stars. Even if they are planets, they are likely to be gas giants like our own Jupiter, and incapable of supporting life for that reason.

Because they are so large, there is too much gravity (inhabitants would be crushed by the enormous pressure — this is why size matters). There are other problems for the ETH and existence of intelligent alien life on these worlds. Many are too close to the heat of their sun to be able to support life, and many others are presumably known because their highly elliptical orbits affect their star in a detectable manner. These irregular orbits would lead to huge variations in temperature (similar to the effect on Mercury — see earlier).

The nearest presumed extrasolar planet is about 15 light-years (about 26,000 times the distance between our sun and Pluto) away in the direction of the constellation Aquarius. Its star is Gliese 876, a dim red dwarf (much larger than the earth) with only about one-third the mass of our sun, and about one-eightieth the sun's brightness. The planet is believed to be about twice the mass of Jupiter and probably a gas giant also.[44] It would be incapable of supporting any life.

Some may argue that these extrasolar objects may indeed support life — but to quote a line from *Star Trek*'s Doctor McCoy — "not life as we know it." This is not a strong argument for the proponents of the ETH because it would be reasonable to assume that supposed visitors to our own planet need to be capable of surviving in Earth's environment. So they would need to be visitors from planets with Earth-like conditions, but no such planets have been observed anywhere. Thus, it would be necessary for the aliens to travel in spacecraft built to replicate their home planet's conditions and insulate them from the effects of the earth's environment. Presumably, such a major undertaking to visit Earth would necessitate an extended stay — many years at least. So this would suggest even more amazing technologies to sustain these conditions for so long.

There is, of course, no good reason why extrasolar planets should not exist, and some may well be discovered to be "rocky" planets like those in our own solar system. However, the likely distances of these objects from the earth make the ETH an unlikely proposition, even if they were inhabited, due to the problems in traveling such immense distances. To date, no habitable planets, within or outside of our solar system, have been observed. Unfortunately for the advocates of the ETH, our search for life on other planets is revealing that the earth itself appears to be a unique place indeed.

Did ancient man know the truth?

UFOlogists often turn to the Bible because it demonstrates insightful knowledge about our universe. This knowledge seems impossible if the Bible was written by ancient men who lacked the skills of modern science and technology. One possible explanation is that a being, or beings, with superior knowledge imparted information to mankind in the distant past. One amazing instance of "modern science" in the Bible is a passage written by a man called Job. Talking about God, whom he believed was his Creator, Job writes:

> He stretches out the north over empty space; He hangs
> the earth on nothing (Job 26:7; NKJV).

Job obviously would have known that you cannot "hang" something on "nothing." Yet, this verse, written around 2000 B.C., correctly describes the earth as being suspended in space, almost 4,000 years before manned space flight provided the first eyewitness view. This scientific insight is easy to explain if the passage was inspired by an outside intelligence.

Looking at this with an open mind, there are two possible sources of the knowledge. Job may have been communicating with an advanced extraterrestrial that he mistook for God. Or, as the straightforward reading of the text suggests, Job was indeed dealing with a supernatural intelligence, such as a divine Creator.

This is not an isolated "science" passage in the Bible. To explain their existence, some subscribers to the ETH believe that ancient extra-terrestrial astronauts visited the earth many millennia ago (as they are still presumed to be doing today), which gave rise to our beliefs, values, and religions. But as many commentators have noted, it is primarily the Bible and the Christian religion that have received special attention from all quarters. This focus suggests that there may be a kernel of truth in there somewhere, but who was right — the original authors who believed they were hearing from a supernatural intelligence, or the modern re-interpreters of the texts, who base their conclusions on modern experiences?

This ancient astronaut theme was promoted to its fullest by Erich Von Däniken in his best-selling book *Chariots of the Gods* (1968). (We will review his beliefs later in this book.) He even founded an "Ancient Astronaut Society," which has several thousand adherents to his view of the history of the world.

Another passage that indicates "outside knowledge" was imparted to biblical authors is found in a book ascribed to the prophet Isaiah. This passage describes the handiwork of Isaiah's purported Creator:

> It is He who sits above the circle of the earth, and its in-habitants are like grasshoppers, who stretches out the heavens like a curtain, and spreads them out like a tent to dwell in (Isa. 40:22; NKJV).

The word *circle* has been translated from the original Hebrew word *khug,* which may be translated "sphere." (Interestingly, the German word *kugel* means "ball, sphere, or globe.") This reference to a circular or spherical Earth is another one of those seemingly inexplicable biblical passages (it is often presumed that ancient man could not have known such things).

Photo courtesy of NASA

Photo of Earth from space

Also, we alluded to another passage earlier about "stretching" the heavens, which would account for the redshifting of starlight.

The Bible contains 66 books by 44 different authors, separated by great distances and as much as two thousand years. Yet, amazingly, they all write accounts of their interaction with God, similarly acknowledging Him to be an Almighty Creator just as the prophet Isaiah did. The Bible also claims that it is the *inspired* (Greek — "God-breathed") Word of the Creator himself (2 Tim. 3:16), and that no words of prophecy came about by human will but by God as men were "moved" by His Spirit (2 Pet. 1:20–21).

History has shown many Bible prophesies to be true, such as Isaiah's prophecy that a Persian king would arise with the name of Cyrus — around 150 years before the event occurred. The Bible has also been confirmed by numerous archaeological discoveries, such as the unearthing of a huge capital of the "Hittites." These were an ancient people mentioned only in the Bible, but presumed to be a myth because no physical evidence had been found. As a result of these findings, the Bible has often been called the "most accurate history book in the world." Is it any wonder that it has come in for so much attention from all quarters? It is historically accurate yet contains so many seemingly unscientific supernatural references.

To many people, it seems apparent that the authors of the Bible must have had "outside help" from ET. But how could any mortal creature — terrestrial or extraterrestrial — predict the future? UFOlogists have not adequately explained how ancient astronauts could do this unless they could travel through time in some capacity, as some have suggested. But even if UFOs were interdimensional, it does not necessarily follow that they could go backward and forward in time. The absence of time-travel visitors ("tourists from tomorrow") suggests that time travel is not a reality, now or in the future. This truly lies in the realm of science fiction, and the space brothers do not claim to be time travelers, anyway. The only plausible explanation for the accuracy of the Bible's predictions and insights is that they were foretold by someone with the capability of seeing outside our time and space. This is consistent with the notion of a greater intelligence who is located outside of our realm but who also possesses intimate knowledge of the construction of the universe — a supernatural being.

Intelligent design in the universe?

Biblical insights show that the authors knew more about their universe than they should have. If ETs have been overseeing mankind's development, then the ETs must have come from somewhere: either they are the product of evolution or they were created by other aliens — or by a supernatural Creator.

Evolution of ETs on habitable planets requires that order come from disorder, by itself. But that is not known to happen in the real world. Our universe shows incredible evidence of design. The planets move with absolute precision, so much so that space scientists can plan with amazing accuracy a spacecraft's rendezvous with a planet years in advance. Although known by ancient civilizations, this clockwork accuracy has recently been confirmed among the stars and galaxies.[45] All the planets in our system orbit the sun in the same direction. Their speed is such that they are held in their orbits by the force of gravity. Without orbital motion, they would be pulled in toward the sun. Too fast and the planets move farther away — too slow and they are pulled in closer. The stability and shape of their orbits also means that they do not get so close as to exert overt gravitational influences on one another.[46] It is believed that a huge dust cloud — around 9.4 billion miles (15 billion km) in diameter —coalesced into our solar system by itself, forming moons and planets with precise orbits and speeds.

It requires great faith to believe that such perfection arises out of a cosmic accident like the big bang. The existence of such precision, order, and design suggests the miraculous work of a supremely wise and intelligent being who created this order and revealed some of the details to ancient people. Is that an unreasonable hypothesis? Many religious UFO buffs believe that the universe was designed by a Creator, but they reinterpret the Bible as a revelation about technological superbeings (e.g., angels and "Jesus") on a mission for the Creator. In most cases, however, this "creator of aliens" used evolution as his creative process, and his messengers are trying to help mankind's evolution.

In contrast, the traditional biblical view holds that the Creator God made the universe and everything in it supernaturally and near-instantaneously. As we have mentioned, there are thousands of eminently qualified scientists who believe this also. Some are the "world's best" in their fields of expertise. One such scientist is Dr. Stuart Burgess, a design engineer at Bristol University. He has won several industry awards, including awards for his work on spacecraft design for the European Space Agency. He is well qualified to comment on "design." He believes that there must be a supernatural explanation to the universe:

> There is a popular misconception that science has shown that miracles do not happen and cannot happen. This is why modern scientists argue that the biblical creation account is not a valid theory of origins. . . . However, science has not proved that miracles do not happen. Science simply shows how things work when miracles are not in operation. One of the useful aspects of scientific understanding is that it actually helps to identify when a miracle has taken place.

Burgess adds:

> The origin of the Universe is a prime example of where natural processes cannot possibly account for what has happened. This is because the creation of the Universe involved physical matter appearing from nothing. Therefore, any theory of origins must take into account that the ultimate origin of the Universe involved a miraculous act. The Bible clearly teaches that the creation of the initial space, time, and matter was a miracle. . . . The consistency between the Bible and scientific principles is also demonstrated by the fact that many scientists, past and present, have had no difficulty in accepting the supernatural creation account.[47]

Burgess, who admits to being a Christian, seeks a rational connection between the design and purpose he observes in the universe and his personal belief in a Creator God. Can he prove such an idea? No. Nonetheless, is his idea any more "fantastic" than the belief that non-demonstrable aliens, traveling in physics-defying spacecraft, are overcoming mathematically impossible distances to visit our planet, even though our planet would have been impossible to observe from their distant home in the first place? Anyone who tries to combine this fantastic claim with the incalculable odds that a finely tuned universe came into existence by itself must also be a strongly religious person like Dr. Burgess.

Each new discovery has shown that the universe is a much "weirder" place than most people imagined or predicted. In one sense, it is almost too incomprehensible to imagine, yet it does exist — it is a reality that we are part of.

Finely tuned for life — the anthropic principle

Copernicus taught us that the sun did not revolve around the earth (a mistaken medieval view known as geocentrism — interestingly, this view did not come from the Bible, as some think, but from Greek and Egyptian sources). The neo — or modern — Copernican view also teaches that there is no "special" place anywhere in the universe.[48] However, observation of our position in the universe would indicate that we are, indeed, in a special place. Our galaxy is at least somewhere near the center of the universe.

Astrophysicist Dr. Russell Humphreys has written extensively on this. A major review of his work concludes:

> The odds for the earth having such a unique position in the cosmos by accident are less than one in a trillion. The problem for big-bang theorists is that they suppose the cosmos was not created but happened by accident — by chance, natural processes. Such naturalistic processes could not have put us at a unique center, so atheistic cosmologists have sought other explanations, without notable success so far.
>
> Over the last few decades, astronomers have discovered that the redshifts of the galaxies are not evenly distributed but are "quantized," i.e., they tend to fall into distinct groups. This means that the distances to the galaxies also fall into groups, with each group of galaxies forming a conceptual spherical shell [like the layers of an onion]. The shells turn out to be about a million light-years apart.
>
> It is remarkable that the shells are all concentric and all centered on our home galaxy, the Milky Way. If they weren't, we would not see groups of redshifts. Russell Humphreys shows that groups would only be distinct from each other if our viewing location were less than a million light-years (a trivial distance on the scale of the universe) from the center.[49]

A well-known concept in astronomy, first coined in 1974, is the "anthropic principle." This is the idea that the entire universe is finely tuned for life — human life in fact. The word "anthropic" comes from the Greek word *anthropos* for "human being." One website explains it thus:

. . . if some of the finely balanced quantities were not finely tuned then our Universe would have grossly different properties. The properties would in fact be so different that it is highly likely that life (as we know it) would not develop and [we would not] be around to ask the question of why the Universe is special.[50]

Astronomer Donald DeYoung also comments:

For any principle of science to be acceptable, there must be experimental results with general validity. The Anthropic Principle which states that the universe is especially suited for the well-being of mankind, is one such assumption. As just one of hundreds of examples, consider the tides that the moon causes on earth. If the moon was closer to the earth, tides would be greatly increased. Ocean waves could sweep across the continents. The seas themselves might heat to the boiling point from the resulting friction. On the other hand, a more distant moon would reduce the tides. Marine life would be endangered by the resulting preponderance of stagnant water. Mankind would also be in trouble because the oxygen in the air we breathe is replenished by marine plants. We can conclude that the moon is in the "correct" position for man's well-being. Even such details as the mass of protons and the strength of gravity have values that give stability to the universe and thus reinforce the Anthropic Principle. . . . The Anthropic Principle is a powerful argument that the universe was designed.[51]

There are hundreds of examples where this is shown to be true, and without going into extensive detail, here are just a few that lend themselves to the idea that the universe is especially designed for life on Earth.

• **Stars and their distance from the earth**
Our neighboring stars in our Milky Way galaxy are nicely spaced apart so that they produce just enough light to be seen, but are not so close that they overwhelm us with dangerous radiation or gravitational forces. On the other hand, if they were farther away, the night sky would be considerably darker, and the stars would not be so useful as navigational aids and markers for the seasons, which mankind has used for many centuries.

• **The solar system's position in the galaxy**

The solar system is located about two-thirds of the way from the center of the Milky Way. If it were closer to the center, where there is a concentration of other stars known as the galactic bulge, we would be overpowered by their brightness, and nothing else in the universe would be observable. If we were too close to the outer edge of the galaxy, the night sky would be too dark.

• **Perfect daylight**

Our sun does not oscillate significantly in size the way many other stars appear to do. This would make conditions unlivable on the earth. The sun provides just the right amount of brightness to the earth and it is the perfect color (its wavelengths) for the job. It has a yellow-white color, unlike many other stars of differing colors. The peak intensity of its light is in the infrared spectrum, which provides warmth to all inhabitants of Earth.

• **The earth spins at the correct speed**

The spin of the earth is ideal for producing day and night. Longer days would cause a greater warming-up effect and, conversely, longer nights — more cold. A faster rate of spin would produce constant violent weather conditions.

• **The right tilt**

The axis of the earth is tilted to an angle of 23.5 degrees. This tilt allows the northern hemisphere to receive more sun from April to September, and the southern hemisphere from October to March, thus spreading the sun's warmth over a greater part of the globe than if there were no tilt. This seasonal change is absolutely vital for triggering the blossoming of plants and fruits, and to the courtship of some creatures. If the tilt were any greater, the ice caps would melt in summer and flood the landmasses. Any less tilt and the seasons would be less marked due to the reduced variation in temperatures.

• **Perfect distance from the sun**

If we were 10 percent closer to the sun, the earth would have furnace-like temperatures, and 10 percent farther away would produce icy deserts. Also, the oceans would boil off or freeze solid respectively, so there could be no life as we know it.

• **Correct orbit of the earth**

The orbit of the earth only varies slightly in its distance from the sun, causing relatively small variations in temperature. A more elliptical orbit (as some other planets have) would be devastating for life on Earth.

• **The right size**

We are aware of the effects of reduced or increased gravity on the other planets in our solar system. There is either too much or too little. The earth is just the right size for its inhabitants. Because of this, water remains in a liquid state. Lesser gravity and the water would be lost to space due to the greater evaporation of cold water caused by lower atmospheric pressure.

• **The water cycle**

Water covers 70 percent of the earth, via its oceans, rivers, lakes, and streams. This arrangement (evaporation from oceans to form clouds that eventually cause rain to fall on the land) is unique within our solar system, and provides a convenient supply of fresh water for the earth's life forms.

• **Right construction**

Earth offers a vast supply of resources, such as wood, metals, animals, plants, and a host of others that are useful for mankind. In addition, Earth has the right conditions to permit the formation and maintenance of the ozone layer in the atmosphere to protect us. It has a magnetic field which helps deflect harmful radiation from the sun. The magnetic field also aids navigation for man and beast. Our atmosphere is composed of just the right gases, unlike some of the noxious combinations found elsewhere in our solar system.[52]

Who knows?

More and more discoveries suggest design, intelligence, and purpose in this amazing universe. As we discover more of these truths, though, we have a paradox because another mystery only increases — that is, the UFO phenomenon. Why is it that, when the search of space is *decreasing* the likelihood of extraterrestrial visitors, the circumstantial evidence for UFO sightings and alien abductions is *increasing*? Could Jacques Vallée be right? Are these creatures from another reality?

In another context, astronomer and author Don DeYoung says:

> It has even been proposed [by those seeking to escape the implications of a universe designed for human beings] that there really is an infinite number of universes [EDH], each with a completely different set of physical properties. According to such thinking, our particular universe just happens to have conditions suitable for human life, and that is why we are here to enjoy it! Of course, there is no way to detect any "other" universes or comprehend their underlying principles.[53]

DeYoung is right: there is no way to scientifically test such things, including Mack and Vallée's "other realities." So if the phenomenon keeps occurring, then perhaps there is some supernatural element beyond the reality that we normally experience. But if we can't test it, and we ourselves can't know, who would know?

The Bible seems to have insight in this regard and is also the focus of much UFO speculation. This is not just my opinion. If you read any UFO literature, the issue of how ancient man could have known so much about the universe will very likely appear on the table for discussion. Besides being a religious book, it is the only such ancient book that has stood up to scientific scrutiny (once you understand the limits of science in really testing the past).

The Bible's knowledge of the universe, and prediction of future events, suggests an interaction with intelligence or forces outside of, but interacting with, our reality. If indeed there were a creator or creators, surely they would not have left us to our own devices. Wouldn't they, or he, or it, want to be known by their created beings? If they do, then almost as surely they would have given us some indication of other dimensions, or other realities, if such things exist. To know how and why any extraterrestrial life may have arisen, and even the reason why we exist, we eventually have to go back to the beginning. All parties, regardless of their philosophical assumptions, realize that understanding what happened in the past is the key to the present, and perhaps the future.

The only physical evidence we have is in the present. In this chapter, we have looked at the present-day evidence for the origin of the galaxies, stars, and life on other planets. In the next chapter we shall look at evidence for the origin of life on Earth. If we can "find" the creator, whether it is evolution, or a group of "supernatural" aliens, or a supernatural "god," we should be better placed to discover the truth about the origin of *all* life, as well as about any other realities or dimensions. So how did life on Earth come about?

Endnotes

1 "Aliens 'Absolutely' Exist, SETI Astronomer Believes," <news.nationalgeographic.com/news/2003/03/0331_030401_setishostak.html>, March 6, 2004.

2 Ibid.

3 "Life on Mars Is a Siren Song in the Human Drive to Know," *Australian* (Features), January 9, 2004, p. 11.

4 "The ET Quandary," *Canadian National Post*, December 8, 2003, p. A13.

5 "Exploring Mind, Memory, and the Psychology of Belief," <www.csicop.org/si/9501/belief.html>, January 6, 2003.

6 Don Batten, Ken Ham, Carl Wieland, and Jonathan Sarfati, *The Answers Book* (Brisbane, Australia: Answers in Genesis, 1999), p. 10–11.

7 Jonathan Sarfati, *Refuting Evolution* (Green Forest, AR: Master Books, 2002), p. 23.

8 "Guth's Grand Guess," *Discover*, vol. 23, p. 35, April 2002.

9 Donald B. DeYoung, *Astronomy and the Bible* (Grand Rapids, MI: Baker Book House, 1992), p. 38–41.

10 Stuart Burgess, *He Made the Stars Also* (Epsom, UK: Day One Publications, 2001), p. 36.

11 Russell Humphreys, *Starlight and Time* (Green Forest, AR: Master Books, 1994), p. 14–17.

12 Latin, meaning "at first view."

13 Edwin Hubble, *The Observational Approach to Cosmology* (Oxford, UK: Clarendon Press, 1937), p. 50, 51, 59.

14 <www.answersingenesis.org/home/area/feedback/2003/0905.asp>, September 8, 2003.

15 Carl Sagan, editor, *Communication with Extra-Terrestrial Intelligence* (Cambridge, MA: MIT Press, 1973), p. 46, cited in Clifford Wilson and John Weldon, *Close Encounter: A Better Explanation* (San Diego, CA: Master Books, 1978), p. 322.

16 P. W. Atkins, *The Creation* (Oxford, UK: Freeman, 1981), p. 3–8, cited in Burgess, *He Made the Stars Also*.

17 Burgess, *He Made the Stars Also*, p. 41.

18 Sarfati, *Refuting Compromise*, p. 154–155.

19 Robert Oldershaw, "What's Wrong with the New Physics?" *New Scientist*, p. 56–59, December 22/29, 1990, cited in Burgess, *He Made the Stars Also*, p. 42–44.

20 Ibid.

21 Ronald D. Story, editor, *The Mammoth Encyclopedia of Extraterrestrial Encounters*, in an article by Thomas Bullard (London: Constable & Robinson, 2002), p. 397.

22 Burgess, *He Made the Stars Also*, p. 115.

23 "Ancient Gullies Suggest Key Ingredient for Life," *Cincinnati Enquirer*, July 8, 1997.

24 R.L. Dione, *God Drives a Flying Saucer* (New York: Bantam Books, 1973), cited in Wilson and Weldon, *Close Encounters: A Better Explanation*, p. 325–326.

25 Ibid.

26 James Mullaney, *Science Digest*, July 1977, cited in Wilson and Weldon, *Close Encounters: A Better Explanation*, p. 59.

27 "Ankle-deep on Mars," <news.bbc.co.uk/2/hi/indepth/sci_tech2003/2769589.stm>, February 19, 2003.

28 Paul Davies (of the Australian Centre for Astrobiology in Sydney), "It's True, Men Really Are from Mars. And So Are Women, Thanks to an Invasion by Red Planet Microbes," *Guardian*, October 30, 2002, p. 22.

29 AWOL is a military term meaning "absent without leave."

30 "NASA Announces Evidence for Water on Mars," <www.answersingenesis.org/docs2004/0304water.asp>, March 5, 2004.

31 Story, *The Mammoth Encyclopedia of Extraterrestrial Encounters*, in an article by Thomas Bullard p. 400.

32 "Life on Mars?" <www.answersingenesis.org/docs/2461.asp>, December 10, 2001.

33 *Creation* 24 (4), p. 4–5.

34 "Conclusive Evidence for Life from Mars? Remember Last Time!" <www.answersingenesis.org/docs2001/0302mars_life.asp>, December 10, 2002.

35 Ibid.

36 "Bradenton Herald," <library.dialog.com/bluesheets.html/b10684.html>, January 30, 2003.

37 Story, *The Mammoth Encyclopedia of Extraterrestrial Encounters*, in an article by Gary P. Posner, p. 221–223.

38 Ibid.

39 Ibid.

40 Story, *The Mammoth Encyclopedia of Extraterrestrial Encounters*, in an article by Frank Stranges, p. 680–681.

41 DeYoung, *Astronomy and the Bible*, p. 38–41.

42 "From Intuition to Discovery," <planetquest.jpl.nasa.gov/science/science_index.html>, February 24, 2003.

43 Wayne R. Spencer, "The Existence and Origin of Extrasolar Planets," *TJ* 15(1):17–25.

44 "Nearest Extrasolar Planet," <www.earthsky.com/1999/es990316.html>, March 2, 2003.

45 Burgess, *He Made the Stars Also*, p. 50–61.

46 Ibid.

47 Ibid., p. 32–33.

48 "Neo" because although Copernicus disproved geocentrism, he himself did not arrive at the conclusion that we are "nowhere special."

49 "Our Galaxy — at the Center of the Universe after All!" <www.answersingenesis.org/docs2002/0807tj.asp?>, December 10, 2002.

50 "Anthropic Principle," <zebu.uoregon.edu/~imamura/209/mar31/anthropic.html>, March 2, 2003.

51 DeYoung, *Astronomy and the Bible*, p. 123.

52 Burgess, *He Made the Stars Also*, p. 62–78 (majority of examples).

53 DeYoung, *Astronomy and the Bible*, p. 123.

Chapter Four

Did Aliens Create
Life on Earth?

Simple cells — really?

If life evolved on the earth, it would be reasonable to presume that life evolved elsewhere in the universe as well. Some leading scientists take this idea further. They suggest that, since such ET beings may be older or more evolved than we are, and therefore more advanced and intelligent, they could have created life on the earth — perhaps even just humans — or at least seeded the planet to kick-start evolution.

The standard theory of biological evolution suggests that non-living chemicals formed into living organisms on the earth about three billion years ago (a theory called "abiogenesis"). Most people picture the first living organisms as some sort of simple, or primitive, cells that later became more complex. But "simple" is a misnomer because there is actually no such thing as a simple cell. Even the "simplest" forms of life that we know — bacteria — are enormously complex (viruses are not alive, they need the machinery of living cells). And when you think about it, any molecular machine that is able to make functional copies of itself would *need* to be extremely complex.

In the early 1800s, the notion of "simple cells" was easy to believe because scientists of the day had no idea about the complexity of the cell's contents or of the information contained in the DNA molecules that guides the development of even the tiniest living organism. At the time, the prevailing theory of origins — "spontaneous generation" — said that life could arise from non-living material. People believed that worms, flies, or even mice simply sprang forth from decaying meat, grain, or other materials. Francesco Redi first demonstrated that flies do not arise from mere chemicals but from the eggs that other flies lay on meat. Redi, and later on, Louis Pasteur, demonstrated what later became known as the biogenetic law — life comes only from life. Both of these men were Christians who believed all life came from an intelligent designer — the supernatural God of the Bible. Their research sought to demonstrate their beliefs.

We now know that every single living cell is so complex that it is virtually beyond our ability to describe it. We could, for example, compare it with a miniature "city" but the comparison would be inadequate because cities cannot reproduce themselves as cells can. However, the "city" is still a useful analogy. The cell's tiny factories constantly retrieve, process, and store food, while highly efficient power plants burn it, producing (and storing) energy without overheating the delicate temperature-sensitive molecular mechanisms. Meanwhile, an elaborate "communication network" allows instant communication both within and without the cell. The transport systems and waste disposal systems are models of efficiency. All of this machinery is manufactured to high precision from the raw materials of nutrient molecules — and the entire city can reproduce itself within a matter of minutes! How could something so complex arise by chance, random processes?

That question remains one of the great mysteries for those who think that life arose out of the disorder of a "big bang." No one today would presume that modern factories arose via an explosion in a brickyard; so if cells are more complex than cities, then their origin begs for even greater intelligent design. Note that natural selection is no help when it comes to how a single cell could have arisen by itself from chemicals. One can't have any natural selection before one has a self-reproducing system, which is horribly complex — a chicken and egg problem. Everywhere we look on this planet we see life giving rise to life — biogenesis — not abiogenesis. There is not a single example of any living creature that has suddenly "come about" by itself. The biogenetic law is a firmly established and universal principle — all life comes from life. Modern evolutionary scientists would balk at being compared with past scientists who believed in spontaneous generation. However, this is exactly what most of them claim happened in a warm primordial ooze billions of years ago, where they believe that lifeless chemicals somehow combined to form "primitive" life. To overcome this, other scientists, and some UFO believers, suggest that life was designed and created by aliens, a topic which will be discussed shortly.

The most efficient system in the universe

Everyone recognizes the absurdity of believing that complex machines form spontaneously through chance, random processes. Machines require a blueprint, and blueprints require a designer. In all living things this blueprint is written on DNA (deoxyribonucleic acid), the complex double-helix molecule that is present in every living organism. DNA carries the code (or instructions) for every "machine" within the cells, telling them what to make — a horse or a human — and also what type of hair, eyes, or skin you will have, and so on.

DNA double helix

The DNA molecule is the most compact and efficient storage information system in the known universe. For example, the amount of information that could be stored in a single pinhead of DNA would be equivalent to a pile of paperback novels 240 times as high as the distance from the earth to the moon, or 100 million times more information than a 40 gigabyte hard drive could hold in your computer.[1]

Even if we could explain the creation of complex coded information by chance, there would be another problem. We would need at the same time to create a mechanism capable of reading and using this coded information; otherwise, the information alone is useless. A fully functional system for writing, reading, and using information is required. This is an example of "irreducible complexity." That is, to be fully functional, the writing mechanism, the reading mechanism, and the mechanism for using the information must all be present at the very first instance it appears. If one of these components is missing, the system won't work. Since life is built on a hierarchy of such "irreducibly complex" machines, the idea that natural processes could have made mere chemicals into living systems is untenable. In his best-selling book, *Darwin's Black Box,* biochemist Dr. Michael Behe describes such biochemical machines:

> . . . systems of horrendous, irreducible complexity inhabit the cell. The resulting realization that life was designed by an intelligence is a shock to us in the twentieth century who have gotten used to thinking of life as the result of simple natural laws. But other centuries have had their shocks, and there is no reason to suppose that we should escape them.[2]

In terms of the volume of information that is constantly working at programming, building, and reproducing our bodies, Dr. Carl Wieland asks us to consider:

> . . . that there are 75 to 100 trillion cells in the [human] body. Taking the lower figure, it means that if we stretched out all of the DNA in one human body and joined it end to end, it would stretch to a distance of 150 billion kilometres (around 94 billion miles). How long is this? It would stretch right around the Earth's equator three-and-a-half million times! It is a thousand times as far as from the Earth to the sun. If you were to shine a torch along that distance, it would take the light, traveling at 300,000 kilometres (186,000 miles) every second, five-and-a-half days to get there.[3]

Design . . . intelligence. Are advanced aliens responsible? Life's enormous complexity is a serious challenge for the theory of evolution. It cannot account for the origin of the first cells, and the problems mount when you consider the development of higher or more evolved life forms (see later in this chapter). Sir Francis Crick, who received a knighthood and the Nobel Prize for his discovery of DNA, admitted:

> An honest man, armed with all the knowledge available to us now, could only state that in some sense, the origin of life

appears at the moment to be almost a miracle, so many are the conditions which would have had to have been satisfied to get it going.[4]

Crick reasoned that such seemingly intelligent design could not have occurred from non-living chemicals under any conceivable Earth conditions. As an atheist, he found the idea of "God as Creator" unpalatable. He proposed, instead, that life originated in outer space and came to Earth. This idea is known as "panspermia," which is from the Greek words *pas/pan* (all) and *sperma* (seed).

The Miller–Urey experiment

In an attempt to prove that life could arise by chance, in 1953 graduate student Stanley Miller conducted experiments based on Harold Urey's proposals about the necessary environmental conditions for life on a primordial Earth billions of years ago.

After concocting a mixture of gases in a flask and injecting an electrical charge, they produced some amino acids, which are building blocks of life. This experiment was regarded as one of the most important breakthroughs supporting the idea that life could have spontaneously arisen, given the right conditions. However, 1970 marked the death-knell for the fleeting hope generated by that experiment. In that year, scientists changed their minds about the conditions of the early earth. Instead of a "reducing," or hydrogen-rich (low in oxygen) environment, they now believed Earth's early atmosphere consisted of gases released by volcanoes (rich in methane and ammonia). Today there is a near-consensus among geochemists on this point. But if you mix those volcanic gases into the Miller–Urey apparatus, the experiment doesn't work. It produces the wrong chemicals; in other words, no building blocks of life. A supposedly irrefutable idea had to be modified or even discarded.

In addition, the major product of the experiment was a noxious mixture of tarry substances (about 85 percent by volume) which are poisonous to life, while the amino acids were only approximately 1.9 percent of the total volume. But even these amino acids were harmful to life. In the real world, the principle of "chirality" requires that all amino acids in proteins be "left-handed," while all sugars in DNA and RNA must be "right-handed." Miller's experiment produced roughly equal amounts of left- and right-handed material, which is detrimental to the production of life.[5]

Although the Miller–Urey experiment had produced [albeit the wrong] amino acids via inorganic processes, the creation of the first proteins began to seem not a small step, but a great — perhaps impassable — divide.[6] Far from proving that life could arise from non-life, Miller and Urey succeeded in highlighting the opposite. A few amino acids (in the wrong amounts) are a far cry from complex proteins, which require that these building blocks be assembled into precise sequences according to all sorts of detailed "city-building" information. In living things, these sequences are the result of pre-existing information passed down from other cells, not "natural processes" of physics or chemistry. How could the first information-laden sequences arise by chance?

On the probability of something like a DNA molecule forming by chance, the late astrophysicist Sir Fred Hoyle illustrated the point this way:

> Now imagine 10^{50} blind persons [that's 100,000 billion billion billion billion billion people — standing shoulder to shoulder, they would more than fill our entire planetary system] each with a scrambled Rubik cube and try to conceive of the chance of them all simultaneously arriving at the solved form. You then have the chance of arriving by random shuffling [random variation] at just one of the many biopolymers on which life depends. The notion that not only the biopolymers but the operating program of a living cell could be arrived at by chance in a primordial soup here on Earth is evidently nonsense of a high order.[7]

Life's origin — from space?

Crick was not the first person to propose the idea of life from outer space. The original idea is attributed to Nobel prizewinning Swedish chemist Svante Arrhenius, back in 1907. He published a book called *World in the Making* after Pasteur had disproved spontaneous generation. His idea was that life had always been present in the universe, and that it traveled from planet to planet as naked bacterial spores. But science fiction writer Isaac Asimov poured cold water on this idea when he pointed out that as far back as 1910, experiments showed that ultraviolet light (UV) would quickly kill such spores. UV is much more intense in space, and in addition, other forms of radiation would kill off any microscopic spores — the problem being accumulated doses over an extended period of time. Around the earth are fields of high-energy particles, which form rings of radiation known as the Van Allen belts (discovered in 1958 by James Van Allen) which would contribute to the radiation dosage.[8] For more complex forms of life, there are additional problems to overcome, such as the nutritional requirements of most organisms, a lack of oxygen, subzero temperatures in space, and the likelihood that any organism larger than one micron in diameter would burn up on re-entry.[9] Recently, there have been discoveries of microbes floating in the stratosphere above the earth, but they appear to be bacteria of Earth origin and not extraterrestrial at all.

Perhaps to overcome such obstacles, Crick co-authored a book called *Life Itself,* which proposed the idea that some form of primordial life was purposefully shipped to the earth by ETs in spaceships. He called this idea *directed panspermia*, but this belief has serious problems, too. Crick reasoned that intelligent life had evolved elsewhere in the universe to produce intelligent beings, and then once again on the earth to ultimately produce people. All this apparently took place following the big bang about nine billion years ago (as was believed in Crick's day).[10]

But evolution itself is undirected, random, purposeless, and wasteful. There is no information contained in matter itself that can produce life, let alone produce similar results time and time again on numerous different planets. It is valid to inquire why supposedly intelligent ETs would seed the earth without knowing what the outcome of undirected evolution would be — unless we are regarded as merely "lab rats" in some grand cosmic wait-and-see science experiment. How could the ETs have known that intelligent life would have definitely arisen in a purposeless process? And who or what life form could expect to exist or survive to see the supposed results of the "experiment" some three billion years later? As we discussed in the previous chapter, how would they find a suitable life-sustaining planet among the trillions of stars in the universe anyway? Crick himself eventually conceded the unscientific basis of his theories:

> Every time I write a paper on the origin of life, I swear I will never write another one, because there is too much speculation running after too few facts. . . .[11]

In any case, as a materialist, his notion of aliens creating life did not solve the problem of how life first arose. It merely pushed it away to an unobservable planet on which those aliens (or their creators, in turn) must have evolved.

After several years of writing science fiction books, famous astronomer Fred Hoyle and colleague Chandra Wickramasinghe published a book that brought serious attention to the idea of panspermia. It was called *Lifecloud: The Origin of Life in the Universe.* This theory had creatures living and breeding in comets and finding their way to Earth, somehow protected from the perils we mentioned earlier. This is truly science fiction. World-famous comet specialist Fred Whipple commented:

> I am charmed but not impressed by the picture of life forms developing in warm little ponds, protected in their icy igloos from the cruel cold and near vacuum of open space, and falling to primitive Earth at speeds exceeding eleven kilometers per second.[12]

Undaunted, Hoyle and Wickramasinghe produced a second book in 1981 called *Evolution from Space,* in which they suggest that genetic material continually enters our atmosphere riding light beams (more accurately, driven by the pressure of light from stars), and that the complex programming for DNA and subsequent evolution had already been "worked out" by a benevolent extraterrestrial intelligence elsewhere. That such famous and learned scientists as Crick, Hoyle, and company can produce such wild speculation is incredible, and highlights yet again that so much of what is called "science" today is merely philosophical guesswork. But their theories are still being discussed to this day and have even gained some credence among others who are also grappling with the origin of the complexity of life. Such fanciful ideas arise because well-informed scientists realize the apparent impossibility of life starting by chance.

Crick conceded this problem when he suggested that the origin of life appears to be nigh miraculous. The complexity of DNA speaks of a design created by a vastly superior intelligence. Hoyle and Wickramasinghe said they faced the same problem:

The conclusion is that the complexity of life on Earth cannot have been caused by a sequence of random processes, but must have come from a cosmic intelligence. Life had already evolved to a high standard of information long before the earth was born, so that our planet received life with the fundamental biochemical problems already solved.[13]

Using the definitions of science that we presented in the last chapter, it is easy to see that such fantastic notions as panspermia are unsustainable. Molecular biologist Michael Denton has also uncovered many serious problems with the evolutionary theory of life forming from non-living matter. In his best-selling book *Evolution: A Theory in Crisis,* he states:

> Nothing illustrates more clearly just how intractable a problem the origin of life has become than the fact that world authorities can seriously toy with the idea of panspermia.[14]

The universal and accepted law of biogenesis simply states that all life comes from life. No one has ever seen lifeless chemicals arrange themselves into the complex, information-bearing bio-molecules needed for life. There are many evolutionary scientists who readily admit this. Yet by faith they believed that this conversion of lifeless chemicals to organic molecules must have occurred early in the history of our planet. Such an unsupported assertion qualifies as religious belief because it deals with the unobserved origin, and therefore the meaning, of life.

The concept of panspermia merely shifts the problem of life's origin further into outer space where it cannot be tested. And did the aliens evolve or were they created? If they were created by other aliens, who created those, and so on? Where does it end, or more importantly, where did it begin?

Mission to Mars (2000)

The movie *Mission to Mars* was a shallow attempt to cash in on the "Mars fever" of the time (probably a result of the "Martian rock" hype some years earlier). Unfortunately, it failed to live up to expectations. A famous director of many successful Hollywood thrillers, Brian De Palma focused on the "face" on Mars in the region of Cydonia. Capitalizing on recent speculation about the possibility of life on Mars, the marketing machine went into over-drive in promoting this movie, with captivating trailers and al-luring posters on the mystery of Mars. Despite a busy opening at the box office, the movie's gross earnings quickly trailed off as the viewing public got wind of its poor script and acting. The movie flopped despite having the best of special effects and brilliant sets, which tried to accurately portray life in space.

The first manned mission to Mars meets with unexpected di-saster, requiring a rescue mission to bring back any survivors and investigate the mystery. The rescue team and one survivor from the original mission encounter an unusual life form at a huge structure on Mars, where our hero-rescuer discovers the secret to the origin of life on Earth. Inside the structure, our hero views the history of the destruction of life on Mars like a video screening. Knowing that their fate was doomed because of an impending asteroid impact, the Martians had dispatched a probe to seed the earth with life — panspermia. However, the movie failed to reveal any more than this. Like all theories of panspermia, it lacked substance and detail. This is one of the first movies to portray panspermia so emphati-cally. The movie's ending basically says, "That's how it was done, the movie's finished, now go home!" One critic wrote:

> The narrative's greatest offense, however, is its hor-rendously simple genesis theory in its horrendously simple plot that needs no more elaboration than the movie's title. It presents a completely vapid narrative with arguably the worst premise for the origin of humanity ever portrayed on film.[15]

In trying to end the movie with an answer, it only posed more questions and left the viewer with an unsatisfactory sci-fi experience.

> *Mission to Mars* is much like space — pretty to look at but empty.[16]

Ockham's razor and SETI's blind spot

If life cannot arise spontaneously from non-life and the simplest living organisms show irreducible complexity, then such organisms must have been fully formed from the very first instant they appeared. That is, the first life must have been designed and created. This is a straightforward conclusion from the available evidence.

In science today, it is generally accepted that the simplest explanation is the best. This view is called Ockham's razor, and one university website explains it so:

> In order to choose among these possible theories, a very useful tool is what is called Ockham's Razor. Ockham's Razor is the principle proposed by William of Ockham in the fourteenth century: "Pluralitas non est ponenda sine necessitate," which translates as "Entities should not be multiplied unnecessarily." In many cases this is interpreted as "keep it simple," but in reality the Razor has a more subtle and interesting meaning. Suppose that you have two competing theories which describe the same system, if these theories have different predictions than [sic] it is a relatively simple matter to find which one is better: one does experiments with the required sensitivity and determines which one give[s] the most accurate predictions.[17]

The simplest explanation for the origin of DNA, using the principle of Ockham's razor, is that it was designed — somewhat like a computer memory chip — and the original life-information was loaded into it by the designer. Since there is no such designer evident here on Earth it is reasonable to conclude that the designing intelligence lives somewhere else.

Note that the SETI program is looking for signs of intelligence, although due to its evolutionary stance, it does not believe in any designer(s) for life. It hopes that an alien intelligence is beaming radio waves across space and that we can recognize the intelligence behind such transmissions. But if advanced alien races somehow evolved differently from us, how would "lowly" mankind be able to recognize or decode their messages? (From an evolutionary standpoint, why should languages evolve similarly? Surely the random numbers of evolution would throw out a "mixed bag" of differing life forms and languages?)

In the DNA of all living things there is already enormously complex coded information that modern technology is only now beginning to decode, such as that revealed in the Human Genome Project (HGP). The simplest living organism known to us has 482 protein-coding genes, or 580,000 letters of information. By comparison, human DNA has three billion (3,000,000,000) letters and all of this information must be precisely arranged. Imagine reading a sentence on this page. If the letters were scrambled, the sentence would cease to carry meaningful information. Similarly, each gene code for a protein is designed to carry out a specific function, and this will not work unless the information is arranged correctly.

The supposed world leader in searching for intelligent messages from space, SETI appears to have an enormous blind spot. Because it accepts evolution as a fact, SETI is either incapable or unwilling to acknowledge that millions of encyclopedias' worth of information has already been transmitted to the earth from an outside intelligence — in the DNA of living organisms. If they ever detect signals from space — and determine that the coded information came from an intelligent source — they will shout to the world that they have discovered an extraterrestrial "language." Yet, the earth already has received tons of coded information, programmed into DNA — a clear sign of such "language" from an outside intelligence!

Dr. Werner Gitt was a director and professor at the German Federal Institute of Physics and Technology and is a world leader in the field of "information science." In several books on the subject, he has made it clear that science makes one thing absolutely sure: information cannot arise from disorder by chance. It *always* takes (a greater source of) information to produce information, and ultimately information is the result of intelligence:[18]

> A code system is always the result of a mental process (it requires an intelligent origin or inventor). . . . It should be emphasized that matter as such is unable to generate any code. All experiences indicate that a thinking being voluntarily exercising his own free will, cognition, and creativity, is required.[19] There is no known natural law through which matter can give rise to information, neither is any physical process or material phenomenon known that can do this.[20]

Genetic manipulation by aliens?

Our look at genetics clearly tells us that genes are designed. Many think that this design is the work of aliens. In his book *Abduction: Human Encounters with Aliens* (1994), Harvard University professor John Mack believed that aliens abduct human beings for sperm and egg collection. Their purpose is to create human/alien hybrids for the purpose of transforming human consciousness; that is, to alter our own perceptions of ourselves as a species. This "transforming" view is common among abduction researchers and UFOlogists who, over the years, have interviewed thousands of "abductees," noting that this "breeding program" seems to be rampant. Many abductees also claim that the aliens themselves have told them such things. These common accounts imply that interfering aliens have been "fiddling" with our genes from the beginning and that we might be the playthings of "superior" races. Such a program, if true, would certainly alter mankind's view of itself.

But how could aliens and humans interbreed? How could we share common DNA that allows interbreeding if they are from other worlds? Presuming they are the creators of Earth life, they must have created some form of "basic" DNA, by using some DNA "threads" from their own bodies or from other creatures on their planet, the theory being that this basic DNA would replicate itself and produce new information and new kinds of creatures. This is similar to Hoyle and Wickramasinghe's proposal when they suggested that this primordial DNA would have all of the engineering and programming bugs ironed out. There are two ways that aliens could have introduced this DNA on Earth.

1. They seeded a primordial Earth and let evolution take over (directed panspermia).

2. They seeded the earth originally and have been overseeing biological, and thus human, evolution along the way.

New information by mutations?

We have already mentioned that evolution is undirected, so point 1 above — a fruitful outcome of human beings after billions of years of undirected change — is an incomprehensible "long shot." Also, masses of new genetic information are required to turn microbes into microbiologists, and, as we shall see, there is no known natural mechanism that can add this information.

In much UFOlogy, DNA is supposed to be a proof that aliens could have "gotten us all started" from one common ancestor, and then "hybridization" could occur between aliens and humans, because the aliens used (tinkered with) their own DNA to start this

Zebras, donkeys, and horses are all from the same original created kind.

process. Yet it is a fact that different kinds of animals cannot cross-breed, even if their DNA is very close (by "kinds" I refer to higher orders than species). The genetic gulf is too great. So for us to interbreed with aliens, our DNA would need to be almost identical to that of the aliens. This difficulty can only be overcome by accepting point 2, that aliens have been directly engineering biological evolution to bring us to this point. However, no scientific study has examined any alien/human "hybrids," so this view remains completely speculative.

There are more problems with both views of seeding. Explaining a "common ancestry" for life on Earth is not as easy as most people think. Although most organisms on Earth use a similar DNA code, some organisms do *not* have a conventional DNA code, and therefore these creatures could not have evolved via a common ancestor. Such differences are like two different papers typed out using two different typewriters with the keys switched — the same keystrokes will produce two entirely different messages. While some creatures (that lack conventional DNA) speak *against* common ancestry, the similarity of the language systems themselves is a strong argument for the common *design* of all living things.

One evolutionary argument for common ancestry is the closeness of genetic material between different species, such as humans and apes. (Some UFOlogists have explained this closeness by claiming that aliens genetically engineered both apes and humans in the distant past.) For example, scientists suggested that there was a 98 percent similarity between human and chimpanzee DNA. This figure has been revised down to as low as 93 percent. On the surface, this percentage still sounds very convincing, but remember that human DNA has three billion base pairs or letters. A 2 percent difference represents a difference of 60 *million* letters of information, while a 7 percent difference equals 210 million letters. How could evolution, through chance random processes and chance selection, keep coming up "trumps" to produce such well-designed and fully functional new lines of information? To even derive humans from the apes (which many believe to be our closest relatives) requires too much of the *right information occurring at the right time* to be credible.

Standard evolutionary theory holds that mutations are capable of giving rise to the new information required. But biological observations have not borne this out. Most mutations are harmful or neutral to the survival of their carriers. Although a handful of mutations are beneficial, in every known case the change represents *a loss of genetic information*. Biophysicist and information theory specialist Dr. Lee Spetner, a former professor at Johns Hopkins University, said this about mutations — dispelling the notion that they help evolution:

> All point mutations that have been studied on the molecular level turn out to reduce the genetic information and not to increase it.[21]

All living creatures possess DNA, which functions as a carrier of information. However, each living organism possesses its own unique library of information. It has been estimated that the three billion letters of information in a single human cell of DNA are equivalent to about 1,000 encyclopedia-sized books of information.[22] If a primordial organism had a single encyclopedia's worth of information (ignoring where this information came from in the first place), to eventually evolve into a human being would require the progressive addition of huge amounts of new information over many steps. This has never been shown to occur through natural processes. Professor Gitt stated the obvious. It takes a greater amount of information to produce information — not less. So how could any other species, like aliens, utilize a method of random chance, like mutations, to create new life forms? It would be like planting a flower seed, and ending up with a forest with all its diversity. There has never been a single documented example of a spontaneous increase in information. Yet, for evolution to take place, it needs to occur constantly. Dr. Spetner says:

> The NDT [neo-Darwinian theory] is supposed to explain how the information of life has been built up by evolution. The essential biological difference between a human and a bacterium is in the information they contain. All other biological differences follow from that. The human genome has much more information than does the bacterial genome. Information

cannot be built up by mutations that lose it. A business can't make money by losing it a little at a time.[23]

What about changes in living things?

Mutations cannot produce new information, so what about the idea of aliens tinkering with evolution along the way? Looking at the changes we see in creatures today will help us understand whether this is possible.

It is true that we do see changes in living things, but the final product is still the same "kind" of creature. For example, there are many breeds of dogs in the world today, but they all came from an original dog that possessed all of the genetic information necessary to produce the variety of dogs we see today. A Chihuahua, now very small, has in fact *lost* genetic information for "largeness" (e.g., a large head, body, and legs), whereas a Great Dane still possesses that information. Similarly, a population of rabbits might have been stranded on an island and is now separated from the parent population on the mainland. In time, and through natural selection, these rabbits could become so different or specialized (this is called speciation) that they might not be able to interbreed with the original population on the mainland anymore. They may even be classified as a new species, but they have once again, through selection, lost genetic information that was present in the original parent population on the mainland.

Why dwell on this? This is not evolution because evolution requires uphill changes. It demonstrates yet again that real science shows downhill changes and losses in genetic information. This finding is consistent with the idea that all the original kinds of creatures needed to be made fully formed and functional, and possessed huge amounts of genetic information from the very beginning. Therefore, aliens periodically visiting the earth to create new kinds of animals would be playing a game of snakes (chutes) and ladders. Natural selection causes the information to head in the wrong direction by reducing it. The aliens would occasionally "top-up" the genetic information, only to see mutations and natural selection reduce it yet again. The "topping-up" could be similar to the methods of genetic engineering that we see today, only it would need to be carried out on a massive scale over all the earth's creatures, repeatedly and near-continually, over millions of years. Wouldn't it be far simpler to engineer humans directly, if that was their goal?

The idea of the earth being seeded by aliens with some ancestor organism which then evolved into higher life forms (point 1) contradicts the science of genetics and information theory. A "classic" quote from Sir Fred Hoyle (who did *not* believe in a supernatural Creator) sums up this dilemma:

Galaxy M31. Galaxies contain billions of stars similar to our own sun.

> The chance that higher life forms might have emerged in this way is comparable with the chance that a tornado sweeping through a junkyard might assemble a Boeing 747 from the materials contained therein.[24]

Evolution overseen by aliens (point 2) would also be a wasteful process. If they are benevolent creators, as many people claim them to be, why use this ugly process of death, struggle, and suffering? Why haven't they revealed themselves openly instead of relying on "middle of the night" kidnappings to interbreed with humans?

It is fair to say that the majority of Western-educated people believe in evolution. But the beliefs of the majority aren't always correct. The majority once believed in spontaneous generation. Some people might defend them "because they didn't know all the facts." But can we honestly say that we possess all the facts today? Tomorrow, mankind will discover something that we don't know today. Ongoing genetic discoveries are likely to continually challenge the 150-year-old theory of Darwinian evolution. Dr. Michael Denton has noted that we have only scratched the surface when it comes to understanding the complexity of design in the biological world. He says:

> It would be an illusion to think that what we are aware of at present is any more than a fraction of the full extent of biological design. In practically every field of fundamental

biological research, ever-increasing levels of design and complexity are being revealed at an ever-accelerating rate.[25]

Do fossils prove evolution in the distant past?

The majority of people on this planet believe that the fossil record
plainly tells the story of evolution, and UFOlogists almost universally
accept this view of origins. So this needs to be briefly discussed. Among
the many thousands of layers of rocks and sediments deposited all over
the globe, people assume that we can see a historical record in stone,
of creatures evolving upward from one kind into another. After nearly
150 years of searching this record, however, have we found the "missing links"? What does the actual evidence show?

Dr. Stephen Jay Gould, a professor at Harvard University (now
deceased), who was arguably the world's most famous paleontologist,
as well as an outspoken humanist and evolutionist, noted about the
fossil record:

> All paleontologists know that the fossil record contains
> precious little in the way of intermediate forms; transitions
> between major groups are characteristically abrupt.[26]

Years later, although an atheist, Gould even added:

> The absence of fossil evidence for intermediary stages be-
> tween major transitions in organic design, indeed our inability,
> even in our imagination, to construct functional intermediates
> in many cases, has been a persistent and nagging problem for
> gradualistic accounts of evolution.

All creatures that appear in the fossil record appear abruptly and
fully functional — just what is predicted by genetics and information
science.

To show that Gould's statements are not unique, consider what Dr.
Colin Patterson has to say. He was, at the time, the senior paleontologist at the world-renowned British Museum of Natural History, reply-
ing to a letter regarding a book he wrote on fossils:

> . . . I fully agree with your comments on the lack of di-
> rect illustration of evolutionary transitions in my book. If I
> knew of any, fossil or living, I would certainly have included
> them. You suggest that an artist should be used to visualize

such transformations, but where would he get the information from? I could not, honestly, provide it, and if I were to leave it to artistic license, would that not mislead the reader? . . . Yet Gould and the American Museum people are hard to contradict when they say there are no transitional fossils. . . . You say I should at least "show a photo of the fossil from which each type of organism was derived." I will lay it on the line — there is not one such fossil for which one could make a watertight argument.[27]

These two leading experts reached the same conclusion, and they are not alone in their assessment. They both believe in evolution, yet the evidence in their own field of expertise does not support the belief that evolution has occurred.

Gould further admits that we do not see humans evolving today, and there is no evidence that, in the future, we will evolve into some alien-like, and supposedly advanced, design:

> We're not just evolving slowly. For all practical purposes we're not evolving. There's no reason to think we're going to get bigger brains or smaller toes or whatever — we are what we are.[28]

L. Harrison Matthews, FRS, in his introduction to the 1971 edition of Charles Darwin's *Origin of Species* — gives a telling commentary on the state of evolutionary theory:

> The fact of evolution is the backbone of biology, and biology is thus in the peculiar position of being a science founded on an unproved theory — is it then a science or a faith?[29]

The purpose of this chapter was to answer the question "Could aliens have 'seeded' the earth to create life?" Here is a summary of the evidence that we have examined so far.

- Scientists have never observed chemicals forming themselves into complex DNA molecules, the blueprint for life. DNA molecules do not produce new genetic information, they reproduce it. DNA appears to be designed, and information science demonstrates that information must be fully present in the beginning.

- Mutations and natural selection reduce *pre-existing* information. There is no evidence of organisms evolving upward (including mankind — technological increase is not biological evolution).

- All life in the fossil record appears abruptly and fully formed; the chains of transitional series hoped for by evolutionists since Darwin are conspicuous by their general absence.

Given these facts, then, aliens needed to create a multitude of fully formed living things at the very beginning.

A third option is that aliens evolved elsewhere and stumbled across our planet with all its life forms. But we have already discussed the related problems of interstellar travel and finding us in the first place. Furthermore, how could DNA have evolved on their world in a form that would enable them to hybridize with humans?

It appears that scientists and UFOlogists who believe the notion of panspermia taking place billions of years ago have many inconsistencies to overcome. Our discussions have deep philosophical and personal implications for every single human being. Why are most people ignoring the obvious evidence? Michael Behe writes:

> Many people, including many important and well-respected scientists, just don't want there to be anything beyond nature. They don't want a supernatural being to affect nature, no matter how brief or constructive the interaction may have been. In other words . . . they bring an a priori philosophical commitment to their science that restricts what kinds of explanations they will accept about the physical world. Sometimes this leads to rather odd behavior.[30]

So, who was responsible for life? Was it aliens (that is, physical beings of unimaginable intelligence and technology) or a supernatural being outside of our space and time, possessing unimaginable powers of creation?

What intelligence could perform such miracles?

Not just any "mortal" alien could have created complex life on Earth. If the evolution of primordial cells is impossible, then aliens with physical bodies cannot be a product of evolution either. As we discussed in chapter 3, matter cannot arrange itself into complex life of any sort by natural processes, so they would also need to have had a Creator. The origin of life is a deeply religious question. It asks, "How and why are we here?" Since we know of no Creator here on Earth, it is reasonable to presume that someone outside of our dimension — our physical reality — has brought everything into existence.

In this regard, many UFO believers express deep interest in the Bible, not only because of its historical value and predictive ability, but because they believe that the biblical texts reflect the interaction between ancient astronauts and Earth's history, and that the Bible provides clues to their "god-like" status. Some believe that alien beings from other, even supernatural, dimensions have been overseeing mankind's affairs, and that early people inaccurately recorded their activity in the Bible.

Yet it is reasonable *first* to consider whether to take the Bible at face value. It claims to be the words of the Creator himself, and many millions of people, including some world-class scientists, subscribe to this view, despite those in the UFO movement who desire to reinterpret the Bible. If this Creator supernaturally and inter-dimensionally transmitted coded information into DNA molecules, couldn't He give further information in written documents via mankind, whom He created, too? As we shall see in the coming chapters, aliens are apparently communicating with modern human beings, who in turn are writing down *their* instructions. Christians claim that a similar method was used by God to inspire the Bible.

In Genesis, this "God" described the creation of the heavens and the earth, bringing matter, space, and time into existence, and then He described the filling of His creation with a myriad of life forms. Physical chemist and author of some leading books on biblical creation Jonathan Sarfati explains the traditional Christian view of the creation account in Genesis:

> . . . creationists, starting from the Bible, believe that God created different kinds of organisms, which reproduced "after their kinds" (Gen. 1:11–12, 21, 24–25). Each of these kinds was created with a vast amount of information. There was enough variety in the information in the original creatures so their descendants could adapt to a wide variety of environments.[31]

This view provides a marked contrast to the views of UFOlogists, and it avoids many of the difficulties associated with the process of evolution. Even though life appears to be designed, there are at least three intractable problems with the notion that aliens were responsible:

1. The entire universe appears to be specially designed for life on Earth, which is not explained by the cosmic disorder invoked by a big bang. This purposeful design would have occurred before any aliens evolved or came into existence. Therefore, they could not be responsible for the design of the universe.

2. Evolution presumably produces undirected results. A wasteful mechanism, it is assumed to have produced many species that simply died out or did not "make it" as a result of survival of the fittest. There is no evidence that evolution is a viable method of "creation" anyway. Therefore, evolution could not have given rise to the aliens in the first place, and they must have been created.

3. The complexity of life on Earth, as evidenced by DNA and the fossil record, appears to have "burst" into existence showing no signs of evolutionary ancestry. Like the universe, it requires an *ex nihilo* (Latin, meaning "out of nothing") creation. Aliens could not have created the matter from which they ultimately came.

The study of origins is invaluable in the study of UFOs. Where could they come from? Are they older and more advanced than us? Are they genetically related to us? Whereas operational (observable, repeatable, and testable) science causes us to marvel at the miracle of life itself, "creation" falls outside the realm of operational science. An open-minded person must weigh which version of creation is most believable: could the Almighty God of the Bible be responsible for the instantaneous creation of life, or was it a result of evolution? A marriage of the two — that the aliens' creation story has been married into the Bible — is not really a viable option because of the difficulties we have discussed with the origin of the universe and biological life.

Why evolution?

At this stage it would be quite reasonable to ask, "If the evidence is so straightforward, why do so many scientists believe in evolution?" A world-famous evolutionist and professor of genetics, Richard Lewontin, gives a clue:

> We take the side of [evolutionary] science in spite of the patent absurdity of some of its constructs . . . in spite of the tolerance of the scientific community for unsubstantiated just-so stories, because we have a prior commitment to materialism [the belief that matter is all there is]. . . . Moreover, that materialism is absolute for we cannot allow a Divine foot in the door.[32]

He is really saying that the only other alternative is a supernatural Creator, which is clearly an unacceptable notion to him.

A leading evolutionist and professor of physics at the University of Manchester, H.S. Lipson, went even further when he commented:

> In fact, evolution became in a sense a scientific religion; almost all scientists have accepted it and many are prepared to "bend" their observations to fit in with it.[33]

Humanism (the belief that we are all just evolved animals, and thus are our own masters) allows us to decide what is truth in our own eyes. On the other hand, if there is a Creator, by definition He owns what He has made and has the right to do what He wants with His creation. If this view is the truth, then it means that we have enormous personal responsibilities to the one who made us. This is an unacceptable position for an atheist who has already declared there is no God or Creator. In reality, this is an emotional decision (not one based on logic or scientific evidence) because mankind wants to believe that we are masters of our own destiny. The big bang and evolution provide man with an easy excuse to evade the idea of the supernatural and the possibility of a divine Creator. Similarly, the extraterrestrial hypothesis (ETH — aliens visiting us from other planets) is both based on and reinforces belief in evolution — in this case, on other worlds.

The last two chapters have examined the limits of science, as a first step in determining the truth about UFOs. So where do we go from here in our search for answers? Science can only take us so far, and at some point we must invoke the supernatural to explain things that we cannot answer in the natural realm. But this does not mean we are invoking a mere "God of the gaps" for the things we cannot scientifically explain. It is a logical step. In the previous chapter, engineer and design expert Dr. Stuart Burgess was quoted as saying that science was useful in demonstrating when the miraculous has taken place. If the big bang and evolution are unsatisfactory causes, and ETs could not have evolved or used evolution, where do these alien creatures come from?

By realizing the possibility of a supernatural or extra-dimensional realm, it will help widen our field of exploration in trying to understand the UFO phenomenon. If UFOs operate outside of our laws of science, then we must also look outside our natural laws to understand who or what they are. But if you and I have never been to other dimensions or realities, we could use a helping hand in understanding this realm. Given the focus of the religious UFO movement on the Bible, can we glean insight from its texts? Although an ancient book, it is the one most referred to and quoted by many UFOlogists. One biblical character who claimed to have come from an extra-dimensional reality is Jesus Christ. Both Christians and many UFO believers claim Jesus Christ as their own. He claimed to have knowledge pertinent to both worlds. In the Bible, when talking about himself and his own origin, Jesus said in John 3:12–13:

> I have spoken to you of earthly things and you do not believe; how then will you believe if I speak of heavenly things? No one has ever gone into heaven except the one who came from heaven — the Son of Man.

Many religious UFO believers interpret this "heaven" to be another planet, galaxy, or extraterrestrial home where technology may have overcome death and sickness.

In the following chapters we shall again use science to help determine the physical evidence and claims for UFOs, but in the spiritual realm, we shall look at the Bible. As already pointed out, this is what many UFO believers do, as they find many parallels for their beliefs in the Bible, particularly in regard to future events. And as we shall see later, mankind is central to the plans of our so-called ET space brothers.

Endnotes

1 *Creation* 25 (2): 26–31.

2 Michael Behe, *Darwin's Black Box* (New York: The Free Press, 1996), p. 252–253.

3 *Creation Ex Nihilo* 17 (4): 10–13.

4 Crick quoted in "Panspermia," <www.creationdefense.org/68.htm>, March 9, 2003.

5 "God: Validated by Scientific Endeavor," <www.god-1.net/God.htm>, March 16, 2003.

6 "Survival of the Fakest," <www.creationinthecrossfire.com/Articles/SurvivaloftheFakestpt1.html>, March 16, 2003.

7 Fred Hoyle, "The Big Bang in Astronomy," *New Scientist*, vol. 92, no. 1280, November 19, 1981, p. 527.

8 "Panspermia," <www.pathlights.com/ce_encyclopedia/20hist11.htm>, March 9, 2003.

9 "Panspermia," <www.creationdefense.org/68.htm>, March 9, 2003.

10 "Panspermia," <www.pathlights.com/ce_encyclopedia/20hist11.htm>, March 9, 2003.

11 Crick, cited in "Panspermia," <www.creationdefense.org/68.htm>, March 9, 2003.

12 Fred L. Whipple, "Origin of the Solar System [review of Hoyle's work]," *Nature* 278 (577:819), quoted in "Panspermia," <www.pathlights.com/ce_encyclopedia/20hist11.htm>, March 9, 2003.

13 F. Hoyle and N. Wickramasinghe, *Evolution from Space* (London: J.M. Dent & Sons, 1981), cover page.

14 Denton, cited in "Panspermia," <www.creationdefense.org/68.htm>, March 9, 2003.

15 " 'Mission to Mars' Presents Great Effects, Confusing Plot," <wildcat.arizona.edu/papers/93/116/04_1_m.html>, March 16, 2003.

16 Ibid.

17 "What Is Ockham's Razor?" <phyun5.ucr.edu/~wudka/Physics7/Notes_www/node10.html>, March 11, 2003.

18 "How Would You Answer?" <www.answersingenesis.org/docs/3270.asp#r16>, March 13, 2003.

19 Werner Gitt, *In the Beginning Was Information* (Bielenfeld, Germany: Christliche Literatur-Verbreitung), p. 64–67.

20 Ibid., p. 79.

21 Lee Spetner, *Not by Chance* (Brooklyn, NY: The Judaica Press Inc., 1997), p. 138.

22 "Human/Chimp DNA Similarity," <www.answersingenesis.org/docs/2453.asp#f6>, March 13, 2003.

23 Spetner, *Not by Chance*, p. 143.

24 "Hoyle on Evolution," *Nature*, vol. 294, November 12, 1981, cited in *The Revised Quote Book* (Brisbane, Australia: Creation Science Foundation, 1990), p. 21.

25 Michael Denton, *Evolution: A Theory in Crisis* (Bethesda, MD: Adler and Adler, 1986), p. 342.

26 Stephen Jay Gould, "The Return of Hopeful Monsters," *Natural History*, vol. LXXXVI (6), June–July 1977, cited in *The Revised Quote Book*, p. 8.

27 Personal letter (April 10, 1979) written to Luther Sunderland, cited in Luther Sunderland, *Darwin's Enigma* (Green Forest, AR: Master Books, 1984), p. 89.

28 In a speech in October 1983, reported in the *Washington Times*, "John Lofton's Journal," February 8, 1984, cited in *The Revised Quote Book*, p. 13.

29 Harrison L. Matthews, Introduction to Darwin's *The Origin of Species* (London: J.M. Dent & Sons Ltd., 1971), p. xi, cited in *The Revised Quote Book*, p. 2.

30 Michael Behe, *Darwin's Black Box*, p. 243.

31 Jonathan Sarfati, *Refuting Evolution* (Brisbane, Australia: Answers in Genesis, 2002), p. 32.

32 Richard Lewontin, "Billions and Billions of Demons," *New York Review*, January 9, 1997, p. 31.

33 H.S. Lipson, "A Physicist Looks at Evolution," *Physics Bulletin*, vol. 31, 1980, p. 138, cited in *The Revised Quote Book*, p. 2.

Chapter Five

Lights in the Sky — Where Are They Coming From?

UFOs defined?

One of the more pervasive beliefs about UFOs is that they contain extraterrestrial beings. Ronald Story, noted UFO researcher and editor of *The Mammoth Encyclopedia of Extraterrestrial Encounters* (EEE), relates a story about his son, Brian, which demonstrates how much the ETH has saturated popular culture. He says:

> This phenomenon was made strikingly clear to me by an experience with my son. He was five years old at the time (in 1979). . . . Without having any prior discussions on the matter . . . I asked my son Brian: "What is a UFO?"
>
> He answered without hesitation, "a flying saucer."
>
> So, I rephrased the question this way: "What is *inside* a flying saucer?"
>
> To which he replied, matter of factly: "People from other planets." Nothing could better illustrate to me that "UFO"

had become a living symbol in our culture for the vehicle that carries "humanoids from another planet.[1]

The origin of the term "UFO" is attributed to Captain Edward J. Ruppelt, a former chief of the U.S. Air Force's Project Blue Book. Although the term technically refers to an *unidentified* flying object, in common language it now means "flying saucer containing aliens."[2] Most modern dictionaries also define the term as a "flying saucer" or some other reference to an extraterrestrial craft. This popularization of the UFO phenomenon makes research extremely difficult. As we previously mentioned, no indisputable empirical evidence (no piece or fragment) of an extraterrestrial craft has ever been recovered. Research relies mainly on eyewitness testimonies, and in the climate of a science fiction–crazed society, we are unlikely to get reports untainted by preconception, even from the average person.

By way of example, let's presume that 150 years ago a farmer "putting his cows to bed" looks up and sees a group of lights flashing across the night sky at incredible speeds. What will he attribute it to? He has never seen airplanes, satellites, or spaceships, and the science fiction age is still many years in the future. Depending on his world view, he may dismiss it as "just one of those things," a trick of the starlight, or perhaps think it to be a spiritual manifestation, such as angels, demons, or the like. There is no doubt that past generations were more religious than ours, in the sense that their outlook was attuned to a more traditional or mainstream spiritual view of the world. Shift forward to the present, and today's farmer is likely to interpret the lights as a UFO (in the common-language sense).

A swarm of UFOs — an eyewitness testimony

It was May 1986 — late autumn in Australia, and in the eastern inland rural areas of this massive island continent, well-known for its heat, dust, and flies, the evenings at this time of year have a definite chill to them. On this particular evening, however, it was a bit warmer than usual due to the cloud cover that blanketed the night sky. So many clouds, in fact, that hardly a star was visible. The moon was not scheduled to appear anyway. Paul and his brother Gary had the run of a friend's wheat and cattle property this weekend for a bit of rest and relaxation.

In the still, quiet evening, they were doing what a lot of young Aussie males do who are brought up in "the bush"[3] — shooting. Sometimes it's for rabbits, but on this evening it was foxes. Neither species is native to Australia, and they have caused immense damage over the years to crops and the native fauna of this unique country.

The silence was broken only by the imitation fox calls that the men were making in an effort to entice their prey out of their "hidey-holes." Perched in the back of their "ute" (pick-up truck), they had two rifles and a spotlight at the ready, but alas there were no foxes this evening. To pass the time, Paul's eyes surveyed the remote landscape. It was cleared, ready for planting, and very little caught the eye on the horizon — except for two lights.

They must be stars, Paul thought to himself. *Hang on, though, there's clouds about, and these things are moving.* He nudged Gary to have a look as well. As they fixed their eyes on these two strange lights, the objects moved more quickly and came closer, changing directions very sharply, as if in response to each other's actions. Paul said later:

> At this stage we couldn't perceive how far away they were, but they were definitely underneath the cloud layer, and moving at "impossible" speeds. I could feel my body tense — I wondered what was going on.

Unable to take their eyes off these lights for several minutes, Paul glanced sideways, and noticed, almost with a sense of horror, that there were other lights — about 18 or more of them. They were closer, the lights were much bigger, and again, they were moving in all directions. Paul describes what he saw:

They were moving faster than anything that I've ever seen or imagined, and turning — doing "u-turns" without even slowing down. It should be impossible for anything to do that — but they were! We were now terrified. We made a decision to get out of there, but when we got into the front seats of the ute to drive away, we realized we needed to turn the headlights on because it was pitch black. We were scared because we didn't want "them" to notice us. But we had to do it, as we didn't want to stay there any longer. It took us about five minutes to get back to the hut where we locked ourselves inside. After a few minutes, we decided to peer outside again. Instead of looking across the fields, we now had to look directly upward to see them. They were even closer. There was a break in the clouds and two of the lights sped through the gap as if they were racing each other. It gave the impression that something intelligent was guiding these things. Then, as we were watching, one of them dropped — no, sped — directly toward the ground, and as it got closer it did a u-turn and then went straight back upwards. It didn't even slow down to change direction, and as it shot upward, there was a blue tinge and a triangle shape coming from underneath it. It was giving off no sound, not even the sound of rushing wind.

Paul and his brother scanned the newspapers and television channels to see if there were any other reports of these sightings. They thought about visiting an observatory that was located nearby, thinking, *Surely they must have seen something*.

Over the years, Paul has shared their experiences with only a handful of trusted friends and family. The doubts "nagged" at him for many years. He kept silent, fearing that people would doubt his sanity — until now. Many sightings must have gone similarly unreported due to such fears.

Paul decided to relate this story to me, that it may help others. Since his experience, he has become a "born-again" Christian. Today, he reasons that no technology, man-made or otherwise, could be responsible for the types of maneuvers he witnessed, and he has reconciled the events within his belief system. However, when I asked him what he thought they were at the time of the sightings, he frankly admitted:

> Oh, there was no doubt in our minds. We thought they were UFOs — spacecraft piloted by aliens. Looking back, I can see that I was influenced by all the UFO stuff we saw and read — like the "Roswell Incident" for example. There was nothing else that I knew of at the time that could explain them.

> Interestingly, Paul's father and grandfather had also seen UFOs. The family (generational) "link" and the "triangle" shape are both common in UFOlogy.

Due to the popularization of UFOs, many people are, to an extent, intentionally looking for sightings, expecting them to occur. In this respect, there is a strong psychological element that plays a part — a "hope" for such sightings. I have personally met many such people over the years who wished for such experiences — in some way being shaped by the desire to come into contact with some force greater than themselves. Many years ago, as a young man searching for meaning, I can recall having similar desires.

Sightings are so numerous that organizations abound that are dedicated to the research of UFOs and associated phenomena. Some, such as FUFOR (Fund for UFO Research), CUFOS (Center for UFO Studies), NUFORC (National UFO Reporting Center), and MUFON (Mutual UFO Network), regard themselves as impartial clearinghouses for UFO reports.

Some of these, such as MUFON and CUFOS, actually engage "field investigators" to determine, where possible, the true nature of reports. It would be fair to say that the majority of these investigations usually conclude that sightings can be explained as natural phenomena or man-made technologies. Figures on this are usually in the vicinity of 90–95 percent. (As we have said previously, residual cases *might* be explained in such ways if one had access to all of the available information, anyway. The hardened skeptic, true to his faith, would simply say that *all* UFOs *definitely could* be explained in this manner.) The most common object mistakenly labeled as a UFO is the planet Venus (27 percent of all sightings). Other mistaken objects include:

- Satellites circling the earth or burning up on re-entry.
- Meteors or meteor showers passing through, or burning up in, our atmosphere.
- Rocket launches or vehicles in the atmosphere, such as the space shuttle.
- High- (and lower-) altitude weather balloons.
- Astronomical phenomena such as the northern and southern lights (*Aurora Borealis* and *Aurora Australis*).
- Noctilucent ("night light") clouds. These are high-altitude ice-crystal clouds that glow at night from reflected sunlight.
- Lenticular clouds — lens-shaped clouds that look remarkably like a "flying saucer."
- Lightning — particularly ball lightning, a very rare phenomenon.
- Flocks of birds.
- Aircraft.
- Reflections of the sun on various objects.
- Car headlights or even streetlights.
- Kites or parachutes.
- Insect swarms, such as moths.

Hypotheses of the heavyweights

These are just some of the widely varying, yet verifiable, objects that have been reported as UFOs. Yet there is always an unexplained residue of sightings. Paranormal investigator and UFO skeptic Joe Nickell comments:

> . . . there remains a residue of unexplained cases which proponents and skeptics interpret quite differently. Proponents treat the residual cases as if — simply by being unsolved — they infer a paranormal cause. But that is, at best, a logical fallacy called "arguing from ignorance" and, at worst, mystery monger-ing. Skeptics may sometimes be too dismissive, but they cor-rectly observe that incidents may be unexplained for various reasons, including insufficient, erroneous, or even falsified evi-dence — the same reasons that many crimes remain unsolved.[4]

Have many of the eminent and aforementioned organizations commenced operations solely on the basis that a few unexplained sightings represent something mysterious to be investigated? Noted UFOlogist J. Allen Hynek (whom we mentioned in chapter 1) was a scientific consultant for the U.S. Air Force on Project Blue Book for over 20 years. Although Blue Book listed 12,618 UFO reports, of which 701 (c. 5 percent) have remained unidentified and could not be explained, it concluded that UFOs did not pose any threat to national security. The government is effectively "off the hook" with this type of explanation. It doesn't say what they are, but it provides an answer which they believe serves the public interest. The later Condon Report came to much the same conclusion. Hynek's role was to study UFO reports and determine whether an astronomical object, such as the moon or planet Venus, for example, may explain them. Initially, he was a UFO skeptic, but he soon became convinced that UFOs were worthy of serious study, and in 1973 he founded CUFOS.[5]

But why did he think so? So far, we have only been discussing whether UFO sightings are potentially of extraterrestrial spacecraft. Surely rational scientists would not decide on a career in UFOlogy just on the basis of a few "Twilight Zone" mysteries?

It is claimed that on occasion there has been some collateral physical evidence. The most difficult to refute are scorch marks, depressions in the ground, and burnt or damaged plants that sometimes take much longer than expected to recover.

Where there's smoke there's no fire. . . .

One event that apparently left physical traces occurred in Socorro, New Mexico, on April 24, 1964. Lonnie Zamora, an experienced and respected police officer, reportedly came across a "landed" UFO after being distracted from the pursuit of a felon. He discovered, at a distance, a saucer-shaped craft standing on tripod-like legs, and two small figures about 4 feet tall dressed in white coveralls. As he moved closer to get a better look, he noticed that they had returned to their craft and it took off, hovering above the ground before it sped away. Zamora contacted his base and requested assistance, and a skeptical Sergeant Chavez was dispatched to investigate. Zamora showed him the site, where they found large imprints in the ground, supposedly from the legs of the craft.

Smoke was coming from a bush that appeared to be burnt, yet it was not on fire, and apparently cold to touch. There were other areas that showed signs of being burnt, including clumps of grass. Charred particles and soil samples were taken for examination, yet they showed no traces of any chemical or foreign residue. No radioactivity emanated from the area, either. Although Zamora was the only person to "sight" the craft, nine separate people viewed the landing traces and burn marks when they were still "fresh." Apparently there was also a concurrent sighting that was described as a "funny-looking helicopter" and ignored at the time.

Some time later, UFO skeptic and investigator Philip J. Klass investigated the case and thought it to be a classic hoax. However, the Project Blue Book team investigated the event, describing the witness as credible. To date it remains as "unexplained" on their files.[6]

There have been electromagnetic disturbances associated with sightings, causing outages and interference in electrical systems, car motors, and communication devices. And of course many UFOs have been sighted on radars.

There are also physical effects on humans and animals. Dogs, cattle, and other types of creatures very commonly give the indication of being "spooked" just prior to and during UFO sightings. Humans have experienced dizziness, headaches, various pains, nausea, and a whole range of differing symptoms during an encounter.

As mentioned previously, it is often the eyewitness testimony that provides the most intriguing clues as to whether there indeed is something more worth investigating, and they often have very interesting tales to tell. Many of these eyewitnesses have also become contactees. That is, according to Hynek, they have had a "close encounter of the third kind" or CE-3 experience, where the alleged alien occupants have been seen by human beings with or without some interaction having taken place. Interestingly, Hynek and others have noticed that there does seem to be a similar pattern of experiences with contactees from all over the world. Messages from the "aliens" appear to be of a similar thread also, and we shall look at these patterns in more detail in later chapters. Here are some of Hynek's observations about the UFO phenomenon, from interviews he conducted over the years:

The conclusion I've come to after all these years is that first of all, the subject is much more complex than any of us imagined. It has paranormal aspects but certainly it has very real physical aspects, too. The attitude we're taking in the Center for UFO Studies [CUFOS] is that since we're going to have scientists involved, we will push the physical approach as hard and far as we can — instrumentation, physical evidence, photographs, radar records. If we are finally forced by the evidence itself to go into the paranormal, then we will.[7]

He was reported expressing these views in *Lumières dans la Nuit,* issue 168, in October 1977:

HYNEK: [The extraterrestrial] theory runs up against a very big difficulty, namely, that we are seeing too many UFOs. The Earth is only a spot of dust in the Universe. Why should it be honored with so many visits?

INTERVIEWER: Then what is your hypothesis?

HYNEK: I am more inclined to think in terms of something metaterrestrial, a sort of parallel reality.

INTERVIEWER: And what then is your personal conviction?

HYNEK: I have the impression that the UFOs are announcing a change that is coming soon in our scientific paradigms. I am very much afraid that UFOs are related to certain psychic phenomena. And if I say 'I am very much afraid,' this is because in our Center at Evanston we are trying to study this problem from the angle of the physical sciences. . . . But it would be absurd to follow up only one path to the exclusion of all others.[8]

This theory was repeated when Hynek was interviewed by *Newsweek* (November 21, 1977):

UFO's, he says, may be psychic phenomena and the "aliens" may not come from outer space but from a "parallel reality."[9]

A former skeptic, Hynek investigated UFOs for nearly 40 years, although he was not a "one-man" show. He surrounded himself with credible and reliable scientists, whom he implored to take a scientific approach to all the data. He was the author of numerous technical papers and textbooks on astrophysics, and also the author of several books on the UFO phenomenon:

> Hynek submitted that perhaps UFOs were part of a parallel reality, slipping in and out of sequence with our own. This was a hypothesis that obviously pained him as an empirical scientist. Yet after 30 years of interviewing witnesses and investigating sighting reports, radar contacts, and physical traces of saucer landings no other hypothesis seemed to make sense to him.[10]

Not a new phenomenon

Unknown lights, objects, and shapes have been observed in the skies for thousands of years. Reports have been handed down through the ages from many nations of the world, including India, China, Japan, England, Ireland, France, Italy, the Americas, Scandinavian countries, and Polynesia. Ancient Romans and Greeks had stories of "fiery globes" and flying shields. Ancient Egyptians left accounts of "circles of fire" and "flaming chariots" that sailed across the heavens. American Indians have legends of "flying canoes" and "great silvery airships." Some of these early "vehicles" were also said to contain occupants.

Note how the descriptions of UFOs (flying shields, for example) seemed to be explained in terms of the technology of the day. Is this because the contactee is unable to adequately describe advanced technology? But one would think that a silvery disk, for example, could be described as such regardless of the age or culture. One cannot discount the possibility that the UFOs may be manifesting themselves in an understandable form of technology for the age.

The first modern wave of documented UFO sightings occurred in what became known as the "airship waves" of 1886 and 1887 in the United States. Despite the description, the sightings occurred several years before any documented flights of airplanes or powered craft of any kind in the United States. At that time, the term "airship" was probably used to describe any sort of flying vehicle. Most of the sightings were described as strange lights, or objects that were "cigar-shaped," "egg-shaped," or "barrel-shaped." These are very similar to the types of man-made airships (zeppelins or balloons) that were to follow in the years to come. It is intriguing to note that the manifestations came in a shortly-to-be-realized technological format. Toward the end of 1887, hints of "airship" activity were also reported in other countries around the world, although it was known that some European countries had motor-powered balloons by that time.

Although traveling slowly by the standards of modern reports, these UFOs were perceived as being able to travel quite fast, ascend, and change directions very rapidly. Colored lights were also commonly reported to be following the craft. On several occasions, there were some CE-3 encounters, as occupants of the ships were apparently seen. According to one report, two men told the Stockton, California *Evening Mail* in 1896 that:

> The strange beings were very tall, with small delicate hands, and large narrow feet. Each creature's head was bald with small ears and a small mouth, yet the eyes were big and lustrous.[11]

Remember also that shortly after this time, the public consciousness had been "alerted" to the possibility of extraterrestrial life. This was the era of Percival Lowell's Martian canals theory. The cigar shape was also a descriptive term that was to remain for many years, although Jacques Vallée noted that in the period from 1914 to 1946, there were relatively few sightings[12] compared to the modern explosion of sightings that occurred

Airship wave woodcut in an 1896 newspaper to
illustrate a reported sighting

after Kenneth Arnold's flying disks of 1947. This follows a pattern; researchers Ankerberg and Weldon noted that between 1920 and 1947 less than a dozen science fiction movies were made, whereas during the period between 1950 and 1980 over one hundred such films were made.[13]

The changing shape of UFOs

We have already commented on the way the sightings seem to pre-empt man-made technologies. Airships are seen a few years before they are manufactured and then Arnold and others see silvery or white craft in a postwar, pre–rocket-savvy culture. This "coincidence" has not been lost on the government conspiracy theorists with their ideas of not-yet-revealed secret government technologies. However, their theory breaks down when applied to sightings by ancient Greeks, Romans, and American Indians.

As has been shown, the shapes of UFOs have followed a pattern of change as well. However, three descriptive characteristics are common over the last few decades. The U.S. Air Force's Project Grudge report of December 1949 concluded that the most common shapes are:

1. Disk-like objects (the commonest of all)
2. Rocket-like or cigar-shaped objects
3. Luminous objects appearing at night

In another emerging pattern, triangular, cone-shaped, and boomerang-shaped objects have been common since the 1980s as well. The *Wall Street Journal*, in October 1990, claimed that in Belgium alone there had been more than 2,600 sightings of triangular UFOs the previous year. There is also photographic evidence of many of these events.[14] A consistent feature of the reports is the description of colored lights. There have been several testimonies of craft changing their shape or "morphing," and even disappearing. On occasions they appear to "slip" in and out of our reality.

The myriad of shapes could not be a result of thousands of differing groups or races of aliens visiting the earth in their various types of uniquely shaped craft, by reason of the technological barriers explained in chapter 2. It was reported that the British *Flying Saucer Review*, which was frequently regarded as the world's leading UFO publication, has objectively and thoroughly researched UFOs for over 40 years through a network of over 50 experts. An official statement by editor Gordon Creighton reads:

There seems to be no evidence yet that any of these craft or beings originate from outer space.[15]

In addition, it has been noted by prominent researcher John Weldon that:

1. Despite the millions of sightings, there has never been a single radar detection of a UFO entering our atmosphere from outer space.

2. "Aliens" seem able to live and breathe in Earth conditions without the aid of respiratory devices.

3. UFOs have been fired upon numerous times by American, Russian, and Canadian pilots, yet not one has ever been brought down.

4. And startlingly, no UFOs sighted on differing occasions ever appear exactly alike.[16]

"Now you see us . . . now you don't!"

From the data, we may draw the following conclusions about UFOs.

- They are already here. Some way and somehow they appear to be emanating from our own planet.

- They are visible yet do not seem to be real physical entities. In other words, they do not seem to be bound by the same physical laws as the rest of our material/natural world.

- They and/or their occupants are sometimes willing to be seen, but do not appear to want to make open and friendly contact on a large scale.

Hynek and Vallée describe some characteristics in their book *The Edge of Reality:*

If UFOs are, indeed, somebody else's "nuts and bolts hardware," then we must still explain how such tangible hardware can change shape before our eyes, vanish in a Cheshire cat manner (not even leaving a grin), seemingly melt away in front of us, or apparently "materialize" mysteriously before us without apparent detection by persons nearby or in neighboring towns. We must wonder too, where UFOs are "hiding" when not manifesting themselves to human eyes.[17]

Why would supposedly intelligent and more "evolved" advanced beings play this game of cat and mouse? On one hand, they provide us with enough evidence, such as sightings and burn marks on the ground, to suggest something is out there. Then with seeming stealth, they engage, interact with, and even abduct, humans (see chapter 7) in the dark of night, subjecting their captives to all manner of scientific examinations and strange sexual practices. And then they seem to act very coyly, as if not wanting to be seen at all. For most, the "why" factor remains one of the great mysteries of UFOlogy.

Many UFO researchers have abandoned the ETH (extraterrestrial hypothesis) for the IDH (interdimensional hypothesis). They, too, have realized that it would be nigh impossible for the millions of sightings to actually be of vast numbers of spaceships that have entered our atmosphere. Notwithstanding this, the same researchers generally still hold to a common belief that there must be millions of other civilizations in this "highly evolved" universe.

Here to teach us new truths

Since 1947, the level of the "game" has continued to step up a few notches with ever-increasing regularity. First, there was an increase in sightings. Next, occupants were sighted, and then contacts frequently occurred. With each new revelation, a media frenzy ensued, and consequently, even accounts of people meeting aliens became commonplace (see section about George Adamski later). Now they hardly rate a mention, until some new experience once again shatters our reality. Is it constantly the work of hoaxers seeking their five minutes of fame, or is this progression the result of deliberate actions by real UFOnauts, perhaps trying to change our perceptions of reality?

When Hynek developed his now-famous "close encounters" classification system, it catered to three levels of experience. But due to the increased levels of interaction with the UFOnauts, two more levels — CE-4 and CE-5 — have been added (where CE-4 experiences relate to kidnappings or abductions of victims, and CE-5 experiences to contact initiated by human beings via methods such as telepathy). Some of these contacts have purportedly resulted in death.

Nowadays, the terrifying experiences of alien abductions are almost at plague proportions. Where will it go to from here? Perhaps the space brothers will land on the White House lawn and abduct the president in full view of the world's press?

Whether these experiences correspond to reality or not, abductees are never the same afterward. They and their perception of the world are forever altered. Many develop a strange interest in the occult and supernatural. Hynek noted in a magazine interview:

> Certainly the phenomenon has psychic aspects. I don't talk about them very much because to a general audience the words "psychic" and "occult" have bad overtones. They say, "Aw, it's all crazy." But the fact is that there are psychic things; for instance, UFOs seem to materialize and dematerialize. There are people who've had UFO experiences who've claimed to have developed psychic ability. There have been reported cases of hearings in close encounters and there have been reported cases of precognition, where people had foreknowledge or forewarning that they were going to see something. There has been a change of outlook, a change of philosophy of persons' lives. Now, you see, those are rather tricky things to talk about openly, but it's there. Many people, like Jacques Vallée and I, to some extent, feel that it might be a conditioning process.[18]

This "conditioning" process seems to be a step-by-step procedure. Nothing would alter our world more than a mass landing in full view of TV cameras. However, the messages from the ETs themselves suggest that we are "not ready" for such a feat, not until a sufficient amount of contactees have instigated a new belief system. The "unreal" characteristics of UFOs, combined with the messages of the space brothers (discussed later), suggest that these reported "aliens" have something to hide. This is also a view almost universally endorsed by all serious UFOlogists. In noting this common view among other researchers, Ankerberg and Weldon comment:

> These researchers believe that the UFO entities are deliberately programming the human observers with false information in order to hide their true nature and purpose.[19]

Vallée adds:

> I propose the hypothesis that there is a control system for human consciousness. . . . I am suggesting that what takes place through close encounters with UFOs is control of human beliefs, control of the relationship between our consciousness and physical reality, that this control has been in force throughout history and that it is of secondary importance that it should now assume the form of sightings of space visitors.[20]

He also adds that:

> . . . human belief . . . is being controlled and conditioned, man's concepts are being rearranged, and we may be headed toward a massive change of human attitudes toward paranormal abilities and extraterrestrial life.[21]

Even famous UFO researcher John Keel (author of numerous UFO books including *The Mothman Prophecies 1975* — later made into a Hollywood movie of the same name) notes:

> The UFOs do not seem to exist as tangible, manufactured objects. They do not conform to the natural laws of our environment. They seem to be nothing more than transmogrifications tailoring themselves to our abilities to understand. The thousands of contacts with the entities indicate that they are liars and put-on artists. The UFO manifestations seem to be, by and large, merely minor variations of the age-old demonological phenomenon. Officialdom may feel that if we ignore them long enough, they will go away all together, taking their place with the vampire myths of the Middle Ages.[22]

When we consider that today most children would describe UFOs as "visitors from other planets" as Ronald Story's son believed, then to some extent, the UFOnauts have already succeeded in substantially shaping our ideas. It is disturbing that so many people are willing to jump on board the "benevolent" UFO bandwagon, despite the seeming evidence that the space brothers — whatever they are — have some sort of secret agenda, and have not been entirely honest with us. Yet many are willing to believe their messages, without even stopping to consider that they might be being deceived.

The IDH has given rise to the new "religious" brand of UFOlogist. We include the UFO cults in this category. Some feel that the UFOs are from parallel universes and/or that genuine ETs have evolved to a new level of consciousness or spirituality and are able to communicate with us from distant galaxies. In the following chapters, we will see evidence that the space brothers are contacting a selected few modern prophets who are being encouraged to rise up and show others how to reach their next stage of evolution.

Ankerberg and Weldon have commented on the disparity between the ETH and what is really occurring:

> . . . how credible is it to think that literally thousands of extraterrestrials would fly millions or billions of light-years simply to teach New Age philosophy, deny Christianity, and support the occult. . . . Why would they consistently lie about things which we know are true, and why would they purposefully deceive their contacts?[23]

For example, a common claim revealed as deception was that ETs were visiting us from Venus. Chapter 3 described Frank Strange's 1959 meeting with a Venusian by the name of Val Thor. Nowadays, most visitors seem to come from farther away, elsewhere in the galaxy where we cannot test their claims.

As Weldon and Ankerberg noted, the denial of the Christ of the Bible and a reshaping of our traditional religious views is a very common thread that runs through UFOlogy. It seems incredible that seeming alien space travelers are so interested in Christian ideas. As the founder of the faith, Jesus Christ had some interesting things to say about the future. His words of warning in Matthew 24:24–25 seem surprisingly relevant to today's UFO phenomenon:

> For false Christs and false prophets will appear and perform great signs and miracles to deceive even the elect — if that were possible. See, I have told you ahead of time.

J. Allen Hynek's book *The Hynek Report of UFOs* argues that, during his years as a researcher on Project Blue Book, the U.S. government intentionally deceived and lied to the American public about the nature of UFOs.[24] Hynek and other cogent UFOlogists such as John Keel and Vallée have shifted from the ETH view and noticed the paranormal link to UFOs. So why does the government have nothing to say in this matter? This remains a mystery, and perhaps it is the religious connotations that prohibit it from "official" classification. Because the occultic and spiritual nature of such claims is not scientifically verifiable, perhaps governments do not want to admit that they cannot explain what is really happening. One could imagine the public disquiet if its leaders actually admitted that "something is happening, we don't know what, and we are powerless to do anything about it." It would be open season for every bizarre claim of the "UFOnuts" and hoaxers professing to have the answer, and could lead to a serious, although unwitting, endorsement of those self-professed UFO messiahs who claim to be in contact with the ETs. It would be even more difficult to weed out the apparently genuine and serious claims from those of the frauds and fame-seekers. Hence, it seems, the blanket statement, "UFOs pose no threat to national security."

Cooper, the high-flyer — what did he see?

Sometimes, even otherwise cautious UFO researchers cite cases as "fact" which are anything but. In chapter 1, we mentioned the UFO sightings of high-profile NASA astronaut Gordon Cooper. A search of the Internet will reveal a myriad of articles reproducing the famous claim of his seeing a greenish-glowing object ahead of his *Mercury* capsule in 1963. It has almost become UFO "fact." As the story has grown and spread over the years, it has been recorded that Cooper saw the object, which was apparently seen by a tracking station at Muchea, just north of Perth, Western Australia. In addition to this, it is claimed that over two hundred people at the tracking station also witnessed this event. It appears that even Hynek and Vallée were swayed by these reports. This point must be stressed because many other high-profile and seemingly credible UFO agencies believed the report to be true. By 1977, yet another story surfaced that Australian scientists also visually sighted the low-level, football-shaped object, and also that cameramen took 16,000 feet of film.[25] However, a closer look will reveal that Cooper never actually claimed to have seen a UFO at all while on that mission.

James Oberg is a computer scientist and a former flight controller at NASA's Johnson Space Center. He is also a UFO skeptic and is a member of the UFO committee for the skeptics' organization Committee on the Scientific Investigation of Claims of the Paranormal (CSICOP). He has researched the Cooper UFOs and claims to have exchanged communications with Cooper himself on the subject. He says:

What was actually happening was that on his third orbit, five hours into the flight, Cooper was describing auroral activity ("Northern Lights"). He reported, "Right now I can make out a lot of luminous activity in an easterly direction. I wouldn't say it was much like a layer. It wasn't distinct and it didn't last long, but it was higher than I was. It wasn't even in the vicinity of the horizon and was not well defined. A good size — it was a good-sized area. It was very indistinct in shape. It was a faint glow with a reddish-brown cast."[26]

Many times since, Cooper has flatly denied seeing a UFO. On a radio show he was quoted as saying:

No, somebody made a lot of money selling . . . lies on that one. . . . It was totally untrue, sorry to say.[27]

Oberg reports that in an OMNI interview published in 1980, Cooper was also asked about his UFO reports, and said:

It got so bad that there were deliberately falsified tapes of communications with the astronauts, where UFO material was simply edited in.[28]

Furthermore, Oberg claims that:

Cooper explicitly denied that there had been UFO sightings on his two flights. In a 1978 letter to me, Cooper stressed the non-occurrence of a sighting on *Mercury 9*. I have the original on-board tapes in my possession which also refute this.[29]

Although Cooper was an avid proponent of the ETH, he stated that the *Mercury* legend was incorrect. This is a strong rebuttal by any standard. Without going into the details of how this "urban myth" became reality, it should suffice to say that this example aptly demonstrates that there are too many willing parties eager to perpetrate a story for notoriety, material gain, or just to promote their pet UFO theory. However, Cooper still held to his claim that he saw a UFO land at Edwards Air Force base in 1957. He says:

. . . the case of one that landed out on the dry lake bed right out from a number of camera crews we had who filmed it. And the film was there and was sent forward to the safekeeping [sic] somewhere in Washington, never to be seen again.[30]

Cooper claimed that the object was:

> . . . hovering above the ground — and then it slowly came
> down and sat on the lake bed for a few minutes.[31]

Sounds compelling, doesn't it? Once again, the prebelief appeared to be at work in Cooper's thought processes, as he already believed that he had seen UFOs early in the 1950s while stationed at an airbase in Munich, Germany. Oberg set about investigating the "Edwards base" claim. In talking firsthand with one of the witnesses, he was sent a file of material on the sighting, which revealed that the claim had already been thoroughly investigated by a leading UFOlogist (and ETH proponent) of the day, James McDonald. Oberg discovered that the "dome-shaped" object was nothing more than a distant weather balloon, the appearance of which was distorted by the desert's atmospheric effects. The film footage was simply exposures made by a tracking camera. And far from disappearing (or being suppressed, as Cooper actually claimed), the film was sent to Project Blue Book at Wright-Patterson Air Force Base.

Brad Steiger is one of the most prolific writers on the paranormal. He has authored and co-authored 148 books on the subject, including 22 on UFOs.[32] He believes in a multidimensional origin for UFOs. Some years after the Edwards AFB incident, Oberg says Steiger revisited the photos in his paperback *Project Blue Book* and wrote the following caption for the photographs:

> UFOs on target! Photos taken by United States military
> personnel for case #4715, Edwards AFB, May 2, 1957.[33]

But Oberg claimed that the case number did not appear on another list in Steiger's book, which included all "unsolved" cases, suggesting that it did not remain a mystery — it must have been solved. But surely the reader would want to know what it was, particularly after the declaration, "UFOs on target!"

This is either a genuine error or a case of "never let the facts get in the way of a good story." In relating the difficulty of getting to the bottom of any UFO report, Vallée noted this about proponents of the ETH:

> I also discovered that I could expect *no* cooperation
> from most of the UFO believers, who were willing to help

me only to the extent that my conclusions would support their preconceived idea that UFOs are extraterrestrial visitors to the earth.[34]

An avid New Ager, Steiger himself has abandoned the ETH, stating that:

> . . . we are dealing with a multidimensional paraphysical phenomenon which is largely indigenous to planet earth.[35]

There are many who, like Cooper, still advocate the ETH. For such "nuts and bolts kinda guys" the interdimensional hypothesis has too many spiritual connotations. After all, based on the belief that cosmic evolution accounts for the origin of the universe, some galaxies may be millions of years older than ours, and therefore more advanced, so, "Who knows what technologies they may possess?"

The origin of the extraterrestrial hypothesis

Coming hot on the heels of a wave of postwar sightings, the theory that the U.S. government knew more than it was letting on about UFOs became the "only game in town." In 1947, pilot Kenneth Arnold saw nine saucer-shaped objects from his airplane. His report seemed to spark a subsequent wave of UFO sightings. Among other ideas, he thought that the saucers could have been a secret U.S. weapon. Earlier we mentioned that a Gallup poll of the same year highlighted that the public thought much the same thing. It revealed that 29 percent of those surveyed thought that saucers were an optical illusion, 10 percent thought they were hoaxes, 15 percent agreed with Arnold, and 1 percent thought it was Russian technology.[36] People were fascinated, but there was nothing to suggest anything more than the public had already concluded. But in 1948, the mood was about to change. This was as the result of the involvement of former Marine Corps Major Donald Keyhoe in an event known as the Mantell incident. There is no doubt that Keyhoe's subsequent writings were a prime catalyst for today's widespread acceptance of the ETH.

On January 7, 1948, the first officially recorded UFO-related fatality occurred. A UFO shaped like an "ice-cream cone topped with red" was sighted over a military base near Fort Knox, Kentucky. Four National Guard F-51 Mustangs were dispatched to investigate. When three of the planes closed in on the object, it was described as metallic and of "tremendous size" and "round like a tear drop, and at times almost fluid."

Flight leader Thomas F. Mantell radioed in to say that he was closing in to take a good look:

> It's going up now and forward as fast as I am . . . that's 360 mph, . . . I'm going up to 20,000 feet, and if I'm no closer, I'll abandon chase.[37]

Mantell was never heard from again. His decapitated body was later found in the wreckage of his aircraft near Fort Knox. It was revealed that Mantell blacked out at 20,000 feet from a lack of oxygen, and it was officially reported that he was merely chasing the planet Venus.[38]

UFO incidents had now taken a serious turn. A death had occurred, and with a wave of recent sightings, the government's not-so-convincing answer and its less-than-prompt response on the matter created rampant speculation. It was discovered that the

Captain Thomas F. Mantell

elevation of Venus in relation to the pilots' position did not correlate. The authorities could not have made such a basic mistake.

Keyhoe and cover-ups

Upon taking a closer look, the editor of *True* magazine thought the official position was "damned queer," so he called in Donald Keyhoe to investigate. Keyhoe believed the Mantell incident had all the hallmarks of a cover-up. Also unimpressed with the handling of a couple of other cases, Keyhoe thought he was on to something big, and he said so in his 1950 magazine article titled "The Flying Saucers are Real." In it he drew the following conclusions that later became part of the reconnaissance theory, i.e., the ETs are watching us:

1. For the past 175 years, the planet Earth has been under systematic close-range observation by living, intelligent observers from another planet.

2. The intensity of this observation and the frequency of the visits to the earth's atmosphere increased markedly during the past two years.

3. The vehicles used for this observation and for interplanetary transport have been identified and categorized as follows: Type I, a small, non–pilot-carrying, disk-shaped aircraft equipped with some form of television or impulse transmitter; Type II, a very large (up to 250 feet in diameter), metallic, disk-shaped aircraft operating on the helicopter principle; Type III, a dirigible-shaped, wingless aircraft which, in the earth's atmosphere, operates in conformity with the Prandtl theory [aerodynamics] of lift.

4. The discernible pattern of observation and exploration shown by the so-called "flying disks" varies in no important particular way from well-developed American plans for the exploration of space expected to come to fruition within the next 50 years. There is reason to believe, however, that some other race of thinking beings is a matter of two-and-one-quarter centuries ahead of us.[39]

Although such ETH theories had abounded before, Keyhoe had hit the big time — he had details! This was the start of an enormous controversy. In the same year, he published a book of the same name as his article. The world and its UFO beliefs would never be the same again. By 1950, Gallup polls added another category as an explanation for UFOs, namely: "comets, shooting stars, *something from other planets*" (emphasis added). Keyhoe subsequently published four more books: *Flying Saucers From Outer Space* (1953), *The Flying Saucer Conspiracy* (1955), *Flying Saucers — Top Secret* (1960), and *Aliens from Space* (1973). The titles leave no doubt as to his particular viewpoint, and the public eagerly consumed all of it.

Keyhoe smelled a conspiracy — a theme he played to the fullest extent, and he was partly correct. However, the government wasn't covering up evidence of alien visitations. It was covering up top-secret technology that even its own Air Force wasn't aware of at the time, and it wasn't even *advanced* technology. Unfortunately, the truth would not be revealed openly until 1985.

A secret project known as Skyhook was being conducted. These were massive weather balloons 450 feet (135 m) tall and 100 feet (30 m) across that were used to carry equipment to listen to radio transmissions around the world. They could ascend to altitudes of 70,000 feet, where the high-altitude, fast jet-stream currents could carry them. Such currents could also cause the balloons to move quite erratically and even stop on occasions. The balloons could also reflect an assortment of colors as the light would be refracted off, and through, their plastic envelope covering.

More conclusively, subsequent investigations by the Blue Book team, years later, confirmed that two other ground-based observers who thought they had also seen a UFO had agreed that it was a balloon when taking a closer look through their telescopes.[40]

But it was all too late. The "gate was open and the horse had bolted." By the time of, and as a result of, Keyhoe's books, the myth of the Mantell incident was growing. It became an "urban legend" similar to Cooper's *Mercury* sightings. Despite the fact that medical examinations showed that Mantell had died from the impact of his plane crashing to Earth, stories circulated that a UFO "death ray" had shot him down.

This demonstrates how little Keyhoe actually had to go on, as is often the case with sensational reports. His provocative conclusions demonstrate that he was already a UFO believer (the prebelief again), and that he did not discern the evidence with any impartiality (another common problem). It should also be remembered that the government of the day contributed to the perceptions of its alleged lack of integrity. Government officials were non-cooperative and became more so after Keyhoe's allegations. In turn, their over-defensive attitude gave the impression that Keyhoe was right, and this gave the government continuing credibility problems. Keyhoe wrote in 1953:

> Three years ago this proposal would have amazed me. In 1949, after months of investigation, I wrote an article for *True* magazine, stating that the saucers were probably interplanetary machines. Within 24 hours the Air Force was swamped with demands for the truth. To end the uproar, the Pentagon announced that the saucer project was closed. The saucers, the Air Force insisted, were hoaxes, hallucinations, or mistakes. Later, in a book called *The Flying Saucers are Real,* I repeated my belief that the Air Force was keeping the answer secret until the country could be prepared. Several times officers at the Pentagon tried to convince me I'd made a bad mistake.

But when I asked them to prove it by showing me the secret sighting reports, I ran into a stone wall. . . .[41]

The whole ETH/government conspiracy theory was now a racing juggernaut that has not abated to the present day.

Martin Kottmeyer is one of the world's leading experts on the psychosocial aspects of the UFO phenomenon.[42] With the benefit of hindsight, he comments on the Keyhoe factor in the heady days of the explosion of the modern UFO era:

> Keyhoe's thesis in these early books was impressionistic and airy speculation. He cites no evidence of downed saucers with TV cameras. He cites no alien informants explaining their missions. . . . There really wasn't any evidence to build on. Some of the cases even argue against it. Keyhoe expresses the opinion: *"The Mantell case alone proves we've been observed from space ships. . . ."* Whatever their faults in retrospect, Keyhoe's writings were seminal in directing the future course of the UFO mythos. Keyhoe was read by many, and heard in the media by many more. UFOlogists adopted his thesis sometimes explicitly, often implicitly [emphasis added].[43]

Trying to stop the juggernaut

So the modern UFO era got off to a flying start, albeit on "something that wasn't." If Keyhoe had had access to all of the information at the time (an issue I have repeatedly highlighted), one wonders whether such conspiracy theories would have accelerated at such a rate. The ETH, and government complicity, quickly became accepted as fact by many. This changed the world view of many observers, further clouding impartiality on the subject. Keyhoe became the first director of the NICAP (National Investigations Committee on Aerial Phenomena). Independent of government, this was a pro-UFO/ETH organization. Notwithstanding this, they quickly became adept at identifying hoaxers and "repeaters" (serial sighters). But the establishment of this group, with Keyhoe at the helm, only served to inspire more claims.

Nonetheless, there are many sightings that remain difficult to explain as mistaken natural phenomena. One such case around that time became known as the "Lubbock lights." In August 1951, several university professors saw a formation of strange lights in the night sky

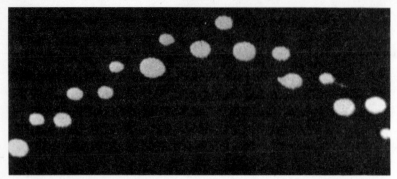

The Lubbock lights (Note that they are flying in formation.)

at Lubbock, Texas. Described as softly glowing bluish-green objects, after initially disappearing, they reappeared an hour after the original sighting. Then on a third occasion, the lights descended and circled over another observer's house, a Mr. Joe Bryant. He thought they were plovers, a common bird in that part of Texas.

Later, it was discovered that a college freshman, Carl Hart Jr., managed to take some amazing photos of the lights. Hart vehemently denied that the photos were fake, a position he maintained even decades later.

The U.S. Air Force and Blue Book chief, Edward Ruppelt, gave the young Hart a very difficult time. But they reported that his story "could not be 'picked apart.' "[44]

The Air Force eventually decided that the objects were birds, and that the reflection of newly installed streetlights in Lubbock caused the glowing appearance. However, this is an inadequate explanation because the lights were seen in many different parts of Texas. Later, Ruppelt was to eventually admit that he never found an explanation for them:

> The photos were never proven to be a hoax but neither were they proven to be genuine.[45]

Welcome to Earth, my Venusian friends

A flood of similarly inexplicable sightings has occurred over the years, but George Adamski added a new dimension with his 1953 book *The Flying Saucers Have Landed*. A Polish immigrant to the United States, Adamski was the first person to widely publicize his claim of meeting an extraterrestrial. This event occurred in the California desert in 1952, when he allegedly met a longhaired blond man from Venus called Orthon. Warning of impending doom for mankind if we did not change our ways, Orthon hopped aboard his ship and flew away. However, there were to be many subsequent contacts, and even free joyrides around the solar system for Adamski, who was even invited to attend a "galactic council" meeting on Saturn, appearing as Earth's representative. He also provided detailed descriptions of the actual spaceships and their interiors.

Adamski's first and subsequent books "sold like hot cakes," and he became an in-demand celebrity all over the world — including meeting European royalty. In many writings he became referred to as "Professor Adamski" (he often signed his name as such, in correspondences) leading many to falsely believe that he was an accredited scientist, when in fact he was never formally educated.

The modern extraterrestrial contact movement can undoubtedly be traced back to the high-profile Adamski. But Adamski's accounts, like the Mantell/Keyhoe episode, were based on fallacy rather than fact.

By 1954, Adamski was "catching flak" from a number of quarters including science fiction writer Arthur C. Clarke, who labeled Adamski's photographs of the Venusian mothership and scout ships as frauds. Clarke pointed out that:

> The uncanny resemblance [of the "scout ships"] to electric light fittings with table tennis balls underneath them has already been pointed out.[46]

Then in October 1957, UFO investigator James W. Moseley (who now writes a satirical UFO magazine called *Saucer Smear*) severely attacked Adamski's credibility. Based on personal interviews with Adamski, he was able to demonstrate deliberate misquotations of prominent witnesses who supported his claims, and prove that one of Adamski's encounters was a preplanned, orchestrated event. He demonstrated this from tape recordings Adamski had played to co-workers about a week before the contact took place. Moseley also showed Adamski to be a plagiarist as well as a fraud. He had "lifted" some passages from an earlier book by another author. Although now dead and widely discredited, he is the "father" of the contactee phenomenon, and many still endorse his work. The George Adamski Foundation in California continues its "work" to this day.[47]

A common trait with the early contactees like Adamski was that the space brothers claimed to be coming from planets within our solar system, including our own moon. It should be remembered that human exploration of the solar system was still many years away, nuclear weapons had already been used against mankind, and the Cold War was heating up. These were unstable times, and perhaps it was the content of the messages that Adamski gave, more so than his speculative contacts, that people wanted to hear. The messages were warnings that mankind needed to stop its warring ways (remember the movie *The Day the Earth Stood Still?*). Of Adamski, it was said:

> Adamski and most of the other leading contactees of the 1950s were *utopians*. "George Adamski had a vision of a better world, and that vision apparently became reality for him."[48]

The messages of the space brothers are no different today, and still have the same appeal. "We are here to help you; we will not let you destroy yourselves. . . . You will be saved." In a time when conventional religious beliefs are waning, the perceived technological answer has mass appeal and a growing credibility. With all those witnesses and their sightings, "something must be happening."

The "real" Mexican wave

In the early 1990s, numerous sightings in Mexico were verified by abundant photographic and video footage, which came in from many areas of the republic.

In April 1991, Adriana Velaquez and her brothers claimed to have seen two "midgets" signaling to them with a red light from one of the craft. In May of the same year, silver-colored vehicles appeared over the town of Huejutla, and over the village of Real del Monte a UFO fired a red beam to the ground. Later that month, hundreds of people confirmed seeing 12 shining objects near the city of Pachuca. This pattern was repeated over the next few days when approximately 15 triangular lights (similar to those of the Belgian UFO wave) appeared in the same location.

In January 1992, an electrical blackout afflicted 22 municipalities in two separate states, and at the same time three UFOs were seen hovering and scanning the ground with some sort of "spotlights." In April 1993, hundreds more people witnessed brightly

UFO over Mexico City

glowing vehicles performing various aerial maneuvers for over an hour one evening. The descriptions fitted that of a mother ship with four accompanying vehicles. Numerous other sightings were also reported.

The Mexican "wave" also saw an increase in contacts. In May 1994, a small humanoid was described by Joaquina Reyes as being dressed in white, with a crown and a belt that constantly changed color.[49]

However, an event over Mexico City in January 1993 became the most verifiable UFO event ever. If reports are to be believed, tens of thousands of people, including several in government and military service, witnessed silvery-looking craft giving an aeronautics display in broad daylight. This continued into the afternoon when two more metallic disk-shaped craft appeared and were recorded by residents with camcorders. Over 700 videotapes, including 100 in broad daylight, have been collected by researchers. Local newspapers and TV stations heavily featured the sightings, which were also claimed to have been verified by civilian and military radar. The front page of the major Mexican newspaper *La Prensa* carried the headline "Astonishment! UFOs over the Capital."[50] Even "60 Minutos," the Mexican version of the well-known current events show "60 Minutes," devoted extensive coverage to this wave. Reporter Jaime Maussan stated:

> Thanks to the video camcorder, Mexico has become the site of the most documented UFO flap in history.[51]

The wave continued for many years, and, amazingly, people seemed to become desensitized to the occurrences. Curiously, not much coverage was given to these sightings in the American press, although Mexican and U.S. UFOlogists worked closely together during this time. Even as late as May 2004, TV news broadcasts all over the world carried footage shot by the Mexican Air Force of UFOs hovering over Mexico.

Sadly, as too often happens, there were those wishing to make a few bucks out of the frenzy that surrounded the wave. The Las Lomas UFO film of 1997, for example, showed a wobbly looking saucer disappearing behind some high-rise condominiums in a suburb of Mexico City.[52] It became the subject of much heated discussion and is not widely regarded as authentic footage. This sort of thing has called the credibility of many sightings into question even where there has been no indication of a hoax.

In the second half of the 1990s, a similarly well-witnessed wave of sightings occurred over Israel, comprising the full gamut of UFO experiences, including electrical outages, cattle mutilations, crop circles, and even abductions. Israel is regarded by some as a UFO hotspot.[53]

A skeptic's paradise

The rise of contactees and believers also gave rise to an active group of non-believers. The UFO skeptics were, and still are, greatly concerned at the transforming of society's beliefs, taking place due to what they see as, at best, mistaken anomalies, and at worst, deliberate frauds and hoaxes.

One major debunking of the UFO phenomenon was the Condon Report of 1969. This research project was also known as the University of Colorado UFO Project. Spearheaded by physicist Edward J. Condon with a $525,000 grant, it was decided that an autonomous panel, with no prior UFO experience (and therefore no predetermined opinions) would collaborate with all relevant agencies to determine the truth about UFOs. But far from being the death knell for UFO beliefs, the mismanagement of the project became a "glaring example" of the government's supposed desire to cover up and deceive the public. Unfortunately, right from the start, Condon himself gave the impression that UFOs were merely a nagging psycho-social problem that the Air Force wanted buried once and for all. There were damning leaked internal memos that further undermined the integrity of the investigation and inflamed proponents of the ETH. Keyhoe's NICAP eventually broke off relations with the study group.[54] Even the world's most famous UFO debunker, a 30-plus-year investigator named Philip J. Klass, conceded that, "I cannot endorse the Colorado investigation as having been well managed."[55]

Nonetheless, despite being badly managed, the Condon Report represents the largest single investigation ever carried out by mainstream scientists on the UFO problem. Its findings eventually led to the closure of Project Blue Book in 1969, and like projects Sign and Grudge before, it reached much the same conclusion, saying:

> Careful consideration of the record as it is available to us leads us to conclude that further extensive study of UFOs probably cannot be justified in the expectation that science will be advanced thereby. It has been argued that this lack of contribution to science is due to the fact that very little scientific effort has been put on the subject. We do not agree. We feel that the reason that there has been very little scientific study of the subject is that those scientists who are most directly concerned, astronomers, atmospheric physicists, chemists, and psychologists, having had ample opportunity to look into the matter, have individually decided that UFO phenomena do not offer a fruitful field in which to look for major scientific discoveries.[56] [The full text of the Condon Report, which contains many details of sightings, including photographs, is readily available online.]

Ever since, UFO organizations, individuals, scientists, and members of Congress have petitioned for a new federal inquiry — without success.[57] It seems the authorities are in the position of being "damned if they do and damned if they don't." On several occasions

UFOlogists have petitioned for the release of classified documents under the Freedom of Information Act (FOIA). In many cases, before the information was released to the public, much of the information in these documents had been erased "in the interests of national security." The authorities have claimed that the information contained details of security protocols and methods for gathering intelligence and information which are top secret. Conspiracy theorists use these points to strengthen their arguments and their criticisms of the government.

But it refuses to go away

For all the attempts at debunking by skeptics, and despite the lack of "hard" scientific evidence, all over our planet the UFO phenomenon continues to escalate. As a researcher of the issue, I believe that this is a much bigger and deeper problem than the average person knows. These are not isolated incidents affecting a couple of thousand "cranks and nutcases."

It is true that the majority of sightings are the result of mistaken identity, and some have proven to be conscious lies or imaginary events. Similarly, in the realm of abductions, a great percentage may be psychological delusions, hoaxes, and shallow attempts to gain attention and fame. But despite the myriad of explanations, too many ordinary people with far more to lose than to gain by telling fanciful stories go to their graves never resiling from their accounts of the events. There is no question that something mysterious, quite real, and very serious is going on. Sadly, much of this is being exploited by those bringing their various agendas to the evidence. However, I have the greatest respect for those involved in genuine UFO research, and enormous compassion for those who have been subject to seemingly inexplicable sightings and the terrifying ordeals of abduction experiences, often with very distressing consequences. To not have closure about why such things are happening to them must be emotionally devastating.

In their desire to believe, many UFO advocates do themselves a disservice. They scream for official inquiries, but often reject the findings if they do not agree with their own hypotheses. The "noise" generated by the ETH and IDH proponents seems to increase the belief that governments are hiding the truth. In a society that appears to thrive on anti-establishment ideas, a good "conspiracy" will always attract attention, as will be evidenced in the next chapter.

Endnotes

1 Ronald D. Story, editor, *The Mammoth Encyclopedia of Extraterrestrial Encounters* (London: Constable & Robinson, 2002), p. 739–740.

2 Ibid.

3 An Australian colloquialism for the more remote country areas of Australia, as opposed to the busier metropolises.

4 Story, *The Mammoth Encyclopedia of Extraterrestrial Encounters*, in an article by Joe Nickell, p. 476–477.

5 Ibid., p. 304–305.

6 Ibid., p. 664–668.

7 J. Allen Hynek, *Fate*, June 1976, cited in Story, *The Mammoth Encyclopedia of Extraterrestrial Encounters*, p. 304–305.

8 Hynek, *Lumieres dans la Nuit*, No. 168, October 1977, cited in Story, *The Mammoth Encyclopedia of Extraterrestrial Encounters*, p. 304–305.

9 Hynek, *Newsweek*, November 21, 1977, cited in Story, *The Mammoth Encyclopedia of Extraterrestrial Encounters*, p. 304–305.

10 Douglas Curran, *In Advance of the Landing: Folk Concepts of Outer Space* (New York: Abbeville Press, 1985), p. 21, cited in William T. Alnor, *UFOs in the New Age* (Grand Rapids, MI: Baker Book House, 1992), p. 81.

11 Story, *The Mammoth Encyclopedia of Extraterrestrial Encounters*, in an article by Loren E. Gross and Lucius Farish, p. 17–21.

12 Ibid., in an article by Randall Fitzgerald, p. 61.

13 John Ankerberg and John Weldon, *The Facts on UFO's and Other Supernatural Phenomena* (Eugene, OR: Harvest House Publishers, 1992), p. 8.

14 Alnor, *UFOs in the New Age*, p. 184.

15 Official policy statement of *Flying Saucer Review*, cited in Ankerberg and Weldon, *The Facts on UFO's and Other Supernatural Phenomena*, p. 12.

16 Ankerberg and Weldon, *The Facts on UFO's and Other Supernatural Phenomena*, p. 12.

17 J. Allen Hynek and Jacques Vallée, *The Edge of Reality* (Chicago, IL: Henry Regnery Company), p. xii–xiii, cited in "The Premise of Spiritual Warfare," <www.alienresistance.org/ce4premise.htm>, March 7, 2003.

18 Hynek, *Today's Student*, April 3, 1978, cited in Story, *The Mammoth Encyclopedia of Extraterrestrial Encounters*, p. 304–305.

19 Ankerberg and Weldon, *The Facts on UFO's and Other Supernatural Phenomena*, p. 10–11.

20 Story, *The Mammoth Encyclopedia of Extraterrestrial Encounters*, in an article by Jacques Vallée, p. 753–754.

21 Jacques Vallée, *The Invisible College* (New York: E.P. Dutton, 1975), p. 207, cited in Ankerberg and Weldon, *The Facts on UFO's and Other Supernatural Phenomena*, p. 19.

22 John Keel, *Operation Trojan Horse* (Lilburn, GA: Illuminet Press, 1996), p. 266, cited in Chuck Missler and Mark Eastman, *Alien Encounters*, (Indianapolis, IN: Koinonia House, 2003), p. 248.

23 Ankerberg and Weldon, *The Facts on UFO's and Other Supernatural Phenomena*, p. 13.

24 Story, *The Mammoth Encyclopedia of Extraterrestrial Encounters*, in an article by Randall Fitzgerald, p. 306.

25 "In Search of Gordon Cooper's UFOs," <www.zip.com.au/~psmith/cooper.html>, January 22, 2003.

26 Ibid.

27 Art Bell's "Coast to Coast" radio show, September 1999, cited in "Gordon Cooper: No Mercury UFO," <www.space.com/sciencefiction/phenomena/cooper.html>, January 22, 2003.

28 "In Search of Gordon Cooper's UFOs," <www.zip.com.au/~psmith/cooper.html>, January 22, 2003.

29 Ibid.

30 Ibid.

31 Ibid.

32 Story, *The Mammoth Encyclopedia of Extraterrestrial Encounters*, in an article by Brad Steiger, p. 673–674.

33 "In Search of Gordon Cooper's UFOs," <www.zip.com.au/~psmith/cooper.html>, January 22, 2003.

34 Jacques Vallée, *Confrontations: A Scientist's Search for Alien Contact* (New York: Ballantine Books, 1991), p. 14, cited in Ankerberg and Weldon, *The Facts on UFO's and Other Supernatural Phenomena*, p. 13.

35 "Blue Book Files Released," Canadian UFO Report, Vol. 4, No. 4, p. 20, 1977, cited in Ankerberg and Weldon, *The Facts on UFO's and Other Supernatural Phenomena*, p. 13.

36 Story, *The Mammoth Encyclopedia of Extraterrestrial Encounters*, in an article by Martin S. Kottmeyer, p. 553–562.

37 Ibid., p. 395–397.

38 Ibid.

39. Ibid., in an article by Martin S. Kottmeyer, p. 553–562.

40 Ibid.

41 Keyhoe, *Condon Report*, Section V, Chapter 2: UFOs 1947–1968, cited in "Scientific Study of Unidentified Flying Objects," <www.ncas.sawco. com/condon/text/s5chap02.htm>, June 1, 2003.

42 Story, *The Mammoth Encyclopedia of Extraterrestrial Encounters*, in an article by Martin S. Kottmeyer, p. 364.

43 Ibid., p. 553–562.

44 Ibid., in an article by Kevin D. Randle, p. 375–377.

45 Ibid., attributed to Edward J. Ruppelt, cited in an article by Kevin D. Randle, p. 375–377.

46 James W. Moseley, "Some New Facts about Flying Saucers Have Landed," *Saucer News*, p. 6, October 1957, cited in Alnor, *UFOs in the New Age*, p. 89.

47 Alnor, *UFOs in the New Age*, p. 87–89.

48 Story, *The Mammoth Encyclopedia of Extraterrestrial Encounters*, in an article by David Stupple, p. 10–13.

49 Ibid., in an article by Scott Corrales, p. 419–420.

50 Missler and Eastman, *Alien Encounters*, p. 12–14.

51 Ibid.

52 Story, *The Mammoth Encyclopedia of Extraterrestrial Encounters*, in an article by Scott Corrales, p. 419–420.

53 Missler and Eastman, *Alien Encounters*, p. 14–17.

54 Story, *The Mammoth Encyclopedia of Extraterrestrial Encounters*, p. 747–751.

55 Philip J. Klass, *The Condon Study*, p. 378, cited in Alnor, *UFOs in the New Age*, p. 79.

56 "Scientific Study of Unidentified Flying Objects," <ncas.sawco.com/ condon/text/intro.htm>, June 1, 2003.

57 Story, *The Mammoth Encyclopedia of Extraterrestrial Encounters*, p. 747–751.

Chapter Six

Mysteries, Myths, Mayhem, and Money

Roswell — the holy grail of UFOlogy

"RAAF Captures Flying Saucer on Ranch in Roswell Region" proclaimed the local newspaper — the July 8, 1947, edition of the *Roswell Daily Record*. This was the first public airing for what became known as the "Roswell incident." It has become the most written-about/watched and talked-about account of a UFO in history. Even people who have no particular interest in UFOlogy have usually heard about the events of June 1947, when a flying saucer allegedly crashed in New Mexico and the U.S. Air Force retrieved alien bodies. This popularity is due to the numerous books, movies, and television shows that the Roswell legend spawned. Recently, movie mogul Steven Spielberg married the Roswell tale with the modern paradigm of abductions and crop circle mysteries, resulting in a multi-million-dollar TV series called *Taken*. Although made for a relatively minor cable TV channel in the United States, the series won Emmy Awards and became the most-watched series ever for its particular channel. The Roswell "incident" is alive and well!

Early in June 1947, something fell onto a ranch operated (but not owned) by W.W. "Mac" Brazel. He first discovered the debris on or around June 14, ten days before Kenneth Arnold's flying disks made major headlines all over the country. (Soon after Arnold's report, flying objects were seen in 39 separate states.)

Brazel's farm was located about 75 miles northeast of the town of Roswell. On a visit to nearby Corona, his relatives told him about the "flying saucer flap." A few days later, he drove into Roswell to buy a new pickup truck, carrying with him several pieces of the debris. He visited the local sheriff, who, on inspecting the material, thought that it might have some military significance. Sheriff Wilcox duly phoned the local Roswell Army Air Base, where he spoke with Major Jesse Marcel. Thinking from the initial report that it might be a downed aircraft, Marcel's commander, Colonel William Blanchard, ordered Marcel and counterintelligence officer Sheridan Cavitt out to Brazel's ranch. On viewing the wreckage, Cavitt immediately thought it probably came from a weather balloon, but Marcel had other ideas. When they arrived back, Marcel woke his wife and son, Jesse Jr., who even today remembers his father talking about flying saucers.[1] On July 8 the public information office at the base made the announcement that they had recovered a flying disk. This created newspaper headlines — it was a sensation!

However, at the intervention of Brigadier General Roger Ramey, who had also inspected the wreckage, a press conference was soon held that included Marcel. The army announced that the fuss was over nothing more than a weather balloon, pieces of which were duly paraded

The July 8, 1947, issue of the *Roswell Daily Record*

for public display. Marcel didn't agree with this conclusion, probably because this was unlike any weather balloon he had ever seen. It is evident that he thought it was a UFO. Prior to the press conference, a weather officer by the name of Irving Newton remembered seeing pieces of what he recognized as a weather balloon laid out in Ramey's office. In the 1990s, Newton told investigators:

> I remember Major Marcel chased me all around that room. . . . He kept saying things like, "Look how tough that metal is. Look at the strange markings on it." While I was examining the debris, Marcel was picking up pieces of the radar target sticks [see later in this chapter] and trying to convince me that some notations on the sticks were alien writings. But I was adamant that it was a weather balloon with a RAWIN [radar] target. I think he was embarrassed as crazy and he would like to do anything to make that turn into a flying saucer.[2]

Despite Marcel's efforts, the Roswell "incident" was dead in the water, at least for the next 30 years or so.[3]

Champions of the cause

In 1978, world-famous ETH proponent Stanton Friedman came across an acquaintance who introduced him to Jesse Marcel. Marcel revived his crashed saucer theory, and Friedman believed he finally had proof of a conspiracy that hid the truth. Marcel claimed that weather balloon material had been substituted for flying saucer wreckage for the 1947 press conference photos. More startling revelations were to come, and Roswell would now truly become an "incident."

The Roswell Incident is the name of perhaps the most famous book written about the events of 1947. Penned by Charles Berlitz and William Moore, the book's 1980 release revived and enlarged the ideas of an earlier 1950 book by alleged hoaxer Frank Scully, which claimed that the government had in its possession several flying saucers and over 30 alien bodies from different regions across the country. It is clear that Berlitz and Moore were inspired by the embellished works of Scully and probably by the enormous sales potential of the subject matter (Scully's book caused a sensation when it was released). Friedman also assisted Berlitz and Moore with the early chapters of their book.

It should be mentioned that Berlitz, an occult writer, has also made a career out of embellishing stories and fashioning them into books.

He has written books about the "Philadelphia Experiment" (in which he claims the U.S. government was dematerializing Navy warships and rematerializing them over vast distances — this became a major urban legend), the Bermuda Triangle, and the legend of Atlantis.

UFO investigator Kal K. Korff investigated some of the claims Berlitz and Moore were making for their Roswell book. One such claim was that over 75 witnesses had been interviewed in it. However, upon careful reading and research of their book, he could find the testimonies of only 25, of whom only 7 were firsthand witnesses of the wreckage.

Some of the other claims in *The Roswell Incident* were that:

- The recovered pieces were made of an unknown and unbreakable material. It would not tear, burn, or break.

- There were alien markings on the wreckage, perhaps writing or hieroglyphics.

- Alien bodies were recovered from the crash.

- The saucers from a nearby crash site were stored in a facility known as Hangar 18 at Wright Patterson Air Force Base.

Over the ensuing years, more and more books have made even more spectacular claims. New witnesses have suddenly appeared, and on one occasion, secret documents turned up on a UFOlogist's doorstep, containing information about a top-secret government organization called Majestic 12 (Majic 12 *or* MJ-12), which will be discussed later. As recently as the 1990s, there have been official government investigations into the incident, some 50 years after the original event.

An official investigation . . . yet again

Roswell refuses to die. The following includes details from a 1994 inquiry by the U.S. General Accounting Office (GAO). Congressman Steven Schiff, who had displayed a keen interest in UFO matters, generated this inquiry. The GAO was involved because it intended to conduct an independent audit of the Department of Defense's policies and procedures with regard to the Roswell incident.

The inquiry reproduced text from the July 8 edition of the *Roswell Daily Record* — citing Brazel's recollections about the discovery on his farm:

[The object] . . . might have been as large as a table top. The balloon which held it up, if that is how it worked, must have been about 12 feet long, he felt, measuring the distance by the size of the room in which he sat. The rubber was smoky gray in color and scattered over an area about 200 yards in diameter. When the debris was gathered up, the tinfoil, paper, tape, and sticks made a bundle about three feet long and 7 or 8 inches thick, while the rubber made a bundle about 18 or 20 inches long and about 8 inches thick. In all, he estimated, the entire lot would have weighed maybe five pounds. There was no sign of any metal in the area which night [sic] have been used for an engine and no sign of any propellers of any kind. Although at least one paper fin had been glued onto some of the tinfoil. There were no words to be found anywhere on the instrument although there were letters on some of the parts. Considerable scotch tape and some tape with flowers printed upon it had been used in the construction. No string or wire were to be found but there were some eyelets in the paper to indicate that some sort of attachment may have been used. Brazel said that he had previously found two weather balloons on the ranch, but that what he found this time did not in any way resemble either of these.[4]

Note how Brazel's original description fits the description of something more benign, like a weather balloon as claimed, although it didn't resemble any he had seen previously. Subsequent interviews revealed that none of the witnesses ever claimed that the material was unbreakable. Incredibly, it was discovered that the hieroglyphics were nothing more than flower patterns and other markings on scotch tape manufactured by a toy company.

In 1989, a new witness by the name of Glenn Dennis came forward, claiming that he was working as a mortician the day the "saucer" wreckage arrived. This staggered his friends, who commented that he had made no previous mention of this in the 30 or so years they had known him. Dennis claimed seeing the bodies of dead aliens and taking part in an autopsy of them. It should be noted that Dennis spoke up only after the Roswell incident had achieved some notoriety. Skeptical investigators found considerable holes in his story; for example, he claimed to know people at the time of the incident who never worked on the base until *after* the events of 1947. He also talked about a nurse who supposedly assisted at the autopsies, but her name has never appeared on any records, and she has never been found to this day. This only served to deepen the mystery in the eyes of some, and she became known as the "disappearing nurse," implying that she had probably been "done away with." It would appear that Dennis's memory is not quite as good as it should have been. After being discredited, he now declines interviews by skeptical investigators.

Another "star" witness who had memory problems was Frank Kaufmann, who claims he watched a UFO explode while he was monitoring a radar screen. He said that he was also part of the military team sent to retrieve the wreckage and alien bodies. Years later, famous skeptic Philip Klass "grilled" Kaufmann, who eventually confessed that he never trained as a radar operator. Several retired Air Force colonels who were stationed at Roswell have been interviewed in subsequent years. None knew anything about the storage of UFO debris or alien bodies.[5]

UFO writer Randall Fitzgerald comments on Major Jesse Marcel's role in the whole affair:

> For a sad case of apparent exaggeration we need look no further than Major Jesse Marcel. UFO researchers Robert Todd and Kal Korff independently obtained Marcel's nearly 200-page long military service file and found, in Korff's words, a pattern of Marcel "exaggerating things and repeatedly trying to write himself into the history books." Marcel had told book authors that he held a college bachelor's degree, had been a pilot of B-24s in World War II, received five air medals for shooting down five enemy aircraft, and was himself shot down. Yet absolutely none of this was true according to his own service file! Marcel frequently changed his testimony about the Roswell debris. First he said he had heard about someone trying to dent the metal with a hammer, then later he said "we even tried making a dent in it with a 16-pound sledge hammer, still no dent in it." Sometimes he said the debris "didn't burn very well," and then other times he claimed it would not burn at all. Marcel's career lasted less than three years after his humiliation at Roswell, when he resigned to open a small-town TV repair shop.[6]

So what really happened?

It should be remembered that when the base at Roswell made the announcement about a flying disk, the term had only been in use for a few days. What was a flying disk anyway? No one knew, but it did cause imaginations to run wild.

During the post-war period, technology grew at a rapid rate. America had the bomb, and they knew that the Soviets possessed it as well. Official documents released only a few years ago have since shown that a very sensitive project, classified TOP SECRET 1A, was being conducted. It became known as Project Mogul. With similarities to Skyhook (Captain Mantell's death and Major Donald Keyhoe's investigation mentioned in the last chapter), it was a balloon array designed to reflect radar and also monitor acoustic emissions from around the world. To achieve this, it needed to float high in the stratosphere. With some 23 balloons in its array, the purpose of this mission was to detect suspected Soviet nuclear tests. The radar reflectors were basically large metal foil kites, made with sticks, called RAWIN targets. The toy company that manufactured the "kites" also used reinforcing tape to hold them together. The balloons, which were made of neoprene rubber, also carried low-frequency microphones, a sonobuoy, aluminum tubes, rings, and battery packs.

On June 4, 1947, Mogul flight 4 was launched from Alamogordo Army Air Field, New Mexico, not far southwest of Roswell. Some of the balloons burst as a result of exposure to the sun, and, as the battery power was depleted, the military lost contact with the array only 17 miles from its eventual crash site. Information about Project Mogul remained classified for over 40 years.[7]

All of this occurred before the age of rockets and satellites. Project Mogul was a forerunner of that technology and was quite a novel way of listening to the "enemy." It was not advanced technology, so why was it top secret? Why couldn't the government reveal the truth and avoid all of the speculation? Quite simply, the U.S. was worried that if the Soviets knew they were being spied upon, they would move their nuclear testing underground.

How could a collection of paper, sticks, foil, and rubber be mistaken for a flying saucer? Perhaps the official Government Accounting Office report sums it up:

> Adding some measure of credibility to the claims that have arisen since 1978 is the apparent depth of research of

some of the authors and the extent of their efforts. Their claims are lessened somewhat, however, by the fact that almost all their information came from verbal reports many years after the alleged incident occurred. Many of the persons interviewed were, in fact, stationed at, or lived near Roswell during the time in question, and a number of them claim military service. Most, however, related their stories in their older years, well after the fact. In other cases, the information provided is second or thirdhand [sic], having been passed through a friend or relative after the principal had died. What is uniquely lacking in the entire exploration and exploitation of the "Roswell Incident" is official positive documentary or physical evidence of any kind that supports the claims of those who allege that something unusual happened.[8]

Some years later, UFOlogist John Keel suggested that dummies (similar to crash test dummies) were thrown from high altitudes for research purposes, which may offer an explanation for the alien bodies myth.

Historical documentation has shown the complete lack of physical evidence for a crashed UFO and alien bodies at Roswell, as well as providing straightforward evidence of what did happen. When mysterious elements appear in an account, human beings seem capable of fabricating fantastic stories to embellish something they want to be true. But the yarn spinning went even further, as "the faithful" desired to keep the Roswell legend alive.

Men in Black, Hangar 18, and MJ-12

One of the claims of pro-ETH UFOlogists is that the Roswell "bodies," and those mentioned in Scully's book, were housed in a secret storage facility known as Hangar 18. (*Hangar 18* was also the name of a popular movie that promoted a similar theme.) Originally thought to be located at Wright Patterson Air Force Base, the mysterious depot has "resurfaced" in a number of locations, including the similarly mysterious government facility known as Area 51 in Nevada. In UFOlogist folklore, the mention of Hangar 18 invokes the implication of a cover-up. The U.S. government has always denied its existence.

In 1984, a roll of unprocessed film anonymously arrived at the door of UFO researcher Jaime H. Shandera. He then contacted William L.

Moore (co-author of *The Roswell Incident*), and they had the film developed. On it, they discovered photos of allegedly top-secret government documents that were claimed to prove that the government had recovered crashed flying saucers at Roswell and other locations. Later, Shandera and Moore added that they uncovered other similar documents filed away in government archives. Then, in 1994, another roll of film came into the possession of Don Berliner (Berliner is co-author of another Roswell conspiracy book).[9] This film supposedly contained a Special Operations Manual (SOM 1-01) on how to handle UFO incidents.[10]

These documents "proved" that the authorities not only knew about the UFOs but, more importantly, that they conspired to cover up the truth. The most startling revelation to come out of these documents was that former President Harry S. Truman, on the basis of events at Roswell, authorized the formation of Operation Majestic Twelve (MJ-12). This was supposed to be a covert military group that operated above the law, and it is claimed that, over the years, MJ-12 operatives used intimidation and disposed of evidence (and even of witnesses) to conceal the truth about UFOs. These operatives became known as the "Men in Black" (MIB), which seemed to tie in with another conspiratorial idea. In common UFO lore, the mysterious MIB had, for many years, been turning up after UFO sightings, harassing and following witnesses, as well as UFO investigators. It was a description that became popular in books and movies over the years, including two recent Hollywood blockbusters of the same name. In reality, the MIB notion could probably be traced back to a scary 1953 book by Gray Barker, called *They Knew Too Much about Flying Saucers* — another story that somehow became "truth."[11]

The most important piece of evidence for the MIB claims came from a memo supposedly prepared by Truman for Defense Secretary James Forrestal, dated September 24, 1947, authorizing the creation of MJ-12.[12]

In profiling these documents, well-known British UFO researcher Timothy Good jumped on board the conspiracy bandwagon, and at the same time tried to rehabilitate the reputation of Frank Scully and his earlier claims. In 1987, Good's big-selling book, *Above Top Secret: The Worldwide UFO Cover-up*, also revealed an alleged briefing document prepared for (then) president-elect Dwight D. Eisenhower, which detailed the history of Roswell and MJ-12.[13]

Who could refute this? They were sensational claims, and for once, no reliance on dubious eyewitnesses and failed memories — this was "proof" of the Roswell incident. Or was it?

It is no wonder that in some quarters UFOlogy is not taken seriously. Once again, these claims turned out to be hoaxes, and Moore and Shandera in particular came in for intense criticism. The Eisenhower briefing document proved to be a forgery. A linguistic expert found clear differences in style between the forgery and original documents by the alleged author. For instance, the way the date was written was not consistent with other documents by the same author. Interestingly, the date format was characteristic of William Moore's style in his own personal letters.[14]

The "Truman memo" also came under critical analysis. Under a microscope the document was shown to be a composite: typed words, characters, and numbers did not align correctly on the page as would be expected if they were typed on a single typewriter. Truman's signature was an exact copy from another document that he had signed. The original document, from which the signature was lifted, has even been located and identified. Because no two signatures are ever exactly alike, this was damning evidence.

Furthermore, the Eisenhower memo (which Moore and Shandera claimed to have found in government archives) was supposedly written by his aide, Robert Cutler, but he was out of the country on that date. UFO debunker Philip Klass hints that the memo, which was found in an unlikely archival location, could have been smuggled into the archives by Moore or Shandera. The document apparently had a double fold, unlike other filed documents, and would have fit nicely into a coat pocket.

And finally, Berliner's SOM 1-01 operations manual contained many inconsistencies. Supposedly printed in April 1954, it said that any recovered extraterrestrial craft should be sent to "Area 51 S-4." Yet that portion of Nellis Air Base did not become known as Area 51 until many years later.[15] This suggests that many UFOlogists who "shout" the loudest about government conspiracies are in fact involved in acts of conspiracy themselves.

Misalignment of type from the Truman memo

Area 51 and other "secret stuff"

Why do people go to all the effort of producing forgeries and lying? Philip Klass alleges one clue to the motive for William Moore's actions:

> Less than two years before Moore made public the initial MJ-12 papers on April 16, 1983 — he had confided to then-close friend and UFOlogist Brad Sparks that he was contemplating creating and releasing some hoax Top Secret documents. . . . Moore explained to Sparks that he hoped such bogus documents would encourage former military and intelligence officials who knew about the government's (alleged) UFO cover-up to break their oaths of secrecy. Sparks strongly recommended against the idea.[16]

It appears that through fraudulent means, they were trying to get the government to "play their hand." For some, the belief in UFOs is so strong that the end justifies the means. This is a common psychological trait of believers in such conspiracy theories, similar to those involved in religious cults. They believe that they have the exclusive truth and that they must reveal it at all costs. The term "exclusive" implies that everyone else is wrong. In many cases, if you do not agree with their beliefs or conclusions, then you are also perceived as being part of the conspiracy, or at best you are grossly deceived.

Berliner and Friedman also claimed in their book *Crash at Corona* (1992) that the government had harvested alien technology and had used it to advance human science. This is a popular theme in UFOlogy, known as reverse engineering. One of the major books to popularize this idea was written by retired U.S. Army Colonel Philip J. Corso. In *The Day after Roswell* (1997), he claimed that although not a firsthand witness at Roswell, he did eventually see an alien body. However, his major claim to fame is that he was involved in "seeding" (farming out) recovered alien technology to American defense contractors, ultimately leading to inventions such as laser technology, night vision equipment, and microchips.[17] Corso and his book were feted widely on TV and media. The book contained four photographs that he claimed were research from Army intelligence files. Skeptics have said that one photo was clearly a 1935 Ford hubcap that was thrown into the air, and the other three were lifted from the official Condon Report, and therefore not originals as claimed.

Although to this point I have seemed to focus on examples that are easily dismissed as nonsense, these people and the events surrounding them were pivotal in shaping modern UFO culture and popular beliefs. Some of these men remain "leading lights" on the UFO circuit, still propagating their ideas.

The fact that they have been proven to be frauds seems to be of secondary importance to UFO believers. Secret technology conspiracies have spawned the belief that the U.S. government was involved in covert alien operations at its highly secret base known as Area 51. Also known as Groom Lake, this top-secret facility really does exist, and is located about 90 miles northwest of Las Vegas, Nevada. It has become a "magnet" for UFO groupies who flock there in droves. Over

A Russian satellite photo of Area 51

the years, locals and visitors have reported and captured footage of strange lights hovering over the base.

Besides the claims of reverse engineering, there have been sightings of alien craft and flying saucers over the area. Proponents of the ETH have several explanations for these sightings:

1. The Air Force has been developing flying saucer technology of its own, as a result of harvesting alien devices. And much of this is also responsible for UFO sightings around the world.

2. The government has been in a collaborative relationship with the ETs for many years, and has allowed many of them to use Area 51 as a secret Earth hiding base.

3. ETs are spying on Area 51 as they carefully watch the development of human technology at the base, regardless of its source.

One of these ideas was reinforced in a 1989 TV interview by a self-described physicist called Robert Lazar. He claimed that theory 1 (above) had been going on for many years, and that he had a "Majestic" (12) security clearance. As usual with individuals who make such spectacular claims, investigations determined that his qualifications and employment history were false. Nonetheless, his claims have brought lasting worldwide attention, not only to himself but also to Area 51, and he is a regular on many UFO specials that appear on TV from time to time. One would think that it would be easy for people to find out for themselves that he deliberately falsified his employment history.

It is quite easy to claim to have worked for a top-secret organization. For example, if I claimed to have been a spy for the CIA, and you asked them if this were true, they would likely reply, "We can neither confirm nor deny this." Because they will not deny it, I could happily go on claiming that I was an operative and that any public employment records were part of the CIA's disinformation campaign to ensure that I remained a covert operative. And if they should openly deny that I ever worked for them — well, they would, wouldn't they? It's classic stuff that only adds to the mystery.

The most self-refuting aspect of Lazar's theory, however, is that if he were indeed a classified Majestic operative, then in true MJ-12 fashion he should have been locked up or "disposed" of long ago for having "spilled the beans" on Area 51.[18]

Adding weight to the conspiracy idea is the fact that the U.S. government has increased its "land grab" around the base, enlarged the facilities, and also beefed up ground security. This is not surprising because there seem to be incessant intrusions into the base by UFO curiosity seekers with something to prove. All around the base there are signs advising that entry is illegal. I recall watching a UFO conspiracy-type documentary on television claiming that Area 51 had something to hide. In full view of the TV cameras, the presenter entered the restricted area, then was duly captured and removed from the base, thus allegedly proving his point. He loudly proclaimed that there are secrets that the government did not want him, or anyone else, to see.

This is the type of nonsense that UFOlogy attracts, and it distracts from the fact that some people really are seeing very serious phenomena.

It is well known that the military *does* develop secret technology for defense reasons, and has done so at Area 51. The area originally commenced operations as a test site for the U-2 spy plane in the 1950s. It is also believed to have served as a test site for the futuristic (as it was back then) SR-71 Blackbird reconnaissance plane, and the site is *known* to have been used for America's "stealth" technology. With this technology, the United States developed radar-invisible planes such as the F-117 stealth fighter and the stealth bomber. Rumors abounded about the stealth weapons even before their existence was officially released. There are similar rumors today about another secret project supposedly called "Aurora." Delta (triangle-shaped) winged craft have also been tested by the United States, and it is now known that Americans have experimented with saucer-shaped craft as well. Given that the majority of sightings remain identifiable craft or natural phenomena, who knows how many top-secret technologies are responsible for UFO sightings.

As expected, the government will neither confirm nor deny to what extent they are testing vehicles or weaponry at Groom Lake. It doesn't matter to the UFO buffs anyway. Area 51 has already taken on legendary proportions. If you were to visit the area, you would drive down State Highway 375, which the state of Nevada has officially named the "Extraterrestrial Highway." Like the town of Roswell, where there is now a UFO museum, a tourist industry has sprung up in the nearby town of Rachel. You can even stop off and have a drink at the "Little A'Le'Inn." As we will now see in more depth, it seems that the truth is not important, especially when money is an issue.

The *Alien Autopsy* movie

In addition to the paranormal and religious agendas of UFO believers, we have highlighted the massive popular, or lay, interest in the UFO phenomenon. If there is one thing our modern culture is good at, it is making money. We have discussed only a few of the numerous profit-seeking books and movies — some were based on complete non-events, and yet they became huge sellers that defined and shaped popular UFO culture.

One pivotal piece of profit-making propaganda that needs to be discussed is the *Alien Autopsy: Fact or Fiction* (1995) film. This movie was, quite simply, huge. After doing the rounds on cable and satellite channels, it eventually made its way onto mainstream TV. Tens of millions of people worldwide have seen it. Unfortunately, most of these same people never heard any of the contravening evidence, i.e., that this was one of the biggest UFO hoaxes in history.

Purporting to be an in-depth documentary, this show was compiled and narrated by Jonathan Frakes, who played Commander Will Ryker in the also hugely popular TV series *Star Trek: The Next Generation*.

This "documentary" is once again based around the Roswell legend. The film claimed to show real archived footage of autopsies carried out on the bodies of dead aliens recovered from the Roswell crash site. The effects were realistic (as you would expect in this day and age) and rather gruesome as the "medicos" carved open the alien body and removed organs. All sorts of experts were called in to examine the footage — anatomists, surgeons, and even special-effects artists, to determine whether it was real or not. Almost unanimously, they roundly condemned it as a hoax.

Because the film was in black and white, and had a grainy, scratched appearance, it provided the illusion of age, and to support the claim that the film was genuine, a sample of footage was sent to Kodak to verify its old age, which Kodak duly did. Upon further investigation, though, Kodak revealed that only the leader tape and a single frame were submitted for examination. A Kodak spokesman told the *Sunday Times* in London:

> There is no way I could authenticate this. I saw an image in the print. Sure it could be an old film, but it doesn't mean it is what the aliens were filmed on.[19]

Portrayals in the film also contradicted some of the statements made by Captain Jesse Marcel with regard to the numbers of appendages and fingers that the aliens possessed. This latest "proof" had all the hallmarks of previous Roswell hoaxes. There was no prior indication that such a film existed or might be in circulation. Why did it suddenly appear after being hidden away for so many years?

It was so popular that the Fox Network in America repeated it quickly after its original screening. However, not only was it widely condemned by experts but eventually one of the actors also came forward and revealed that he was paid to take part in the hoax. Fox then aired another special called *The World's Greatest Hoaxes; Secrets Revealed*. Along with Bigfoot and other seemingly solved mysteries, they announced that the *Alien Autopsy* movie was one of the biggest orchestrated hoaxes ever presented.[20] Along the way, though, someone made an awful lot of money on a gullible and UFO-hungry public.

Not only in America — the secret KGB files

Most of the reports that catch the media's attention seem to occur in the United States, but UFO sightings have been common all around the world, including Third World countries. There also seems to be a strong UFO link in countries where mystical-type Eastern religions such as Buddhism are practiced. In the West, the UFO link is more associated with New Age beliefs, which readily incorporate these extraterrestrial ideas. Researcher Bill Alnor says that the messages from the space brothers, via their earthly representatives, reflect a kind of a "non-judgmental universalism." They transcend conventional beliefs, yet at the same time bind them all together. He says that a man in Brazil, who now has 70,000 followers, was quoted as saying, "We believe everyone is a natural medium, and that all roads to God are good." Apparently he mixes flying saucers with Christianity, Hinduism, and many occult ideas.[21]

In countries where mystical beliefs dominate the culture, it would appear that the perception of UFOs generally takes on spiritual dimensions. The ideas of cover-ups and conspiracies are less prevalent in these Third World countries.

The 1950s was much more than the decade of the UFO. In Western nations, the Cold War led to mistrust and an emphasis on "secret stuff." Citizens were told to keep a watch out for "Reds under the beds" (communist spies). McCarthyism[22] was rampant, and the communist threat, rightly or wrongly, took on paranoiac proportions. Much of the perceived technology behind UFOs, if not attributed to aliens, was thought to be secret U.S. technology to counter the Soviet threat. But a prevalent mindset in American society was "If we can do it, so can the communists." So, to some people, UFOs might be secret Soviet technology.

However, the Soviet Union was having its own UFO flaps, though the West did not know much about them because little information flowed freely out of Moscow. It is reasonable to assume that, in turn, the Soviets could believe that UFOs were a result of secret U.S. technology. Ideas abounded in the USSR that the Americans deliberately orchestrated a saucer flap as a campaign of disinformation to cover up the truth about their own technological advances. After all, some of America's own citizens were claiming this, and America's UFO obsession was well publicized for all to see — including the Soviets.

In the 1960s and 1970s, though, Soviet news channels started to report sightings of UFOs. This seemed incredible in a nation where all news was controlled by the state. In 1967, one detailed account told of a commercial Russian airline crew sighting a UFO that maneuvered around their plane.[23] UFOlogists seized upon this opportunity — "If the Soviets are reporting them, it must be true." There were dozens of sightings, and in recent years, even the formerly state-controlled Russian newspaper *Pravda* ("Truth") began referring to the KGB's (Russian Secret Service) involvement and investigation into UFOs. UFOlogists in Western countries have picked up on these reports, and in some cases used them as evidence at UFO hearings in the U.S. Congress and the British House of Lords. Then, amazingly, no sooner than the Russian UFO wave started — it stopped. Private UFO groups in the Soviet Union were banned, and sightings ceased to be reported in the state media.[24] However, that did not mean that Soviet citizens no longer experienced such things. Years later, in 1979, an amazing Soviet government about-face occurred. A report was released by the Academy of Sciences in Moscow. Headed by astronomer Lev Gindilis and a team of investigators, the Gindilis Report concluded that no known natural or man-made stimulus could account for such phenomena. The implication was that it was something alien. Former NASA flight controller James Oberg investigated the strange goings-on in the former Soviet Union. He discovered:

> Like many other official Soviet government reports, the Gindilis Report turned out to be counterfeit science. In effect,

and probably in intent, it served to cover up one of Moscow's greatest military secrets, an illegal space-to-earth nuclear weapon. What the witnesses really saw back in those exciting days in 1967 were space vehicles all right, but not from some distant, alien world. They were Russian missile warheads, placed in low orbit under false registration names and then diverted back toward the planet's surface after one circuit of the globe. As they fireballed down toward a target zone near the lower Volga River, they seared their way into the imaginations of startled witnesses for hundreds of miles in all directions. . . .[25]

Although the tests themselves were not illegal, they were a trial run, intended to demonstrate the feasibility of launching nuclear weapons from space. This scheme itself *was* illegal under an international treaty forbidding orbiting nuclear weapons. Oberg adds:

> Pentagon experts soon dubbed this fearsome new weapon a "fractional orbit bombardment system," or FOBS. . . . So when Russian UFO witnesses concluded that they had been seeing alien spaceships instead of treaty-busting weapons tests, Soviet military officials were all too willing to permit this illusion to prosper. [26]

Unlike the USA, where the majority of rocket launches were well advertised, the Soviets conducted many tests under a veil of secrecy. Many of the UFO sightings can be attributed to rocket and missile launches, or the re-entry of vehicles back into the atmosphere. It is now known that the Soviets had many top-secret launch sites in their territories.

The hostile and secretive political climate in the former Soviet Union has created an even more conspiracy-driven mindset than in the United States. Russian UFOlogists abound, and as with Roswell and so many other cases, the stories and events have taken on a life of their own. The Russian government, along with many individuals in that country, has also become a master of disinformation.

The number of sightings in the former Soviet Union are probably second only to the United States, and some have remained unexplained to this day. One of the most famous that remained unsolved for many years was the "Cape Kamenny UFO." Oberg's account of it appears in the feature box.

"One of the best" encounters

"Top American UFOlogist Jacques Vallée cited this encounter in a 1992 book as one of the best in the world. His casebook coding-scheme gave it the highest marks: 'Firsthand personal interview with the witness by a source of proven reliability; site visited by a skilled analyst; and no explanation possible, given the evidence.'

"A graphic account of this UFO was given by American UFOlogist William L. Moore [of MJ-12 document fame] based on casebooks compiled by Zigel [a Russian UFO enthusiast]. 'On December 3 [1967], at 3:04 p.m.,' wrote Moore, 'several crewmen and passengers of an IL-18 aircraft on a test flight for the State Scientific Institute of Civil Aviation sighted an intensely bright object approaching them in the night sky.' Moore reported that the object 'followed' the evasive turns of the aircraft.

"But years later I discovered that the aircraft, passing near Vorkuta, in the northern Urals, had by chance been crossing the flight path of the Kosmos-194 spy satellite during its ascent from Plesetsk. The crew had unwittingly observed the rocket's plumes and the separation of its strap-on boosters. All other details of maneuvers were added in by their imaginations. Yet this bogus UFO story is highlighted as authentic by nearly every Western account of Russian UFOs in the last 20 years. . . .

"The Russian UFOlogists have failed. The ultimate test of the Russians' ability to perform mature, reliable UFO research is how they treat 'the smoking gun' of Russian UFOlogy, the Petrozavodsk 'jellyfish' UFO of 1977. The jellyfish was a brief wonder in the West before being quickly solved as the launch of a rocket from Plesetsk. Western UFOlogists readily accepted the explanation, but now it turns out that Russian UFO experts never did. They have assembled a vast array of miracle stories associated with the event, including reports of telepathic messages and physical damage to the earth."[27]

— James Oberg

Another movie — a Russian UFO crash

It was bound to happen. A supposedly Russian movie mysteriously appeared showing alleged secret KGB footage of a crashed alien saucer. Turner Network Television (TNT) achieved worldwide syndication for its documentary called *The Secret KGB UFO Files* (1999). It was narrated by Roger Moore (of James Bond movie fame and official goodwill ambassador for UNICEF), and it showed an autopsy being carried out on a deceased and badly mutilated alien body. In a very convincing fashion, uniformed Soviet soldiers paraded around a half-buried flying saucer that allegedly crashed in Sverdlovsky, USSR, in 1969.

This was conspiracy theory at its best, but sadly done in a B-grade fashion, including a computer-altered voice of a former CIA agent who claimed to have infiltrated the Russian UFO team. One scene that was trumpeted as footage of secret Soviet rocket tests was actually footage from a test firing of NASA's space shuttle solid rocket boosters.

UFOlogists, like the pro-ETH Friedman, were canvassed for their opinion. One ex–NASA worker claimed to have in his possession secret Stalin documents that showed Soviet interest in the Roswell crash. Unfortunately, he did not produce them for the program and, to date, never has. Even if he did, it would not be surprising. After all, Roswell eventually demonstrated that the U.S. was spying on the U.S.S.R.

However, the biggest clue about the authenticity of the "KGB-UFO" footage came from the disclaimers at the beginning and end of the show, which stated that the contents of the documentary "may or may not be true" and that the producers bore no responsibility as to the accuracy or truthfulness of the claims and sources.[28] So much for journalistic integrity!

Von Däniken, aliens, and big business

Many people fail to realize the popularity of the UFO phenomenon and dismiss it lightly. But as a gauge of common interest, one need look no further than the writings of Erich von Däniken.

In 1968, while manager of a Swiss hotel, von Däniken wrote his first book, *Chariots of the Gods*. It was an instant smash success. The enormous appeal of von Däniken's writings is that he has blended much of traditional religion with the ETH, claiming proof that the earth was visited by extraterrestrials in the distant past. These ETs, according to von Däniken, are "the gods" of ancient writings and religions, including Christianity. He quickly became the most high-profile advocate of this "ancient astronaut" theory. Many have latched onto these ideas as a means of understanding how religious beliefs may have arisen. They are uncomfortable with the idea that miracles, as recorded in the Bible, for example, could have occurred, because they are not scientifically verifiable today. In *Chariots of the Gods,* von Däniken proposes that many of these seemingly inexplicable supernatural events are descriptions by primitive cultures of advanced technologies — things that the writers could not comprehend. His theories also try to account for the origins of intelligent life on Earth.

Researcher and editor of *The Encyclopedia of Extraterrestrial Encounters* (EEE) Ronald Story points out how today's population is divided on the issue of origins. He says that (in Western nations) roughly 50 percent believe in the Darwinian doctrine of evolution, where, given enough time, simple matter gradually evolved, through chance, random processes, into complex organisms such as human beings (discussed in chapter 4). The other half believes that life is not the result of the accidental processes of "time and chance," but of the will and purpose of a divine Creator, namely the Judeo-Christian God of the Bible. He also describes another view called "astrogenesis," which is in effect a marriage of the two ideas. That is, a type of space-age Book of Genesis that once again places man at the center of creation. However, this creation is a localized biological event that has been engineered by ETs, who triggered and oversaw the evolution of mankind.[29] Von Däniken (and indeed Arthur C. Clarke) has been an advocate of this view, which is not only increasing in popularity in modern UFOlogy, but also among the general public — particularly among young people who have been raised on a diet of science fiction. Not surprisingly, von Däniken has usurped this appeal to great effect, and has a new generation of fans. To date, he has written 26 books, in 32 languages, which have sold over 60 million copies.[30] This makes him one of the most popular authors of all time, not just in the science fiction realm. In understanding this appeal, let's consider what he wrote:

> Religious people, regardless what faith they belong to, hope for "salvation from above." The greater part of the UFO followers do exactly the same. The Ancient Astronaut movement, however, sees the problem from the opposite side.

The extraterrestrials were here thousands of years ago. They have left behind rules and regulations but also a promise to return in the remote future (time dilation). Considering that the "Gods" of ancient times did not always treat mankind gently and quite often became angry and punished brutally, a "hope from above" is not realistic. Rather the contrary! Mankind should be prepared technically and also morally for the return of the "Gods."[31]

Von Däniken is an ex–Roman Catholic and very hostile toward organized religion. He proposes that the judgments of God, as recorded in the Bible, were invoked by ETs to shape moral law. For example, he believes that the destruction of the city of Sodom (Gen. 19:1–28) was caused by space beings using nuclear weapons. Similarly, the story about the Hebrews under Egyptian slavery, as recorded in the Book of Exodus, is somehow supposed to be a human breeding experiment conducted by aliens, and man — in his ignorance — began to worship these beings. Von Däniken claims to be able to explain and support his ideas scientifically. However, he has a presupposition (a religious belief) that ETs have previously visited this planet. He sees his ideas of ancient astronauts as "true science" and uses this "UFO science" to discredit traditional religion.[32]

Evidence of ancient astronauts

To support his theory, von Däniken traveled the world looking at the archaeological records and artifacts of past civilizations. He has used rock carvings (petroglyphs), the Egyptian and Mayan pyramids, Stonehenge, the massive stone idols on Easter Island, plus any form of ancient technology to claim that "primitive" man could not have possessed the skills and technology to visualize and build what they did. Although von Däniken claims to use the scientific method, his theories, though popular, are very speculative. They show a distinct lack of understanding of operational science, and proper research is sadly lacking.

One simple but glaring example is pointed out in archaeologist Dr. Clifford Wilson's book *Crash Go the Chariots* (1972), a million-copy best seller, which is a devastating refutation of von Däniken's claims. Von Däniken "sees" extraterrestrials all through the Bible whenever it refers to miraculous or angelic events. He states that Enoch, "according to tradition, disappeared forever in a fiery heavenly chariot." However, the Bible describes Enoch as a righteous man in the eyes of God, and in Genesis 5:24, it simply states that "God took him away," which just means that God took him to heaven, bypassing the process of death. There is no mention of a fiery chariot. It appears that von Däniken is relying on memory because he thinks the Bible says one thing, when in fact, it actually states another. Clearly, he is confusing the event of Enoch with Elijah (2 Kings 2:13) some 2,500 years later in biblical history, when Elijah disappeared in a fiery chariot.[33] This is a very poor and basic mistake, suggestive of dubious research, which seems to be endemic in von Däniken's books.

Two of the most enduring icons of von Däniken's theories are the "Palenque astronaut" and the "Nazca lines."

The Palenque Astronaut

In the ancient Mayan city of Palenque, Mexico, there is a large stone pyramid. Excavations after World War II revealed hidden chambers inside the structure, including a tomb for the Mayan king Pacal, who died around A.D. 683. On the lid of the tomb is a highly detailed carving. Von Däniken gives his impression:

> On the slab [covering the tomb is] a wonderful chiseled relief. In my eyes, you can see a kind of frame. In the center of that frame is a man sitting, bending forward. He has a mask on his nose, he uses his two hands to

The detailed carving from the lid of the tomb of the Mayan king Pacal, who died around A.D. 683

manipulate some controls, and the heel of his left foot is on
a kind of pedal with different adjustments. The rear portion
is separated from him; he is sitting on a complicated chair,
and outside of this whole frame you see a little flame like an
exhaust.[34]

This is a grandiose description, and von Däniken clearly sees what
he wants to see. A casual glance at the carving clearly shows that the
man is naked and barefoot, except for a loincloth. If pictured in his
spaceship, it hardly seems appropriate clothing for a technologically
advanced extraterrestrial to be flying around the galaxy in. Moreover,
there is no mask attached to his face — it is merely an ornament; the
pedal is a seashell (a Mayan symbol associated with death); the hand
controls are nothing of the sort and merely represent a panorama of
the background view in the carving; and the exhaust appears to be a
representation of the sacred maize plant. In short, the carving is simply
a religious depiction to adorn the tomb of a deceased royal figure.[35]

The Nazca lines

The mysterious Nazca lines are to be found near the ancient city of
Nazca in Peru. Covering an area of some 37 square miles, von Däniken
says:

> At some time in the past, unknown intelligences landed
> on the uninhabited plain near the present-day town of Nazca
> and built an improvised airfield for their spacecraft which were
> to operate in the vicinity of the earth.[36]

On the Nazca plains, there are very long, and sometimes inter-
connecting, lines or markings (known as geoglyphs) covering a massive area. Some of the lines run for several miles, many are absolutely
straight, others run parallel to each other and some are circular. Adherents to von Däniken's beliefs refer to this as the "Nazca spaceport,"
claiming that the full splendor and meaning can only be appreciated
from the air. Von Däniken assumes that the feat of constructing such
markings, let alone air travel, was beyond the ancient Peruvians, and
so he invokes the ET factor once again, claiming that the markings are
signals and landing strips for alien spaceships.

Many of the lines are only a few inches across. They are hardly
big enough for a landing strip or runway. Although massive in scale,

representations of animal figures, including a giant condor (a South American bird) can be clearly seen from the air. The lines themselves were not difficult (in the engineering sense) to construct, either. Many were made by simply moving stones and pebbles to one side to expose the yellow soil underneath. In an area that averages only half an inch of rainfall per year, they have remained virtually undisturbed for centuries. The meaning of the lines is not entirely clear, but further research is suggesting that they align with star constellations, and that some of these have been superimposed onto the animal figures. History has shown that the South American Indians had an amazing understanding of astronomy. In short, the huge lines were probably built for religious reasons. It is a ridiculous notion to suggest that extraterrestrials, who were capable of flying many light-years across the galaxy, needed some sort of "markers" on the earth to find their way around.

In the semi-arid plains near Broken Hill, located in the outback of western New South Wales, Australia, local artist Peter Anderson single-handedly created the world's largest piece of art. Covering an area of almost 5 million square yards (4 million square meters), using nothing more than a hand mower and a tractor, Anderson carved the impressive giant image of a smiling stockman. He was a lone operator who achieved the feat without the aid of satellite navigation (GPS), and he

Photo courtesy of Corbis

An aerial photo of the Nazca lines in Peru

did so undetected. Yet, it requires a trip into the air to fully appreciate the detail and grandeur of his work. Obviously, the Nazca Indians, with greater manpower, could have easily created the images despite not having the advantage of a tractor.

Von Däniken's claims are extreme beyond belief with regard to the Palenque astronaut and the Nazca lines, and other claims too numerous to mention here. Besides Clifford Wilson, UFOlogist Ronald Story has also written two books dismissing von Däniken's claims — *The Space Gods Revealed* (1976) and *Guardians of the Universe* (1980). Many other serious UFOlogists completely reject von Däniken's evidences, although some do believe in the astrogenesis theory.

On 22 occasions, publishers rejected *Chariots of the Gods*. After a science fiction writer helped rewrite the manuscript, it was eventually accepted and the rest is history, as they say.

Honesty on trial

A program on Britain's Channel 4 TV reported that after finally gaining some success, von Däniken was arrested by Interpol for non-payment of £7,000 of business tax. Continued investigation by the courts revealed a further £350,000 of personal debts, and von Däniken was eventually imprisoned for three and a half years for embezzlement. Undeterred, he continued to write while in jail, which resulted in his second book, *Return of the Gods*. This time he claimed that the massive sculptures on Easter Island were built by aliens. Despite his personal reputation being in tatters, this book was another best seller.[37] They added:

> Von Däniken's credibility was finally undermined after he was unable to substantiate claims made in another book — *Gold of the Gods* — that he had photographed metal plaques containing the wisdom of extraterrestrials. In 1977, a BBC *Horizon* programme, *The Case of the Ancient Astronauts*, took a rational look at his theories and showed them to be pseudo science.
>
> Numerous other wonders cited by von Däniken as corroboration for his theories were similarly debunked. In the late 1970s he rapidly disappeared from the public arena, and in 1982 he could not find an English or American publisher for his tenth book.

In the past few years, however, his ideas have again started to become popular in a culture fascinated by programmes such as *The X Files*. He is also working on a huge theme park in Switzerland, called the Mysteries of the World, and money is gushing into the project. Scientist or pseudo scientist, heretic or visionary, he is certainly tenacious and a master at whipping up a frenzy in the public imagination.[38]

Undeterred by criticism and the thorough refutation of his "evidences," von Däniken knows what makes a good story and continues to market his business. But maybe there is another source of inspiration for his ideas. He was reported as saying:

> I know that astronauts visited the earth in ancient time. . . . I was there when the astronauts arrived. Why should anyone believe I am able to leave my body whenever I desire and observe the past, present and future — all at the same time? Nonetheless it is true. It has been for many years.[39]

His method is also known as astral traveling, or an out-of-body experience (OBE). This is a New Age occult practice, also common to some Eastern religions. And as we shall see later, the New Age movement and occultism in general have hijacked the modern UFO movement.

A top man in "his" field

Besides von Däniken, there are others who invoke extraterrestrial interference in human origins. One such person is high-profile UFOlogist Zecharia Sitchin. Rather than the airy speculation of von Däniken, Sitchin claims to be a scholar. Although he graduated in economics, he claims to be an expert in Hebrew and ancient Sumerian texts.

He has concluded that all modern Bible translations are interpretations that do not accurately portray the real beliefs of ancient times and the original Hebrew authors. Like von Däniken, he also sees ETs throughout the Bible. His most popular theme is the description of the "sons of God" marrying with the "daughters of men" in Genesis 6 (see the appendix for a thorough examination of this UFO/Bible text). Sitchin, von Däniken, and many others believe this to be the "intermarriage" of extraterrestrials with a humanoid or subhuman species. However, their source book itself, the Bible, clearly states that intelligent man already existed and flourished before these events took place.

Besides ETs, Sitchin sees flying saucers throughout many ancient texts, pictures, and tablets. His books have taken on almost legendary proportions among the UFO movement. They are so voluminous and detailed that they cannot fail to impress and give the idea that he knows what he is talking about. He claims his sources are ancient clay tablets. The average UFOlogist has never had to deal with this type and weight of information, and most wouldn't know whether he is telling the truth anyway. Very few serious scholars have yet undertaken the task of unraveling his work.[40]

He believes that Sumerian tablets refer to God or the gods as *Anunnaki,* meaning "those who from heaven to Earth came," and believes that these are the same as the biblical *Anakim* — who, he claims, came from a planet called Nibiru. He says:

> It took additional decades of research and study, of both ancient and modern astronomy, to reach a startling conclusion: There is one more planet in our solar system, a post-Plutonian planet with a large elliptical orbit that brings it to our vicinity (passing between Mars and Jupiter) every 3,600 Earth-years; it is then that the comings and goings between Nibiru and Earth take place.[41]

It sounds studious, grand and factual, but is short on substance. Although extra objects might exist around our solar system (mainly large rocks or asteroids), there is no evidence to support his version of biblical events, and his speculations about the planet Nibiru are most certainly incorrect. A quote from a NASA website bluntly states:

> There is no known Planet X or tenth planet in our solar system. Scientists have been looking for about a hundred years. It was believed that such a planet was required to explain the orbital characteristics of the outer planets Uranus and Neptune. Many searches have been performed and, to date, no evidence of such a planet has emerged. In addition, better information about the masses of outer planets has also now shown that no other planets are necessary to explain the planetary orbits.[42]

In addition, it is quite simple to determine the unlivable planetary conditions that would be created by a large elliptical (oval, not circular) orbit of a planet orbiting our sun — passing in and out of our solar system. According to Sitchin, it only passes between Jupiter and Mars every few thousand years, and this is supposedly as close as it gets. But we already know that such a distance from our sun would provide harsh and unlivable conditions. These hypothetical aliens not only have to endure extreme below-freezing temperatures, but are apparently so prescient and patient that they can plan their excursions to Earth thousands of years ahead.

Most serious UFOlogists dislike the religious connotations that the New Age movement brings to UFOlogy. However, Sitchin's popularity transcends both camps. He appears as a scholarly authority to the proponents of the ETH, and to the New Agers he is a hero for attacking the historicity of the Bible and God as Creator by claiming the Bible has been misunderstood, and is not to be taken as literally and historically true. Researcher and cult specialist Bill Alnor notes that, like von Däniken's books, Sitchin's are clearly designed to:

> . . . demolish the foundations of every ancient tradition in favor of his notion of ancient astronauts coming to earth.[43]

Yet, as we discussed in earlier chapters, attributing the creation of life on Earth to extraterrestrials only shifts the "original" creation problem to outer space. We cannot explain the origin of complex life and subsequently the appearance of human beings simply by the cross-species breeding of humanoid space aliens and primitive ape-like creatures, or the genetic engineering of animals, as discussed in chapter 4. Despite the scholarly impression of such claims, they show a distinct lack of basic knowledge of genetics.

Beamships from the Pleiades

Swiss contactee Eduard "Billy" Meier claimed to have had his first meeting with an alien at age five in 1944. An elderly extraterrestrial male named Sfath regularly visited him, traveling in his pear-shaped flying machine, speaking to Meier telepathically. Meier had been selected for a mission, and he was being conditioned and educated to prepare the world for a "New World Order" (millions of contactees have been told this same thing). Sfath taught him until 1953, when Sfath was replaced by another ET, but this time it was a female named Asket. Meier's relationship with Asket took on new proportions as she took him back in time to see Earth's history as it happened. During this time he also traveled extensively and studied the world's religions.

In 1975, Meier began a new contact with a female alien called Semjase who was apparently from the star system Pleiades, and it was she who would help catapult Meier to the forefront of the extraterrestrial contact movement. (Semjase has "popped" up to meet a few other people, but her name seems to have links with an ancient past. Remember this name when reading the appendix.)

One of the photos presented by Billy Meier, which he claimed was of a beamship

The teachings of Meier and his alien friends were spectacularly appealing to large numbers of people. They combined traditional values with New Age concepts. "Look after the earth, don't damage the environment, we are here to help you, and be good to your parents." These tales give everyone "warm fuzzies" — they are the same messages that the "space brothers" have been feeding us for over half a century, particularly since the advent of the nuclear age. It encompasses a universal theme, and when combined with the so-called "misunderstood" writings of traditional religions, it has mass appeal. Meier quickly became the prophet of a new generation and a new world, compiling thousands of pages of contact notes. Along the way, Meier was also given instructions on how to find an ancient Aramaic document which was supposedly unearthed in a tomb in Jerusalem. This text is claimed to contain the original teachings of Jmmanuel, or Jesus, which were, they claim, later corrupted as the Christian Bible. Now called the *Talmud Jmmanuel,* it has effectively become a new "Bible" for Meier devotees.

However, skepticism rose because of the frequency of supposed contact Meier was having, so he claimed that Semjase provided him with "proof" that would stun the world. She allowed Meier to take approximately 1,000 photographs and 12 movies of the supposed visiting spacecraft. These pictures, in amazing clarity, showed the "beamships" (as they are called) performing a variety of maneuvers, including descents which were characterized by a side-to-side swaying motion. Although they obviously looked as if they were being suspended from a string and hence rocking from side to side, this characteristic has been described as the "falling leaf" motion in UFOlogy,

Meier's pictures and photos have become famous and infamous. They have been sold to TV stations and many publishers. After so many years of sightings, but such scant pictorial evidence, this breakthrough appeared almost too good to be true. But that's the problem — it was.

Crude forgeries that fooled everyone . . . almost

Recently, a group known as Underground Video, former advocates and fans that sold and marketed Meier's materials, launched a class action suit against Meier, his company, and associates, alleging fraud. Meier defenders rallied to the cause, claiming the photos could not be debunked. Pro-Meier scientists had apparently verified that they could not be duplicated artificially, and other supporting witnesses confirmed their authenticity. However, on an Internet website, a representative from Underground Video wrote:

> Our investigation first began as a supportive effort to verify the known facts of the Meier case to present the truth of alien-human contact to skeptics. With the assistance of members from the Hollywood special effects team of the Ultra-Matrix Corporation, we studied the Meier photographs and claims. . . . After six months of intense inquiry, with the assistance of cinematographers, physicists, and computer analysis from Total Research [another UFO research group], we found the claims of the representatives of the Meier case to be absolutely untrue. We discovered miniature models and a variety of deceptive methods used to create this hoax.[44]

> Underground Video was one of the foremost defenders of the Meier material. We are DISAPPOINTED to now learn the ENTIRE case is a hoax. Representations of any authenticity with regard to this case made by alleged scientific examination has [sic] proved to be totally unreliable and misleads [sic] the general public into believing a carefully fabricated lie. The persons who authenitcated [sic] the Meier case are not credible scientists nor [sic] investigators.

Along with Underground Video's statement is a photo-graph showing one of Billy Meiers [sic] alleged Pleiadian beam-ships taken in 1981. After computer enhancement and careful scrutiny, it has been shown the Beamship is really a miniature model made out of an upside-down cake pan, disconnected copper hose fitting, a bracelet, carpet tacks and various other identifiable objects [emphases in original].[45]

The Total Research Group referred to is run by Kal K. Korff, an investigative journalist who traveled to Switzerland undercover to in-vestigate Meier. Korff claims he is not a UFO debunker but wants to see serious study of the UFO phenomenon. During his time in Swit-zerland, he also interviewed Meier's ex-wife, Kalliope (or Popi), who duly "blew the whistle" on Meier, claiming he used crude models and strings for the Pleiadian beamships, which he then superimposed onto the Swiss countryside.

Korff's 400-plus-page book also details Meier's criminal back-ground, and includes interviews of former friends and supporters who claim he started the hoax for financial gain.[46] In addition, Dennis Stacy, editor of the *MUFON* (Mutual UFO Network) *UFO Journal*, wrote, "Photographic analysis [of Meier's photographs] . . . reportedly revealed that Meier's amazing array of flying saucers consisted of small models suspended from strings."[47] Subsequent photos of the beautiful blond aliens Asket and Nera were discovered to be a blurred photograph of a TV screen featuring girls from an episode of the *Dean Martin Show*. Similarly, a picture of Semjase was found to be a photocopy of a model from a Sears catalog. Bill Alnor comments:

The scientific UFO community with few exceptions has thoroughly trashed the Meier claims.[48]

There is a substantial weight of evidence against Meier, but it doesn't seem to matter to the "true believers." A large organization has built up around him, including a cult following known as FIGU (in English, Free Community of Interests in Fringe and Spiritual Sciences and UFOlogical Studies), which is based around his substantial Swiss compound. Those who speak out against the fraud risk a flood of pro-tests and even threats. However, like Adamski before him, it is the blending of religion and science, albeit pseudo on both counts, that seems to elevate Meier to a messiah-like status in the minds of many.

Some have claimed he is a crook, a crude forger, and a liar. But, like Adamski before him, it is what he says, not what he is, that is seen as important. Sadly, Meier's descriptions of his ET encounters and subsequent references have become a "standard" in UFOlogy. Serious study suffers as a result.

Capers in the crops!

Crop circles seem to have mystified people for many years. But are they really as mysterious as many are led to believe?

Although it is claimed that crop circles have been around for hundreds of years, the records in support of this claim are scant. They are really a modern occurrence, first appearing in significant numbers around the mid to late 1970s and early 1980s. Initially, farmers around southern England started to find circular depressions in fields of wheat and other crops. Who made them was a mystery. As they increased in number, they gained notoriety and the interest of investigators. A new research field (pun intended) was born, and crop circle experts, called cereologists or croppies, started to take a closer look at what some believed was a phenomenon created by UFOs. It was thought that they might have been saucer nests; that is, depressions created by landed flying saucers. Circles started appearing in locations other than the south of England, and as publicity increased, they started to turn up in other countries, too. They increased in complexity, as well; rather than just plain circles in the maize, they started to appear as geometric shapes, such as circles within circles, triangles, spirals, and a huge variety of other designs. If indeed it was the work of UFOs, it gave the impression they were involved in a game of one-upmanship with each other, or leaving the world a massive calling card.

Over the years, cereologists such as Delgado, Andrews, Levengood, Silva, and others have made some startling claims about characteristics of crop circles. Some of the more general beliefs about crop circles include:

- They are made by "ionized plasma vortices." This was an idea popularized by Dr. Terence Meaden. These are supposedly eddies of wind that cause downward pressure on the crops. Although this might be possible to account for a crop marking of a plain circular design, it could not account for complex ones. Despite the claims that some witnesses have seen such eddies making crop circles, more people have claimed to see flying saucers create them. So-called eyewitnesses are not as reliable as one might think.

- They are radioactive. Analyses of soil samples have proven this to be untrue.

- There are cellular changes within the plants. No such changes have been documented, casting doubt on the authenticity of the claims.[49]

However, just as quickly as claims like the above are debunked, explanations arise to counter the scientific conclusions. Here are some further claims by those proposing construction by ETs, which, as we shall see, have really left egg on their faces:

- They are too precise or accurately constructed to have been man-made, suggesting they were made by an advanced technology.

- The bending of stalks, without being broken, was impossible to achieve by human means.

- Humans could not have constructed them without being detected by others. (But remember the outback artist Peter Anderson who carved the image of the smiling stockman undetected for over a year.)

Signs, the movie — God versus the aliens (2002)

Although *Signs* was billed as a science fiction movie, the reviews claimed that it was about a spiritual journey and a restoration to faith. This is an intriguing notion because practically all "sci-fi" ignores traditional religions and particularly the Christian God of the Bible.

The film is set in a small American farming community where the central character, Graham Hess (an ex–Episcopalian priest, played by Mel Gibson), has turned his back on God as a result of the horrific death of his wife in a roadside accident. Things go from bad to worse for Hess when strange crop circles appear in his cornfields and things start going "bump in the night." It soon becomes apparent on the nightly TV news that aliens are visiting the earth and harvesting human beings (the reason is never explained). His crisis of faith deepens and he even forbids prayer at the dinner table. He exclaims to his brother and children that "we are on our own" (in the context that there is no God to help them). This is ironic because later on in the movie he "confronts" God and exclaims, "I hate you!"

This movie has some genuinely scary and tense moments, particularly during the final confrontation with a left-behind alien intent on revenge against Hess. It is at this point that the real meaning of the title *Signs* is revealed. The irreconcilable events in his life that caused him to turn his back on God, now viewed with meaning and purpose, ultimately restore him to faith.[50]

The movie never suggested that Hess had any difficulty reconciling the concept of extraterrestrial life with his Christian faith. Alien life can only exist from one of two causes — God created it, or it evolved (made itself by "natural" processes). This movie presumes that there is a God. However, if sentient aliens are part of His creation, then mankind cannot be the focal point of His created universe as the movie, and also the Bible, implies. The secular concept of intelligent alien life is implicitly based on the premise that, if life evolved on the earth, it must have evolved elsewhere in the universe. Evolution requires millions of years of death and suffering as "normal," and is therefore opposed to the biblical account of the entrance of death through man's sin.

In the movie, God uses death and tragedy in the priest's family as a tool for helping him in the future. The priest may have been satisfied with the answer because he regained his faith. But in the real world, not everyone who experiences these tragedies readily gains such an answer.

Although this is an entertaining and well-crafted "thriller," it invoked this spiritual conundrum without satisfactorily answering the "big-picture" question of why there is death and suffering in the world in the first place.

The prank hatched in a pub

In 1991, two gentlemen in their sixties from Southampton, England, confessed to being the original crop circle "engineers" for over 15 years. Doug Bower and Dave Chorley said they dreamed up the idea over a pint of stout at a local pub one evening. They had seen reports of a UFO saucer nest in Australia and thought they would have some fun recreating them in England.

Initially, using a steel bar, they created some simple circles. As Meaden's vortex theory was used to explain them, the men started to create more and more complex designs to scuttle the vortex idea, and to further the notion of construction by intelligent aliens. Others obviously caught on to the "gag" as crop circles started appearing all over the place with increasing complexity in design. It suggests that other hoaxers had no problem in guessing that these designs were man-made, so they duly copied them. But UFO buff Pat Delgado obviously didn't think so. He championed the ET connection throughout the media, and he combined with Colin Andrews to produce a colorful best-selling book called *Circular Evidence*.[51]

Naturally, when Bower and Chorley stepped out and "spilled the beans" — claiming responsibility for over 250 circles — Delgado and Andrews were less than impressed and denounced the two "creators" as hoaxers. However, Doug and Dave had the last laugh. Under the watchful eye of video cameras, they created an elaborate crop circle using what is now the common method of just rope and planks. Not knowing that it had been filmed, Delgado and Andrews, by now "world" authorities, inspected the circle and duly declared it to be the "real thing" — a "genuine" construction by an outside intelligence that no hoaxer could have made.[52]

Thus, as in most cases in UFOlogy, there was a simple explanation to crop circles despite the wild speculations of the pro-UFO lobby. To this day, cereologists denounce the work of hoaxers (this is really a misnomer because "hoaxers" are the *real* creators of crop circles) by claiming that there are telltale signs differentiating the man-made ones from so-called "genuine" ET-crafted ones. But if supposed experts were all fooled so easily before, why should we treat their claims any differently now?

A few years ago, a famous video clip appeared in a documentary showing supposed flying saucers hovering over a field, magically creating crop formations in a matter of seconds. This has also been established as a hoax, but it is nonetheless doing the rounds on the Internet. Farmers have also learned how to make a "quick buck" — some charging an entrance fee for viewing circles in their fields. So who is to say what other motivation inspires these "mysterious" patterns?

Crop circles have become a modern art form. A group known as Circlemakers has a website (<www.circlemakers.org>) where you can view the story of these modern artists. Despite being denounced by cereologists, they have repeatedly constructed elaborate crop circles under the gaze of TV cameras and press, in the darkness of night and undetected by others. They have even created giant advertisements for companies like Weetabix and Mitsubishi, which commissioned them to create crop circle logos to promote their wares.

Despite claims that it is impossible to create these designs in one night, Circlemakers say they were filmed by the BBC producing 100 circles in 100 minutes.[53]

And in a measure of the silliness, and as a comical response to the other hoaxers that were copycatting their activities, the "two Dougs" produced a pattern that stated "WE ARE NOT ALONE." Even this was taken to be a message by aliens. No one stopped to think that if it were crafted by ETs, they would surely have written, "YOU ARE NOT ALONE!"[54]

As if we needed any more indication of the "power" behind the crop circle phenomenon, a BBC report commented that during the foot-and-mouth epidemic in 2002, the British government, in an effort to halt the spread of this disease afflicting livestock, established strict rules about crossing the English countryside. However, they also noticed that during this time there was a virtual halt in the occurrence of crop circles. It appears that the aliens, or wind vortices, duly obeyed the wishes of Her Majesty's government, or were worried about catching the dreaded disease.[55]

Once again, despite evidence to the contrary, many continue to hold on to the belief that several crop circles cannot be accounted for by human origin, leaving only one other explanation — the one they want to hear!

A supernatural link or another hoax?

Interestingly, even though a group like Circlemakers does not credit ETs with the construction of circles (they are hated by pro-UFO cereologists for debunking their pet theory), they *have* reported the occurrence of strange phenomena during and after their construction. In a very public press release, they commented:

> Our crop formations are intended to function as temporary sacred sites in this landscape. Whilst constructing crop formations in the fields we have experienced a series of aerial

anomalies including: small balls of light, columns of light, and blinding flashes. All apparently targeting ourselves and our crop formations. We are unsurprised at the numerous visitors who have reported a diverse assortment of anomalies associated with our artworks. These have included physiological effects, such as headaches and nausea. Healing effects such as one report of a cure for acute osteoporosis. Physical effects such as camera and other electronic equipment failure. We are certain that our artworks are subject to the attention of paranormal forces and act to catalyze other paranormal events.[56]

Similar unrelated occurrences have also been reported all around the world and skeptics claim that these are part of the hoax, yet these are the same type of phenomena that accompany some UFO sightings. If some form of paranormal activity is accompanying the manufacture of these circles, it might also have something to do with their increasing appearance around the world. Have hoaxers discovered and provided an opportunity or portal for supernatural "forces" to manifest themselves? We have already demonstrated that, besides the orchestrated frauds and hoaxes that have shaped modern UFOlogy, there seems to be a deceptive supernatural characteristic to sightings, contacts, and, as we will see, the abduction scenario.

Humanity has been fascinated with the occult and supernatural for as long as we have been on the earth. People have built temples, shrines, and obelisks in an effort to appease and attract supernatural forces. Have these "capers in the crops" inadvertently become a beacon for such forces? Or was there a more overt intention all along?

A little-known fact about Circlemakers is that before they entered the lucrative commercial market, they called themselves Team Satan. This is a very bold name and might be suggestive of their intent. It is unlikely that anyone would label themselves with a moniker so representative of all that is evil in the spiritual sense without a good reason. Indeed, satanic worship continues to be quite prolific in the world today, and many are drawn into it by its allure and mysticism. Have crop circles become modern shrines of occult worship? Most certainly, Team Satan is not ashamed to publicly draw attention to the "supernatural side" of its work and, perhaps deliberately, draw more folk into the dark world of the occult using the curiosity factor.

Short on substance

In this chapter, we have highlighted many of the dubious claims of some UFOlogists and fame-seekers. However, it should be pointed out that there are many honest, respectable, and hardworking researchers whose work makes books such as this one possible. I have the utmost regard for those who have devoted themselves to finding answers for this often-baffling mystery.

Many supporters of what can now be called the UFO movement feel that they get a "raw deal" from the popular media and, as a result, the general public. They have an overwhelming desire to be taken seriously. But because this is often not the case, a mindset is manifested that they are misunderstood, and that the public is being "hoodwinked" in a global cover-up about UFOs. As I sat through a prestigious UFO conference, I listened to speaker after speaker, supposedly experts in their field, relate this same theme. Their contempt of the establishment was very evident. On several occasions, where there have been "nuts and bolts"-type sightings, the lack of corroborating evidence always seems to be the government's fault. ("Surely they must have seen something — why don't they tell us?")

At such conferences, pictures abound of saucers which they allege to be real but which are known frauds, and booths display crop circles which they endorse as alien-made, but which have been verified as man-made (at least they should display ones for which no one has claimed credit, to keep some mystery). I found it amazing to hear so many allusions to the "cover-up" at Roswell, the harassment of UFO investigators by government officials, and references to the teachings of George Adamski and Billy Meier. Although these "legends" may have had encounters of some kind, they have been clearly exposed as frauds who have been only too willing to lie to advance their cause. Surely, by any critical standards, once someone has been involved in deliberate deception, the rest of their testimony should be treated with some suspicion.

As mentioned previously, a normal scientific approach is to start with a hypothesis and then explore, test, and try to disprove every aspect of your hypothesis until you are left with what is scientifically valid, testable, and observable. The approach of modern UFOlogy fails on many of these counts. If it wants to be taken seriously, it needs to clear its decks and apply a proper level of scientific rigor to the evidence.

I have listened to many UFO speakers expounding, as they frequently do, many scientific-sounding notions. Unfortunately, it is often glaringly obvious for anyone with critical analytical skill that their words lack substance. Many of their claims are riddled with "I knew a guy once" stories, often second or thirdhand, full of sweeping statements and generalizations that would not be acceptable at any scientific gathering.

I recall meeting one gentleman, smartly dressed in a suit and proudly displaying his "official UFO investigator" badge on behalf of one of the longest-running UFO groups in the world. He told me he had been an investigator for many years, yet had only investigated one case, plus his own "close encounter." I asked him if he had undergone any training, to which he replied in the negative. Upon further discussion, I realized that this particular organization merely goes and "has a chat" with the contactee. I asked, "Do you take note of the weather conditions and cloud cover? Do you talk to the neighbors? Do you contact air traffic control to find out whether the UFO was seen on radar or whether there were any official craft in the area? Do you have a checklist to catalog and compare cases?" Although I was trying to find out what objective investigations are usually undertaken in such cases, he obviously felt concerned that I was attacking his belief in UFOs and defensively replied: "No, but UFOs are real." Perhaps I'm a little naïve, but I thought it would have been necessary to exclude all other possibilities. This sort of approach is not the case with all UFO organizations and there are serious exponents, but these days they are few and far between. Yet I heard many comments at one conference to the effect that UFOlogy is mature enough to merit accreditation as a college or university course. Obviously, the bar would need to be raised considerably before this could occur.

In my opinion, rather than being so critical of others, the modern UFO movement needs to be more introspective and take a long, hard look at itself. Its conspiracy-driven mentality makes it a beacon for every type of misunderstood pseudo-scientific, eccentric, and quasi-religious idea. Unfortunately, the study of UFOs in the modern era has been hijacked by those I call "religious UFOlogists." Many of its adherents hold strong pre-existing New Age ideas, and many are psychics, spiritualists, and others involved in occult practices. The desire for UFOlogy to be taken seriously as a valid science is not helped by an embrace of those who make unwarranted claims and propose many scientific-sounding ideas that are merely based on an "opinion" or a spirit guide from the "other side." I have seen these unsubstantiated claims firsthand, and sadly, the gathered assembly seemed to receive such comments as fact.

Although they give the impression that they are all-embracing, these "religious" adherents of UFOs are very intolerant of traditional religious views. They made this very evident at a conference I attended, when a former Christian missionary recounted his now-world-famous sightings, which occurred during his time of service in a Third World country. It was a well-documented event with plenty of corroborating witnesses. Although he was treated with respect (mainly because he was one of the "fortunate few" to have had an experience), when asked for his view of what he saw, you could hear the disappointment when he said, "I thought they were angels," meaning angels as they are described in the Bible. This does not sit well with the view that UFOs are, in fact, ETs visiting the earth, whether they appear physically or in some spiritual form. The religious UFOlogist believes that these ETs are on a religious mission, but it is a transforming one designed to take the world into a new age. They have no time for old-fashioned views.

Although every person has a preconceived world view — a bias with which we interpret the evidence — the modern UFO movement is notable for its marked lack of objectivity. More disturbing is that they themselves fail to realize that their own New Age view is in fact a religious view and one that is held to the exclusion of other more traditional religious views.

In addition, they are only too keen to imbibe the stories told by these visiting entities, though they cannot scientifically establish their origin or indeed their reality in the physical realm. We do know that the so-called space brothers have established a pattern of telling us things that have been proven to be demonstrably false. One should then ask, "Should *they* be trusted either?" After all, if they have lied, should they not be treated as liars? Apparently it doesn't matter, as long as one's desire for something to be true is strong enough. This attitude explains why truth suffers in the UFO phenomenon as a whole.

Endnotes

1 Ronald D. Story, editor, *The Mammoth Encyclopedia of Extraterrestrial Encounters*, in an article by Randall Fitzgerald (London: Constable & Robinson, 2002), p. 606–618.

2 Ibid.

3 "What Really Happened at Roswell," <www.csicop.org/si/9707/roswell. htm>, December 10, 2002.

4 "Report of Air Force Research Regarding the Roswell Incident 1994," <www.af.mil/lib/roswell.html>, December 10, 2002.

5 Story, *The Mammoth Encyclopedia of Extraterrestrial Encounters*, in an article by Fitzgerald, p. 606–618.

6 Ibid.

7 Ibid.

8 "Report of Air Force Research Regarding the Roswell Incident 1994," <www.af.mil/lib/roswell.html>, December 10, 2002.

9 Don Berliner and Stanton Friedman, *Crash at Corona* (New York: Paragon House, 1992), in which they claim that the government retrieved two alien spacecraft in and around Roswell, New Mexico.

10 Story, *The Mammoth Encyclopedia of Extraterrestrial Encounters*, in an article by Joe Nickell, p. 387–390.

11 William T. Alnor, *UFOs in the New Age* (Grand Rapids, MI: Baker Book House, 1992), p. 77.

12 "The New Bogus Majestic-12 Documents," <www.csicop.org/si/2000-05/majestic-12.html>, June 1, 2003.

13 Alnor, *UFOs in the New Age*, p. 82–84.

14 "The New Bogus Majestic-12 Documents," <www.csicop.org/si/2000-05/majestic-12.html>, June 1, 2003.

15 Ibid.

16 Ibid.

17 Story, *The Mammoth Encyclopedia of Extraterrestrial Encounters*, in an article by Randall Fitzgerald, p. 181.

18 Ibid., in an article by Arlan K. Andrews, p. 96–98.

19 "Alien Autopsy Film a Hoax Concludes Scientific Organization," <www. csicop.org/articles/roswell_film.html>, December 10, 2002.

20 "Fox Show Says 'Alien Autopsy' Was Hoax [news]," <www. aliensonearth.com/misc/1998/dec/d13-001.shtml>, December 10, 2002.

21 Alnor, *UFOs in the New Age*, p. 82–84.

22 McCarthyism (named after 1950s U.S. senator Joseph McCarthy) was the name given to a movement to purge the United States of communist (Soviet) influence.

23 "TNT's The Secret KGB UFO Files," <www.csicop.org.cmi/reviews/ TNT-KGB.html>, December 10, 2002.

24 Ibid.

25 Ibid.

26 Ibid.

27 Ibid.

28 Ibid.

29 Story, *The Mammoth Encyclopedia of Extraterrestrial Encounters*, p. 102–104.

30 "Welcome to the World of Mysteries of Erich von Däniken," <www. daniken.com>, June 9, 2003.

31 Story, *The Mammoth Encyclopedia of Extraterrestrial Encounters*, in an article by Erich Von Däniken, p. 761–762.

32 Ibid., in an article by Barry H. Downing, p. 578–582.

33 Clifford Wilson, *Crash Go the Chariots* (San Diego, CA: Master Books, 1976), p. 95–96.

34 Story, *The Mammoth Encyclopedia of Extraterrestrial Encounters*, p. 483–484.

35 Ibid.

36 Ibid., in articles by James W. Moseley and Joe Nickell, p. 469–476.

37 "Real Lives," <www.channel4.com/history/microsites/R/real_lives/ daniken_t.html>, June 9, 2003.

38 Ibid.

39 Quoted from von Däniken manuscript on file at the Christian Research Institute, Irving, California, cited in Alnor, *UFOs in the New Age*, p. 204.

40 Alnor, *UFOs in the New Age*, p. 200–201.

41 Story, *The Mammoth Encyclopedia of Extraterrestrial Encounters*, in an article by Zecharia Sitchin, p. 661–663.

42 "Is There a Planet X or 10th Planet?," <starchild.gsfc.nasa.gov/docs/ StarChild/questions/question4.html>, June 11, 2003. Note that in March 2004, NASA announced the discovery of another object in our solar system, which some claim to be a planet. Named "Sedna," it is only 1,413 miles (2,274 km) in diameter, and is obviously not a candidate for Sitchin's ET planet; it was detected at its closet proximity to the sun, a massive three times farther away than Pluto. It has below-freezing temperatures and a highly elliptical orbit (it is presumed to be this close once every 10,000 years).

43 Alnor, *UFOs in the New Age*, p. 200–201.

44 "The Meier Hoax," <www.virtuallystrange.net/ufo/updates/2000/sep/m21-006.shtml>, June 17, 2003.

45 "Billy Meier Hoax," <www.geocities.com/Area51/Corridor/8148/scam.html>, June 16, 2003.

46 Story, *The Mammoth Encyclopedia of Extraterrestrial Encounters*, in an article by Randall Fitzgerald, p. 671.

47 Dennis Stacy, "New Books," *MUFON UFO Journal*, February 1987, p. 11, quoted in Alnor, *UFOs in the New Age*, p. 165–166.

48 Ibid.

49 "Sci Skeptic FAQ UFO's and Flying Saucers," <home.xnet.com/~blatura/_3.html>, December 10, 2003.

50 This concept rings true today, as many seem willing to blame God for difficult circumstances in their lives. Although the Book of Genesis describes God as the Creator of an originally perfect world, the theory of evolution has caused many to view God as a "cruel Creator," apparently because God used the sordid and wasteful mechanism of evolution to create life. So it is thought that He cannot be a God of love (see chapter 10).

51 Story, *The Mammoth Encyclopedia of Extraterrestrial Encounters*, in an article by Jenny Randles, p. 175–178.

52 "Circlemakers," <www.circlemakers.org/mythmen.html>, April 19, 2004.

53 "Circlemakers," <www.circlemakers.org.freddy.html>, June 10, 2003.

54 "Circular Reasoning: The 'Mystery' of Crop Circles and Their 'Orbs' of Light," <www.csicop.org/si/2002-09.crop-cirlces.html>, April 19, 2004.

55 "Disease Brings Poor Crop of Circles," <news.bbc.co.uk/2/hi/sci/tech/1496296.stm>, June 18, 2003.

56 "Circlemakers," <www.circlemakers.org/press.html>, June 10, 2003.

Chapter Seven

Abducted — Close Encounters of the Fourth Kind

ET takes it up a notch

As we have seen, the "evidence" for alien intervention in human affairs has escalated to a new level in recent years. Today, the most controversial aspect of UFOlogy is the claim that people are actually being abducted by aliens. Research polls, such as the Roper poll, suggest that as many as four million American citizens, from all walks of life, claim to have been kidnapped against their will and subjected to medical and examination procedures aboard alien spacecraft, along with bizarre sexual encounters. This phenomenon is occurring all over the world, and if true, it is a far cry from the benign and friendly contacts that have been claimed in previous years. Have the aliens suddenly turned "nasty," or is it that we just don't understand their culture and methodology? Perhaps they don't say "please" on Pleiades! Despite the allegedly (sometimes) horrific treatment of abductees, the overall message of the space brothers has remained the same. They still claim that they are here to help us, prophesying about the future events of the earth and mankind's fate in general. In the next chapter, we shall examine these messages more closely, but before that let's take a background look at this disturbing phenomenon of abductions.

First, it should be remembered that our investigation of UFOs (specifically unidentified flying objects) has revealed that there is no "hard evidence" for ET craft, and that the majority of sightings could be accounted for as man-made or natural phenomena. Within the small percentage of incidents that were unexplainable (in the natural sense), many respected researchers, such as J. Allen Hynek, Jacques Vallée, John Weldon, and John Keel, have noted that UFOs appeared to behave deceptively. Moreover, when people have claimed contact, the messages of the ETs have perpetrated falsehoods, as we shall see. Vallée was convinced that the entities were trying to alter our perceptions of reality — to induce a paradigm shift in our consciousness.

The abduction scenario is a "giant leap" from just having seen some lights in the sky. Most abduction accounts are based on individual testimonies rather than any physical evidence, and reports from abductees suggest that the behavior of the "space brother" abductors is similar in nature to the deceptive behavior of flying objects, albeit more dark and sinister.

One of the earliest claimed abduction cases occurred in October 1957. A Brazilian farmer by the name of Antonio Villas Boas, while driving his tractor, saw a light descending to Earth. As it headed for him, he noticed it was a shiny oval object, and although he tried to escape its path, it landed ahead of him. He claims that he tried to avoid capture, and that several small figures wearing suits and helmets seized him and took him aboard the spacecraft. While on board, he tried to resist further, but they apparently stripped him naked and performed medical-like experimental procedures on him, including the taking of a blood sample. A mixture of fear, cold, and a strange gas that was pumped into the room caused him to vomit. After they smeared him with some sort of aphrodisiac cream or lotion, a naked human-like female entered the room and seduced him. After having sex with Villas Boas, she pointed to her tummy and then the sky. Villas Boas believes he had been used for breeding purposes. When he was removed from the craft, he noticed that over four hours had passed since he was first abducted.

Although this occurred in 1957, it was not well publicized until some years later, mainly due to the sexual nature of his story (not repeated in full here — the source in the footnote has more details). His claims initially gained him much notoriety, but he later withdrew from public life, studied, and became a lawyer.[1] Many UFOlogists doubt that this was a "real" abduction. As bizarre and disturbing as it seems, this was to become a forerunner for millions of similar abductions in the future.

Under the influence

Although the Villas Boas abduction has many similarities to modern cases, it differs markedly in that he had a lucid recollection of events. The majority of modern abductees only recall their experiences after hypnosis — a method that in itself has become controversial.

Most commentators would agree that the first "classic" abduction case involved a mixed-"race" couple, Barney and Betty Hill. In September 1961 the Hills were driving home one night when they observed a bright-colored object which seemed to be following them. Barney stopped to observe the object through binoculars, and was shocked to see faces staring back at him from windows in the craft. Scared, Barney got back into the car and drove off. Soon after, the couple heard beeping sounds emanating from the back of their car. That was the last thing they remembered before they arrived home feeling a bit disoriented after a journey that took nearly two hours longer than expected. The "missing time" is very common among abductees.

Betty started to read books on UFOs and also began to experience disturbing dreams about having gynecological medical procedures performed on her while inside a flying saucer. This included the insertion of a long needle into her navel, which she remembers being told was a pregnancy test. Barney was also having problems. He started suffering from stomach ulcers and genital complaints. Both Barney and Betty now linked their problems to the UFO sighting. Some years later, they visited a hypnotherapist, convinced that

Photo courtesy of Betty Hill (Jeeves Studios)

Betty and Barney Hill

they had been subjected to experiences that they could not consciously remember.

After being individually hypnotized over many hours, the Hills recalled their alleged experiences, both telling fairly similar stories. After hearing the initial "beeps" in their car, Barney remembered that he was telepathically controlled and instructed to drive to a nearby forest area, where aliens led them from the vehicle into their ship. They both described the beings as around five feet tall (152 cm), having the classic dark and large wrap-around slanted eyes, with a small, narrow mouth (although Betty recounted them as having big noses, which Barney did not claim). Medical procedures ensued, including the removal of sperm from Barney. Betty apparently asked one of the beings where he was from, and he produced a star map. Later, under posthypnotic suggestion, she was able to recall details of the map, which, even today, some claim is a valid diagram of a star system surrounding Zeta Reticuli.

At the time, many people offered explanations about the reasons behind their recollection of such incredible events. Their psychiatrist believed that they were subconscious images based on emotional conflicts (due, he thought, to their mixed-"race" marriage), and that these had been brought to the surface through fear resulting from the UFO sighting. The implication was that their ailments were probably purely psychosomatic. Others have claimed that Betty's dreams were the result of her indulgence in UFO books after the original sighting, and that during the time elapsed between the alleged event and their hypnotherapy, she had told Barney about her dreams, accounting for the similarity of his stories when under hypnosis.

Another popular theory arose suggesting that their subconscious memories were merely recounting aspects of the 1953 movie *Invaders from Mars*, as it bore marked similarities to their own experiences. Although a low-budget movie, it was a terrifying tale for its day, which portrayed aliens with large, slit eyes and large noses. These aliens kidnapped humans, being able to pacify them with strange lights. The captives then had implants inserted into the backs of their necks with a long needle — the implants serving as a sort of mind-control device. Given that accounts of abduction experiences were not commonplace yet, this is a strong argument because the movie would no doubt have been featured on television by the time of the Hills' abduction experience. It should also be remembered that such "out of this world" movies were regarded as horrifying for their day, and likely to have a greater impact on the viewer compared to today, when such themes are commonplace. Some also believe that the differences in Barney's story also drew a close parallel with an episode of *The Outer Limits* called "The Bellero Shield," which aired on TV only 12 days before their first hypnosis sessions.[2] The Hills' abduction has served as a stereotype for the myriad of alleged occurrences that were to follow, and their own experiences formed the basis of a TV movie called *The UFO Incident* (1976).

A mirror of cultural beliefs?

As we have already demonstrated, there can be no doubt that science fiction is a major factor in influencing the beliefs of the masses. Most skeptics would attribute the UFO phenomenon as a whole entirely to this influence. Skeptic Robert Todd Carroll writes:

> There have been many reports of abduction and sexual violation by creatures who are small and bald; are white, gray, or green; have big craniums, small chins, large slanted eyes, and pointed or no ears. How does one explain the number of such claims and their similarity? The most reasonable explanation for the accounts being so similar is that they are based on the same movies, the same stories, the same television programs, and the same comic strips.[3]

Yet, the abduction phenomenon is occurring all over the world, including Third World countries. If millions of people have been abducted, as polls supposedly claim, then in medical terms this would be regarded as an epidemic. It is unreasonable to assume that everyone involved is a sci-fi buff. Demographically, people are being abducted across the social, political, economic, ethnic, intellectual, and geographical spectra. It is fair to assume that most people have read or seen some form of science fiction at some point in their lives (remember, it is overwhelmingly the most popular entertainment genre of today). But the fantasy-driven explanation cannot account for every individual's experience.

The skeptic Carroll also noted something very important concerning UFO beliefs:

> The delusions of the ancients and the medievals are not couched in terms of aliens and spacecraft because these are our

century's creations. We can laugh at the idea of gods taking on the form of swans to seduce beautiful women, or of devils impregnating nuns, because they do not fit with our cultural prejudices and delusions. The ancients and medievals probably would have laughed at anyone who would have claimed to have been picked up by aliens from another planet for sex or reproductive surgery. *The only reason anyone takes the abductees seriously today is because their delusions do not blatantly conflict with our cultural beliefs that intergalactic space travel is a real possibility and that it is highly probable that we are not the only inhabited planet in the universe. In other times, no one would have been able to take these claims seriously* [emphasis added].[4]

This quote notes that strange phenomena have been going on, as far as we can determine, for hundreds of years (and, as we shall see, these early phenomena link strongly to many aspects of modern "abductions"). With regard to Jacques Vallée's "multiverse" (interdimensional hypothesis — IDH), both he and other researchers have recounted "abduction" stories of fairies, goblins, elves, and the "Good People" who snatched away children and adults, taking them to fairyland. Vallée also claimed to have studied many religious traditions, folk stories, and even occult texts, and found other similarities, such as missing time, the abductee's perceptions of reality being profoundly altered, and stories of a place where "changelings" (offspring that are half-human, half-goblin, etc.) are born, midwifed by the abductee (the person who has been abducted).[5] Vallée wrote:

> I pointed out in *Invisible College* that the structure of abduction stories was identical to that of occult rituals. I had shown in *Passport to Magonia* that contact with ufonauts was only a modern extension of contact with non-human consciousness in the form of angels, demons, elves, and sylphs. Such contact includes abduction, ordeal (including surgical operations), and sexual intercourse with the aliens. It often leaves marks and scars on the body and the mind, as do UFO abductions.[6]

Some abductees even acquire psychic powers, and as we shall see, these are similar characteristics to those featured in what is now known in UFOlogy as the Classic Abduction Syndrome (CAS).

Carroll's earlier quote alludes to two popular cultural ideas that are integral to abduction accounts. They are that intergalactic space travel is a possibility (highly unlikely, if not impossible, and based on sci-fi beliefs), and the belief that evolution is true and could account for life elsewhere in the universe (another unprovable belief). No one is immune from the influence of their bias or world view when they view the "evidence" for UFOs. The skeptic, who already "knows" that UFOs cannot be real, might say that *all* sightings are potentially explainable in "naturalistic" ways (e.g., cases of mistaken identity by inexperienced observers), and that *all* abductions have a medical or psychological explanation. Similarly, a UFO believer might regard virtually every experience as a real alien encounter because that is what he is looking for and wants to believe. It seems that most people want a "one-size-fits-all" explanation for what is occurring. An open-minded inquirer will realize that the whole UFO phenomenon is a complex issue, involving a variety (and often a mixture) of explanations and factors. Commentator Mark Pilkington highlights the symbiosis between sci-fi and UFO experiences, but also notes a deeper issue:

> . . . UFO lore can be traced back to various visual and thematic elements from science fiction. In my view, however, rather than being reason to dismiss the entire UFO problem as a fantasy generated in human psychology, the relationship demonstrates the overwhelming complexity of such phenomena. At most it shows that what people see in the sky is to some extent governed by the popular cultural motifs of the day, in our case flying saucers and little gray aliens, but it doesn't solve the problem of what is happening in the first place. . . . But it is the CAS which is most visible and media friendly, its proponents attempting to standardise the abduction experience by pushing [them] aside as "screen memories." . . . Reports from countries other than America, and to a lesser though increasing extent Britain, feature an amazing variety of colourful creatures, often rooted in the cultural history of the area. But America's cultural dominance of the world is fast spreading into the realms of UFO experience and the "grays" [classic "gray"-looking aliens] have started to proliferate elsewhere.

There is no doubt in my mind, however, that something extremely strange is happening to these people; the narrowing down and categorising of their experiences is just a human way of dealing with what we do not understand, and it is here that the influences of popular culture are felt most strongly.[7]

The alien abduction phenomenon itself is fast becoming a modern cultural icon. Famous UFO debunker Philip Klass has noticed a trend:

> When I first entered the UFO field in the mid-'60s, even the pro-UFO organizations like NICAP exercised appropriate caution when evaluating claims from "repeaters," and especially from "abductees." Now, no tale is too wild to be embraced by a large segment of the UFO community. How very sad.[8]

Even famous popularizers of modern science, like Carl Sagan, have devoted a large percentage of their time and writings to dismissing the notion of alien abductions. For such well-known and prolific authors to spend so much of their time on this subject, the phenomenon must have taken deep root in our modern culture.[9]

Fire in the Sky — The Travis Walton abduction

The alleged abduction of a young woodcutter in 1975 has become the most high-profile abduction case in history. The abduction of Travis Walton was originally recounted in a *National Enquirer* report, but has since grown to include three books, a major movie, and countless articles. It has been a "nice little earner" for Travis Walton, despite his claims to the contrary. It is also one of the most controversial abduction accounts, as opinions about its authenticity still divide much of the UFO community.

It is claimed that as seven young woodcutters were returning from a day's work of forest clearing, they saw a flying saucer hovering nearby. Walton alighted from their vehicle, stood underneath the UFO, and then was apparently knocked backward by a ray or a beam of light which emanated from the craft. Terrified, team leader Mike Rogers (Walton's brother-in-law) and his workers fled the scene. They returned later but found Walton missing. Strangely, they did not report the event to the local sheriff until two hours later.

While Walton was missing, Rogers and his men were forced to undergo a polygraph (lie detector) test, which five of them passed.

Then five days later, after a phone call from Walton, his sister and older brother traveled over 30 miles to find him in a disturbed state, lying in a phone booth.

Walton claimed that he had been abducted by aliens, taken aboard their craft, and subjected to a variety of medical-type examinations. Three months later, Walton and his brother were asked to also take polygraph tests and, judging from the surrounding publicity, they passed. In short, it was cited as a classic abduction case and not a hoax for the following reasons:

1. Walton passed his lie detector test.

2. Out of the six other witnesses, five passed similar tests.

3. Walton was of good character with no motivation to concoct a story.

4. Walton and his family had no prior interest in UFOs, and therefore were unlikely to be hoaxers.

5. The other witnesses had no reason to lie or participate in a hoax.

APRO (Aerial Phenomena Research Organization) was one pro-UFO organization that thought it to be a genuine case. However, NICAP (National Investigations Committee on Aerial Phenomena) concluded that it was a hoax. A deeper look uncovered plenty of damning evidence to refute each of the above reasons:

1. Arch debunker Philip Klass discovered that Walton had already failed a polygraph test some months earlier, which was paid for by the *National Inquirer* (NI), which was then complicit, along with APRO, in covering up the results. An inexperienced examiner conducted the second test, which Walton passed. Apparently, Walton was allowed to provide the questions himself. It looks like the NI needed a good front-page UFO story.

2. It has been alleged that the other tests performed on the so-called corroborating witnesses involved questions to determine only if there had been foul play, and not to substantiate the UFO story. Remember, they were being treated as suspects in Walton's disappearance. No one gave

credibility to the UFO story until Walton returned. The tests only asked if a crime had been committed.

3. Walton had a criminal record relating to burglary and forgery offences he committed with Charles Rogers (Mike's brother). As for motivation, the NI was offering a cash reward for any proof of UFOs (see 5 below). Walton also received remuneration from the NI for his story.

4. Investigators discovered that Walton was a "UFO freak." Both he and his family had claimed many sightings in the past. It is said that when authorities notified the family about Travis's abduction, they were not overly perturbed, suggesting that the aliens would return him because they were always friendly.

5. Motivation for the crew was not a problem either. Mike Rogers had under-quoted on a forest-thinning contract. It was taking longer than expected to do the work, and winter was setting in. After asking for an extension, he would have been financially penalized for falling behind. After they failed to complete the work in the set time, 10 percent of the contract price was withheld. The UFO claim gave Rogers and the crew a valid reason to claim the withheld funds, as his "scared" crew refused to return to the site to finish the work.[10]

In addition, Walton did not seem to suffer from the post-abduction preoccupation with UFOs that seems to befall many others. He showed little interest in further investigation. You would presume that most people in such a position would want to get to the bottom of their experience.

A urine test for uric acid levels determined that he must have eaten during the five absent days he claimed to be on board the alien craft.[11] His urine also showed no trace of acetone. After going without food for more than a couple of days, the body begins to break down its own fat. The waste product of this is acetone, which is excreted in the urine. Yet Walton claimed he did not eat, and lost 10 pounds during his ordeal.[12] Also, there was no evidence of marks or burns on his chest where, it was claimed, a beam of light hit him with such force that it knocked him over.

Mike Rogers has since sold artwork based on Walton's description of his "abduction," and Walton now earns a living as a guest speaker at UFO conferences all over the world, even though he says he is unhappy with the attention that was focused on him after the abduction. Once again, one of the great shaping events of modern UFO lore is not what it seems.

The Classic Abduction Syndrome (CAS)

Abductions are becoming commonplace. It seems that the more experiences are recounted and retold, the more stories of abductions appear bearing similar characteristics.

The CAS is so named because of features common to abduction cases. UFO folklorist Thomas Bullard lists eight common categories of experiences, noting that not all will apply in every case. The headings are Bullard's,[13] but the details include my own observations and comments.

1. **Capture**

The experience usually occurs at night when an individual (or sometimes a group) is driving a car, sitting at home, or sleeping in bed, when a light(s) or a UFO appears nearby. This is often the abductee's last conscious recollection. Subsequent details are often recalled under hypnosis, although some have been triggered by an event, such as an image on TV, a conversation, or *déjà vu*–type experiences. Some abductees do claim abductions during the daylight hours. (For example, one lady named Joyce says that her abductions started at age five, and that she was levitated out of a classroom while in the presence of other people. When she returned, she was woken from what the teacher thought was a bout of daydreaming. The abductee experienced a huge amount of missing time, and no one else in the classroom witnessed her "abduction.")

Usually, the abductee (often called an "experiencer") remembers feeling a sense of stillness over the physical world, and a feeling of paralysis, which overtakes their bodies. Most are gripped by fear and are unable to resist as they are levitated out and upward in a beam of light (commonly blue) to a waiting ship. Sometimes they are accompanied by alleged alien beings of varying descriptions, but most commonly, the grays.

Interestingly, the grays appear to be the most common type in American cases, with "Nordics" (tall, blond, European-looking beings) predominating in England and Europe, and bigfoot or monster types in South America.[14]

Many have claimed that they were transported through solid objects, such as a wall, roof, or car. Shortly after being beamed up, there may be periods of lost consciousness, with the experiencer waking up on board the ship.

These accounts are similar to those of people who engage in occult activities such as astral traveling, or other "out of body experiences" (OBEs). Beaming toward a light source is also similar to the accounts of people who claim near-death experiences (NDEs). Some who say they've had an NDE have claimed seeing alien-like creatures on "the other side," and also report seeing dead relatives in the presence of aliens.[15] This large body of anecdotal evidence is not to be ignored, and it once again points to the psychic/spiritual nature of UFOs. Researchers have already shown that many UFOs can change shape (or morph), and as we shall see, the aliens themselves appear in a variety of guises.

2. **Examination**

Once on board, the captives are usually undressed, and made to lie on an examination table of some sort. Often their eyes or bodies are scanned, or an "alien" captor peers directly into their eyes. Experienced abduction researcher David Jacobs claims that this is to create sexual stimulation via the "optic nerve," i.e., creating images in the abductee's mind in preparation for alleged sexual medical procedures.

Using what are often described as "primitive" devices (compared to what one might expect for a supposedly advanced race), every imaginable body orifice is probed. Jacobs believes that these thorough examinations are not the real reason for abduction, but are meant to

David Jacobs

give the abductee (or possibly us) the impression that the whole episode is some sort of study or scientific experiment.[16]

Eggs and sperm are routinely removed from victims, and sometimes the captives are forced to have sex with each other. On occasion they are also forced to have sex with their alien captors, heterosexually, homosexually, and even with "hybrids" (who are supposedly the offspring of previous interrelations between aliens and humans). Jacobs claims that the abductors have no particular interest in sex, but that it is part of the process of sperm collection or egg fertilization for breeding purposes.

Sometimes women are impregnated artificially, and told via telepathic means that they are pregnant. Jacobs and others claim that experiencers have subsequently had pregnancy tests to confirm this event. Apparently, when this type of implantation occurs, it is common for another abduction event to take place for the purpose of removing the fetus. One can only imagine the deep emotional scarring that occurs with experiencers who genuinely feel that they have undergone these events.

Sometimes, blood, skin, and hair samples are taken, and implants (commonly known as alien implants) are inserted into victims. Some abductees have subsequently had objects surgically extracted, but upon examination it appears that they are simply of biological origin, and not some form of advanced technology (although it is claimed that some resemble a ceramic-like substance). Photos abound of alleged implants, as do "scoop" marks in the abductee's skin, as well as bruising and scratches. Skeptics refute these claims, stating that there is no proof they have been caused by ETs and that the more reasonable explanation is that the experiencer merely forgot how the marks originally got there.

3. **Conference**

At this stage, the abductors conduct school lessons for their captives. Once again, using telepathic methods, they sometimes communicate the reasons for their activities, or tell the abductee that they have been specifically chosen for a mission. The beings often tell of future events, not only concerning individuals but also events on a global scale. Sometimes these prophetic events are portrayed on large screens or as some type of holographic image. Although he is not a Christian, Bullard relates the UFO messages using biblical language:

> The beings often warn of a time of tribulation ahead and prophesy disasters to come, and may school the witness for an obscure mission to be performed "when the time is right."[17]

These prophecies often bear a close resemblance to events forecast in the Bible. UFO literature is riddled with biblical references, as we have indicated earlier in this book. Many of the ETs' messages have *paralleled* biblical events, stories, and prophecies. At the same time, the biblical texts are often misquoted and misrepresented. Members of the pro-UFO lobby, such as von Däniken and Sitchin, have twisted the Bible to read into it what they want to believe. This is deceitful. The original Bible authors — intelligent people in their own right — should be fairly represented and their writings portrayed accurately — not with the biased view that they must have been primitive and ignorant because they lived long ago.

As to the unreliability of the ETs' predictions, one of the world's leading experts on the psychosocial aspect of the UFO phenomenon, Martin Kottmeyer, says:

> Over two hundred predictions premised in the extraterrestrial hypothesis by encounter claimants and UFOlogists have been offered over the past half-century and they have uniformly failed. Further belief in it is not recommended.[18]

4. **Tour**

On rare occasions, the abductee is given a tour of the ship, including the bridge. If a "tour" occurs, the most common experience is to be shown the "incubatorium." This is a special room where they will see numerous containers of liquid that contain fetuses of "hybrids." The abductee is told that one or more of the fetuses belong to them.

Sometimes women are shown rooms containing hybrid babies or children. They are often forced to hold or make contact with individual babies, and are told that they are their own children, who need their mother's contact. Many recount memories of breastfeeding them, even though they are not actually pregnant or lactating at the time.

Occasionally, experiencers say they meet older children or adult hybrids in these rooms.

5. **Otherworldly Journey**

In a small number of cases, it is reported that the beings fly the witnesses to another environment, but not necessarily another planet. It may be an underground or undersea location with no sunlight, yet displaying a uniformly lit sky. When taken to another planet, it is often dark, desolate, and showing signs of ruin or destruction.[19]

6. **Theophany**

Witnesses may claim to have met a divine being, or had a religious experience while on board the spacecraft. Some have said they have heard the voice of God, or have participated in some seemingly religious ritual. The aliens have sometimes disguised themselves as Jesus, the pope, well-known celebrities, and even the dead spouses of the abductees. On occasions, this was done in order to gain the cooperation of the abductee, even for the purpose of having sexual intercourse with them.[20]

7. **Return**

The victim is returned to their home, car, bed, or wherever, to resume normal everyday activities. They are often told to forget their experiences (which they do until later).

8. **Aftermath**

Although initially the abductee may have no conscious recollection of events, they may suffer from significant aftereffects for weeks, and even years to come. Physical effects include nausea and pain or lesions in various parts of the body, particularly in the region of the genitalia.

The most telling effects occur on the experiencer's personality and outlook on life or world view. It has been noticed by the majority of researchers that the person undergoes a type of religious transformation. They have also suggested that instigating a belief change in the abductee could be the reason for the whole enterprise.

Surveys have overwhelmingly shown that the majority of
abductees subsequently develop an interest, and openly participate,
in New Age/occultic or Eastern-type mystical religions.[21]

Some also claim to be able to regularly astral travel after their experience. It is also interesting to note that many describe their astral
traveling experiences as being "real." That is, they testify to the sensation of movement — up and down, side to side, as they move along.
One lady described this travel, as well as her abduction experience, as
"more real than reality."

Abductees also report developing psychic powers, such as ESP or
a form of precognition. However, an even more common effect is that
the abductees start to witness a range of seeming paranormal experiences including poltergeists.

It seems ironic that in an age where traditional religious values and
beliefs are being discarded as unscientific, mainly due to the materialistic ("matter-is-all-there-is") interpretations of modern science, many are
willing to accept the bizarre (even hostile) and illogical demonstrations
and messages of the so-called alien visitors. Although many pro-UFO
researchers would justify the aliens' bad behavior as being simply mat-
ter-of-fact and business-like, it makes little sense, especially since their
messages are often ones of salvation, claiming the high moral ground
and condemning poor human behavior. If they are so technologically
advanced and have been visiting the earth for hundreds, or even thousands, of years, why are they not friendlier or more reasonable in their
behavior toward us? Surely they would understand our human nature
and sensibilities, and seek our cooperation. And if they are genuinely
concerned about our environment, why do they not use their technology to help us?

Listed above were the common characteristics of alien abductions that you would find in many standard UFO books and articles.
Now look at some of the facts the pro-UFO lobby does not widely
publicize.

What the experts *don't* tell us

Pro-UFO writer Bullard, who developed the aforementioned categories, adds:

Though polite, the outward courtesy of the beings hides
an innate coldness. They show little concern or understanding

for human feelings and care only for accomplishing their mission.[22]

Former abductee-turned-researcher, the late Dr. Karla Turner, also derived some disturbing conclusions based upon her own experiences, and her research of other victims. Some of her observations follow:

- Aliens can alter our perceptions of our surroundings.

- Aliens can control what we think we see. They can appear to us [in] any number of guises and shapes.

- Aliens can be present with us in an invisible state and can make themselves only partially visible.

- Abductees receive marks on their bodies other than the well-known scoops and straight-line scars. These other marks include single punctures, multiple punctures, large bruises, three and four fingered claw marks, and triangles of every possible sort.

- Female abductees often suffer serious gynecological problems after their alien encounters, and sometimes these problems lead to cysts, tumors, cancer of the breast and uterus, and to hysterectomies.

- A surprising number of abductees suffer from serious illnesses they didn't have before their encounters. These have led to surgery, debilitation, and even death from causes the doctors can't identify.

- Abductees often encounter more than one sort of alien during an experience, not just the grays. Every possible combination of gray, reptoid, insectoid, blond, and widow's peak have been seen during single abductions, aboard the same craft or in the same facility.

- Abductees report being scoffed at, jeered at, and threatened by their alien captors. . . . Unknown fluids are injected into some abductees.

- Abductees — "virgin" cases — report being taken to underground facilities where they see grotesque hybrid creatures, nurseries of hybrid humanoid fetuses, and vats of colored liquid filled with parts of human bodies.

- Abductees report seeing other humans in these facilities being drained of blood, being mutilated, flayed, and dismembered, and stacked, lifeless, like cords of wood. Some abductees have been threatened that they, too, will end up in this condition if they don't cooperate with their alien captors.

- Aliens come into homes and temporarily remove young children, leaving their distraught parents paralyzed and helpless. In cases where a parent has been able to protest, the aliens insist that "The children belong to us."

- Aliens perform extremely painful experiments or procedures on abductees, saying that these acts are necessary, but give no explanation why. . . . Painful genital and anal probes are performed, on children as well as adults.

- Aliens make predictions of an imminent period of global chaos and destruction. They say that a certain number of humans . . . will be "rescued" from the planet in order to continue the species, either on another planet or back on Earth after the destruction is over. Many abductees report they don't believe their alien captors and foresee instead a much more sinister use of the "rescued" humans.[23]

Turner also made the following comment:

> In every instance from this list, there are multiple reports from unrelated cases, confirming that such bizarre details are not the product of a single deranged mind. These details are convincing evidence that, contrary to the claims of many UFO researchers, the abduction experience isn't limited to uniform pattern [sic] of events. This phenomenon simply can't be explained in terms of crossbreeding experiments or scientific research into the human physiology. . . . Before we allow ourselves to believe in the benevolence of the alien interaction, we should ask, do enlightened beings need to use the cover of night to perform good deeds? Do they need to paralyze us and render us helpless to resist? Do angels need to steal our fetuses? Do they need to manipulate our children's genitals and probe our rectums? Are fear, pain, and deception consistent with high spiritual motives?[24]

Vallée was right. These beings do act deceptively. They also act dishonestly. One would have good reason to be suspicious of their motives, despite their yarns about being here to help us. These beings say one thing and do another. They talk about doing good but they actually behave abominably. People are scarred, physically and emotionally, for the rest of their lives by such experiences. This is hardly something people would wish upon themselves — or is it? Strangely, some repeat abductees eventually start to welcome their experiences. This is markedly reminiscent of "Stockholm Syndrome," a phenomenon that occurs when hostages, such as in a kidnapping or terrorist plot, start to sympathize, and even cooperate, with their captors. One example is the experience of the famous horror fiction writer Whitley Strieber (see box).

Communion [1987] — Whitley Strieber

Whitley Strieber is undoubtedly the world's most famous abductee. As a writer of horror stories (*The Wolfen,* 1978; *The Hunger,* 1981), his "alien" experiences in December 1985 enabled him to effectively communicate the alien abduction experience to a UFO-hungry society. Both of the aforementioned horror novels were subsequently made into motion pictures, so it is hardly surprising that his publisher, knowing the potential of the UFO subject matter, paid an enormous one-million-dollar advance for his abduction tale, called *Communion.*

In graphic detail, he described his childhood abduction experiences, mind control, alien implants, and rectal probes. It was a sensation, eventually selling ten million copies, and was also made into a very scary movie of the same name, starring Christopher Walken. In *Communion,* Strieber wrote:

> Tiny people were now moving around me at great speed. . . . I had the thought I was being taken away, and remembered my family. It was a truly awful sensation, accompanied as it was by the same sense that I was absolutely helpless in the hands of these strange beings.[25]

Strieber's experiences were recalled under hypnosis. Over the years, his visitations continued. By the time of his second book, *Transformation* (1988), he was indeed undergoing a transformation of sorts. Although initially horrified by his experiences, he now started to welcome them, almost as a religious experience, and this started to put him at odds with the pro-ETH UFO community. He claims that these beings ultimately helped him develop further occult talents, such as OBEs and astral traveling. He also started to link his visitor experiences with other religious ideas, claiming them to be the gods, fairies, ghosts, and UFO sightings of history, as well as the miraculous events of the Bible. This in turn led him deeper into the occult, attending witchcraft ceremonies and the like.

However, Strieber was already a "supernatural" believer long before his "visitor" experiences (as he called them). He was a New Age devotee. He had been a long-time follower of an occultic mystic called Gurdjieff, whose practices included Zen, tarot, and shamanism, among others. He was even reported as saying:

> I am a student of the great thirteenth-century mystic, Meister Eckart. I have been a witch. I have experimented with worshipping the earth as a goddess/mother.[26]

Yet again we see a demonstrable link between occultic New Age beliefs and UFO/alien experiences. Although it is likely that Strieber didn't initially link his New Age practices with his UFO experiences, he eventually realized the significance himself. He was quoted as saying, "I made choices a long time ago that brought me this experience."[27]

His books have made an enormous impact on UFOlogy, and have thrust the UFO/alien experience deep into the public consciousness. UFO researcher Bill Alnor believes that Strieber, more than anyone else, is responsible for promoting UFOlogy into the mainstream of the New Age movement.

Why do so many researchers seem blind to the obvious ill treatment of humans? For many, the answer can be found in the belief that "the end justifies the means." In other words, they believe the whole UFO phenomenon to be true and of vital importance. It must therefore be revealed, no matter the cost. The study of UFOs also has an addictive quality about it. It involves the mystical, containing fantastic stories, conspiracies, and intrigue. This feeds on itself — and carries other risks. Experienced UFO investigator John Keel explained that it causes a "suspension of disbelief." He said:

> I'm seeing more and more excellent UFO investigators going off the deep end. . . . They take in any strange theory, because they've been desensitized by all the strangeness for so long.[28]

The "wackiness" of it all may account for why so many have lost their objectivity. And as we have already seen, many deliberate frauds and hoaxes have been orchestrated in an effort to force the authorities to "tell the truth." This only adds to the strangeness of it all. If the aliens want to change our world view, it would appear that we are already making it very easy for them.

Why is it so important for them to change our traditional spiritual beliefs? One cannot deny the consistency of the ET messages from across a huge and varied "landscape." It is no secret that the space brothers have been threatening a global catastrophe — via our own carelessness or imposed by them — unless we change our ways. In some cases, they claim to have created humankind and therefore they have the right to do with us as they want. The way of salvation, it appears, is by following these new religious leaders into the New Age. And if the inhabitants of the earth do not change, then the select few who believe will be spared and saved. In the next chapter we shall look closely at the religious messages of the ETs.

The "big guns" of abduction research

The abduction phenomenon has been studied intently, and there are now researchers who have devoted their careers to this topic. Despite this, I think even the experts would agree that nobody really has a "handle on it." Possibly the three highest-profile players in this area are Budd Hopkins, Dr. David Jacobs, and Dr. John Mack.

Budd Hopkins may be regarded as the pioneer in this field. He uses the method of hypnosis to garner reports, and was one of the first to report that abductees suffered from physical markings, lesions, and so on. He also noticed patterns of repeated abductions of the same individuals, and generational abductions; that is, occurrences among several members within a family group, including successive generations. He is a strong advocate of the idea that aliens are visiting the earth and conducting breeding experiments with humans, thereby producing the hybrids. His three books, *Missing Time* (1981), *Intruders* (1987), and *Witnessed* (1996), have all been best sellers, and *Intruders* was made into a CBS miniseries. It remains one of the most influential books about abduction research ever written.[29]

Hopkins introduced David Jacobs to this field. He holds similar beliefs but is not so enamored by the ET abductors. Currently, he is the associate professor of history at Temple University, Philadelphia, and has amassed nearly 40 years of research on UFOs. His doctorate came as a result of a dissertation about UFOs, and it was only the second time that a degree has been granted on the basis of a UFO-related theme. He says that initially he was excited at the thought of extraterrestrial contact but says that his years of research have led to a better understanding of the ETs' motivation. He describes it as:

> . . . a clandestine programme of physiological exploitation by one species of another for an alien agenda. I dislike what the phenomenon does to the lives of individual abductees, and I like even less the changes that the abductors intend for the society in which the abductees live.
>
> I fully understand the fringe position that I occupy within the UFO research community, but I have, unfortunately, not found an alternative theory to account for the data.
>
> . . . I confront the subject with dread. Studying its motivations results in my anxiety. I find myself in the position of having spent my entire adult life studying a phenomenon that I have come to abhor. I desperately wish I could say otherwise.[30]

Jacobs should be congratulated for his honest and candid assessment. His conclusions have put him at odds with many of his peers. One gets the impression that he would be happy to find the truth and a genuine solution to the abduction scenario. He has founded the International Center for Abduction Research (ICAR) and has written two books, *Secret Life* (1992) and *The Threat* (1998).

John Mack was a professor of psychiatry at prestigious Harvard University, and founded the Program for Extraordinary Experience Research (PEER). Mack claimed he was initially a skeptic and that he initially did everything he could to look for other root psychological causes, such as childhood abuse.[31]

In 1990, he met veteran abduction researcher Budd Hopkins and began working with experiencers, or abductees — over 100 of them were interviewed by Mack over the next few years. After what he described as a thorough psychoanalysis of these people, Mack concluded that they were solid citizens and of sound mind. He became convinced that something important was going on. It should be noted that Mack was already a Pulitzer Prize winner for his biography on T.E. Lawrence. However, like Hopkins, Mack became a true believer, and his fame grew with the publication of his best-selling 1994 book *Abduction: Human Encounters with Aliens*, for which he received a $200,000 advance.

It is said that this was not the first time Mack had flirted with the fringe of psychiatry. Douglas Jacobs, an assistant professor of psychiatry at Harvard, who has known and admired Mack professionally since 1975, commented:

> His whole career has been about blazing trails. . . . There are people who think he's an embarrassment to Harvard, that he's gone off the deep end. . . . Many of my colleagues have rejected John Mack's research outright.[32]

Mack built up a thriving business around his abduction research. He published further books, and received considerable financial advances for his publications. This, say some, caused him to lose his objectivity, and many skeptics have cast doubt on his methods of gathering evidence, particularly his hypnosis sessions (discussed later).

Like the UFO phenomena, abduction theories lack a "smoking gun"; that is, physical evidence to substantiate the claims of abductees. Hardened skeptic Philip Klass comments:

> If you assume that we do have extraterrestrial visitors who are engaging in crossbreeding and that they are very advanced, why don't they abduct Olympic athletes? . . . And why is it that not one person who claims to have been aboard a flying saucer has ever brought back a paper clip or cigarette lighter or some other souvenir?[33]

Mack would have loved to have physical evidence. What abduction researcher wouldn't? But he defended his research by saying:

> If someone did bring back an artifact, though, the debunkers would just argue over its pedigree. . . . I'm not trying to prove this with physical evidence. I take the whole package. These abduction accounts are so congruent among healthy

people, from all over the United States — people who are not in touch with each other, who have nothing to gain and every-thing to lose by telling their stories.[34]

Mack's observations are very valid. Years of research led him to a conclusion similar to that of other researchers, namely that the aliens are interdimensional, from another reality or spiritual realm. However, despite their being from a spiritual (a presumably non-physical) realm, Mack agreed that there was a real breeding program being conducted by these entities:

> Now, the effect of that is . . . in a number of abduct-ees — not just people I see, but the ones Budd Hopkins and other people see — is to produce some kind of new species to bring us together to produce a hybrid species which — the abductees are sometimes told — will populate the earth or will be there to carry evolution forward, after the human race has completed what it is now doing, namely the destruction of the earth as a living system. So it's a kind of later form. It's an awkward coming together of a less embodied species than we are, and us, for this evolutionary purpose.[35]

Once again, we can see the reference to evolution — that these beings have masterminded, or have been overseeing, human evolution. But what exactly is a "less embodied species?"

Are they spirit beings?

John Mack provides further insight into the form of these beings.

> It's both literally, physically happening to a degree; and it's also some kind of psychological, spiritual experience oc-curring and originating perhaps in another dimension. And so the phenomenon stretches us, or it asks us to stretch to open to realities that are not simply the literal physical world, but to extend to the possibility that there are other unseen realities from which our consciousness, our, if you will, learn-ing processes over the past several hundred years have closed us off.[36]

What Mack is saying is that they are both spiritual and physical be-ings, and that our scientific age has closed its mind to the possibilities of these other existences. One is mystified as to how something can be ethereal, spiritual, or ghost-like — whatever it is — and physical (or potentially manifesting as physical) at the same time. Yet this is what the experts are suggesting. Although this sounds unbelievable, it may give us a clue as to the origin and nature of these beings (remember that they can appear and disappear, pass through walls, and so on).

Interestingly, the Bible has already recorded experiences similar to those that Mack describes (see chapter 9). One such occasion involved the founder of Christianity, Jesus Christ. After His reported resurrection from the dead, many witnesses saw Him, as He walked, talked, and even ate with them. The apostle Thomas doubted Christ's resurrection, but soon became convinced. In John 20:25–28, the Bible records the event:

> So the other disciples told him, "We have seen the Lord!" But he [Thomas] said to them, "Unless I see the nail marks in his hands and put my finger where the nails were, and put my hand into his side, I will not believe it." A week later his disciples were in the house again, and Thomas was with them. Though the doors were locked, Jesus came and stood among them and said, "Peace be with you!" Then he said to Thomas, "Put your finger here; see my hands. Reach out your hand and put it into my side. Stop doubting and believe." Thomas said to him, "My Lord and my God!"

Thomas was able to feel him, and yet Jesus could appear and disappear at will. The apostle Paul also recorded that after His resurrection, Jesus appeared to over 500 other people (1 Cor. 15:5–8), not just a select few who could have conspired to make up such a story. The account of the resurrected Christ is one of the most well-documented and witnessed events in history. Yet, scientifically, dead men do not rise from the grave. Jesus appeared in a form that seemed to be physical, yet it had ethereal qualities, according to the biblical testimonies. His body had been transformed in preparation to go to another place. Notably, Jesus himself said that He came from elsewhere:

> . . . I am from above. You are of this world; I am not of this world (John 8:23).

And,

My kingdom is not of this world. . . . But now my kingdom is from another place (John 18:36).

If we are to take the Bible at face value, it suggests that Jesus was, and is, a visitor from another dimension — and one who may give us some insight into this phenomenon, this other dimension or reality, as Mack calls it. Moreover, it may lead us to discover the origin of the alien beings who are supposedly abducting people. In fact, the Bible frequently talks about other beings, such as angels, who reflect the same bodily characteristics that Mack describes.

Many in the pro-UFO lobby regard Jesus as an extraterrestrial visitor who was on the same "spiritual" mission as the current ET visitors. Cultists — such as Billy Meier and Rael, who claim to have met Jesus in His flying saucer — say they believe this. Many of these same UFO cultists also believe the Bible's claim that Jesus will return to the earth again. Christians call this event the Second Coming or Second Advent.

However, the Bible clearly indicates that Jesus did not need a flying saucer to travel, nor did He even pretend to have one. It tells of His ascension to heaven in Acts 1:9–11.

He was taken up before their very eyes, and a cloud hid him from their sight. They were looking intently up into the sky as he was going, when suddenly two men dressed in white stood beside them. "Men of Galilee," they said, "why do you stand here looking into the sky? This same Jesus, who has been taken from you into heaven, will come back in the same way you have seen him go into heaven."

The Bible says that one of the ways that the world will recognize the real Jesus Christ is that His return will be in the same manner in which He left (note, there is no description of a craft of any kind — in the description of such an important event, surely a craft would have been mentioned). In addition, He will still bear the scars of his crucifixion as a further demonstration of His true identity.

In the aforementioned passage, the two people who appeared in white were angels. These are likewise beings that the Bible records as being able to manifest in and out of our reality. Note also that when manifesting in human form, they were recognized as men. This is a consistent feature of the angels that the God of the Bible sent on missions, and they were recorded as male in appearance throughout the thousands of years of history in the Old and New Testaments. We shall look at this in greater detail in chapter 8.

Non-supernatural explanations

The concept that aliens are traveling millions of light-years to stealthily abduct human beings has little appeal for most thoughtful persons, regardless of their background. But the idea that spirit beings are appearing from another dimension is totally abhorrent to atheistic, materialist skeptics. Quite simply, it doesn't fit within their world view, which says that such things must have a naturalistic explanation.

Probably their most common view is that alien abductions are the psychological manifestations of the human mind, and that researchers like Hopkins, Jacobs, and Mack were complicit in perpetuating the delusions.

One of those views is called the "The Psycho-Social Theory;" that is, the aliens originate in the *psychology* of the individual and take their shape from social factors.[37] Debunker and psychologist Dr. Robert A. Baker says:

> Raised on a steady diet of *Star Wars, Star Trek*, and *The X-Files*, and aided by wishful thinking, pseudo-science and pop-psychology, the average citizen was ready to be persuaded that the truth was, indeed, "out there" and that an evil and conspiratorial government was denying him and her their "right to know."[38]

Some researchers tried to prove that abductees were typically "fantasy prone" or even "encounter prone," suggesting that UFO events were likely to be experienced by some people more than others. The idea is that a certain percentage of the population is unable to separate inner fantasies from reality. Scientific testing has been unable to establish either of these theories, and they are not widely regarded today. Some have even suggested that the abduction experience resembles "birth trauma" and that the experiencer is subconsciously revisiting it. Research is also being done to understand the effect of magnetic fields on the temporal lobes of the brain, with the claim that it produces feelings and images similar to abduction experiences. One wonders, though, where the magnetic fields might come from when lying in bed at night.

It appears that skeptics have a multitude of psychological explanations, but one of the more popular ones is the idea of "sleep paralysis." Dr. David J. Hufford defines this as:

> . . . a period of inability to perform voluntary movements, either when falling asleep or when awakening, accompanied by conscious awareness. This condition has been ascribed both to hypnagogic [in the process of falling asleep] and hypnopompic [waking up] states.[39]

It is claimed that while in either of these states, hallucinatory images can be formed in one's mind, which can be recalled later. Hufford claims that as many as 15 percent of the general population could have experienced this paralysis, and it has been estimated by some that as many as 50 percent of abduction cases could be explained by this phenomenon. One of the strongest evidences for the sleep paralysis explanation is that most abductions occur at night and while people are in bed.[40] The similarity of descriptions, such as the presence of others in the room, or feeling as if one is floating out of the room, suggests that sleep paralysis may well explain many episodes of abductions. But the sleep paralysis theory fails to account for the in-depth, fine details of the interaction between humans and these strange beings in many instances. In short, how could a barrister in Birmingham have exactly the same experiences and receive the same messages as a bus driver in Bombay?

There is no question that pro-abduction researchers are keen to foster the idea of alien abductions and, as we have said, pursue this view to the exclusion of all other explanations. They might claim that polls suggest that 3 or even 4 percent of the general population have been abducted, and that this many people can't be delusional. One such poll that fosters this idea is the oft-quoted "Roper poll." Based on this poll, a report by abduction researchers Hopkins, Jacobs, and Westrum (1992) concluded that aliens had abducted almost four million Americans.

The Roper organization allows for other questions to be tacked onto the end of its own regular polls. A representative sample of almost 6,000 were surveyed. Respondents were not directly asked if they had ever been abducted by aliens; instead, they were given a series of indicator questions about whether they had ever undergone the following experiences:

- Waking up paralyzed with a sense of a strange person or presence or something else in the room.

- Experiencing a period of time of an hour or more, in which you were apparently lost, but you could not remember why, or where you had been.

- Seeing unusual lights or balls of light in a room without knowing what was causing them, or where they came from.

- Finding puzzling scars on your body but neither you nor anyone else remembering how you received them or where you got them.

- Feeling that you were actually flying through the air, although you didn't know why or how.[41]

A "yes" answer to four out of the five questions was taken as evidence of alien abduction. The 62-page report, with its introduction by John Mack, was vigorously defended by Hopkins and Jacobs on the basis that they were experienced researchers who had worked with nearly 500 abductees. It is true that they were already "true believers" — and skeptics would claim that they were looking for concurring evidence. Amazingly, this evidence was interpreted to conclude that up to 4 million Americans and 185 million earthlings have been abducted by aliens. The findings were mailed to over 100,000 psychiatrists, psychologists, and mental health professionals in the United States. Such conclusions would surely create an impact on the medical profession.

Hypnosis and repressed memories

Not so long ago, court judges recognized that memories of child abuse, if unlocked from a victim's mind through the method of "regressive hypnosis," must have constituted a real event in that person's life. In short, it was evidence. This evidence was admissible until the courts rejected it for reasons explained below. Many innocent people have been sent to jail on the basis of events that never actually happened.

One of the problems with this method is the chance that the therapist, or the person conducting the hypnosis session, can inadvertently (or intentionally) plant suggestions into the patient's mind. In turn, it is claimed, these can become false memories that hypnosis brings to the fore. Many of today's health professionals also claim that hypnosis unlocks a person's imagination (not just the memory), and when imaginative events come to the surface, they can be mistakenly interpreted as memories.

UFO researchers such as Hopkins and Mack have commonly used the method of memory regression when interviewing experiencers. They have been seen conducting such sessions on television for documentary purposes, and on the surface everything seems innocuous and straightforward. Their critics claim, however, that they are always looking for evidence of abductions, as shown by their biased Roper poll conclusions. So how can they be objective or impartial when questioning patients in a hypnotic state?

At a 1994 skeptics' conference, John Mack defended his methods, saying that he had considered all other possibilities, such as sleep paralysis and nightmares, but he said that UFO abductions have "a quality all of their own."[42] However, a virtual bomb was about to explode on Mack.

Donna Bassett, a former patient of Mack's, who had participated in one of his studies, got up to speak. She revealed that she had been working undercover in an effort to find out more about his methods. In short, she had been "faking it." Critics chimed in, claiming that if Mack did not detect her as a fraud, his methods were unreliable. Bassett seemed to suggest that Mack did not intentionally lead his patients, but that his scientific methodology was flawed. The conference reported on Bassett's observations:

> . . . many patients would often practice "overlay," a term she said they invented to refer to their embellishing their stories. "They [the abductees] told John what he wanted to hear," Bassett added. She said she felt that many of the patients were seeking attention.[43]

Journalist Mark Pilkington examines all the confusion in an effort to get to the bottom of what actually happens to experiencers:

> Many people who undergo these experiences want to be told what has happened to them, calling on the visible "experts" who appear on TV or write books to do so. Often they are referred to abductee support groups where beliefs are reinforced and memories reshaped; this is how the mythology becomes reality. Gradually the inherent flaws in the CAS are becoming more widely recognized; but while the media can

still make mileage out of alien kidnappers, change is likely to be a slow process, especially when the alternatives are complex and undefined. That some UFOs are truly unidentifiable is beyond doubt. There have been too many reports from reliable and multiple witnesses, too many radar and visual correlations by pilots, too many films and photographs, too many blacked out military and government documents. For them all to be hoaxes, misidentifications, and hallucinations seem more unlikely than most of the other explanations put forward over the years.[44]

Some psychologists suggest the power of emotional belief is enough on its own. Professor Richard McNally from Harvard University says:

> If you genuinely believe you've been traumatized and recall these memories, you'll show the same psycho-physiologic emotional reactions as people who really have been traumatized. . . . "Abductees" also believe in their experiences so deeply that they display real stress symptoms similar to those of traumatized battlefield veterans.[45]

Many other researchers have also noticed a strong predisposition of these experiencers to what many describe as "religious beliefs." From an atheistic point of view, a religious belief would include any faith that entails the supernatural or mystical. However, McNally and other researchers have shown that this is not entirely the case. During his work with "abductees," McNally noticed that the "religious" trend was distinctly toward one area alone — New Age beliefs:

> Most of them had pre-existing new-age beliefs — they were into bio-energetic therapies, past lives, astral projection, tarot cards, and so on.[46]

The occult — real phenomena

There is a clear pattern. Impartial research shows that most abductees have, in the past, dabbled in what is commonly known as the occult, even if it was on a relatively minor basis. For some, they may not have been aware of the potential of unlocking this doorway to the supernatural when they dabbled in New Age practices. But regardless, their involvement in the occult subsequently increases, and they also become more prone to New Age beliefs and practices.

Many links can be made between UFOs and the occult.

Even for seasoned New Agers who already believed and practiced the occult, the escalation in occultic activity after their "abduction" still comes as a surprise. Why? I don't believe that anyone can expect, and be prepared for, the experience of being abducted by "alien" beings. The whole concept of what has taken place is so earth-shattering and so profound (e.g., "the space brothers chose me") that it completely changes their world view and attitude toward such phenomena. For example, if they subsequently perceived the aliens to be real, then they would have no doubt that their New Age messages are true as well, and then shape their lives according to these ideas. It's as if the so-called aliens are mimicking Jesus by providing their victims with a "Damascus Road" experience[47] and then proclaiming "follow me" — sadly, many do just that.

Far from the abductee population including all those with religious beliefs, there is one group of people that, by and large, is notably absent. They are Christians. Here we have to be careful about the definition of what constitutes a Christian. Many people in the world claim to be a Christian; that is, they have Christian ideals or morality, and may even regard themselves as good people. Some in this group still regularly claim abduction. But I am talking about what are known as "born-again," Bible-believing Christians — those who are often (these days unflatteringly) described as "Christian fundamentalists." It is as if ETs tend to avoid this select group of people. This reality has been largely ignored by many UFO researchers. But one group gets credit for discovering this startling fact.

CE-4 is an alien abduction research group founded by Joe Jordan and Wes Clark. The group has a dozen or so members based in Florida. Each member is also a trained field investigator for MUFON (Mutual UFO Network), arguably the most respected clearinghouse for UFO reports in the world. Joe Jordan, CE-4's president, is also a state section director of MUFON.

Because there were so many experiencers in the Florida area, CE-4 decided to conduct their own research independently of MUFON. They wanted to see if they could establish any significant patterns or factors that may have been overlooked by other researchers. The cases they studied had all the usual hallmarks of the CAS. They wondered, *Where to go from here.* Perhaps it was time for a completely new approach. One of the researchers posed the question, "Are Christians being abducted?" Clark says about himself at the time:

> I had a belief in God, but that was about the extent of my spirituality. Joe was a crystal-rolling New Ager. Neither one of us had ever even considered a spiritual origin of the phenomenon. We had a hunch we were onto something.[48]

At first, this line of investigation bore no fruit. Muslims, Buddhists, Jews, agnostics, all seemed to claim abduction experiences. As more case studies were examined, a puzzling trend emerged:

> The Christians reporting the abduction experience tended to be people who intellectually espoused the existence of God, but didn't apply it personally. But there seemed to be an obvious absence of devout, Bible believing, "walk the walk" Christians. Where were they in this equation?[49]

Jordan and Clark then remembered an earlier interview with an experiencer named Bill D. (see box).

Bill's paradigm-changing abduction

What follows is the case of Bill D. (written by, and reproduced here courtesy of, CE-4 Research Group Inc.).

Bill's experience took place at Christmas in Florida in 1976. His abduction started out typically, i.e., late at night, in bed. Earlier in the evening he saw some anomalous lights through his living room window over a forest north of his house. He assumed it was a police helicopter searching for drug runners or something. Whatever it was, it agitated his dogs for several hours thereafter. He eventually went to bed.

He was lying in bed, kept wide awake by the barking dogs, when paralysis set in. He was unable to cry out. He could see nothing but a whitish gray, like a mist or fog, although he sensed someone or something was in his room. His wife didn't waken. The next thing he knew, he was being levitated above his bed. He then had the sensation he was being suspended by what felt like a pole inserted into his rectum. By this time, he was alive with terror, but he couldn't scream. Here is where the story becomes very interesting. The following is an excerpt taken directly from the transcript of Mr. D.'s interview:

> I thought I was having a satanic experience; that the devil had gotten a hold of me and had shoved a pole up my rectum and was holding me up in the air. . . . So helpless, I couldn't do anything. I said, "Jesus, Jesus, help me!" or "Jesus, Jesus, Jesus!" When I did, there was a feeling or a sound or something that either my words that I thought or the words that I had tried to say or whatever, had hurt whatever was holding me up in the air on this pole. And I felt like it was withdrawn and I fell. I hit the bed, because it was like I was thrown back in bed. I really can't tell, but when I did, my wife woke up and asked why I was jumping on the bed.[50]

The answer to halting abduction experiences

It was the first time these experienced field investigators had ever heard of an abduction being stopped, and this man did it by just calling on the name of Jesus. Many researchers had previously recognized the spiritual nature of abductions, but no one had attempted to specifically research the spiritual aspects on their own merits. The folks at CE-4 began to look a bit closer at the data and the findings of other researchers.

Rita Elkins, a reporter with the well-known *Florida Today* newspaper, was interested in this research and she extensively interviewed both Jordan and Clark. The published article drew an immediate response from experiencers in the local area, like this one:

> Recently I read the *Florida Today* account of your research. I'm especially interested in the "religious component" that you seem to be discovering in some UFO abduction cases. Back

about 1973 my wife had a strange experience in the middle of the night. At the time we knew nothing about UFO abductions, so we had no category in which to place it other than extremely "lucid nightmare." It has many of the abduction "components." The point is that she stopped the entities and the whole experience with the name of "Jesus." . . . It's vital to get this information out.[51]

Clark said that many of the respondents claimed to be Christians who told of their own abduction experiences. He felt that they were happy to have someone to talk to; they usually felt uncomfortable talking about their experiences because most UFO investigators had New Age inclinations and ideas that opposed their own beliefs. In addition, the Christian church is not equipped to deal with such reports because the UFO phenomenon has been largely misunderstood and dismissed by organized religions. Clark comments:

> As the number of cases mounted, the data showed that in every instance where the victim knew to invoke the name of Jesus Christ, the event stopped. Period. The evidence was becoming increasingly difficult to ignore.[52]

The *Florida Today* article also appeared online, and it then made its way to an Internet news journal called *CNI News*. From here it turned up in Europe's most high-profile and respected UFO journal, *The Flying Saucer Review*. CE-4 received responses from all over the world, with dozens of reports of abductions being halted in the name of Jesus Christ. Another three major researchers told Jordan, off the record, that they had similar cases, but they would not officially report them, fearing damage to their credibility. Jordan gives some insight into why anyone would suppress such findings. He says that most UFOlogists share his former New Age beliefs (he has since become a Christian), and would not trade their religious beliefs for another more traditional view. He adds:

> These people go from one thing to another looking for development of a higher consciousness. . . . Any place but in traditional religion.[53]

CE-4 then tried to canvass Christians to hear of any abduction experiences that this group of people might have encountered. They claim that most of the responses were of a type that said, "I'm a Christian, and

I'm abducted all the time, and I've seen Jesus on the ship." This was initially confusing to Jordan and Clark in trying to understand why certain types of Christians were being abducted, and others not. For further insight, they researched the Christians' own book — the Bible — by taking Bible study courses. Gradually, things became a little clearer. They started to understand that these events were *completely* spiritual in nature, and resembled ancient stories and descriptions of what the Bible calls "demons." It seems amazing that the ET-believing UFOlogists, and even skeptics, have noticed that modern alien abductions resembled ancient stories of demons, yet they have ignored the world's most famous and best-selling book, which explains their origins. The similarity was not lost on John Keel. He wrote:

> Demonology is not just another crackpot-ology. It is the ancient and scholarly study of the monsters and demons who have seemingly coexisted with man throughout history. Thousands of books have been written on the subject, many of them authored by educated clergymen, scientists, and scholars, and uncounted numbers of well-documented demonic events are readily available to every researcher. The manifestations and occurrences described in this imposing literature are similar, if not entirely identical, to the UFO phenomenon itself. Victims of demonomania (possession) suffer the very same medical and emotional symptoms as the UFO contactees. . . . The devil and his demons can, according to the literature, manifest themselves in almost any form and can physically imitate anything from angels to horrifying monsters with glowing eyes. Strange objects and entities materialize and dematerialize in these stories, just as the UFOs and their splendid occupants appear and disappear, walk through walls, and perform other supernatural feats.[54]

Yet many investigators disregard these similarities, due to their own particular beliefs. The UFO believers think that these were merely primitive descriptions of aliens, and the skeptics think they were imaginary. Consequently, the Bible's account has been treated with disdain by both groups, despite seeming to have the answers to explain the phenomenon. Unlike others, Clark and Jordan were doing their homework. Despite not being Christians at the time, they wanted to know what the Bible had to say.

War in another dimension

CE-4 had discovered that the Bible described a battle fought in the spiritual realm. To Bible-believing Christians, this concept is known as "spiritual warfare." In explaining this premise of spiritual warfare, Jordan and Clark attempted to describe why some Christians are abducted, why some are left alone, and why abductions can be halted easily in the name of Jesus Christ.

They describe Christians as falling into two categories. One type is the person who has given mental assent to Christian ideals but who is still what the Bible calls carnal; that is, mostly guided by his natural impulses. He does not necessarily apply Christian concepts to his lifestyle because he hasn't learned to, or he doesn't want to. He cannot discern spiritual things, and he remains subject to spiritual attack from these entities. They describe this Christian as a "talk the talk" Christian. It is possible that some who fall into this category might not be truly "born again," and therefore not truly Christian by the Bible's own definition (John 3:3–7).

The other type is a person who has given his life over to following Jesus Christ, the author of Christianity, and the one whom the Bible claims is the Creator of the universe. This type of Christian applies biblical/Christian principles in his daily life, and he looks for a spiritual reality beyond the world around him. Because of this discernment, these Christians would view abduction experiences by entities/demons as a spiritual attack, and deal with them in the appropriate manner — in the authority of the name of Jesus Christ. Clark describes this type of person as a "walk the walk" Christian.

Some might argue that genuine born-again believers have been abducted, too, citing the "Andreasson affair." Betty Andreasson claimed to be a Christian, but she experienced ongoing abductions over many years. This is a well-documented and researched case, but the reports indicate that she presumed they were real aliens and she accepted their invitation to participate.[55] The evidence suggests that very few born-again Christian believers show up among abductees.[56] Of course, you can be a Christian and believe that aliens do exist on other planets, but it would imply that you have not taken the Bible's history of origins seriously — see the section "Did God create aliens?" in the appendix. Some Christians might also accept the idea that God used evolution on the earth and/or elsewhere. However, this is adding external religious philosophies to the Bible, violating its own clear warnings against this compromise. If Christians can be deceived, then it would appear that they can also be subject to abduction experiences, albeit this is much rarer than with the general population. (And, as shown, if they call on the name of Jesus, the experience stops.)

Such an experience befell Robert Prentiss, a former California policeman with degrees in sociology, nursing, psychology, and counseling. Shortly after he became a Christian, he and his wife saw a multitude of UFOs in a variety of shapes and colors over a period of weeks. After watching an apparent landing, they ventured to the site where they came upon an area of red-colored scorched earth with depressions in the ground. Prentiss said:

> During these weeks of tantalizing sightings, I became totally obsessed with the UFOs, convinced that something *great* was about to happen. I abandoned my daily Bible reading and turned my back on God [emphasis in original].[57]

Many evenings he would wait in anticipation of contact, waiting for some great event to happen, at the same time immersing himself in UFO literature. But the sightings stopped. Feeling betrayed, confused, and angry, Prentiss immersed himself in a debauched lifestyle and alcohol. Having abandoned his Christian lifestyle, he entered into a period of deep depression. In hindsight, he believes that God used these experiences to open his "spiritual" eyes to a Bible-based world view. He says he realized he was being deceived:

> . . . my thought processes were influenced . . . to embrace the concept of extraterrestrial beings with its concomitant theory of naturalistic evolution which would, of course, serve to negate the biblical truth that Christ died *once for all*. Since then . . . as I have allowed Jesus Christ to become Lord of my life . . . inner convictions have been reinforced through study of the Scriptures, as well as the preponderance of scientific evidence supporting the biblical account of creation [emphasis in original].[58]

The evidence suggests that meddling in the occult can open a doorway to the spiritual realm where there is a battle going on, and that you could become a casualty of war. Former abductee Virginia Miller-Witmer, who halted her abduction in the name of Jesus, said:

Although I accepted Jesus Christ as my Savior as a child, I have not always lived as I should. After being hurt by molestation, I sought a way to bring power and control in my life. I dabbled in occult practices. I made a childish attempt at witchcraft, participated in childhood séances and as a teen, experimented with meditation. . . . During all these experiences and many more, I believe God never left me. I grieved Him tremendously but He never left me.

Alien encounters were the last thing on my mind in 1987. But one night I found myself in the clutches of an evil presence. I believe that if it had not been for the experience, I might not have ever repented my occult involvement. I had not thought about my occult involvement for years and considered it experiences of a child. *Now I know that both God and Satan took my involvement seriously. It really made no difference if I took it seriously or not* [emphasis added].[59]

Many researchers, notable abductees (like Strieber), and others (like the lady above), have clearly understood the link between abductions and occultic New Age beliefs. Let's briefly recap. Clark says:

After 50 years of the modern UFO era we have literally millions of eyewitness accounts, hundreds of photographs, and in recent years many examples of video documentation, but we still do not have one single piece of hard physical evidence, in spite of thousands of eyewitness reports over the years. This suggests they are not physical, but spiritual manifestations. Even physical landing traces can be explained as a type of "counterfeit creation," or manipulation of mass and energy, not to mention shapeshifting and many UFOs' ability to make 90 degree turns [at impossible speeds] and other maneuvers that are considered to be impossible in the physical realm.[60]

Even the world's most respected UFO researcher, J. Allen Hynek, was forced to confront the obvious:

Another peculiarity is the alleged ability of certain UFOs to dematerialize. . . . There are quite a few reported instances where two distinctly different UFOs hovering in a clear sky will converge and eventually merge into one object. These are the types of psychic phenomena that are confronting us in the UFO mystery.[61]

Substitute "spiritual" for "psychic," and then compare the spiritual nature of UFO sightings with the character of alien abductions, and surely we have to begin to realize that these entities are not real physical ETs from other planets. They are from another dimension, just as Vallée, Keel, Mack, and so many other UFO researchers, from differing sides of the fence, have concluded. So, to find their source, one needs to wear "spiritual glasses." Unfortunately, most of these modern-day researchers have embraced a humanist-based view of the world, with the theory of evolution serving as the creator of both them and the aliens. This opens them up to spiritual deception and, in turn, has blinded them to the claims of the Bible, which makes God the Creator. I suggest that the answers they have been looking for but do not want to hear may be — "God is real, and the Bible is true."

This possible interpretation is further supported by the space brothers' single-minded obsession with undermining the Bible's account of the nature and mission of the only "One" who appears to be able to stop them — Jesus. In the next chapter we are going to attempt to wear "spiritual glasses" to discern exactly where these beings might have come from and what is motivating them.

Endnotes

1 Ronald D. Story, editor, *The Mammoth Encyclopedia of Extraterrestrial Encounters*, in an article by Scott Corrales (London: Constable & Robinson, 2002), p. 759–761.

2 "Screen Memories: UFO Mythology and Science Fiction Films," <www. hedweb.com/markp/ufofilm.htm>, December 10, 2002.

3 "Alien Abductions," <www.skepdic.com/aliens.html>, January 6, 2003.

4 Ibid.

5 "Paradigm Wars: Examining Competing Views on Alien Abductions, by Michael Miley," <www.visibiliti.com/mmiley/paradigmwars.htm>, January 6, 2003.

6 Jacques Vallée, *Confrontations* (New York: Ballantine Books, 1990), p. 159, cited in Chuck Missler and Mark Eastman, *Alien Encounters* (Indianapolis, IN: Koinonia House, 2003), p. 253.

7 "Screen Memories: UFO Mythology and Science Fiction Films," <www.hedweb.com/markp/ufofilm.htm>, December 10, 2002.

8 Story, *The Mammoth Encyclopedia of Extraterrestrial Encounters*, in an article by Philip J. Klass, p. 362.

9 "Aliens are Coming . . . or Are They Here?" <www.shootthemessenger.com.au/pre_dec97a_life_dec97/1_aliens.htm>, June 12, 2003.

10 Story, *The Mammoth Encyclopedia of Extraterrestrial Encounters*, in "Report by NICAP," p. 763–768.

11 "The Skeptical Believer: Pitfalls of UFOlogy," <www.darkecho.com/skepticalbeliever/pitfalls.html>, August 2, 2003.

12 "The Selling of the Travis Walton 'Abduction' Story," <www.debunker.com/texts/walton.html>, August 2, 2003.

13 Story, *The Mammoth Encyclopedia of Extraterrestrial Encounters*, in an article by Thomas Bullard, p. 4–10.

14 "Paradigm Wars: Examining Competing Views on Alien Abductions, by Michael Miley," <www.visibiliti.com/mmiley/paradigmwars.htm>, January 6, 2003.

15 Ibid.

16 "International Center for Abduction Research — Straight Talk," <www.ufoabduction.com/straighttalk.html>, January 16, 2003.

17 Story, *The Mammoth Encyclopedia of Extraterrestrial Encounters*, in an article by Thomas Bullard, p. 4–10.

18 Ibid., in an article by Martin S. Kottmeyer, p. 364.

19 Ibid., in an article by Thomas Bullard, p. 4–10.

20 Dr. Karla Turner, "Aliens — Friends or Foes?" *UFO Universe*, spring 1993, cited in "The Premise of Spiritual Warfare," <www.alienresistance.org/ce4premise.htm>, March 7, 2003.

21 "UFOs and Alien Abductions," <www.christianinformation.org/ufo2.html>, December 20, 2002.

22 Story, *The Mammoth Encyclopedia of Extraterrestrial Encounters*, in an article by Thomas Bullard, p. 4–10.

23 Turner, "Aliens — Friends or Foes?" *UFO Universe*, spring 1993, cited in "The Premise of Spiritual Warfare," <www.alienresistance.org/ce4premise.htm>, March 7, 2003.

24 Ibid.

25   Whitley Strieber, *Communion* (New York: Beech Tree, 1987), p. 26, cited in William T. Alnor, *UFOs in the New Age* (Grand Rapids, MI: Baker Book House, 1992), p. 100.

26   In an interview with Douglas Winter in the book *Faces of Fear*, cited in Alnor, "UFO Cults are Flourishing in New Age Circles," *Christian Research Journal*, p. 5, 1990, cited in Alnor, *UFOs in the New Age*, p. 105.

27   Ibid.

28   Panel discussion on hoaxes, The International Fortean Organization, Fortfest '90 conference, Mclean, Virginia, November 10, 1990, cited in Alnor, *UFOs in the New Age*, p. 229.

29   Story, *The Mammoth Encyclopedia of Extraterrestrial Encounters*, p. 300–302.

30   Ibid., in an article by David M. Jacobs, p. 331–332.

31   "Nova Online/Kidnapped by UFOs/John Mack (Interview with John Mack)," <www.pbs.org/wgbh/nova/aliens/johnmack.html>, January 6, 2003.

32   "Are Aliens Already Here? Harvard's Controversial John Mack," <www.skepticfiles.org/misctext/mack.htm>, July 29, 2003.

33   Ibid.

34   Ibid.

35   "Nova Online/Kidnapped by UFOs/John Mack (Interview with John Mack)," <www.pbs.org/wgbh/nova/aliens/johnmack.html>, January 6, 2003.

36   Ibid.

37   Story, *The Mammoth Encyclopedia of Extraterrestrial Encounters*, in an article by Hilary Evans, p. 545–547.

38   Ibid., in an article by Robert A. Baker, p. 113–114.

39   Ibid., in an article by Kevin D. Randle, p. 663–664.

40   "Abduction by Aliens or Sleep Paralysis," <www.csicop.org/si/9805/abduction.html>, January 6, 2003.

41   "Alien Abductions," <www.skepdic.com/aliens.html>, January 6, 2003.

42   "Exploring Mind, Memory, and the Psychology of Belief," <www.csicop.org/si/9501/belief.html>, January 6, 2003.

43   Ibid.

44   "Screen Memories: UFO Mythology and Science Fiction Films," <www.hedweb.com/markp/ufofilm.htm>, December 10, 2002.

45 "BBC News/Alien 'Abductees' Show Real Symptoms," <news.bbc. co.uk/1/hi/in_depth/sci_tech/2003/denver_2003/2769875.stm>, February 18, 2003.

46 "BBC News/Alien 'Abductees' Show Real Symptoms," <news.bbc. co.uk/1/hi/in_depth/sci_tech/2003/denver_2003/2769875.stm>, February 18, 2003.

47 In Acts 9:3–18, Saul, a persecutor of Christians, had an encounter with Jesus (after Jesus' ascension to heaven) on the road to Damascus, resulting in him becoming a Christian. His name was later changed to Paul, the famous Apostle of the early Christian church.

48 "A Letter to the *Mufon UFO Journal,*" <www.alienresistance.org/ ce4mufonletter.htm>, August 1, 2003.

49 "The Premise of Spiritual Warfare," <www.alienresistance.org/ ce4premise.htm>, March 7, 2003.

50 Interview with CE-4 Research Group, August 1996, cited in "The Premise of Spiritual Warfare," <www.alienresistance.org/ce4premise. htm>, March 7, 2003.

51 "CE-4 Case Files," <www.alienresistance.org/ce4casefiles.htm>, August 2, 2003.

52 "The Premise of Spiritual Warfare," <www.alienresistance.org/ ce4premise.htm>, March 7, 2003.

53 " 'Spiritual Warfare?' Some Look to Bible for Answers to Alien Abductions," <www.flatoday.com/space/explore/stories/1997b/ 081797b.htm>, January 6, 2003.

54 John Keel, *Operation Trojan Horse* (Lilburn, GA: Illuminet Press, 1996), p. 192, cited in Missler and Eastman, Alien Encounters, p. 247–248.

55 "Return of the Nephilim? by Chuck Missler," <www.khouse.org/article. phtml?article_code=22>, September 11, 2003.

56 "UFOs and Alien Abductions," <www.christianinformation.org/ufo2. html>, December 20, 2002.

57 Robert B. Prentiss, December 25, 1976, cited in Clifford Wilson and John Weldon, *Close Encounters, A Better Explanation* (SanDiego, CA: Master Books, 1978), p. 297–302.

58 Ibid.

59 "Encounter by Virginia Miller-Witmer," <www.alienresistance.org/ ce4encounter.htm>, August 2, 2003.

60 "The Premise of Spiritual Warfare," <www.alienresistance.org/ ce4premise.htm>, March 7, 2003.

61 J. Allen Hynek, interview in *UFO Report Magazine*, p. 61, August 1976, cited in "The Premise of Spiritual Warfare," <www.alienresistance.org/ce4premise.htm>, March 7, 2003.

Chapter Eight

The Gospel
According to ET

Who are you going to believe?

All the evidence we have looked at points against these "alien" entities as being "extraterrestrials," i.e., from other planets. However, they seem to be interdimensional, in the sense that they seem to be emanating from another dimension or realm. The evidence suggests that, despite their capability of interacting within our own physical reality, both they and their source are spiritual in nature. Despite *their own claims* to be an advanced or highly evolved alien species, the entire hypothesis that aliens come from other planets, star systems, or parallel universes appears to be an elaborate masquerade. In other words, they are lying and trying to create an illusion of something that is not real. If this interpretation is correct, what could possibly be their motive?

Given the deceptive behavior of these spiritual beings and their intentional campaign of misinformation, they must be trying to hide their real motives. They appear to be operating in a covert manner, similar to a "fifth column." Their efforts resemble a propaganda war that tries to convince the enemy that their intentions are not hostile, that is, that "we're the good guys." Human combatants have used similar methods in conventional warfare on this planet, where one side tries to "soften up" a country prior to invasion, giving the impression that they are no threat. It is classic deception.

As the CE-4 researchers discovered, there is a battle going on in another dimension or a spiritual realm, and control of humankind and the earth appears to be the goal. Remember the conclusions of researchers Vallée and others: they noticed that these beings seem intent on changing our traditional view of the world — in short, our view

An artist's depiction of a "gray"

of reality. Achieving this goal is not as difficult as one might think. As we have repeatedly shown, the evolutionary world view, coupled with a diet of science fiction and a decline of traditional religious beliefs, has prepared the world for the arrival of the space brothers and their new religion.

It appears that these beings want to bring the world into a new order; that is, one great unifying religion under their auspices. Yet this religious agenda is not new. It is one that has been around for as long as mankind has been on the earth — this new religious order is supposed to embrace all faiths, but it is noticeably intolerant of biblical Christianity. Therefore, it should be of no surprise that the abductors have generally left genuine Bible-believing Christians alone because these Christians may be able to "spiritually discern" the true nature of this attack on their beliefs. Unfortunately, many Christians believe the whole ET scenario is nonsense, probably because they have never been exposed to this phenomenon. And although they may recognize some aspects as spiritual in origin, most do not realize how widespread this "enemy campaign" appears to be.

CE-4 discovered, by means of practical research and not a preexisting belief in Christianity, that the Bible provided answers to the nature of this spiritual battle. It has been written of these researchers:

Jordan and Clark didn't start out as "Bible pounders with a point." In fact, quite the opposite. They were just looking for truth like everyone else, and what they have found will cause the UFO/abduction phenomenon to never be viewed in exactly the same way again. It was the research they did and the data they found that made believers out of them.[1]

Researcher Jordan not only spoke with fellow directors in MU-FON, but he contacted several of the leading abduction researchers in the United States. They all requested anonymity, but off the record *every single one of them* claimed to have cases of abductees halting their experiences in the name of Jesus Christ. These experts, not knowing how to deal with this knowledge, simply disregarded it.[2] The fact that they wanted anonymity also suggests that they didn't want their own pre-existing belief system challenged, which was likely to be already entrenched in New Age concepts and practices. In addition, with the abduction phenomenon at plague proportions, one can make a good living by being a "specialist."

Why is it that the mention of the name of Jesus affects these beings so badly? Why are they afraid of a name that is often disregarded and derided or used as a swear word in our modern culture? The messages of these beings are often aimed directly at discrediting the traditional view of Christ. The space brothers frequently claim that Jesus is not the Savior of all mankind but one of a few good religious leaders who have appeared on this earth, or even that he is a UFOnaut like them. All their efforts seem focused on undermining the Bible and the Christian view that Jesus is the Savior of mankind, and replacing it with the view that they are the saviors instead. It is hard to avoid the conclusion that these beings actually believe Jesus is the One He claims to be. If He is God incarnate, and they are merely deceivers, we can now realize their motives for seeking to discredit Him.

Should one trust these deceptive beings' claims to be our saviors? Be careful — to be "deceived" means to believe a lie. Who should we believe? Beings with questionable origins who abuse humans and treat them with disdain? Remember that people who have encountered so-called aliens have been transformed emotionally and religiously as a result of an encounter with a spirit, but often it is an unpleasant experience that leaves them with a sense of being violated, depressed, and even suicidal.

Abduction researcher and hypnotherapist Donna Higbee became alarmed at the dramatic change in the attitude of people who had undergone an abduction experience. She wrote:

> I noticed a drastic change . . . in the attitudes of several of the abductees from one meeting to the next. People who had been traumatized all their lives by ongoing abductions and had only anger and mistrust for their non-human abductors suddenly started saying they had been told/shown that everything that has happened to them was for their own good, that the abductors are highly spiritual beings and are helping them (the abductee) to evolve spiritually. By accepting this information, the abductees stopped fighting abduction and instead became passive and controlled. When I checked with other researchers, I found that this was a pattern that was repeating itself over and over again around the country. I became concerned that abductees were accepting these explanations from entities that we know can be deceitful, use screen memories to mask real memories, use virtual reality scenarios to implant images into abductees' heads, and manipulate and abuse. I wrote an article for the *MUFON UFO Journal* (September 1995) and encouraged abductees to seriously think about what they were accepting as their truth, in light of the evidence, not the explanations offered them by these non-human entities.[3]

A spirit of love

Contrast this with the claims of Christians about their encounter with Christ, who, rather than controlling people against their will, laid down His life in the service of human beings. No one could deny that the theme of Christ's ministry on this earth was one of love, forgiveness, and acceptance. Most people today would like to live in a world with these Christian values, but they don't want to accept what they regard as the "religious baggage" that goes along with it. This attitude results from the common view that Christianity is just another religion. But as we shall see, the UFO debate is not just about a religious point of view, but about a spiritual battle of epic proportions and of such importance that not a single person alive on the planet should ignore it.

It is commonly observed that people who make a conscious choice to become Christians undergo a transformation. They become passionate about their newfound beliefs, and try to tell everyone else about it because they believe they have hit upon the foundational truth that gives meaning to their existence. That's big news in a world where the prevailing world view teaches that life, including you and me, is nothing more than evolved pond scum, and that there is nothing but death and oblivion at the end of our lives. The Bible implores Christians to love, forgive, and serve others, using Christ as their model. According to the Bible, Christians are transformed because they've met with a spiritual being who changed them. But unlike alien abductees who encounter a spirit of deception, for Christians it is a "close encounter" with a spirit called the Holy Spirit who comes from Jesus Christ. The Bible says that Christ is actually God the Creator, who came in the flesh so that we might understand the nature and person of God himself and believe in Him. The Bible says, in Hebrews 1:3:

> The Son [Jesus] is the radiance of God's glory and the exact representation of his being. . . .

Although this may sound a little confusing, the Bible claims that God exists in three persons but He is one God (historically called the Trinity). The three "persons" are God the Father, God the Son (Jesus), and God the Holy Spirit. This God claims to be unique. There is none like Him.

Change can be dramatic among folk who become Christians. Murderers, criminals, the abused, the broken-hearted, suddenly become full of life and become new people. The Bible says they have become "born again," which is a far cry from the transformations that take place among alien abductees. Many are startled at the rapid transformation that Christians undergo. In John 3:3, Jesus says:

> I tell you the truth, no one can see the kingdom of God unless he is born again.

The very words of Jesus indicate that no one can see, enter, or understand God's kingdom until they have had this new (spiritual) birth. Christians have available to them "spiritual glasses" to help them discern a spiritual realm that we cannot naturally see or understand. This lack of understanding about the spiritual realm helps to explain why so many researchers and abductees fail to determine the true nature of an encounter with a "space brother." Not only do they fail to see through the charade, but they can become very much aligned with the "mission" of their abductors. Researchers Missler and Eastman explain:

> The tragic lesson here is that while the UFO phenomenon has the ability to engender tremendous personal devotion and self-sacrifice, it also has the ability to perpetrate a massive deception.[4]

The apostle Paul was initially hostile to Christianity (he even killed some of Jesus' followers), but when he had a personal encounter with Jesus he became a believer and laid down his own life in the service of his faith. He was born again, and as a result, the Bible says he received the Spirit of God (the Holy Spirit), who dwells in every Christian believer. To explain why non-Christians are unable to easily understand the true nature of spiritual things, Paul wrote, in 1 Corinthians 2:12–14:

> We have not received the spirit of the world but the Spirit who is from God, that we may understand what God has freely given us. . . . The man without the Spirit does not accept the things that come from the Spirit of God, for they are foolishness to him, and he cannot understand them, because they are spiritually discerned.

Paul says that the world cannot correctly understand spiritual things. In the past, traditional Christian views caused many to believe and understand that there was a spiritual dimension to our existence. But evolution, masquerading as modern science, now advances the belief that "atoms are all there is." The New Age movement (NAM) has also embraced this idea, saying that matter itself is a unifying force — a god or self-perpetuating energy or entity in its own right, similar to the "force" of *Star Wars* fame. The idea that there is an *impersonal* god or some "force" behind the universe has become the most popular view today. Once again, this is in sharp contrast to the message of a supreme deity who has personally communicated through Christ and the Bible. New Age beliefs, which the space brothers endorse in a variety of forms, appear to be a counterfeit or substitute religion designed to keep people away from the knowledge of the true Creator God of the Bible.

This is an immense effort on the part of the deceivers, and you may wonder why. It is clear that the "space beings" believe in the God of the Bible, or else they would not be expending so much effort to convince us otherwise. Simply stated, they are the adversaries of God. One of Jesus' disciples, a man named John, saw this spiritual battle and wrote warning Christian believers to be careful about what we believe, and also warning them to be mindful of God's enemy, which he called "the spirit of the antichrist." This phrase describes a being who is "anti," that is, *against* or *instead of* Christ, the Son of God, and who is presently working to deceive non-believers. John wrote:

> Dear friends, do not believe every spirit, but test the spirits to see whether they are from God, because many false prophets have gone out into the world. This is how you can recognize the Spirit of God: Every spirit that acknowledges that Jesus Christ has come in the flesh is from God, but every spirit that does not acknowledge Jesus is not from God. This is the spirit of the antichrist, which you have heard is coming and even now is already in the world (1 John 4:1–3).

In earlier chapters we mentioned that these "ET" entities and their earthly evangelists seemed to be obsessed with the Bible. We shall now look more closely at its teachings to find out what it really says about the origin of this battle and who is really overseeing this deceptive plan — and as we shall see, the Bible explains that the lie is as old as time itself. Well in advance of this modern era, that book warned the world that God's spiritual enemies would try to deceive us.

Back to the beginning

According to the first book of the Bible, before the world or even the universe began, there was God. He is self-existent and needs nothing to sustain Him (see Appendix: Who Made God?). When God created the universe, at that same moment, space and time, as we understand them, came into existence. Although God is outside of our space and time, He interacts in it. He also created a spiritual realm or another dimension (although the "spirit" beings in their dimension may have "physical" attributes — though different from ours). The Bible describes Jesus Christ as the Creator:

> He is the image of the invisible God, the firstborn over all creation. For by him all things were created: things in heaven and on earth, visible and invisible, whether thrones or powers or rulers or authorities; all things were created by him and

for him. He is before all things, and in him all things hold together (Col. 1:15–17).

Note that the passage says that Jesus created visible and invisible things for himself. By definition, if He made the universe and everything in it, then He owns it. The invisible things — "whether thrones or powers, rulers or authorities" — include beings from the spiritual or unseen realm. If God created "all things," it must also include these spirit beings and their realm. Therefore, some of these beings must be the same ones who are now waging war against him. The Bible claims in Ephesians 6:12:

> For our struggle is not against flesh and blood, but against the rulers, against the authorities, against the powers of this dark world and against the spiritual forces of evil in the heavenly realms.

This makes a pretty clear claim. There is a war going on in the unseen or heavenly realms. According to these passages of Scripture, the beings discussed in this book are commonly known as angels. I have deliberately avoided using that expression for them until now because the word "angels" usually invokes the image of a beautiful heavenly being, dressed in flowing white robes and "fairy" wings. This is far from the teaching of the Bible, which describes that there are good angels and bad ones. But to find out how it became this way, we need to go back to the very first book of the Bible. It tells us about all the players in this conflict.

First, there was God. According to Genesis 1:1, "In the beginning God created the heavens and the earth." The word translated as "God" is the Hebrew word *Elohim,* which is a plural word (implying the Trinity), but the word is used singularly (with a singular verb) to describe (the one) God as the Creator. (The Raelian cult deliberately misuses this word to imply that we had multiple creators, namely ancient alien astronauts.)

According to verse 26, on the sixth day of creation, God said to himself, "Let us make man in our image, in our likeness," and so Adam (his name means "man or mankind") and subsequently the first woman, Eve, were created. This does not mean that Adam was created in God's physical likeness but in His spiritual likeness. This verse teaches that we have a spirit, too.

So when were the angelic beings created? In the Book of Job 38:4–7, a dialogue is recorded between the man Job and God himself. God is reminding the man Job that He is the Creator:

> Where were you when I laid the earth's foundation? Tell me, if you understand. Who marked off its dimensions? Surely you know! Who stretched a measuring line across it? On what were its footings set, or who laid its cornerstone — while the morning stars sang together and all the angels shouted for joy?

Although it is poetic language, this passage also conveys historical truth. The passage tells us that the angelic spirit beings had already been created and were watching God perform His handiwork. Therefore they knew that God was their Creator also.

Angel, a Greek (the language of the New Testament) word and its parallel Hebrew word *malak* (the Old Testament was originally written in Hebrew), both mean "messenger." These messengers were used as agents of God to carry out His purposes. These angelic beings are mentioned in the Bible on literally dozens and dozens of occasions. Here is what we can glean from some of the passages (it would be prudent to look at a Bible and check out these references for yourself):

> They are spirits (Heb. 1:14), yet they always appeared to humans as men/males when doing God's bidding (Gen. 19:1; Luke 24:4).
>
> They number in the hundreds of millions or perhaps more (Heb. 12:22; Rev. 5:11).
>
> They were given names such as Gabriel, Michael, and even Lucifer (Luke 1:19; Jude 9; Isa. 14:12).
>
> There are various types and categories of angels mentioned, e.g., cherubim (Gen. 3:24; Ezek. 10:1–20), seraphim (Isa. 6:2, 6) and watchers (Dan. 4:17, Authorized Version). They also appear to differ in rank and dignity, some being described as archangels, princes or rulers (1 Thess. 4:16; Jude 1; Dan. 10:20–21, 12:1; Eph. 6:12).
>
> They are/were called holy and elect (Luke 9:26; 1 Tim. 5:21).

They are more powerful than mankind (2 Thess. 1:7; 2 Pet. 2:11).

They can appear among, and interact with, humans, even killing them on occasion (Gen. 16:9, 19:15; 1 Chron. 21:15; Ps. 78:49; John 20:12). In Exodus 12:23 God's destroying angel killed all the firstborn in Egypt (except for those of the Hebrew families who followed God's instructions for protection), and in 2 Kings 19:35 an angel sent by God killed 185,000 soldiers in one evening.

They can appear so real to humans that we do not recognize them as angels (Gen. 18:1–16; Heb. 13:2).

They are not to be worshiped (Rom. 1:25, NKJV; Col. 2:18; Rev. 19:10).

Many of the descriptions of these angelic beings conform to the "spiritual yet physical" characteristics attributed to aliens. It enables us to understand why, when masquerading as aliens, angelic beings are able to perform such incredible physics-defying feats.

Here's where the trouble begins

In the beginning, though, God created one particular high-ranking angel. He was described as a "guardian cherub," and many believe that he was in charge of all the other angels. His name was Lucifer. In parallel with a description of an earthly king, God apparently describes Lucifer's position:

> You were in Eden, the garden of God; every precious stone adorned you: ruby, topaz and emerald, chrysolite, onyx and jasper, sapphire, turquoise and beryl. Your settings and mountings were made of gold; on the day you were created they were prepared. You were anointed as a guardian cherub, for so I ordained you. You were on the holy mount of God; you walked among the fiery stones. You were blameless in your ways from the day you were created till wickedness was found in you (Ezek. 28:13–15).

Lucifer had it pretty good. He was the number one spirit in the neighborhood, and was in charge of at least several million other angels. But he had a problem — pride. Having authority delegated to him wasn't enough. He wanted it all, including God's throne, and so he conspired against the One who made him. Of course, he is now generally known as Satan (which literally means "adversary" or "accuser") or the devil. The name change was apt, as we shall see.

Most people are familiar with the account of Adam and Eve in the Garden of Eden. The Bible says that Eve[5] was deceived by the serpent that lured her into eating from the Tree of the Knowledge of Good and Evil. God had already warned Adam and Eve that to eat of this tree would result in the curse of death befalling them and their descendants. It didn't refer to instantaneous physical death, but literally meant "dying you shall die," i.e., the process of death shall begin and "you will surely [inevitably] die." It also caused a spiritual separation from God their Creator. This curse of death has befallen all mankind because we have all sinned (rebelled against God and broken his laws). Romans 3:23 says:

> . . . for all have sinned and fall short of the glory of God.

Like Lucifer, the first people had everything they would ever need, as God their Creator had provided for them. They could have lived forever in fellowship with God, who used to walk with them in the garden at a time when everything, including Adam and Eve, was perfect.

Then the accuser struck. He turned on God. By trying to win man's allegiance (and the allegiance of the other angels), Lucifer thought he could usurp God's throne and authority. This corrupted and destroyed the focus of God's creation and that which, according to the Bible, God loves more than anything else — us. Lucifer uttered those infamous words that still resonate today:

> For God doth know that in the day ye eat thereof, then your eyes shall be opened, and *ye shall be as gods*, knowing good and evil (Gen. 3:5, Authorized Version, emphasis added).

In one sense, the first people did become like God in now knowing the difference between good and evil, but Lucifer lied to them. Genesis 3:4 says:

> "You will not surely die," the serpent said to the woman.

By getting man to rebel, he knew that Adam and his descendants would now be spiritually, and eternally, separated from God. For once sin had come upon them they could no longer be in the presence of a pure and holy God. Satan thought he could spite God and destroy

His eternal purposes for mankind by telling people they could aspire to godhood — this is fundamentally *the same message the space brothers deliver today.*

Most people assume that Lucifer took the form of, or perhaps indwelt, a snake or serpent. While this is entirely possible, if he appeared as a talking reptile, then why was Eve not more cautious? Some may argue that she was still innocent and had no experience of evil yet. But one would think a talking snake would have aroused her suspicion — none of the other animals are recorded as speaking. She wasn't stupid — she was perfect in every way. Is it possible that Satan was not a typical serpent? Whatever form he took, it deceived Eve enough to lower her defenses, despite God's warning. She was *deceived,* and it was the beginning of a long war of deception. The original Hebrew word for serpent in this passage comes from the root word *nachash,* which can mean to whisper a spell or to enchant. In addition, Lucifer literally means "light-bearer" or "shining one" (also morning star). Figuratively, the Bible also describes God as light, so is it possible that Eve was deceived by an entity appearing as a being of light? In 2 Corinthians 11:14, the apostle Paul warns that:

> . . . Satan himself masquerades as an angel of light.

Right here at the beginning of creation we can see the counterfeit plan of God's adversary coming into action. Adam and Eve were deceived, tricked or conned into believing a benevolent-appearing entity. These are exactly the same methods that the deceiving spirits, appearing as aliens, UFOs, space brothers — whatever you want to call them — employ today. They:

- Use false appearances — Satan, an angel, was able to appear as something he wasn't, possibly altering his form to do so. UFOs commonly manifest as objects of light.

- Pretend to be the good guys — "I'm here to help you."

- Lie about human potential to reach godhood — using the classic yarn, "You shall be as gods." But Satan didn't warn Adam and Eve about the consequences of death and eternal separation.

From the very beginning, humans have been lied to, have believed the lies, and are still accepting them today. As we shall see, these lies constitute the central theme of New Age ideology.

God tells us of Satan's planned coup in Isaiah 14:12–15.

> How you are fallen from heaven, O Lucifer, son of the morning! How you are cut down to the ground, you who weakened the nations! For you have said in your heart: "I will ascend into heaven, I will exalt my throne above the stars of God; I will also sit on the mount of the congregation on the farthest sides of the north; I will ascend above the heights of the clouds, I will be like the Most High." Yet you shall be brought down to Sheol [grave or hell], to the lowest depths of the Pit (New King James Version).

We can understand, in some small way, the vanity and wickedness of Satan by comparing him to the evil earthly despots that history shows had similar visions of grandeur. When they know their days are numbered, it still doesn't stop them. They embark on a crash-and-burn policy designed to take as many down with them as possible, to spite their enemies.

Satan is not alone in this. Satan had some angelic followers. We cannot be sure of the number, but the Bible gives us indications that approximately one-third of the created angels were ejected from heaven and cast down to the earth (Rev. 12:4). They are also now roaming about the earth (Job 1:7). Their focus is now the eternal destruction of mankind through lies and deception designed to take our eyes off Jesus the true Creator and His plan of redemption for mankind. Quite simply, these evil angels, under the leadership of Satan, want to deceive and destroy as many human beings as they possibly can. Even when they appear to be our friends, they are the enemies of God.

But Satan and his hordes of evil angels cannot win, according to the Bible. Jesus is their Creator, and thus He has authority over them. He says that their fate is already established:

> Depart from me, you who are cursed, into the eternal fire prepared for the devil and his angels (Matt. 25:41).

But more importantly, Christ says He loves and cares for those who are part of His family. His authority is absolute and He will protect them from the evil ones, so they do not need to fear the evil deceivers any more. Two-thirds of the heavenly host are still doing God's bidding and directly engaging the enemy.

Deceptive spirits

According to the Bible, these evil spirits can influence the way some people think and act. They can even possess (indwell) humans. We find such a description in Luke 11:24–26:

> When an evil spirit comes out of a man, it goes through arid places seeking rest and does not find it. Then it says, "I will return to the house I left." When it arrives, it finds the house swept clean and put in order. Then it goes and takes seven other spirits more wicked than itself, and they go in and live there. And the final condition of that man is worse than the first.

This is similar to the pattern of repeated abductions where the victims have completely given themselves over to their abductors. In Mark 1:24–26, the Bible gives an account of a man afflicted by these evil spirits:

> "What do you want with us, Jesus of Nazareth? Have you come to destroy us? I know who you are — the Holy One of God!"
>
> "Be quiet!" said Jesus sternly. "Come out of him!" The evil spirit shook the man violently and came out of him with a shriek."

Notice how these spirits recognized Jesus and obeyed Him. This pained shriek is also reminiscent of Bill D.'s abduction in the last chapter when he described that the application of Jesus' name somehow hurt the entities that were trying to abduct him. Similar stories have been reported elsewhere.

In Mark 5:1–15, Jesus encountered a disturbed man who would even mutilate himself. When Jesus ordered the spirits (demons) to leave the man, they recognized Jesus as "the Son of the most high God," and confessed their name to be "Legion . . . for we are many" (verse 9). When they left the man they entered a herd of pigs and destroyed them by running them over a cliff.

New Age author Whitley Strieber's increasing contacts with spirit beings masquerading as aliens leaves us in no doubt about the progressive nature of the deception that enveloped him. In Strieber's first book, *Communion,* he describes his first encounters with the visitors (only recalled through hypnosis). In *Transformation* the visitors started to teach him deeper things that he linked with the spiritual realm, although he recalls that they were always vague about their point of origin.[6] Because of his New Age beliefs, Strieber refused to believe that the beings were those as described in biblical terms. He wrote:

> So far the word *demon* had never been spoken among the scientists and doctors who were working with me. And why should it have been? We were beyond such things. We were a group of atheists and agnostics, far too sophisticated to be concerned with such archaic ideas as demons and angels.[7]

However, and true to New Age form, Strieber started to connect his visitors to all the religions of the world:

> Whatever the visitors are, I suspect that they have been responsible for much paranormal phenomena, ranging from the appearance of gods, angels, fairies, ghosts, and miraculous beings to the landing of UFOs in the backyards of America. It may be that what happened to Mohammed in his cave and to Christ in Egypt, to Buddha in his youth and to all our great prophets and seers, was an exalted version of the same humble experience that causes a flying saucer to traverse the sky or a visitor to appear in a bedroom or light to fill a circle of friends.[8] [Note that the boy Christ was taken to Egypt short-term by his earthly father, but there is no biblical record of Christ receiving any divine instructions while there.]

Strieber and his visitors are advocating a new religion, and one that he hopes will unite all of humanity. But from the titles of his following books, it becomes apparent how deeply he fell into the occult phenomenon of "alien" worship. After *Transformation*, there came *Breakthrough* (1995), *The Secret School: Preparations for Contact* (1997), and *Evenings with Demons* (1997).

It has been said that Strieber is one of many people who have been increasingly deceived to a point where they have become continually *possessed* by spirits — in similar fashion to the biblical occurrences mentioned earlier. In true counterfeit fashion, demonic possession has even been given a New Age technological facelift. They are now called "walk-ins." This is the belief that a more evolved or "ascended" alien form has literally taken over a human being. (See later in this chapter.)

Power over life and death

If we take the Bible at face value, Jesus had, and still has, authority over these powerful lying spirits. How? Because the Bible claims He is the Creator of the universe and therefore the Creator of these beings as well.

There is abundant historical evidence that Jesus walked this earth as a man. Many UFO believers agree with this. They also like the teachings of Jesus because He showed a better way to live in accord with the "benevolent" teachings of the "space brothers." However, many of them would dismiss His express command for humans to follow Him, and they would reject the Bible's claim that He is the Creator God who became man with the express purpose of becoming mankind's Savior. (The next chapter will examine the Bible's description of the "way" to know Christ as Savior.) Jesus also promised the Holy Spirit as a "helper" (John 14:16, 26; 15:26). The Holy Spirit indwells, lives with, and helps the believer — He does not take over, in the manner of a demonic (alien) possession (walk-in).

The consistent "big picture" of the Bible repeats that Jesus sacrificially chose to lay down His heavenly glory to become a man in order that we might believe in God. Since it was a choice, then at anytime He could have changed His mind. When He was being arrested, just before His crucifixion, His disciples tried to forcibly prevent His arrest, and Jesus said:

> Do you think I cannot call on my Father, and he will at once put at my disposal more than twelve legions of angels? (Matt. 26:53 — at that time, a Roman legion was about 6,000 men.).

Christ explained (and at other times showed) that He could use his power immediately at any time. The evidence of the halting of abductions by calling on His name indicates that He is indeed still alive and powerful. The death and resurrection of Christ is the focal point of Christianity, and is also a well-documented and historical fact. Because He rose from the dead, it adds credence to the claim that He is the Creator and thus has power over life and death.

Many UFO believers would suggest Christ rose from the dead via extraterrestrial technology. But the Bible says He was disfigured more than any man (Isa. 52:14). He was beaten, bruised, speared, flogged, and lay dead for three days. Some sort of resuscitation is one thing, but to restore an unimaginably broken, torn, and bruised body is another. If Jesus was a UFOnaut who could foretell the future, why did He let himself undergo such torture? What could possibly be the point of this demonstration, unless He was willingly paying the penalty for mankind's sins, as the Bible says?

There is a great risk for anyone who overlooks this cosmic act of Christ and dismisses the Bible's claims. Those who impose a "UFO view" on the Bible must reinterpret Bible verses or take them in isolation to fit their view. This approach creates irreconcilable differences with other Bible verses, and violates the big picture of the Bible, which clearly lays out, from the very first book to the last book, God's plan to redeem mankind through the sacrifice of His son, thus restoring paradise lost. Anyone who believes in, or has contact with, UFOs or aliens does not need to be deceived any longer.

The very words of Christ declare:

> Then you will know the truth, and the truth will set you free (John 8:32).

Since He is a holy and sinless God, He cannot lie. Unlike Jesus' adversaries, who are known liars, Christians claim that He has never lied. Even non-Christians generally regard Him as an example of moral flawlessness. He said of himself:

> I am the way and the truth and the life. No one comes to the Father except through me (John 14:6).

Despite the claims of the so-called space brothers that they are the gods, or have come from the kingdom of God, Jesus says there is no other way to God the Father except through believing in Him. What better method can the lying spirits employ to serve their ends than to teach the world that it is mistaken about Jesus, or that Christianity is one of only many ways to the kingdom of God? Numbers 23:19 and Titus 1:2 say that God does not and cannot lie. If Jesus failed to tell the truth about one single thing, then His claim to be God would be invalid because He would be a liar. In contrast, the record shows that our so-called alien saviors have lied repeatedly.

We are now going to look at the not-so-subtle deceptions that are being employed to keep people away from the Creator God.

Pseudo-biblical beliefs

Although the majority of the population, including the UFO skeptics, believe that there is extraterrestrial life somewhere in the universe (shown by poll results mentioned earlier), a good number of them think that people who claim to be in touch with ETs are crackpots. They do not even consider the possibility that these UFO-believers are being deceived by powerful spirit beings. However, the world suddenly realized the serious and dangerous nature of such beliefs when, in March 1997, 39 members of a UFO-believing group committed suicide.

The suicides were an act of devotion in a cult known as Heaven's Gate. Their leader, Marshall Applewhite, claimed to be an incarnation of Jesus Christ after being told that he was specially chosen. In the months prior to their suicides, the cult had been warning of impending Armageddon (a climactic global "last days" battle) on the earth. Applewhite was "graciously" providing advance notice and offering a last chance for salvation. Where was this salvation coming from? He believed that it was coming from a flying saucer that was trailing the Hale-Bopp comet, and that it was coming to redeem their souls and take them to the kingdom of heaven. The cult even produced advertising posters claiming to know "the only way out of this corrupt world," suggesting that their physical bodies were merely containers for their souls[9] and that they would be transformed into angel-like or ethereal bodies just like their ET saviors. Applewhite's answer was to commit suicide, thus leaving his earthly container behind. Claiming to be Christ, he said he had already done this nearly 2,000 years ago. Tragically, it is likely that Applewhite had a serious case of the "walk-ins." "Devotion unto death" demonstrates the tragic depth of his deception.

They believed that man's next stage of evolution was a spiritual one — not a physical one — calling it "Evolutionary Level above Human" (the Kingdom of Heaven), i.e., to become like "gods." They even believed that the higher beings, regarded as space aliens, had previously and deliberately crashed spacecraft in staged events, and left their discarded bodies for the government and military to find. Apparently these crashes occurred in the 1940s and are obvious references to the non-events known as the Roswell incident and the "crashes at Corona."

Heaven's Gate's beliefs are riddled with pseudo-biblical references that reinterpret the intended meanings of the biblical text. The most

significant teaching is that Christ is not the Son of God but an interstellar being who ascended to the next level. This is the most common
view of Christ among the UFO/New Age lobby. Jesus is lumped in
with all the so-called "great teachers" of history — Buddha, Mohammed, and so on.

This is also a prominent view held by a New Age couple, Brad and
Sherry Steiger, who, between them, have probably written more books
on UFOs than anyone else. Sherry Steiger is a former student of the
Lutheran School of Theology in Chicago, who started to delve deeper
into the UFO phenomenon and even worked with Dr. J. Allen Hynek.
Like a Martini cocktail, she blends many biblical events with a "UFO
twist and a dash of von Däniken." She believes, for example, that the
destruction of Sodom and Gomorrah is a nuclear blast at the hands of
the angelic visitors. Like Whitley Strieber, she also claims that these
angelic UFOnauts are embedded in our history and in many of the
ancient religions of the world, saying:

> I have come to see through my continued study from the
> 1960s on, that all the world religions have similar descriptions
> of astral vehicles and supernatural beings and their interac-
> tions with humankind. I believe the UFOs to be the "Powers
> and Principalities" — as stated in the New Testament. . . .[10]

I believe that she is correct, except for her belief that they are extraterrestrial, which is the viewpoint that these fallen angels are eager
for us to believe. Unfortunately, the well-meaning and amiable Steigers
have accepted it. Their beliefs are straight out of the New Age textbook.
Brad Steiger says the ETs have been guiding us all along:

> I believe that, through the ages, they have been provoking
> humankind into higher spirals of intellectual and technologi-
> cal maturity, guiding men and women toward ever-expanding
> mental and spiritual awareness, pulling our species continually
> into the future.[11]

A relatively consistent feature of the Steigers' prolific writings is
that they advocate an almost complete reinterpretation of the Bible.
They are not alone. It would be possible to fill volumes with a mélange
of "creative" ideas by contactees and New Age writers on how conventional religions formed as a result of extraterrestrial interference
in human affairs. But, particularly, we see in such notions a continual

reinterpretation of the Bible according to modern UFO/New Age beliefs.

There is a simple and reasonable question for those who take such liberties with the well-detailed events recorded in the Bible. Quite simply, "Were you there?" It is a touch arrogant for modern people to presume they can reinterpret the Bible authors' intent on the assumption that those early writers were technologically ignorant or didn't understand. In fact, they were in some ways savvier than generations today because they were more spiritually attuned. Our understanding of spiritual things has been stolen by our preoccupation with the physical world and our trust in operational science to be our "savior." In addition, if the Bible mistakes alien interference as the handiwork of God or angels, then why are the Scriptures so clear about *having nothing to do with these types of practices* (see later)? If the space brothers have been guiding and overseeing mankind's development, then you would think that the Bible would encourage such contacts. But it does not! God expressly forbids such contacts. This "reinterpretation" fails on its own logic.

The New Age/UFO view of the world precludes its adherents from accepting the Bible for what it claims to be — the very words of God (see 2 Tim. 3:16). But from where do they get such a myriad of strange interpretations? Directly from the horse's (alien's) mouth, it would appear. This mode of communication has all the appearances of another age-old occult practice that has been given a technological facelift. It's now called channeling.

Just tune in — messages from another dimension

Many of the prominent movers and shakers in the UFO movement claim to have had direct and open contact with extraterrestrials. These privileged few are called contactees. Billy Meier and George Adamski are two notables that we have previously mentioned. Like many others, they were told that they had been chosen to spread the cosmic wisdom of the space brothers (this is how the term was first derived) to all mankind. Even in the early days of such contacts, it was clear that the "missions" given to contactees were to "raise a cosmic awareness and consciousness," sometimes by spearheading new religions. More recently these messages and missions have been imparted to abductees, many of whom have subsequently allowed themselves to become the subject of walk-ins and channeling sessions. Channeling occurs where a being from another source or level supposedly communicates through a human who has entered into a trance-like state. In other words, the human acts as a medium or channel for the other being. Today, there is a plethora of modern gurus who claim to be in contact with extraterrestrial beings, interdimensional ones, and/or both. Whitley Strieber claimed that he came to a point in his relationship with his visitors where he could call upon them almost at will. This reinforces the spiritual nature of his experiences.

This is a dangerous practice. How can one be sure about who or what is "transmitting" the message? Indeed, Strieber himself remains unsure as to the origin of his visitors. It is often claimed that the sources must be genuine because they impart tales and stories to the recipients that only they could know are true, such as life histories or incidents from their past. This may be true (discussed later), but once again, we should recall that the space brothers have also told people things that we know are demonstrably *not* true.

Channeling is closely related to the walk-in phenomenon and can incorporate other practices, such as automatic writing (dozens of books have supposedly been written by extraterrestrial beings who control a person while they type or write messages) or remote viewing (where the individual sees pictures or images of an event, sometimes on other planets or in space). Attempts have been made to validate remote viewing as a scientific method. There are many claims that even the U.S. government experimented with remote viewing by predefining categories or questionnaires for the viewers to answer — a bit like filling out a multiple-choice form while "under the influence." I have heard firsthand claims from self-proclaimed experts that just about anyone can be trained for this task. "It's just a case of emptying yourself completely of any earthly thoughts before you begin a session, allowing streams of thoughts or pictures to transcend from other sources." But is it reasonable to allow a powerful, unknown being from an unknown origin to do this to you?

Lynn E. Catoe was a senior bibliographer for the Library of Congress (USA). In 1969 she wrote an insightful document compiled for the United States Air Force called *UFOs and Related Subjects*. She felt that she had some insight into the origin of such practices, writing:

> A large part of the available UFO literature is closely linked with mysticism and the metaphysical. It deals with

subjects like mental telepathy, automatic writing and invisible entities as well as phenomenon [sic] like poltergeist manifestations and possession. Many of the UFO reports now being published in the popular press recount alleged incidents that are strikingly similar to demonic possession and psychic phenomenon that have long been known to theologians and parapsychologists.[12]

Although Brad Steiger does not use the term "walk-in," he takes this a step further by suggesting that many people alive on Earth are in fact from other worlds. In his early books, he says he started to look for similarities among people who claimed extraterrestrial contacts that resulted in increased paranormal ability (which is usually a subsequent sign of contact). He claims that many of these people started to feel that their "soul essences" were from another place. UFO researcher Randall Fitzgerald comments about the Steigers' book, *The Star People* (1981):

> Brad and Francie Steiger not only believe that many humans are descendants of space beings who mated with our species to prepare Earth for transformation, but they themselves are Star People here to assist the aliens in that work.[13]

In a later book called *Starborn* (1992), the Steigers used information derived from questionnaires completed by thousands of people. Steiger, and his second wife, Sherry, claimed they found a pattern of physical and psychic similarities that were initially triggered by what they described as an "activating incident" at a very young age in their subjects. They say this could have been an encounter with an alleged angel, elf, holy figure, or a UFO entity. The idea then ballooned to suggest that even children's invisible playmates were indicators of their childhood ET experiences. The Steigers' New Age conclusions were summarized as follows:

> Currently, the Steigers state that the greatest single commonality among the Star People is a desire to be of service to the planet and all of Mother earth's children. It is such a sense of mission that seems to distinguish those who believe that they have interacted with some facet of a Higher Intelligence or with an extraterrestrial or multidimensional being.[14]

History redefined

On the surface, these appear to be noble ideals, but once again, where is the God of the Bible? Surely the highest goal is to attain knowledge about the Creator of the universe, but if the Steigers, who claim they come from Christian backgrounds, had taken the Bible at face value, they would have found the answers without the need for their continually "evolving" ideas. Besides recognizing their countless falsehoods, what else can we glean about these deceptive entities?

Interestingly, in Brad Steiger's 1989 book *The Fellowship*, he wrote about contacts with an alien by the name of Semjase — the very same name of the blond alien who supposedly visited Billy Meier. It is claimed that Semjase also visited another famous contactee by the name of Fred Bell to inform him, among other things, that the Bible has been edited incorrectly. She also told him about the future — apocalyptic events to come — in similar fashion to the Book of Revelation in the Bible. It is no coincidence that all three became decidedly anti-Christian and anti-biblical in their outlook, especially after their contact with Semjase, who told them that the Bible had "holes."

Francie Steiger, Brad's first wife, claimed to have channeled messages from an angelic being named Kihief. UFO researcher William Alnor writes:

> Kihief gave her an alternate history of the world and explained a way of salvation — a different gospel — from the one outlined in the Bible and believed by Christians for twenty centuries. . . . According to Kihief, the serpent people, who, he says, were represented by the serpent described in the biblical Garden of Eden, helped create humankind. Francie Steiger says we should believe him because "he speaks only of God and of goodness."[15]

Is it any coincidence that Kihief appears as a good guy? Note that he even redefines the serpent in the Garden of Eden, who for centuries has been the embodiment of the evil angel known as Satan or Lucifer. To a Christian, this version of Bible history is reminiscent of Holocaust-deniers who rewrite history by saying, "The Holocaust never really happened," and "Hitler was just a misunderstood genius." Many channelers and contactees report similar "corrections" of history (see example in the next chapter). Kihief also told her that humans were being conditioned for change and being prepared for a transformation into the New Age.

One of the most prominent New Age religious leaders on the planet is a man by the name of David Spangler. It is little known that he also claims to be in contact with alien entities. He has even reinvented the role of Lucifer:

> Spangler teaches that Lucifer is an agent of God's love. He believes that Lucifer is the angel of man's inner evolution, that "the light that reveals to us the path to Christ comes from Lucifer . . . the great initiator. Lucifer comes to give us the final initiation that many people in the days ahead will be facing, for it is an initiation into the New Age.[16]

Spangler claims this information was dictated to him by spirit entities, and he calls this the "Luciferian Initiation" and says that those who follow this path will become "light" bearers. The aliens seem to be obsessed with (masquerading as) light!

Apart from Semjase, who keeps popping up to visit contactees, there are some other names of space brothers that warrant further investigation. Ashtar is supposedly an ET who commenced his visitations in the 1950s, which have continued to the present day. On one occasion he appeared and apparently spoke through an author by the name of T. James (by literally taking over the vocal chords), claiming that people lived with Satan on the moon (demonstrably wrong, yet again!) Billy Meier also claims to have been told by his Pleiadean visitors about a being called Ashtar, who used to be an evil alien but is now a good guy working with Jesus. Ashtar also visited another "world-famous" contactee, George Van Tassel, and gave him a mission to save the world from itself. World-renowned UFOlogist and archaeologist Dr. Clifford Wilson is only one of several who have pointed out how this entity "Ashtar" keeps appearing in the UFO literature as well as in ancient texts. John Keel, one of the world's most published and well-respected UFOlogists, also noted this, and highlighted the element of deception, when he wrote:

> Thousands of mediums, psychics, and UFO contactees have been receiving mountains of messages from "Ashtar" in recent years. . . . Ashtar is not a new arrival. Variations of this name, such as Astaroth, Ashar, Asharoth, etc., appear

in demonological literature throughout history, both in the Orient and Occident. Mr. Ashtar had been around a very long time, posing as assorted gods and demons and now, in the modern phase, as another glorious spaceman.[17]

In addition to the demonological literature Keel spoke about, we can trace the ancestry of some of these space beings/gods from the Bible. That Book is full of instances where people turned away from worshiping the true God to follow false gods and deities based around the stars and planets. Ashtaroth appears in the Old Testament several times as an evil object of worship condemned by God. On several occasions, when the ancient Israelites started to worship "foreign gods" and false deities, instead of the one true God, God let them have their own way and removed His protection from over them. This resulted in many calamities befalling them until they realized the error of their ways, repenting and returning to worship the true Creator. In 1 Kings 11:33, God says:

> . . . they have forsaken me and worshipped Ashtoreth the goddess of the Sidonians, Chemosh the god of the Moabites, and Molech the god of the Ammonites, and have not walked in my ways, nor done what is right in my eyes, nor kept my statutes and laws. . . .

Ashtoreth was the female consort of Baal (just one of many names for the devil — also called Baalzebub, who was sometimes worshiped as a sun god). Some Bible scholars claim her name literally means "star." There is no doubt that she was also worshiped as a moon goddess and also the goddess of the planet Venus (an object of fertility). In other passages, similar names appear in various forms and often in the plural (Ashtaroth, Baalim), probably signifying modifications of the original form. Ashtoreth was the Ishtar of the Accadians, Astarte of the Greeks (1 Kings 11:5, 33; 2 Kings 23:13), Ishtar of the Assyrians, and Astarte of the Phoenicians, and she was also called the "queen of heaven" (Jer. 44:25).

In addition, we see Chemosh, a "god" which *Strong's Bible Concordance* says is associated with "Baal-peor" and "Baal-zebub" (also mentioned in the New Testament in several instances), which signifies the worship of Mars and Saturn. The idol Molech (associated with evil and cruel practices) was also an Assyrian-Babylonian god of the planet Saturn, and is transliterated as Chiun in Amos 5:26, and as Remphan (or Repham in some translations) in Acts 7:43. In Egypt, the worship of the "creator" sun god Ra is well known. As Keel noticed, they have been deceiving mankind for a long time.

The worship of heavenly bodies is also common throughout Asia, where mystical religions abound, and in ancient North and South American beliefs, particularly the Mayan culture, which incorporated human sacrifices. New Age UFOlogy is linked to spiritism, a practice found all over the Western countries, but which is even more pronounced in "developing" countries.[18]

Well-known Christian author Dave Hunt, when presenting a paper at the "Human Potential Foundation" conference, was reported as saying:

> What we are seeing is staggering, not only spirit mediums, psychics, yogis and kooks, but now top scientists are seriously attempting to contact "spirit beings" whom they believe are highly evolved, godlike entities with great knowledge and more powers than humans possess. It takes little insight to realize that the attempt to contact non-physical entities opens the door for all kinds of satanic deception. . . .[19]

Nothing new under the sun

In Ecclesiastes 1:9–11, the wise Israelite king Solomon wrote:

> What has been will be again, what has been done will be done again; there is nothing new under the sun. Is there anything of which one can say, "Look! This is something new"? It was here already, long ago; it was here before our time. There is no remembrance of men of old, and even those who are yet to come will not be remembered by those who follow."

As already pointed out, the modern UFO/New Age movement has as a major source of influence the practice of channeling, or communicating with "spirits," "a higher evolution," "vibration," "frequency," or whatever technological pseudo-speak they care to call it. However, the Bible speaks very openly about things that are unmistakably the same practices. In Deuteronomy 18:10 God commands:

> Let no one be found among you who sacrifices his son or daughter in the fire [the worshipers of Molech sacrificed their own children in a fire that burned in the belly of this bronze

god], who practices divination or sorcery, interprets omens, engages in witchcraft, or casts spells, or who is a medium or spiritist or who consults the dead. Anyone who does these things is detestable to the Lord. . . .

On numerous occasions it is made clear that God detests such practices. One of these practices is also called divination (foretelling the future by supernatural means). God tells us why He does not want people to dabble in these things:

> Their visions are false and their divinations a lie. They say, "The Lord declares," when the Lord has not sent them; yet they expect their words to be fulfilled (Ezek. 13:6).

Can they tell the future? Apparently not. The contactee movement is a "train wreck" when it comes to the reliability of future prophecies. But the lying spirits manage to deceive many by revealing secrets only known to the contactees. This is no different than the popular TV mediums who supposedly contact the dead relatives of participants, and then go on to reveal intimate personal details. Their "prophetic" words are very convincing — if you are ignorant of spiritual things. As we saw in the last chapter, dabbling in the occult is like opening a doorway to the evil side of the spiritual realm. Of course it is possible for these spirits to know intimate details of your life — once you have invited them in and they have been following and watching you very carefully in order to perpetrate the deception.

An example of this occurs in Acts 16:16–19, where the apostle Paul encounters a person who is able to do such things. The author of Acts (a doctor by the name of Luke) writes:

> Once when we were going to the place of prayer, we were met by a slave girl who had a spirit by which she predicted the future [or at least claimed to]. She earned a great deal of money for her owners by fortune telling. This girl followed Paul and the rest of us, shouting, "These men are servants of the Most High God, who are telling you the way to be saved." She kept this up for many days.
>
> Finally Paul became so troubled that he turned round and said to the spirit, "In the name of Jesus Christ I command you to come out of her!" At that moment the spirit left her.

See how it obeyed the authority of Christ's name spoken by a believer? But some others, who were not Christians, tried to replicate Paul's efforts and they experienced a different outcome.

> Some Jews who went around driving out evil spirits tried to invoke the name of the Lord Jesus over those who were demon-possessed. They would say, "In the name of Jesus, whom Paul preaches, I command you to come out." . . .
>
> One day the evil spirit answered them, "Jesus I know, and I know about Paul, but who are you?" Then the man who had the evil spirit jumped on them and overpowered them all. He gave them such a beating that they ran out of the house naked and bleeding. When this became known to the Jews and Greeks living in Ephesus, they were all seized with fear, and the name of the Lord Jesus was held in high honor (Acts 19:13–17).

Many may consider such biblical accounts, and even the practices of witchcraft and sorcery, to be remnants of primitive ideas and cultures. In the Book of Exodus 7:8–13, Moses approached Pharaoh to seek the release of the Hebrew people, and on God's instruction, Moses threw a wooden staff to the ground and it became a snake. The book then says that each of Pharaoh's sorcerers also conjured up a snake, but their efforts were overcome by God. Is this any different than the shape-shifting and illusional characteristics of UFOs in the night sky, leaving landing traces, burn marks, or even depressions in the ground? In talking about UFOs, researchers Ankerberg and Weldon noted:

> . . . it seems evident that these phenomena are produced in the same manner that other occult manipulations are produced. They involve dramatic manipulations of matter and energy. Although they originate from the spiritual world, they can produce very powerful, temporarily physical manifestations at the material level. . . . However the UFO is produced, it is frequently of small dimensions — an area where an extremely large amount of energy is concentrated.[20]

"We're all brothers" — the "many-ways-to-God" idea

The modern New Age/UFO movement is happy to embrace those of other religious persuasions. It has roots in Buddhism, Shintoism

(Japan is a UFO-mad society), Hinduism, Taoism, Animism, and most other mystical religions that are steeped in the worship of spirits, deities, dead ancestors or reincarnated ones, and even the heavenly bodies. Christians are embraced, too, providing they are not too dogmatic about their faith and don't mind a reinterpretation of the Bible here and there.

Notice what happened in an interesting account of a young Israeli king by the name of Manasseh, who departed from his father's practice of worshiping the one true Creator. In 2 Kings 21:3–6, we see:

> He rebuilt the high places his father Hezekiah had destroyed; he also erected altars to Baal and made an Asherah [remember Ashtar] pole, as Ahab king of Israel had done. He bowed down to all the *starry hosts* and worshipped them. He built altars in the temple of the Lord, of which the Lord had said, "In Jerusalem I will put my Name." In both courts of the temple of the Lord, he built altars to all the *starry hosts*. He sacrificed his own son in the fire, practiced sorcery and divination, and consulted mediums and spiritists. He did much evil in the eyes of the Lord, provoking him to anger [emphases added].

Notice that Manasseh led his people astray. They followed their leader in a manner similar to those who follow cult leaders today. Also note that the passage clearly relates the worship of false gods (Baal and Asherah) with the "starry hosts" (or the hosts of heaven) and with the practices of witchcraft, divination, and spiritism. God makes no distinction among these practices. They are one and the same, and evil in his sight.

God gave another clear command:

> You shall have no other gods before me. You shall not make for yourself an idol in the form of anything in heaven above. . . . You shall not bow down to them or worship them; for I, the Lord your God, am a jealous God, punishing the children for the sin of the fathers to the third and fourth generation of those who hate me (Exod. 20:3–5).

God viewed this so seriously that He made it one of the Ten Commandments. He was not being egocentric. This warning was, and is, for our own good. Note how the warning passes on to the next generation. This is strikingly similar to what occurs in the UFO and abduction cases in which several generations of family members appear to be afflicted — until the cycle is broken in the name of Christ. Lifelong UFOlogist, and author of some of the biggest-selling UFO research books of all time, John Keel, says:

> Millions of people have been affected at least temporarily by UFO contact, [and] thousands have gone insane and ended up in mental institutions after their experiences with these things began.[21]

Such problems help to explain why God is not tolerant of the worship of other beings, which He created (Rom. 1:25). True Christianity, which claims to be solely based on the teachings of the Bible, cannot, by definition, be all-embracing like the New Age movement. The Bible expresses intolerance of other religions because they keep people away from the truth of the Bible and its way of knowing and worshiping the one true God. We have already noted that many ancient Eastern religions, which involve spirit worship, are very open to these UFO experiences. But there is a link to the UFO/deceptive contact phenomenon in many other major religions as well, often at a foundational level.

The Church of Jesus Christ of Latter Day Saints (Mormons), with nearly eight million members worldwide, was founded by Joseph Smith after his contact with an angelic being. Bill Alnor writes:

> In 1823, in an era when more people believed in angels than visitors from space, an "angel" named Moroni allegedly appeared at Smith's bedside in upper New York state and re-commissioned him as a prophet to launch a new dispensation of Christianity that would restore the apostate church. In 1820, Smith allegedly received a vision claiming that he was God's new prophet.[22]

Note how the entity appeared to be representing God with "pure and honest" motives. No wonder that Mormons, like alien contactees, are not very open to traditional Christian claims about the truth. They find it hard to believe that they were manipulated by something appearing so "good."

Alnor also writes about James Walker, an ex-Mormon (fourth-generation), who says that Mormons actually believe God used to be a man named Elohim who lived on a planet named Kolab. He was eventually allowed to become one of the gods and marry numerous goddesses, and we are their resultant offspring. By joining the Mormon Church and obeying the church's secret rituals, followers will have a chance of godhood, too, on another planet somewhere. In addition, Smith believed that the moon was inhabited and that he would preach his gospel there someday (now who gave him that incorrect prophecy?).[23] Joseph Smith's encounter was with a being called "Moroni" (supposedly a good angel) which selected him for a special mission. Over the years, thousands of contactees and abductees have been told a similar thing — "You have been chosen." The Mormons even have an "extra Bible" — their own "holy" writings known as the Book of Mormon.

The Islamic religion also appears to have its origins in a visitor experience. In A.D. 610, after six months of spiritual meditation in a cave, Mohammed claimed that the angel Gabriel appeared to him. After many years of visitations, Mohammad recited to his band of followers the words he claimed to have heard, much of which came after visions and trances (some of his own contemporaries actually thought he was demon possessed). Some of these pronouncements were memorized and some were written on animal bones, parchments, and pieces of leather. About 15 years after his death, these writings were authorized and compiled into Islam's holy book, the Quran.[24]

Although the good angel Gabriel is mentioned in the Bible, it does not necessarily follow that it was the real Gabriel that appeared to Mohammed. (Remember, people have claimed that the beings appearing to them on spaceships have sometimes called themselves Jesus, too.) It makes no sense that one of God's faithful angels (the one who appeared to the virgin Mary, no less) would provide new revelation that reinterprets the Bible and denies the deity of Jesus. The Bible makes no mention of, and in fact warns about, any extra instruction other than what is already written in the Bible. In Luke 1:32, 35, Gabriel twice says Jesus is God's Son, but the Quran's Gabriel says that Jesus is an ordinary man, although a prophet, and not God's son. Both cannot be true.

> See that you do all I command you; do not add to it or take away from it.
>
> If a prophet, or one who foretells by dreams, appears among you and announces to you a miraculous sign or wonder, and if the sign or wonder of which he has spoken takes

place, and he says, "Let us follow other gods" (gods you have not known) "and let us worship them," you must not listen to the words of that prophet or dreamer. The Lord your God is testing you to find out whether you love him with all your heart and with all your soul (Deut. 12:32–13:1–3).

This is incredible. Here is a warning from the Old Testament against being impressed by supernatural manifestations, and the New Testament offers an even more direct warning about listening to angels:

But even if we or an angel from heaven should preach a gospel other than the one we preached to you, let him be eternally condemned! (Gal. 1:8).

Although Muslims follow Allah (which is Arabic for God), who they claim is the same as the God of the Bible, many religious commentators believe that there is abundant evidence, historically and archaeologically, that the name Allah is derived from the name "al-ilah." They claim that this is the Moon god who was married to the goddess of the sun, and the stars were their daughters. They also believe that the worship of these deities was common in pre-Islamic times throughout the Middle East and Arabia. Many dispute this, although it is interesting that statues and artifacts from archaeological discoveries suggest that the famous crescent, which is representative of Islam, was derived from this occultic source.[25]

Louis Farrakhan, the popular leader of the Nation of Islam movement founded in the United States, was a former UFO contactee, according to a popular American newspaper (the *Washington Post*, September 18, 1995, p. D3). As a young man, he was taken aboard a UFO where he met "Master Elijah Muhammed" (the former Nation of Islam leader, then deceased), the builder of the ship.[26] Although not widely reported, Farrakhan and his followers apparently believe that Armageddon is coming and that the spaceships will return again someday. He and his Nation of Islam group were the organizers of the Million Man March that took place in Washington, D.C., in the mid-1990s.[27] Elijah Muhammad's widow, Mother Tynetta, also predicted that 2001 would be the "Year of the End" (Armageddon), citing UFOs seen in the vicinity of the September 11 (2001) destruction of the World Trade Center in New York.[28]

The "doctrines of demons"

In 1 Timothy 4:1, the Bible says:

> The Spirit clearly says that in later times some will abandon the faith and follow deceiving spirits and things taught by demons.

Besides the religions that have their origins in the dubious "you are the chosen one" experiences of their leaders, there are many other religious movements based on science fiction and UFO/New Age beliefs. At the head of most of these is a charismatic leader who has had a vision, visitation, or message delivered in a manner that says they have been selected for a mission. The more modern UFO-based movements are often referred to as UFO cults. For example, they often refer to their leaders as the Messiah, including the Raelians (mentioned in chapter 1), whose leader is Rael (a.k.a. former French motorsport journalist Claude Vorhillon).

This infamous group believes that they can awaken the mind, body, and spirit through the pleasures of the flesh. Mass orgies are common at their "spiritual retreat," which doubles as an alien theme park in Florida. Rael (his name is supposed to mean "messenger") claims to have met Jesus, Mohammed, and Buddha on a flying saucer. His "given" mission is to build an embassy near Jerusalem in readiness for the return of our alien creators to Earth.[29] He could be a fraud or a self-deluded madman — or both. Who knows? But it is no joke — the Raelians' following is increasing at an astonishing rate.

One of the trendiest cults around is the Church of Scientology. Founded by the late science fiction writer L. Ron Hubbard, its beliefs could have come straight out of one of his novels. Some have said that his ideas were birthed from those of the world's most famous self-declared Satanist, Aleister Crowley. A *New York Post* article, reporting on investigations by a Boston University researcher, claimed:

> Hubbard had met Crowley in the latter's Los Angeles temple in 1945. . . . Hubbard's son reveals that Hubbard claimed to be Crowley's successor: Hubbard told him that Scientology was born on the day that Crowley died. . . . Scientologists perform some of the same rites that Crowley invented, all designed to free practitioners from human guilt.[30]

Crowley was often described as the "wickedest man on Earth." He even called himself the "Great Beast" of 666, after the description of the devil contained in the Bible's Book of Revelation. Believing that guilt or remorse were to be done away with, he openly used hallucinogenic drugs and advocated complete sexual freedom, including bestiality. Some modern pop stars have made not-so-subtle references to Crowley in their songs, advocating his practices.[31]

So how did these practices form part of a UFO-based religion? Hubbard claimed that "Thetans" or gods — uncreated and eternal beings that were free from all laws — populated the universe. These Thetans gathered together to create time, space, and energy (our creators, once again). However, they were banished to Earth by an evil galactic ruler named Xenu, where they now inhabit the bodies of humans. They were originally incarnated into plants and animals but, through the process of evolution, became humans (another example of how evolutionary ideology is woven into the tales of the deceiving space brothers).

To attain a higher spiritual level in Scientology it is necessary to have these Thetans released from your body. They are currently "negative" spirits because they have been asleep inside of humans for countless millennia. There is a cost for this process, believed to be in the range of two to four hundred thousand dollars. To determine your body's level of Thetans, they supposedly use electronic gadgets known as "e-meters."[32] In a well-known statement, Hubbard was supposed to have said:

> Writing for a penny a word is ridiculous. If a man really wanted to make a million dollars, the best way would be to start his own religion.[33]

This is exactly what he did. The Church of Scientology is extremely wealthy, and no wonder, because it boasts some Hollywood "royalty" as adherents. They include actors Tom Cruise, John Travolta, Lisa Marie Presley, Hilary Swank, Juliette Lewis, Jenna Elfman, and Kirstie Alley. Such revered icons unfortunately give this cult an undeserved air of respectability. Some families have lost children to this group, with the children subsequently becoming even unwilling to relate to their once-loving kin. Distraught families often claim brainwashing and mind-control techniques have been used upon their children and other members. Some countries, such as Germany, are presently trying to outlaw this cult.

It may surprise some to know that groups such as the Aum Supreme Truth sect (Aum Shinrikyo) also have some "spaced-out" beliefs. This was the group responsible for the deadly sarin gas attack in a Tokyo subway, which killed 12 people and afflicted 5,500 others. Once again, it is staggering how ordinary folk are drawn to such lunacy. At their zenith, the cult had 40,000 followers. The cult's leader, Shoko Asahara, also declared himself to be Christ. On one occasion, a rally drew 19,000 people to Moscow's Olympic Stadium. A huge video screen played images of Asahara being crucified in Christ-like manner.[34]

Asahara thought he was the one "chosen" to be the savior of the world. He also claims he received a message from God while on a Himalayan retreat in 1986. But his ideas come straight out of Isaac Asimov's *Foundation* series of novels, in which a select group of brilliant individuals formed a secret society to save mankind and control the future. Asahara's murderous attack on innocent people was designed to hasten Armageddon, and bring the world into a state of chaos, opening the door for his rise to power. But he and most of his followers are now in jail. It would be fair to say that he obviously did not hear from the real omniscient God; otherwise, the prophecies and his plans *would* have come to pass.

Death on demand

Besides the awful tragedy of the Heaven's Gate suicides, there have been similar episodes where many followers have been led astray, even to the point of death. This is a satanic strategy that ensures people never get to hear the truth before they die.

The "Order of the Solar Temple" is a murderous cult whose beliefs are most certainly based in "outer space." Their object of worship was the star Sirius in the Orion constellation. Aleister Crowley also had a preoccupation with Sirius. He claimed to channel messages from a Sirian ("from Sirius") named Lam, as well as a demonic alien being named Aiwass. UFO researcher Bill Alnor has also noticed that some of the more "out-and-out" devotees of black magic, witchcraft, and even Satanism, like Crowley, were interested in Sirius, and that most ET messages today come from this source. He writes:

> Is this a coincidence or are there real, demonic forces at work helping to spark humankind's interest in particular heavenly bodies?[35]

This is nothing new, of course. We have already seen the preoccupation with the heavenly bodies as recorded in the Old Testament, but Alnor notes that it is still occurring.

Founded by Luc Jouret (another leader who claimed he was Jesus Christ) and Joseph Di Mambro, the "Solar Temple" was a cult that had followers in many Western countries. The leaders often made references to the Bible, but as expected, the cult was steeped in New Age practices. Like many other UFO doomsday cults, they had apocalyptic overtones, believing that the earth would eventually be destroyed. It is reported that they were obsessed with the declining state of the planet, marred by the effects of pollution, violence, and immorality. This is astonishing because the group appeared to have no problem with participating in "sex magic" rituals with multiple partners in open acts of adultery. There was also an alleged misappropriation of funds, which may have been one of the catalysts that ultimately led to demise of the cult and its members.

During the middle of the 1990s, fragmentation and rivalry in the group ensued, which is not surprising when leaders determine truth to suit their own evil desires. Under the auspices of a ritual known as the "Christic fire," cult members were shot, stabbed (including women, children, and babies), and suffocated; and their bodies were burned so they could undergo a spiritual transformation, depart this earth, and return home — to a planet orbiting Sirius. In Canada and Switzerland, 74 people were murdered or committed suicide in a period of 30 months. It seems incredible that they willingly followed their leader's instructions without hesitation, whether performing unusual sex acts on demand or committing suicide. Were their members young, impressionable, and disillusioned teenagers who were vulnerable to authoritarian figures? No! The typical member was middle-aged and middle class, and included company directors, sales managers, a former mayor, and a former Olympic champion.

These people apparently sensed a spiritual void in their lives and looked for something to fill it. Unfortunately, they apparently never considered the possibility that their own sinful state had separated them from God, the real Heavenly Father — hence the void. The spiritual forces of the satanic realm take full advantage of this lack of understanding.

Followers of Jesus say they experience a new beginning that not only equips them for this life, but also for the next one. The deception of the space brothers brings only death — in this life and beyond. Jesus says:

If [the true] God were your Father, you would love me, for I came from God and now am here. I have not come on my own; but he sent me. Why is my language not clear to you? Because you are unable to hear what I say. You belong to your father, the devil, and you want to carry out your father's desire. He was a murderer from the beginning, not holding to the truth, for there is no truth in him. When he lies, he speaks his native language, for he is a liar and the father of lies (John 8:42–44).

Why are people attracted to bizarre cultic ideas, and even more strangely, willing to act out these bizarre rituals even to death? For one thing, lies can be very powerful. When a lie is grand enough, it deceives on the basis that "it's so farfetched, it must be true." Another reason is that these cults often use biblical language, providing just enough familiar-sounding truth to make their ideas enticing.

UFO-believers aren't the only reinterpreters

When much of the traditional church has questioned, abandoned, or reinterpreted the validity of its own divinely inspired book (leaving people with the impression that the Bible doesn't literally mean what it says), then it's open to anyone's interpretation.

The theory of evolution has caused many to discount the first book of the Bible (Genesis) as the real history of how the world came to be. On the issue of origins, there is much division in the church, leaving cults with an open playing field. If the church has failed to make a stand on its own origins, its own foundational teachings, and failed to counter the "prophets" who reinterpret the Bible, is it any wonder that people are drawn to cults where there is strong leadership? If the first book of the Bible has to be reinterpreted to fit reality, then what about the rest of the Bible? In other words, "Where does the truth begin in the Bible?" If it's not all true, then the Christian's whole belief system is *founded* on a lie.

Perhaps the popularity of cults is not surprising in a confused world where so many mainstream Christian churches don't know what they believe any more. Jesus knew such a time would come. He said:

At that time many will *turn away from the faith* and will betray and hate each other, and many false prophets will appear and deceive many people (Matt. 24:10–11, emphasis added).

And in Matthew 7:15–20, Jesus tells us that nothing good can come from the deceivers among us:

> Watch out for false prophets. They come to you in sheep's clothing, but inwardly they are ferocious wolves. By their fruit you will recognize them. Do people pick grapes from thorn-bushes, or figs from thistles? Likewise every good tree bears good fruit, but a bad tree bears bad fruit. A good tree cannot bear bad fruit, and a bad tree cannot bear good fruit. Thus, by their fruit you will recognize them.

Sex and ETs — common bedfellows

A key to understanding the popularity of these alien beliefs is the shocking sexual element. It seems impossible to understand the ab-duction/UFO issue without addressing the sexual nature of so many encounters. But why do UFOlogists rarely discuss this topic in great detail? One reason is the apparent "secondary nature" of the sex. For example, as we mentioned in the previous chapter, abduction researcher and hypnotherapist David Jacobs believes that the ETs have no real interest in sex, and also that the sexual medical-like procedures are just a charade to hide the real purpose of their mission — the collection of human sperm and ova for the cultivation and growth of half-human/half-alien offspring. Some Christian researchers actually argue that this production of hybrids is happening at both a spiritual and physical level (based on the return of the *nephilim* that arose when the "sons of God" intermarried with the "daughters of men" in Genesis 6 of the Bible — see appendix). Some UFOlogists, and all UFO skeptics, would relegate such intergalactic sexual relations to the human psyche and even folklore. Writer Nigel Watson notes the neglect of this side of the story:

> The early contactee literature provides a rich variety of such stories and, whatever their validity, it is a pity they have been largely neglected or ridiculed.[36]

Yet, I believe these early accounts offer some valuable clues about the often-sordid nature of such experiences. UFOlogist John Keel ap-parently visited college communities in Northeast America in the 1960s where several young women claimed aliens had raped them, and young men had had their semen extracted. Famous abductee Whitley Strieber describes being painfully sodomized, as do many others. Former Harvard psychiatrist John Mack, in his book *Abduction: Human Encounters with Aliens* (1994), details the episodes of 13 abductees who have had their religious outlooks changed by virtue of their encounters — most of them involved sexual experiences. Of them, one lady called "Jerry" has since become a prolific writer of New Age material, but more notably, the trauma she suffered causes her difficulty in distinguishing the difference between normal sex and being raped.[37]

Once again, I dispute the popular idea (propagated by the "ETs" themselves) that they are here to help us. If they are so interested in human welfare, why do they treat humans so terribly? After all of these years, don't they know the deleterious effects that forced physical sex has upon human beings? (Whether this is really physically occurring or not is beside the point — the abductees believe that it is occurring). It is hard to avoid the conclusion that these spirits do know, and that one of the reasons they are using it is for psychological control and manipulation, and possibly their own gratification as well. Remember Donna Higbee's earlier quote in which she and fellow researchers noticed how passive and controlled abductees became?

Many abductees have reported falling in love with, or being enamored with, their alien captors. In his later books, Whitley Strieber started to write in "loving" terms about his abductors. With any sexual contact there is a level of intimacy that transcends the right or wrong of the encounter. The emotions are even more powerful when the victim has been told they are special and have been chosen for a mission that could potentially save mankind — or when they shared this level of intimacy with a supposedly "divine" being. This is no different from the guru-like hold that many cult leaders, such as Joseph Smith (Mormons), Mohammed (Islam), Moses David (the Children of God cult), David Koresh (Branch Davidians/Waco tragedy), Jouret, Rael, and others have had over their many female followers. All of these religions, including Islam, and their charismatic leaders have advocated multiple sex partners — polygamy and/or having concubines. In the more extreme UFO cults, women and men are only too willing to satisfy the "needs" of their leaders, even to the extent and horror of offering their own children for such practices. Such is the power of control if one is deceived into thinking one is serving someone from God. We know that these leaders have left a trail of shattered lives and wrecked emotions — evidence in accordance with what Jesus said about the fruit of the devil.

In addition, it is obvious that fallen angels would not be interested in sex for the same gratification or purpose that God originally ordained it — a loving human activity within the bounds of marriage. They defile the human body, which was created by God and intended to be a temple for the Holy Spirit of God (1 Cor. 6:19).

As mentioned in the previous chapter, researchers have found similarities of a sexual nature between the ancient stories of fairies, elves, and demons, and the modern abduction scenario. Since we have already established that real, physical ETs could not reasonably be the perpetrators behind abductions, the simplest alternative is that fallen angels are the ones responsible for these modern manifestations, as well as these ancient sexual happenings. Watson writes:

> In the past, hundreds of men and women confessed (not always under torture) to sexual intercourse with demons. Some shapeshifting demons were said to lie with a man (as a succubus) to obtain sperm and then (as an incubus) impregnate a woman with it. Ufologists, in particular, have been aware of the structural similarities between accounts of fairy and alien encounters.[38]

The succubus and incubus encounters are well known throughout history as the acts of demons. This was a long time before science fiction and the possibility of advanced alien technology invaded our psyche. St. Augustine of Canterbury (died A.D. 604), who founded the church in Southern England, wrote:

> It is a widespread opinion, confirmed by direct or indirect testimony of trustworthy persons, that the Sylvans and Fauns, commonly called Incubi, have often tormented women, solicited and obtained intercourse with them. There are even Demons, which are called Duses [i.e., lutins] by the Gauls, who are quite frequently using such impure practices: this is vouched for by so numerous and so high authorities that it would be impudent to deny it.[39]

Throughout the Middle Ages, the idea of fallen angels co-habiting with human beings was a common view (covered in detail in the appendix). Even though theologians of the day argued about the "mechanics" of such a union, these acts were forbidden by the church and often resulted in excommunication.[40]

The "shapeshifting" qualities of these "ancient rapists" are also similar to those of UFOs and aliens. Some aliens have been described as changing into "beings of light," giving, once again, the illusion of a divine encounter.

The Bible describes Satan as a counterfeiter (2 Thess. 2:9). He twists and inverts everything that God has ordained for his own glory. Satanists wear Christian crosses upside down. They take communion in mocking similarity to the practice of Christians. But whereas the Christian tradition uses wine and bread to symbolize the blood and body of the crucified Christ, Satanists will use real blood and real flesh, sometimes from the bodies of aborted fetuses. In the instances of Crowley and the practices of the cults — inspired by satanic deception — it is well known that perverted rites, sexual practices, and orgies form part of worship rituals in occult circles. Such activities fall outside the boundaries of normal loving relationships, and leave a trail of anger, jealousy, and low self-esteem — the fruit of which is more human carnage by way of emotional (and sometimes physical) damage.

But why use sex? Let's be very frank. Humans are sexual creatures. In fact, psychologists recognize the sex drive as possibly the most powerful of all natural physical human drives. In an inappropriate environment, sex can have an addictive quality about it. For many people, it is one of their greatest weaknesses, and many find it difficult to escape once they have entered the promiscuous lifestyle. It's no secret that sexually abused people often mistakenly feel that their only sense of self-worth can come in the form of the next sexual encounter, which, in turn, only leaves them feeling more hollow and degraded. People addicted to pornography find it similarly difficult to escape this sexual trap. Many victims of abductions have also fallen into this web. Sexual abuse victims often have feelings of being used and unworthy, and unfortunately many reach out for comfort and reassurance to the very ones who triggered the emotional collapse — their abusers/abductors — hence the ability to control.

I am therefore postulating that the space brothers' sexual agenda has nothing to do with breeding programs. It is primarily a tool to manipulate and control humans. The descriptions of alien/human hybrids, incubatoriums, and nurseries aboard flying saucers are elaborate illusions to cover this to make the abuse somehow more palatable to the victim. (Many researchers believe that the sexual "experiences-in-common" of so many different abductees is the strongest evidence that advanced extraterrestrial beings are visiting the earth. So a secondary purpose of the whole "hybridization" charade by these deceptive entities might well be to reinforce this whole ET notion.)

Critics will no doubt regard this theory as being too simplistic. Some researchers do accept that certain details of these encounters — like the video screens and the messages they propagate — are part of pretence. But they think that the purpose of the charade is to hide a real hybridization program and somehow to make it more acceptable. But how can this be so, when these masquerading fallen angels have always been "up front" in telling abductees about the breeding program? It's no secret, and it is part of the effort to make themselves appear to be a more evolved and advanced species.

If these are the same demons that have had encounters with humans throughout the ages, then the sexual/medical pretense would seem to be a charade to cover up the connection between their "alien agenda" and the destructive demonic sexual rites in the historical record. Remember that these are the same beings who have apparently gone to great lengths to manufacture the illusions of arriving in spacecraft to cover up who they really are (whether they do this through hallucinogenic suggestion, manipulation of energy, or whatever).

Consider this evidence against the claim of a breeding program: if the aliens have been breeding hybrid offspring for countless millennia, where are their offspring now? Of the explanations offered, a plausible one has yet to emerge.

People seem to be looking everywhere for answers about UFOs and abductions — everywhere except the Scriptures. These say that Satan wants to destroy human lives and keep mankind from the knowledge of the true God:

> For since the creation of the world God's invisible qualities — his eternal power and divine nature — have been clearly seen, being understood from what has been made, so that men are without excuse. For although they knew God, they neither glorified him as God nor gave thanks to him, but their thinking became futile and their foolish hearts were darkened. Although they claimed to be wise, they became fools and exchanged the glory of the immortal God for images made to look like mortal man and birds and animals and reptiles. Therefore God gave them over in the sinful desires

of their hearts to sexual impurity for the degrading of their bodies with one another. They exchanged the truth of God for a lie, and worshiped and served created things [including fallen angels] rather than the Creator — who is forever praised. Amen. Furthermore, since they did not think it worth while to retain the knowledge of God, he gave them over to a depraved mind, to do what ought not to be done (Rom. 1:20–28).

A brief background of the New Age movement [NAM]

A "cult watcher" group known as the Watchman Fellowship defines the term *occult* as coming from the Latin *occultus,* meaning "hidden," and says that the word is used of secret or mysterious supernatural powers or magical, religious rituals. Generally, it refers to witchcraft, Satanism, neo-paganism, or various forms of psychic practices. It also describes New Age as:

> . . . an umbrella term to describe organizations which seem to exhibit one or more of the following beliefs: (1) All is one, all reality is part of the whole; (2) Everything is God and God is everything; (3) Man is God or a part of God; (4) Man never dies, but continues to live through reincarnation; (5) Man can create his own reality and/or values through transformed consciousness or altered states of consciousness.[41]

Generally, the NAM borrows its theology from pantheistic (everything is God) Eastern religions, notably Hinduism, Buddhism, and Taoism, blended with the practices of 19th-century Western occultism.[42]

Although the space brothers often refer to "god," or the "creator spirit," they do not mean the Creator God of the Bible. Even if they refer to this god as creator, it is an impersonal god that they believe is an energy, consciousness, power, love, or force that binds the universe together. There is even a Christian-sounding church/cult called "Christian Science" that believes god is "mind."[43]

The NAM believes that man is not fundamentally (or born) sinful, as the Bible teaches, because he is actually divine in nature and has unlimited spiritual potential. They claim that the problem is that our disconnection from this higher evolutionary plateau is supposedly caused by our ignorance of how to attain it. (Satan said this same thing to Eve. He advised that if they ate from the Tree of the Knowledge of Good and Evil, they would be like gods). In this world view, there is no ultimate authority, and absolute truth is replaced by relative, subjective experience, which can be defined as humanism, the foundational driving force of which is the theory of evolution — "we are evolved and still evolving." The NAM states that the highest goal of humanity is to achieve a Christ-like state or "Christ-consciousness" (they say Jesus was just a man who achieved this higher state).

The woman who, probably more than anyone else, popularized these ideas in the West was Madame Helena Petrovna Blavatsky (1831– 1891). She was already steeped in the occult and Eastern mystical beliefs when, in 1875, she and her husband, Henry Olcott, founded the Theosophical Society in New York. She made many incredible claims about her past, including a visit to Tibet, where she claims she was trained by disembodied "spirit masters." She also claimed to be channeling messages from spirit/alien beings who were highly evolved and part of a governing hierarchy of the universe. The messages she received would be recognized today as "classic" New Age. She was eventually exposed as a fraud and a drug addict. Yet her books (which she allegedly plagiarized) are still in use today all over the world, and various offshoots of her ideas were instrumental in the beliefs of many of the aforementioned Satanists and cult leaders.[44]

One can clearly see a New Age pattern in the messages of the space brothers and why they claim to be helping us attain this next evolutionary level. We can also see how Christianity stands — seemingly alone — in opposing these "God is in everything" beliefs. Historically, Christianity has played a unique role in its portrayal of the spiritual dimension and its definition of absolute truth and wrong and right. According to Christianity, we cannot attain a higher level than to enter a relationship with God the Father, who is a real person. The Bible says we need look no further than Jesus Christ, the real Son of God, to see what God is like:

> The Word [Jesus] became flesh and made his dwelling among us. We have seen his glory, the glory of the One and Only, who came from the Father, full of grace and truth (John 1:14).

Endnotes

1 "The Premise of Spiritual Warfare," <www.alienresistance.org/ce4premise.htm>, March 7, 2003.

2 Ibid.

3 "New Abductee Trend," <users1.ee.net/pmason/new_trend.html>, August 27, 2003.

4 Chuck Missler and Mark Eastman, *Alien Encounters* (Indianapolis, IN: Koinonia House, 2003), p. 295.

5 First Timothy 2:14 says, "And Adam was not the one deceived; it was the woman who was deceived."

6 Whitley Strieber, *Transformation: The Breakthrough* (New York: Avon Books, 1989), p. 79, cited in William T. Alnor, *UFOs in the New Age* (Grand Rapids, MI: Baker Book House, 1992), p. 102.

7 Ibid., p. 103.

8 Ibid., p. 102.

9 Alnor, *UFOs and the New Millennium* (Grand Rapids, MI: Baker Book House, 1998), p. 36.

10 Ronald D. Story, editor, *The Mammoth Encyclopedia of Extraterrestrial Encounters*, in an article by Sherry Steiger (London: Constable & Robinson, 2002), p. 676.

11 Ibid., in an article by Brad Steiger, p. 674.

12 Lynn E. Catoe, *UFOs and Related Subjects — An Annotated Biography*, United States Government Printing Office, 1969, quoted in "The Premise of Spiritual Warfare," <www.alienresistance.org/ce4premise.htm>, March 7, 2003.

13 Story, *The Mammoth Encyclopedia of Extraterrestrial Encounters*, in an article by Randall Fitzgerald, p. 672.

14 Ibid., p. 672–673.

15 Brad Steiger, *Gods of Aquarius* (New York: Berkeley Press, 1983), p. 115, cited in Alnor, *UFOs in the New Age*, p. 124.

16 David Spangler, *Reflections on the Christ*, p. 36–39, cited in "The Lucifer Connection: The NAM 'Light' Experience," <www.spiritual-wholeness.org/churchte/newage/lucifer.htm>, August 17, 2003.

17 John A. Keel, *UFOs: Operation Trojan Horse* (New York: G.P. Putnam's Sons, 1970), p. 230, cited in Alnor, *UFOs in the New Age*, p. 139.

18 Alnor, *UFOs and the New Millennium*, p. 131.

19 Dave Hunt, *A Reason to Fear*, a paper presented in Washington, D.C., May 27–29, 1995, cited in Strieber, *Transformation: The Breakthrough*, p. 79, cited in William T. Alnor, *UFOs in the New Age*, p. 172.

20 John Ankerberg and John Weldon, *The Facts on UFO's and Other Supernatural Phenomena* (Eugene, Oregon: Harvest House Publishers, 1992), p. 36–37.

21 Keel, *Strange Creatures from Time and Space* (Greenwich, CT: Fawcett Publishing, 1970), p. 189, cited in Ankerberg and Weldon, *The Facts on UFO's and Other Supernatural Phenomena*, p. 16.

22 Alnor, *UFOs in the New Age*, p. 193–193.

23 Ibid.

24 "The Man from Mecca," <www.christianmissions.net/islam/man.html>, August 17, 2003.

25 "Allah, the Moon God," <www.biblebelievers.org.au/moongod.htm>, August 17, 2003.

26 "Alien Nation: Louis Farrakhan, Phone Home," <www.lasvegasweekly.com/2002/03_21/news_coverstory_1.html>, August 25, 2003.

27 Alnor, *UFOs and the New Millennium*, p. 30.

28 "Alien Nation: Louis Farrakhan, Phone Home," <www.lasvegasweekly.com/2002/03_21/news_coverstory_1.html>, August 25, 2003.

29 "The Man Who Says He Has Met Jesus, *Sunday Mail* (Brisbane), December 29, 2002, p. 7.

30 Camille Paglia, cited in "Scientology: A Satanic Link," *New York Post*, March 16, 2003, p. 10, <www.rickross.com/reference/scientology/scien467.html>, August 22, 2003.

31 Ibid.

32 Scanning scientology and anti-scientology literature reveals a seemingly contradictory use of terms. A person who gets rid of enough of these negative influences, in another context called "engrams" which themselves were somehow imposed on disembodied "thetans," can themselves become an "operating thetan," a desirable state. Contributing to this complexity/confusion is the level of secrecy involved, and what appears to be an increasing amount of "knowledge" imparted to disciples at deeper levels of involvement.

33 L. Ron Hubbard, speaking at a writer's conference as cited in Alnor, *UFOs in the New Millennium*, p. 103.

34 Alnor, *UFOs and the New Millennium*, p. 95–100.

35 Alnor, *UFOs in the New Millennium*, p. 85.

36 "Loving the Alien," <www.forteantimes.com/articles/121_aliensex.
shtml>, August 23, 2003.

37 Story, *The Mammoth Encyclopedia of Extraterrestrial Encounters*, in an
article by Joe Nickel, p. 380.

38 "Loving the Alien," <www.forteantimes.com/articles/121_aliensex.
shtml>, August 23, 2003.

39 Augustine's classic *City of God*, chapter 23, cited in Missler and
Eastman, *Alien Encounters*, p. 279.

40 Ibid., p. 279–280.

41 Watchman Fellowship's "2001 Index of Cults and Religions," <www.
watchman.org/cat95.htm#New>, August 25, 2003.

42 Ibid.

43 Not to be confused with "creation science," which is the recent endeavor
to study the scientific aspects of God's created universe through the
interpretive framework of the Bible.

44 Alnor, *UFOs and the New Millennium*, p. 53.

Chapter Nine

Look to the Sky — Change Is Coming

The space brothers — rewriting the future

As we saw in the last chapter, fallen angels under the leadership of Satan (that is, the enemies of God banished from heaven) have been attempting to deceive as many as they can about both the past and the future. The "gospel according to ET" has involved rewriting the Bible's history of the universe and then offering an alternative view of mankind's hope for the future. It appears to be part of a climactic battle being waged over the future of mankind.

Everyone recognizes that beliefs about where we came from are instrumental in shaping ideas about our future. On the one hand, if God has a plan or purpose for the existence of the universe and thus our lives, then he has a plan for the future also. Conversely, if benevolent extraterrestrials have been overseeing our evolution, then presumably they would have something to say about the things to come as well. Apparently, the "extraterrestrials," who have already convinced many to reinterpret the *history* in the Bible — particularly on the issue of origins — are attempting to convince people to reinterpret what the Bible says about *future* events as well.

But from where have they acquired their convincing-sounding stories about the future? As mentioned previously, no believer in the ETH has provided a satisfactory explanation as to how alien beings could foresee the future. Even if they were interdimensional, one would presume that if they are somehow linked to our universe, then they would be part of our time and space as well. So the only reasonable explanation for any knowledge they might have about the future would be their access to a proven source of prophecy — such as the Bible.

The most famous book on future events is the last book of the Bible, known as Revelation. It is named so because Jesus himself "revealed" the future to His friend, the apostle John. It is full of vivid imagery, with descriptions of angels and demons and their final state. The book is prophetic and concerns a time to come (which explains why so many people argue about the meaning and reliability of these prophecies). Why trust these prophecies? For one thing, we know from hindsight that many other prophecies made during the time of the Old Testament have been fulfilled in astonishing ways.

For example, there were over 80 particular prophecies pertaining to the life of Christ alone, written long before His incarnation on the earth, yet they were all fulfilled during His short life of about 33 years. This is hardly coincidental, although some might want to explain it away as such. If you were able to calculate the mathematical possibilities that a few, let alone all, of them could be fulfilled by chance, the odds would be almost immeasurable. Therefore, there is good reason to believe that the Bible's remaining prophecies will also come to pass.

Knowing the Bible's reputation, the extraterrestrial deceivers apparently feel a compulsion to "rewrite" its vision of the future. The story in Revelation, as John told it, is not encouraging to people who might turn to the ETs for help. Although John acknowledged that there is a spiritual battle occurring right now, he prophesied that all of the angels will be involved in a climactic finale that will seal the fate of Satan and his followers. For example, in Revelation 16:14–16 he said:

> They are spirits of demons performing miraculous signs, and they go out to the kings of the whole world, to gather them for the battle on the great day of God Almighty. "Behold, I [Jesus] come like a thief! Blessed is he who stays awake and keeps his clothes with him, so that he may not go naked

and be shamefully exposed." Then they gathered the kings together to the place that in Hebrew is called Armageddon.

The Bible here refers to a great battle known as Armageddon (after the valley of Megiddo, in Israel). Although Christians have differing eschatological views of the Bible (that is, relating to "end-times events"), they are in agreement about one surety. Jesus Christ will physically and literally return to this earth, and God will thereafter create a new heaven and a new Earth, in which the righteous — those made right with God by believing in Jesus Christ — will be with Him in glory forever.

John gives a twofold warning. He warns every reader to be prepared because Jesus says He will come like a thief in the night. But notice in the aforementioned passage how demons (deceiving spirits) are able to influence earthly leaders. From beginning to end, the Bible is consistent in recording how these beings influence people. As we mentioned in previous chapters, angels have been given dominion or areas of influence over the earth. According to the Gospel of John, Jesus himself described Satan as the "ruler of this world" (John 12:31, 14:30, 16:11), and He said that the whole world and its ungodly practices are under the control of the "evil one." The Bible ascribes incredible power to Satan:

> The god of this age [Satan] has blinded the minds of unbelievers, so that they cannot see the light of the gospel of the glory of Christ, who is the image of God (2 Cor. 4:4).

Several Scriptures allude to Satan's seductive power and Christ's ultimate triumph. They teach that when Christ came to this earth 2,000 years ago, He laid his majesty aside. After He was baptized, He went to the desert and fasted for 40 days and 40 nights. During this time, the devil came and tempted Jesus because he knew that Jesus was now a man, similar to the millions of others he had successfully tempted and led astray. But Jesus was no ordinary man; He was perfect and sinless — He had come from heaven. Satan even offered Jesus the "kingdoms of the world" if He would follow him and depart from His mission. Because He had now taken human form, Jesus could starve, be thirsty, and be in pain just like any other man. At this time Satan also said to Jesus:

> If you are the Son of God . . . throw yourself down. For it is written: "He will command his angels concerning you, and they will lift you up in their hands, so that you will not strike

your foot against a stone." . . . Jesus answered him, "It is also written: 'Do not put the Lord your God to the test.' " . . . Then the devil left him, and angels came and attended him (Matt. 4:6–11).

Notice Satan's method of seduction. The devil tempted Jesus with Scripture. When he said, "It is written," he was quoting from Psalm 91. These are words that the Psalmist had previously authored under the inspiration of God's Holy Spirit. Quite simply, the devil knows the Bible, too. This tactic explains why the messages of the space brothers parallel, and try to usurp, biblical texts. This deception is particularly prevalent in the area of "end-time" events that have already been prophesied under the inspiration of the Holy Spirit. The UFO literature and the messages of the cults have not only reinterpreted the Bible's history, but their doctrines are saturated with pseudo-biblical references about the future. Satan can read the Bible like anyone else. When he does, he reads that he is eventually going to be destroyed. No wonder he is trying to hoodwink everyone, and it's no surprise that he hates Christians who take the Bible as written. He is waging an enormous spiritual war for the souls of human beings.

The time is right for mass deception

We live at an incredible time. Technology accelerates at such a rate it leaves the average person in a daze. Many people find it difficult to distinguish science-fact from science-fantasy. It is often stated that the majority in Western nations believe that there is life on other planets. In popular belief, then, would anyone really be surprised if UFOs appeared on a global scale? Christians have long believed that during the time before Christ's return to Earth, the enemies of God would perform miraculous signs to deceive many, including, if possible, some Christians. Jesus warns in advance, once again in Matthew 24:

> For many will come in my name, claiming, I am the Christ; and will deceive many (v. 5). For false Christs and false prophets will appear and perform great signs and miracles to deceive even the elect [Christians] — if that were possible (v. 24).

Note that alleged "appearances" of Jesus are more common among UFO contactees and people who have undergone abduction experiences than among any other group of religious believers.

Is it possible that the "great signs" Jesus refers to (in addition to "false prophets") include the modern UFO phenomenon? The Old Testament prophet Jeremiah warned the Israelites in a similar vein:

> This is what the LORD says: "Do not learn the ways of the nations or be terrified by signs in the sky, though the nations are terrified by them" (Jer. 10:2).

God was warning people not to follow the religious or occult practices of others, and he was clearly referring to the time when the pagan nations were worshiping the heavenly bodies.

Interestingly, as we have seen, when people today invite "alien" visitors into their lives, they often experience an increase in UFO "signs." This not only happens on a personal spiritual level, but it can occur on a grander scale. For example, today's crop circles, even though manmade, seem to also generate all manner of strange activity that is similar to the appearances of UFOs. In the Old Testament, Ashtoreth poles and shrines were placed in fields by rebellious Israelites. The worship of false deities like Ashtoreth and Baal was accompanied by occult practices.

> They forsook all the commands of the LORD their God and made for themselves two idols cast in the shape of calves, and an Asherah [same as Ashtoreth] pole. They bowed down to all the starry hosts, and they worshiped Baal. . . . They practiced divination and sorcery (2 Kings 17:16–17).

It is a fact that nowadays the culture is ripe to believe in such things. Therefore, is it any coincidence that this phenomenon is escalating like never before? As people are desensitized to the spiritual nature of occult practices, which are dressed up in a pseudo-technological guise, they unwittingly create vast opportunities for Satan and his minions to perpetrate mass deceptions. Because so many have not given the UFO phenomenon a second thought, and because evolutionary beliefs are increasing in the church, could even many Christians, who are supposed to be able to spiritually discern such things, be caught unawares and deceived by a massive "extraterrestrial" visitation?

The New Age, or "many-ways-to-God," movement is growing, inviting and welcoming the escalation of paranormal and paraphysical phenomena. These include UFO and alien visitations. Jesus said that one day there would be a time of trouble, or "tribulation," on the earth like never before. Many Christians believe that this is to occur before

He returns, although some hold to different views about the timing of Christ's second coming, such as the premillennial (PreM), the amillennial (AM) and the post-millennial (PM) views. The UFOnauts have similar variations on these themes. The PreM view says that just before this time of Tribulation (a seven-year period), Christ will return in the clouds and will "rapture" (from the Latin for "caught up") — that is, resurrect — the dead in Christ, and transform those who are living, taking them away to heaven. This is based on 1 Corinthians 15:51–52. It says:

> Listen, I tell you a mystery: We will not all sleep [die], but we will all be changed — in a flash, in the twinkling of an eye, at the last trumpet. For the trumpet will sound, the dead will be raised imperishable, and we will be changed.

The PreM view says that after the Tribulation and the battle of Armageddon is over, Christ shall return with His saints and reign on the earth for a literal one thousand years, before the devil is loosed again briefly, and the end of the earth comes. The AM view has Christ returning only once (His second coming) after a "church age" and toward the end period of the world. Whatever the case, some sort of "rapture" view is also favored by the UFOnauts, who have imparted many variations to their "missionaries." Such views include:

- Those who refuse to change and allow Mother Earth to evolve (presumably Christians) will be removed by flying saucers and destroyed, or taken to some other place. (This is a counterfeit of the Christian premillennial view, in that if millions of Christians were to suddenly disappear from the earth, flying saucers could be blamed. In turn, New Agers might think their prophecies have come true.)

- That during a "rapture," at the end of time, all UFO believers who have spiritually evolved will be taken away to heaven or another planet, leaving behind the earth for its destruction.

- The ascended ones (UFO believers) will be whisked away. Some believe they will be returned after the earth has been cleansed (Armageddon).

Among the many versions that exist, some include Jesus returning in His spaceship, or UFO believers being whisked away to meet Him on another planet called Heaven (an ethereal New Age/ascended paradise, or even to a golden city — reminiscent of the New Jerusalem of Revelation). However, UFO researcher Bill Alnor says:

> I believe the UFOnauts' view of future events and their concept of the Second Coming strikes at the very core of Christianity itself. Virtually every extraterrestrial message I know today denies what the church has always called the blessed "hope:" Jesus' personal, physical return to Earth that the Bible refers to more than *five hundred times* (emphasis added).[1]
>
> . . . after reading literally thousands of messages from the space brothers . . . and carefully analyzing their views of the Second Coming, the coming millennium, new age, Armageddon, the rapture, and the new Jerusalem, I am convinced that these entities are trying to sell humanity one of the biggest deceptions of all time.[2]

Christ's return has long been called "the blessed hope" by Christians, who know that it will usher in what they will ultimately inherit for eternity. The Bible says a time is coming when the whole universe will be destroyed with a "fervent" heat. God will then create a new heaven and a new earth, in which there is no death, bloodshed, or suffering. (This is similar to many of the messages of the space brothers, which claim that UFO-believers will inherit some form of deathless utopia.) Only those whose names are found in the "Lamb's Book of Life" (Rev. 21:27) will inherit it. This refers only to Christians.

Change is coming

Famous New Age author Barbara Marciniak believes, as do many other UFO/New Age prophets, that the earth is going to undergo a dramatic change. She holds an "evacuation" view that will rid the world of those with old "fuddy duddy" ideas. In her book *Bringers of the Dawn: Teachings from the Pleiadians* (1992), she wrote:

> The people who leave the planet during the time of Earth changes do not fit in here any longer, and they are stopping the harmony of Earth. When the time comes that perhaps 20 million people leave the planet at one time there will be a tremendous shift in consciousness for those who are remaining.[3]

This view gives the impression that it was completely derived from outside of the Bible, yet its form mirrors the Bible's description of end-time events. The Pleiadians' website provides an insight to the source of this counterfeiting operation of the space brothers.

> Compiled from more than four hundred hours of chan-
> neling by Barbara Marciniak, *Bringers of the Dawn* imparts to
> us the wisdom of the Pleiadians, a group of enlightened beings
> who have come to Earth to help us discover how to reach a
> new stage of evolution. . . . We learn . . . how the original hu-
> man was a magnificent being with twelve strands of DNA and
> twelve chakra centers [so-called centers of spiritual energy],
> and who our "gods" are. . . . These teachings offer essential
> reading for anyone questioning their existence on this planet
> and the direction of our collective *conscious* — and uncon-
> scious. By remembering that we are [sic] Family of Light, that
> we share an ancient ancestry with the universe around us, we
> become "bringers of the dawn," consciously creating a new
> reality, a new Earth.[4]

The whole gamut of satanic deception is revealed here in one short passage. False creation, an endorsement of evolution and its "you shall be as gods" philosophy, a vision of a new earth, and a claim that we are part of Satan's family of light and we are part of the universe.

One of the most popular and well-read alternate versions of end-time events comes from a book called *Project World Evacuation* (1992), supposedly channeled by the ET known as Ashtar (there he is again!). But this time he is a commander of an intergalactic, interdimensional fleet of spacecraft known as "The Ashtar Command." Their fleet of spaceships will come to Earth and evacuate only worthy persons while the planet undergoes a "cleansing." The Ashtar command is apparently assisted by none other than Lucifer (who has become a good guy now), and they all operate under the supreme command of Lord Sananda (which is a common UFO term for Jesus).

The following Bible passages describe what some refer to as the rapture of the church:

> Brothers, we do not want you to be ignorant about those
> who fall asleep [die], or to grieve like the rest of men, who have
> no hope. We believe that Jesus died and rose again and so we
> believe that God will bring with Jesus those who have fallen
> asleep in him. According to the Lord's own word, we tell you

that we who are still alive, who are left till the coming of the Lord, will certainly not precede those who have fallen asleep. For the Lord himself will come down from heaven, with a loud command, with the voice of the archangel [Michael] and with the trumpet call of God, and the dead in Christ will rise first. After that, we who are still alive and are left will be caught up together with them in the clouds to meet the Lord in the air. And so we will be with the Lord for ever (1 Thess. 4:13–17).

The following verse was mentioned earlier, but it is relevant to repeat it here in the context of the rapture event.

Listen, I tell you a mystery: We will not all sleep, but we will all be changed — in a flash, in the twinkling of an eye, at the last trumpet. For the trumpet will sound, the dead will be raised imperishable, and we will be changed (1 Cor. 15:51–52).

Compare this to the account in *Project World Evacuation*, supposedly channeled by Ashtar to contactee Thelma Terrell, who goes by the "spiritual" name of "Tuella."

Our rescue ships will be able to come in close enough in the twinkling of an eye to set the lifting beams in operation in a moment. And all over the globe where events warrant it, this will be the method of evacuation. Mankind will be lifted, levitated shall we say, by the beams from our smaller ships. These smaller craft will in turn taxi the persons to the larger ships overhead, higher in the atmosphere, where there is ample space and quarters and supplies for millions of people.

. . . Earth changes will be the primary factor in mass evacuation of this planet. There is method and great organization in a detailed plan already near completion for the purpose of removing souls from this planet, in the event of catastrophic events making a rescue necessary. . . . The Great Evacuation will come upon the world very suddenly. The flash of emergency events will be as a lightning that flashes in the sky. So suddenly and so quick in its happening that it is over almost before you are aware of its presence. . . .[5]

This is a not-so-subtle ploy to usurp the biblical account. There are many differing versions of UFO end times, and some contactees, such as Billy Meier, vehemently disagree with Barbara Marciniak's Pleiadian exhortations. This causes any particular Bible interpretation to become just one of many, in the same way that a proliferation of religions causes many to think that "just one can't be right." If millions of Christians do disappear from the earth, then this deception also provides a way, on an unprecedented scale, for Satan's minions to explain the event and deceive those left behind.

Bringing the Bible up to date?

Many Christians also believe that prior to enormous destruction taking place on the earth, there will be a period of unprecedented peace and a global system, either an economic or religious one, that will unite all of humanity.

Former U.S. President Ronald Reagan understood that the world would suddenly become a small place if an alien attack were real. During an address to the United Nations General Assembly, he said:

> In our obsession with antagonisms of the moment, we often forget how much unites all the members of humanity. Perhaps we need some outside universal threat to make us recognize this common bond. I occasionally think how quickly our differences worldwide would vanish if we were facing an alien threat from outside this world.[6]

Even one of the most powerful men in the world thought it was a possibility. One could think of no better "scare tactic" to deceive mankind than the perceived extraterrestrial threat. Noted UFOlogist Jacques Vallée noticed the following during his UFO studies:

> Increased attention given to UFO activity promotes the concept of political unification of this planet. This is perhaps the most commonly recurring theme in my entire study of these groups. Through the belief in UFOs, a tremendous yearning for global peace is expressing itself. . . . Contactee philosophies often include belief in higher races and in totalitarian systems that would eliminate democracy.[7]

Sadly, by "believing" in the space brothers, many think they will be saved. New Ager Brad Steiger attempts to reconcile the scriptural record and channeled messages from entities who reveal that there is going to be a time of enormous change on the earth. He says:

Although these paraphysical, multidimensional entities have always coexisted with us, in the last half-century they have been accelerating their interaction with us in preparation for a fast-approaching time of transition and transformation. This period, we have been told, will be a difficult one; and for generations our prophets and revelators have been referring to it as "the great cleansing," "Judgment Day," "Armageddon." But we have been promised that, after a season of cataclysmic changes on the Earth plane, a New Age consciousness will suffuse the planet. It is to this end that the UFO is a transformative symbol.[8]

Steiger claims he used to be a Christian (although some would argue that he probably wasn't to begin with). Nonetheless, a clear indication of the strength of the prophesied end-time delusions is that Jesus says they could possibly deceive the "elect" (the elect specifically refers to Christians, or believers chosen by God). If such an undemocratic world system as Steiger describes is going to come, then presumably, Christians alive at such a time would reject it, because they would see it as a prelude to coming end-time events. It is likely then that they would be isolated and hated for failing to go along with the majority. The Bible says there will be a "falling away" toward the end and that many will depart the faith (Matt. 24:10; 1 Tim. 4:1–2). Could that be partly as a result of that sort of pressure from the majority?

Steiger is not the only former "believer" to have been deceived and to have fallen away. The Reverend Dr. Barry H. Downing is the pastor of a Presbyterian church in New York. He has been an advisor to MUFON (Mutual UFO Network) and is a board member of FUFOR (Fund for UFO Research). His book *The Bible and Flying Saucers* (1968) is a work that seeks to harmonize the biblical texts with UFO beliefs. This "matrimony" of the two is a type of universalism that is adored by UFO believers. The fact that Downing is well credentialed theologically does no harm to his cause among the UFO faithful. In fact, it seems to add credibility to his "UFOs in the Bible" views. His book is revered as a benchmark text among the more religious UFO believers, who hail him as a UFO "master."

Downing believes that UFOs are angelic in nature and have possibly been guiding the Christian religion. His book mainly concerns the time of the Exodus of the Hebrews from slavery in Egypt, and he leaves room for the possibility that many of the supernatural events, such as the parting of the Red Sea, and the burning bush that Moses saw, were UFO encounters. Moreover, he believes that these extra-terrestrial angels are aliens from another planet, and thus we should understand that the Bible is a mythological document rather than an historical one.[9] Bill Alnor notes that in a speech to MUFON, Downing argued that:

> The Judeo-Christian tradition can mostly be saved by go-ing in the direction I have gone.[10]

Downing advocates exactly what masquerading fallen angels want to hear — "a reinterpretation of the Bible according to new revelation." It would appear that he has been deceived and has accepted the messages of the alien benefactors, which he places on par with the Bible itself. Downing even thinks that the account of the transfiguration of Christ (Matt. 17:1–9), where He was manifested in His heavenly glory along with the Old Testament prophets Moses and Elijah, was caused by UFO activity. But on reading the Bible at face value, it clearly explains what occurred. Downing is relying on his own wishful notions when it comes to this, and he is imposing his view upon the text, as so many others have done through the ages. When the apostle Peter was reminding some followers about the deity of Christ in one of his letters, he specifically mentioned the transfiguration event, at which he was present. He wrote:

> We did not follow cleverly invented stories when we told you about the power and coming of our Lord Jesus Christ, but we were eye-witnesses of his majesty (2 Pet. 1:16).

Although Downing is influential and well liked among the UFO community, he resorts to cleverly invented stories. As a result, much of his work fails the "Scripture test." This is the straightforward, traditional method where Christians use Scripture to interpret Scripture as a safeguard, not allowing passages to be taken in isolation or out of context. Downing's doctrines, like the fallen angels whose stories he believes, are fulfilling a need that the world wants satisfied — a desire for a non-supernatural interpretation of the Bible. By definition, any intervention by a supernatural God would suggest that the Bible really is what it claims to be — the inspired Word of God (2 Tim. 3:16).

There are consequences for this idea. If the Bible is a true, literal, and historical record of the past, then we should be able to trust its record of the future. It says that God will judge the world again and those outside of Christ will be eternally separated from God. A non-literal approach allows one to choose one's own beliefs about the past and the future. So, which belief system inspired by the so-called extraterrestrials is the right one? There are literally hundreds of different versions, so logic dictates that they can't all be right. But the majority of them do seem to be centered on the Bible, as we have often pointed out. They also seem to be squarely aimed at discrediting a plain or straightforward interpretation of the texts, and the notion that there is but one true God, and that "the way" (the only way) is the one that He has already supplied by suffering a cruel death on our behalf.

The Bible makes it clear that we cannot become gods like Him. We see the incredible prophetic value of the Bible once again as it seems to foretell today's beliefs:

> For the time will come when men will not put up with sound doctrine. Instead, to suit their own desires, they will gather around them a great number of teachers to say what their itching ears want to hear (2 Tim. 4:3).

In recent years, many individuals have claimed to be the person of, or the reincarnation of, Jesus Christ. The number of false christs is increasing in accordance with the warnings that Jesus provided. It is even possible that, as well as counterfeiting a possible rapture of Christians from the earth, fallen angels masquerading as Christ could also try to counterfeit His second coming. UFO contactees have already provided many accounts of meeting (a false) Jesus, either on a spaceship or another planet. Traditional Christian views are constantly under attack and being altered.

With an escalation of deception during these days, one should also expect a resultant increase in false teaching. Once, the Bible was considered the benchmark, or the tool, for discerning such false doctrines. Today, it is more under attack than ever before. Although many people in the pro-UFO movement are quick to claim Jesus as one of their own, they choose to ignore that Jesus himself clearly believed the Bible to be the Word of God. He also believed it to be literal history, particularly with regard to the Book of Genesis and its account of the origin of the earth and the universe. Jesus was no subscriber to evolution, and since He was the Creator of all life, as the Bible claims, aliens could not have evolved or even be overseeing evolution. Jesus warned His followers:

> Watch out that no one deceives you. For many will come in my name, claiming, "I am the Christ," and will deceive many. You will hear of wars and rumors of wars, but see to it that you are not alarmed. Such things must happen, but the end is still to come. Nation will rise against nation, and kingdom against kingdom. There will be famines and earthquakes in various places. All these are the beginning of birth-pains. Then you will be handed over to be persecuted and put to death, and you will be hated by all nations because of me. At that time many will turn away from the faith and will betray and hate each other (Matt. 24:4–10).

The Bible says that during this difficult time, ungodliness, fear, despair, and destruction would reign for a short time. For the benefit of Christian believers alive at that time, Jesus tells what it will be like and warns not to give up hope or look for salvation anywhere else:

> Men will faint from terror, apprehensive of what is coming on the world, for the heavenly bodies will be shaken. At that time they will see the Son of Man coming in a cloud with power and great glory. When these things begin to take place, stand up and *lift up your heads*, because your redemption is drawing near (Luke 21:26–28).
>
> At that time the sign of the Son of Man [Jesus] will appear in the sky, and all the nations of the earth will mourn. They will see the Son of Man coming on the clouds of the sky, with power and great glory. And he will *send his angels* with a loud trumpet call, and they will gather *his elect* from the four winds, from one end of the heavens to the other (Matt. 24:30–31, emphases added).

Jesus' very own words describe that those who have faith in Him will be separated from those who have ignored His warnings:

> When the Son of Man comes in his glory, and all the an-gels with him, he will sit on his throne in heavenly glory. All the nations will be gathered before him, and he will separate

the people one from another as a shepherd separates the sheep from the goats. He will put the sheep on his right and the goats on his left. Then the King will say to those on his right, "Come, you who are blessed by my Father; take your inheritance, the kingdom prepared for you since the creation of the world" (Matt. 25:31–34).

The Bible provides a clear, straightforward account of Jesus' sobering warnings. Just as many of the UFO texts also state, some will be saved and some will not. In short, "both sides of the fence" believe "crunch time" is coming. But whose version of events are we to believe? They can't both be right. One must be truth and one not. In whom should we place our trust? It appears that we must choose carefully — our decision has eternal consequences.

Endnotes

1 William T. Alnor, *UFOs in the New Age* (Grand Rapids, MI: Baker Book House, 1992), p. 54.

2 Ibid., p. 53.

3 Barbara Marciniak, *Bringers of the Dawn: Teachings from the Pleiadians* (Rochester, VT: Bear and Co., 1992), cited in "Rapture: The New Age Version," <www.redmoonrising.com/contrapture.htm>, September 30, 2003.

4 "Books written by Barbara Marciniak," <www.pleiadians.com/frame_books.htm>, September 1, 2003.

5 Tuella, *Project World Evacuation* (New Brunswick, NJ: Inner Light Publications, 1993), cited in "New Age Rapture," <www.redmoonrising.com/newage.htm>, September 1, 2003.

6 *Professional Verbatim Record of the Fourth Meeting*, September 21, 1987, quotes from "Prominent World Government & Military Officials," <www.etcontact.net.Other/QuotePages/QuotesGovernment.htm>, January 22, 2003.

7 Jacques Vallée, *Messengers of Deception: UFO Contacts and Cults* (Berkeley CA: And Or Press, 1979), p. 218–219, cited in John Ankerberg and John Weldon, *The Facts on UFO's and Other Supernatural Phenomen* (Eugene, OR: Harvest House Publishers, 1992), p. 36.

8 Ronald D. Story, editor, *The Mammoth Encyclopedia of Extraterrestrial Encounters*, in an article by Brad Steiger (London: Constable & Robinson, 2002), p. 674–675.

9 William T. Alnor, *UFOs in the New Age* (Grand Rapids, MI: Baker Book House, 1992), p. 222–223.

10 Barry Downing, "E.T. Contact: The Religious Dimension," *MUFON 1990 International Symposium Proceedings*, MUFON, Seguin, Texas, 1990, p. 55, cited in Alnor, *UFOs in the New Age*, p. 225.

Chapter Ten

The Gospel According to the Creator

The author's perspective

Having researched material for this book and met people who are involved in the UFO phenomenon, I am concerned for their welfare — we all should be. There is an enormous spiritual battle going on which has eternal consequences for those involved, and it is more widespread than most people realize.

For example, I remember the call from a desperate mother who had contacted several Christian organizations looking for help for her daughter, who had a history of illicit drug use. The daughter subsequently claimed she was being visited by aliens in the middle of the night. After some discussion, I asked if Mary (not her real name) and I could meet because I felt there was something missing in the puzzle. Over coffee, we discussed her daughter's problems. I mentioned, among other things, "If this is what I think it is, there is either something you are not telling me or something that your daughter has not shared with you. Have there been encounters of a sexual nature? Does she believe that she is 'specially chosen' for their mission?"

I'll never forget Mary's jaw-dropping reaction. Confirming my worst fears, she said, "Yes — oh my goodness! Something really *is* happening to her."

I went on to explain that similar experiences are being reported by people all over the world — thousands of miles away in some cases. Mary was staggered, and realized that what was happening to her daughter was of a completely spiritual nature. She now realizes her daughter's bizarre stories and behavior are a result of deception by very powerful and influential spiritual beings. As noted earlier in this book, abuse, drugs, or even dabbling in the occult seem to provide an entry point for spiritual deception. While psychologists would say (and probably correctly so) that drugs and severe trauma can cause dissociation and even fragmented personalities at a psychological level, it seems increasingly evident that sinister spiritual forces take these opportunities to advance their cause, taking advantage of those who may be at a stage where they are physiologically and emotionally weakened.

The word "deception" is actually a dangerous one to use with someone who is directly involved. Their experiences are real to them. The word implies that we are denying their "reality" and that we don't understand. It appears to dismiss their experience and usually invokes a dramatic reaction. It's almost as if an invisible barrier is raised, preventing further communication.

On another occasion I was giving a lecture on the subject and a young married woman attended who said she had been involved with UFOs for over 12 years. At the end of my lecture, she politely asked if she could respond. For over 20 minutes she quoted chapter and verse of the Bible better than most Christians I know. Each verse was given a UFO interpretation. Apparently, aliens were our creators and had been visiting us for millennia, overseeing our evolution and the Christian religion. Every time I raised an inconsistency in her interpretation of the biblical texts, she promptly moved on to the next subject. She even suggested that some of the original Hebrew words in the Old Testament had been mistranslated into English. Little did she know that I had one of the world's foremost Christian apologists attending that evening with me, who also happens to be Jewish and has a good grasp of biblical Hebrew, and he easily refuted her claims. I don't mention her sharing her viewpoint to disparage her, but the experience was the closest thing that I could imagine to observing the results of brain-washing. She also spoke openly about visitations and stated that she, as well as her young children, had "met Jesus." She had been introduced into what are basically occult phenomena and the "dark side" of the supernatural realm.

These true stories demonstrate the dramatic level of deception, which can even take someone to a point at which logical and rational arguments are not even considered. The tales that experiencers are being told constitute, in my opinion, "alternative truths." How could the real Jesus or His angels impart such "truths"— ones that are in conflict with His own words and history as recorded in the Book that is claimed to be the source of these "truths" in the first place? This is self-refuting. To help overcome this prevalent deception, I have extended my study of biblical truth in this chapter. The real Jesus said in John 8:32:

> Then you will know the truth, and the truth will set you free.

The need to believe

"Why are we here? Where did we come from? Is there any meaning to my existence? Is there life after death?" At some point in life, most people question their existence. We have a spiritual void, or if you like, a piece missing from our understanding of why life exists at all. Some fill this gap with sport, romance, or money, but if we are entirely honest, there must be more.

It is easy to see why religious beliefs have proliferated, as people seek answers to the "big question" of life. Increasingly popular is the hope of salvation via the technologically advanced "space brothers." An atheist might dispute the claim that people need religious answers, pointing out that he can get on quite well without any religious beliefs or God. But in one sense he is a religious person, too. He has decided on an answer for the "big question." That is, there is no God, and he (the atheist) is the product of chance random processes. He has chosen this belief, even though he cannot *disprove* the existence of God or *prove* that the universe came into existence for no purpose. For example, an atheist accepts the "big bang" ultimately on faith, even though he knows of no scientific mechanism that could have caused it to happen.[1]

The question of origins is central to what we believe about ourselves. If we believe that we came from nothing and are destined for nothing, then there is no ultimate meaning or purpose to our existence. However, if God is Creator, then He brought this universe into existence for a reason, and by implication, humans have a reason for existence, too. In fact, the Bible explicitly says that we are central to the Creator's plans and purpose.

Regardless of their religious beliefs, most people would admit that the world is a mess. Many worry about the environment, poverty, food shortages, diseases, and so on. The breakdown of law and order is a major problem, too, not just in Western countries but everywhere in the world.

But is this turmoil any wonder when people have been told that they are just rearranged stardust in some endless cosmic merry-go-round, and that there is no life after death, no Creator to be responsible to, and ultimately no consequences for our actions? Moreover, why should we treat each other with any respect? If evolution is true, it's survival of the fittest. If you are weak and helpless, well, that's just too bad. If we teach people they are just evolved animals, then why should we be surprised when they act like it? The wise King Solomon, under the inspiration of God, explained what makes us act the way we do:

> For as he thinks in his heart, so is he (Prov. 23:7; NKJV).

One of America's worst serial killers, Jeffrey Dahmer, explained the *thoughts* that made him what he was. He believed there were no eternal consequences for his actions:

> If a person doesn't think there is a God to be account-able to, then — then what's the point of trying to modify your behavior to keep it within acceptable ranges? That's how I thought anyway. I always believed the theory of evolution as truth, that we all just came from the slime. When we, when we died, you know, that was it, there is nothing. . . .[2]

The Bible says that breaking God's laws, or even living as if God does not exist, is sin. Could you imagine living in a world where there were no rules? Despite all of us knowing the difference between wrong and right, we seem to have the propensity to get it wrong. The distractions of society subtly encourage us to look after "number one," and our culture empowers us to disregard and challenge authority.

But sin has become a relative term. These days most define wrong or right for themselves. However, the meaning of anything is tied up in its origins. The Bible teaches that sin originated when the first people,

Adam and Eve, rebelled against their Creator and His "rules to live by." So whose rules should we live by, anyway?

Let's be honest and ask ourselves this question: "Did our parents have to teach us how to do wrong things?" There is no need to give the answer. We can't help ourselves — we are constantly getting it wrong. The problem is not the degree of the sin or the offense we commit, but against whom we have committed it. The Bible tells us that we have ignored our responsibilities to the one who made us:

> We all, like sheep, have gone astray, each of us has turned
> to his own way (Isa. 53:6).

The idea that "sin is relative" extends to modern society as a whole. Most of Western societies' laws had their origin in the Bible (they were originally God's laws), but man has corrupted and changed these laws to suit himself. Is it any surprise that we see declining standards of behavior, along with an increase in crimes like murder and tragedies like suicide, when our young people believe that life is without meaning and purpose?

That angelic being of light, the leader of all deceiving "UFOnauts," Lucifer, tricked mankind into actions that had grave, eternal consequences. Because we were originally created as eternal beings, Lucifer knew that sin would *eternally* separate mankind from God. Yes, that's right — forever! Ephesians 2:1–3 says to us:

> As for you, you were **dead** in your transgressions and sins,
> in which you used to live when you **followed** the ways of this
> world and of the ruler of the kingdom of the air [the devil], the
> spirit who is now at work in those who are disobedient. All of
> us also lived among them at one time, gratifying the cravings of
> our sinful nature and following its desires and thoughts. Like
> the rest, we were by nature objects of wrath (emphases added).

What sobering but amazing truth this is. Death and eternal separation are a final state for those outside of God's salvation. The passage describes how we have ignored God, and are following the ruler of the kingdom of the air (also called the prince of the power of the air). This spirit of the "air" (meaning atmospheric regions) is none other than Lucifer/Satan. It is no surprise that he and his minions pose as alien astronauts, telling us there is no God and that we can basically do anything we want. In contrast, God's holy justice means that everyone who has sinned is destined to go to hell, a place far removed from God. When Jesus Christ returns to this earth again, He says God the Father will

> send out his angels, and they will weed out of his kingdom everything that causes sin and all who do evil. They will throw them into the fiery furnace [hell], where there will be weeping and gnashing of teeth. Then the righteous will shine like the sun in the kingdom of their Father. He who has ears, let him hear (Matt. 13:41–43).

What really happened

We are "lost" before we even begin, because we are born sinners. Ours is a hopeless state. However, nothing takes an all-knowing God by surprise. Man's actions brought a response from God — a Curse and a promise. God spoke to the lying serpent in Genesis 3:14–15:

> So the LORD God said to the serpent, "Because you have done this, cursed are you. . . . And I will put enmity [hostility] between you and the woman, and between your offspring and hers; he will crush your head, and you will strike his heel."

The Curse was the "curse of death" (Gen. 3:16–19). All mankind would now die. Surely this is why we grieve at funerals. We have an inner spirit that cannot be reconciled to the loss of loved ones, even though we know we are all destined to die from the moment we are born. If evolution were true, one would think we would have evolved some emotional immunity to death.

Satan and his followers, though, sometimes masquerading as alien entities, have promised an eternal life via a process of reincarnation (a higher-evolved state) if we follow them. This is counterfeit. It's like initially being excited that you found a $100 bill, only to discover that it's worthless. God's enemies cannot restore our fellowship to God.

Lucifer's plan of corruption backfired when God also promised that there would be a male child ("He") who would ultimately defeat Satan, metaphorically crushing his head.

The promised offspring would be one who would pay the penalty for our sins and restore our relationship with God. But how could this be, if we die? No one thinks death is good, so how could a good God institute this penalty? But He knew what He was doing. If we were to live eternally in the flesh, in a fallen world, we would be eternally separated from God. But God sent His Son (also God) to die and pay this penalty for us. Jesus was sinless because He came from heaven, and as the aforementioned passage in Matthew said, only the righteous, bought with the blood of Christ, will enter the kingdom of heaven, because:

> God made him who had no sin to be sin for us, so that in him we might become the righteousness of God (2 Cor. 5:21).

We were already dead in our sins but God has provided a means of escape. Jesus Christ came from the glorious paradise of heaven to die a horrible death on a cross in order that we might know God, and to save us from a fate worse than death. Jesus took the penalty of the Curse upon himself.

> For the wages of sin is death, but the gift of God is eternal life in Christ Jesus our Lord (Rom. 6:23).

Help is on its way

So what must we do now to accept this gift? The Bible says:

> That if you confess with your mouth, "Jesus is Lord," and believe in your heart that God raised him from the dead, you will be saved. For it is with your heart that you believe and are justified, and it is with your mouth that you confess and are saved (Rom. 10:9–10).

And 1 John 1:9 says:

> If we confess our sins, he is faithful and just and will forgive us our sins and purify us from all unrighteousness.

So all you need to do is confess your sinful state before God, believe that He sent Jesus to die for your sins, and accept Him as your Savior. If you can truly believe this and allow Him to enter your life, then you will truly become born again by the Spirit of God. Just as the first living man brought the curse of death upon us, Jesus offers us the gift of eternal life and a reversal of the effects of the Curse:

> So it is written: "The first man Adam became a living being," the last Adam [Jesus], a life-giving spirit (1 Cor. 15:45).

Jesus promises in John 5:24:

> I tell you the truth, whoever hears my word and believes him who sent me has eternal life and will not be condemned; he has crossed over from death to life.

After being buried in a tomb for three days, Jesus rose from the dead. He conquered death, demonstrating to us that He is the Creator and thus has power over life and death. The Bible says that in Christ death has been defeated for all who believe in Him.

> The last enemy to be destroyed is death (1 Cor. 15:26).

It is far better to have a "close encounter" with the Spirit of Jesus Christ than with a fallen angel posing as some technologically advanced alien. As I reported in the last chapter, people claim to have been transformed by an encounter with one of these deceivers, but not for the better. There are accounts of "walk-ins" (demonic possession) and all sorts of "devilish" psychic and paranormal experiences that ensue. Powerful as they may seem, it is a lie (they are known liars, remember). They are not spirits from God; they are spirits destined for destruction, who want to take us with them through their deceptions.

Is He a God of love?

Let's recap succinctly and speak plainly. In the beginning, God created everything good, or perfect, if you like (Gen. 1:31). Although He directly created possibly billions of angels, mankind was at the center of His purposes. Deceived by a fallen angel, we rebelled against God and brought sin, death, disease, and suffering into this world. We spoiled God's creation, and although it is still beautiful, it is broken (Rom. 8:22).

There is nothing we can do to get ourselves off this speck of a world spinning in the vastness of space. There is nothing we can do to save ourselves. But the Bible says that God the Son took our place for the penalty that was deserved — and reserved — for us. He stepped out of heaven to teach us, to show us what He is like, to save us, and to restore relations with us.

Under the threat of death, Jesus, who is God in the flesh, did not waver from telling these shocking truths. He told the Roman governor of Judea, Pontius Pilate, that:

> My kingdom is not of this world. . . . My kingdom is from another place (John 18:36).

And Pilate replied, "You are a king, then!"

Jesus answered, "You are right in saying I am a king. In fact, for this reason I was born, and for this I came into the world, to testify to the truth. Everyone on the side of truth listens to me" (John 18:37).

Jesus could have lied and told the Romans what they wanted to hear in order to escape the coming crucifixion, or He could have called upon vast numbers of heavenly angels to rescue Him. Instead, He chose sacrifice in an unimaginably horrific manner on a wooden cross. Even with the agony of death creeping upon Him, He sought forgiveness for the very ones who were crucifying him, declaring,

Father, forgive them, for they do not know what they are doing (Luke 23:34).

Later, knowing that all was now completed, and so that the Scripture would be fulfilled, Jesus said, "I am thirsty." A jar of wine vinegar was there, so they soaked a sponge in it, put the sponge on a stalk of the hyssop plant, and lifted it to Jesus' lips. When he had received the drink, Jesus said, "It is finished." With that, he bowed his head and gave up his spirit (John 19:28–30).

It was finished. His "mission" to save mankind was completed (He came from another dimension, too). Is God a God of love? *This is an incredible story of love!*

Death and suffering are part of this broken world and our finite existence on Earth. However, eternity waits for everyone (our spirits will leave our bodies when we die), but it is our decision as to where we want to spend it. You are not required to "evolve" to a higher level — there's no such thing! How would you know when you had attained the new level, anyway? If only a few "good teachers" have achieved it (or so the space brothers teach), then there's not much hope for the average Joe like you and me.

God has done the hard work for us. Just believe and follow *the* Holy Spirit. Consider these words from Jesus himself:

For God so loved the world that he gave his one and only Son, that whoever believes in him shall not perish but have eternal life. For God did not send his Son into the world to condemn the world, but to save the world through him (John 3:16–17).

Do we need to follow cleverly contrived stories? The Bible speaks very plainly that the truth is before us and can be easily discovered. We just need to take God at His Word (the Bible).

Whether you are outnumbered, ridiculed, or even persecuted, and regardless of what the majority of people in the world believe or what religious ideology or system they impose, even if technologically advanced "aliens" were to perform great signs, wonders, or miracles — God is the Creator and the One who is in control. He has already expressed His love through the sacrifice of his Son, Jesus Christ, and we can believe His promise to "save" all who believe in Christ based on His revealed nature. We know that He is the only One who can know and determine the future. Fallen angels, the space brothers (or whatever moniker you choose to use) cannot foretell the future. They are created beings; sinful, fallen, fallible, and not omnipotent. Only God is all-knowing (omniscient), all-powerful (omnipotent), and everywhere at one time (omnipresent). By definition, that is why "He is GOD," and that is why we should trust His promise to love us and provide eternal life.

> Who shall separate us from the love of Christ? Shall trouble or hardship or persecution or famine or nakedness or danger or sword? As it is written: "For your sake we face death all day long; we are considered as sheep to be slaughtered." No, in all these things we are more than conquerors through him who loved us. For I am convinced that neither death nor life, neither angels nor demons, neither the present nor the future, nor any powers, neither height nor depth, nor anything else in all creation, will be able to separate us from the love of God that is in Christ Jesus our Lord (Rom. 8:35–39).

Endnotes

1 He may see faith in the big bang as a reasonable faith, because it is supported by certain interpretations of the evidence. But faith it is, nonetheless. The Christian's faith in Genesis creation is also supported by interpretations of the evidence. Both are ultimately held on faith, and both can be supported by "scientific evidence."

2 Jeffrey Dahmer, from an interview with Stone Phillips, *Dateline NBC*, November 29, 1994.

Appendix

UFOs in the
Bible and Other
Questions

DOES THE BIBLE MENTION ETS?

As we have seen, the Bible is central to the debate about UFOs. Even if you subscribe to the extraterrestrial hypothesis (ETH) or the interdimensional hypothesis, the question remains, "Did God create the alien beings elsewhere?" If extraterrestrial life exists, it creates a problem for the big picture of Christianity and the very reason that God incarnate — Jesus Christ — came to this earth and died for mankind. Australian Professor Paul Davies[1] believes that traditional Christian beliefs are under threat due to the possible existence of extraterrestrial life. He says:

Christianity, in particular, has difficulties with regard to the very special role that Jesus Christ plays. If they wish to retain Jesus Christ as the savior, is he the savior of mankind only, or of all sentient beings throughout the universe? Or will each community have its own saviour? Doesn't it all start to become a little ludicrous?[2]

Davies ridicules the Christian faith because he thinks that extraterrestrial life elsewhere in the universe is more or less a given. This assumption is based on his belief that evolution is true, but as we have seen, the evidence for life occurring through chance random processes weighs heavily against this.

If you take an approach to the Bible which allows you to interpret it according to your *own* beliefs, you can fit aliens into the scheme of things, in as many other dimensions as you like. You could even claim the world is going to end tomorrow. But you would be adding information to the Bible based on your own beliefs rather than letting the Bible speak for itself. People often question the validity of the Christian faith when they see so much evil, corruption, violence, and distorted sexual practices committed by those who claim to follow Christ, such as followers of many pseudo-Christian cults. However, if one takes a closer look at such groups and their followers, it is easy to demonstrate that they have not attempted to adhere to the words of the Bible, but that they have imposed their own outside ideas (that is, their own belief system) on the Bible. If you let the Bible speak for itself, it is easy to identify those who claim to follow Christ but in reality don't.

One such area where outside ideas have been added to the Bible is the theory of evolution. In this case, it is commonly believed that scientists have proven the idea that simple chemicals can transform themselves into more and more complex organisms over millions of years. This has not been proven at all, but it is *believed* to have happened by the majority of scientists. A "herd rule" mentality causes others to *believe* that the majority must be correct, and so it is not openly questioned.

Many Christians *believe* that this *belief* system is infallible, then try to fit the idea of evolution and millions of years into the Bible somewhere.

But a plain reading of the Bible allows no such thing. It clearly states that God created the heavens and the earth in six literal 24-hour days and rested from this process of creation on the seventh day (Exod. 20:11). In addition, by looking at the Gospels of Matthew and Luke, and then the genealogies throughout the Old Testament, we can trace Jesus' ancestry all the way back to Adam and Eve. These two were real people — we know that Jesus believed in them because He referred to them. By a simple calculation of the ages given in these chronologies, it is easy to estimate that the time of creation, as recorded in the Scriptures, was only about 6,000 years ago. (Space does not permit us to go into exhaustive reasoning or scientific details on this, but there is a "Recommended Resources" section at the back of this book that covers the subjects of creation/evolution, radiometric-dating methods, natural selection, cosmology, etc.).

If creation occurred a few thousand years ago and the Scripture records that God finished on day 6, there was no time for any processes of evolution to have taken place, here or on any other planet.

If there was intelligent alien life elsewhere in the universe, it must have been created by God during the creation week, because the Bible says that everything, without exception, was created during those six days. But does the Bible mention the creation of intelligent alien life? Before we proceed, let us define what we are looking for. God *has* created intelligent life other than life on the earth. These creatures are mentioned dozens of times in the Bible, and as we discovered, they were the central focus of our study. They are angels. They do not live on other planets (although it is quite possible they could visit them if they so wanted). They exist in the heavenly realms, and have been created as specific agents of God to do His will.

But the "aliens" that most people really want to find are extraterrestrial beings, *Star Wars*–like, and perhaps displaying all of the unusual features that are shown in science fiction movies. Or perhaps they could look like us.

The modern English translations of the Bible mention the word *aliens* only in the context of people being "strangers" or "visitors from a foreign country." It was even used of believers in God (Christians), in recognition that their eternal home is with Jesus Christ in heaven, and therefore Earth is a temporary residence. Many have pointed out that the Bible does not mention intelligent alien life, and therefore conclude that God could have created it elsewhere without telling us. However, this is known as an argument from silence; and conversely, one could argue that it means he didn't.

I use the word "intelligent" because it may be possible to find simple life forms elsewhere in the solar system. Discoveries on other planets may turn up bacteria, for example. But does that mean it originated there? If scientists believe that Martian rocks have found their way to Earth, surely it would be possible for Earth life — even deep rocks contain micro-organisms — to contaminate other planets.

However, the reason I draw the conclusion that there is no intelligent ET life elsewhere in the physical universe is by "strong inference," looking at the many Bible verses that explain how humans are at the center of God's stated purposes for His creation (more shortly). I am surprised at the number of solid Christian researchers, even in the UFO field, who are sitting on the fence with regard to the possibility of ET life, unsure what to believe.

DID GOD CREATE ALIENS?

It would be fair to say that, even for Christians, whether to fit "alien life" into the Bible has been a tricky issue. But the confusion results from two main sources. Firstly, no one is immune to media saturation. Alien themes are so commonplace that it has become almost a given that aliens exist. "Harmless" product advertising on TV commercials, and even children's cereal boxes, promotes these alien space themes. I believe that popular culture has subconsciously caused most people to think that aliens are out there somewhere.

Secondly, our discoveries about the enormous and incomprehensible size of the universe have caused many to think that we cannot be the only "race" in space. Otherwise, the universe would be an awful waste. Similarly, if God created, then why did He create such a vast universe with our little speck of dust (the earth) as the only inhabited place (see the section later, "Why is the universe so big?")?

The major influence here is the belief that evolution occurred on the earth, and by erroneous extrapolation, elsewhere in the universe. Even Christians who don't believe in evolution end up thinking they have to accept that God created aliens elsewhere. I repeat, though, that this is a case of allowing outside ideas to influence our view of Scripture.

Quite simply, the straightforward reading of the Bible is as follows. Genesis 1:1 says: "In the beginning God created the heavens and the earth." Although this opening passage of the Bible describes the creation of the entire universe, it specifically mentions the earth, and only later the sun and moon in our solar system. Stars are mentioned later on in the text, almost as an aside, and the context makes it clear that they were made specifically to benefit mankind, thus placing man as the focus of God's creation. There is never a single case where a verse refers or alludes to any other reason for the creation of stars, such as for the purpose of harboring extraterrestrial life.

The whole of God's creation was "very good," as God pronounced it on day 6. God could hardly have called the process of evolution, with its death and struggle and survival of the fittest, "good," so the texts imply that there was no death before Adam and Eve. When mankind sinned or rebelled against God, the "curse" was brought upon all of God's creation, not just mankind. God cursed the earth (Gen. 3:17), the plants (vs. 18), and the animals (vs. 14); and in fact, Romans 8:21–22 says that the *entire creation* suffers from the Curse:

> . . . the creation itself will be [has not yet been] set free from its bondage to decay. . . . We know that the whole creation has been groaning in travail together until now (Revised Standard Version).

The whole of creation (the universe) was subject to decay as a result of the Curse. This would mean that any inhabitants on other planets, initially created good by God, would now be subject to the curse of death as a result of Adam's sin on Earth. That would hardly seem fair to innocent aliens.

When God, in the form of Jesus Christ (the second person of the Trinity), stepped out of heaven, He came to the earth (this planet only) as a human being, not a Pleiadian or a Vulcan, and He came not only to redeem mankind (who are descendants of Adam) back to himself, but His creation also. God says He will ultimately destroy this cursed creation and restore (or return) it back to the way it was in the beginning. He is going to create a new heaven and a new Earth. If there is intelligent alien life, not only have they been subjected to the curse of death through no fault of their own, but also they have no chance of redemption because that event took place on Earth for the human race only (Heb. 9:26–28). And ultimately they would be destroyed at the end, through no fault of their own. The Scriptures are very clear that Christ did not, and will not, be visiting other planets to undergo crucifixion for alien races. 1 Peter 3:18 says:

> For Christ died for sins once for all, the righteous for the unrighteous, to bring you to God.

He died once. That's it. Moreover, in the new creation, ruled by Christ, redeemed humanity is going to live as Christ's "bride" throughout eternity (Eph. 5:22–33; Rev. 19:7–9). Not only is it clear that even the *new* creation will be designed for mankind, but the idea of Christ separately visiting the planet Vulcan to redeem aliens living there falls down here, too. Because marriage is defined in Genesis as monogamous—one man for one woman, and the marriage of Christ and His church, born from the spear wound in His side, is a clear parallel to the first man and his bride, born from a wound in the side of Adam. In other words, Christ will not be a bigamist or polygamist. He will have *one* bride in eternity, not two (an earthly and a Vulcanian one). The Bible makes no provision for God to redeem any other species, any more than to redeem fallen angels (Heb. 2:16). Mankind and the earth are clearly the spiritual center of God's universe. When we consider the uniqueness of what God has done for us, it makes His redemptive work all the more wonderful.

Did Ezekiel see a UFO?

One of the most infamous claims about UFOs appearing in the Bible is the "sighting" by Ezekiel in Ezekiel 1:1–28. Erich von Däniken is just one of many leading writers who claim that the prophet Ezekiel saw a spaceship.

In the case of the mighty prophet Ezekiel, he was given an amazing experience, and a picture of something that no other person had seen. The text clearly describes the events that took place, and Ezekiel says his vision was imparted to him by God (Ezek. 1:1, 3).

A prophet is a specially chosen person. He is a spokesman for God, and God communicates with his chosen person in such a style that the prophet knows for sure he is hearing only from God. "Knowing the voice of God" is one of the reasons that the biblical prophets were always 100 percent accurate, unlike modern "prophets," whether in the Christian church or outside of it. Ezekiel had a similar problem with a proliferation of false prophets in his day. Ezekiel 13 records that he was told to prophesy against the false prophets of his day. People did not always like God's true prophets because they often spoke directly and personally about people's lives, particularly in the area of revealing and condemning their sin. Often the hearers would reject God's warnings via His prophets because they wanted to continue in their own way.

In Ezekiel's case, God used dramatic imagery to get His message across. For example, in chapter 37, Ezekiel was given a vision of a valley of dry bones. Step by step, sinew and flesh attached to these bones until they came to life as a vast army. Was it meant to be taken literally? Not in this case, because God told Ezekiel that the story was "symbolic" of Israel's restoration to their homeland (they were in exile at the time).

The so-called UFO that Ezekiel saw was no different. No one saw it except Ezekiel. He describes wheels, wings, and living creatures that looked like burning coals and moved like flashes of lightning. Above this strange contraption were a throne and a figure that looked like a man with a brilliant light surrounding him. But right at the very beginning of the passage (vs. 1) and at the end (vs. 28), Ezekiel unmistakably pronounces that it is a vision of God. In verse 17, the "vehicle" is described as going in all directions at the same time, which a real vehicle cannot do. This description is a reference to the fact that God is everywhere at the same time (omnipresent) and that He is not constrained to our understanding. The vision of a man was probably that of the preincarnate Christ, or God the Father in all His glory being carried along by four cherubim (angels).

Many UFO believers claim they place great store in the biblical texts but only when it suits their purposes to do so. It is incredible how often people take a passage of Scripture completely out of context to prove a pet theory. Masquerading angels have also concocted a pseudo-philosophy to closely parallel the texts for their own evil aims. The Bible has become "fair game" for those with their own agenda. I recall an investigator at a UFO meeting glowingly using the passage in Ezekiel to say that "even the Bible mentions UFOs." When I challenged his comment, pointing out that nowhere does Ezekiel use the term "ship," "craft," or any other word to describe a vehicle of any sort, and when I made the more important point that the text clearly describes the thing as a vision from God, he replied, "Yeah, but it's still a UFO."

I didn't say what he wanted to hear. He had already made his mind up and brought his outside ideas to the Bible. He wanted to believe that it is a UFO, despite the intent of the author and the actual words written. This misreading of the Bible is sadly common in UFOlogy.

WHO WERE THE "SONS OF GOD" IN GENESIS 6?

Probably the most often-used and controversial passage of Scripture by pro-ETH UFOlogists is the account of "the sons of God" and their resultant offspring, the Nephilim. The description in Genesis 6:1–7 reads:

> When men began to multiply on the face of the ground, and daughters were born to them, the sons of God saw that the daughters of men were fair; and they took to wife such of them as they chose. Then the LORD said, "My spirit shall not abide in man for ever, for he is flesh, but his days shall be a hundred and twenty years." The Nephilim were on the earth in those days, and also afterward, when the sons of God came in to the daughters of men, and they bore children to them. These were the mighty men that were of old, the men of renown. The LORD saw that the wickedness of man was great in the earth, and that every imagination of the thoughts of his heart was only evil continually. And the LORD was sorry that he had made man on the earth, and it grieved him to his heart. So the LORD said, "I will blot out man whom I have created from the face of the ground, man and beast and creeping things and birds of the air, for I am sorry that I have made them" (Revised Standard Version).

For proponents of the ancient astronaut and astrogenesis theories, the "sons of God" or even the Nephilim refer to extraterrestrial visitors to the earth. Erich von Däniken and Zechariah Sitchin, among others, believe these interfering aliens had sexual union with humans and/or genetically engineered humans or prehuman creatures in an effort to oversee mankind's evolution. This is a grand assumption based on an interpretation of the text that is clearly incorrect. These writers advocate, for example, that the "sons of God" is merely a description by "primitive" biblical authors who did not understand the technology, describing alien visitors from the sky. However, the unity of Scripture, the Scripture test (where passages are cross-referenced with each other to ensure they are not used out of context), and the way that expressions were used similarly throughout all of the books of the Bible do not warrant one particular expression to be rendered differently to other cases where it appears.

The text itself readily refutes the "primitive authors" idea. In the first chapter of Genesis, we read that God created mankind fully formed and intelligent. Adam was even given the job of naming all of the land animals (Gen. 2:19–20). In the subsequent chapters, we see Adam's offspring described as musicians and craftsmen (Gen. 4:21–22), demonstrating they were not primitive. The Scriptures are full of detail to show that, prior to the account in Genesis 6, man was already fully human, vastly intelligent, and engaging in spiritual worship — facts so readily ignored by those looking for the slightest opportunity to "squeeze" a UFO or two into the Bible. Unlike their rejection of earlier passages in Genesis as being real history, they readily accept that the Nephilim incident in Genesis is based on true events. But their "primitive authors and UFO" interpretation is *impossible* if we accept that the earlier descriptions in Genesis are also true.

However, even among Christians, the meaning of this passage is sometimes hotly debated. There are probably four major views regarding the expression "the sons of God" in Genesis 6, with some surprising connections to UFOlogy.

1. It refers specifically to "fallen" angels.

2. It represents the "godly" descendants of Seth, one of Adam's children.

3. They were kings or rulers who were described as "gods."

4. They were human beings possessed by demonic fallen angels.

1. The fallen-angel view

The early verses in Genesis 6 serve as a prelude to the "great flood" of Noah's day. They give the wickedness of man on the earth as the reason that God invoked this global catastrophe. Noah and his family, who were aboard the ark, were the only humans to survive this enormous world-destroying and land-reshaping cataclysm. (Many of the world's present geological formations and fossils were laid down by the catastrophic effects of the floodwater.) Although the space brothers have told many UFO contactees that the flood was a real event, in true counterfeit fashion they have also said that it was triggered by their intervention to cleanse the earth from its impurities.

In addition, some Christian commentators believe that another reason for the flood was not only to destroy sinful mankind but also to wipe out the offspring that resulted from the sexual union of the sons of God and the daughters of men — the Nephilim (see later).

This view is common among those who believe that the sons of God are fallen angels. They argue that these angels cohabited with, or had sexual relationships with, human women. The strongest argument for this view comes from the simplest understanding of the text itself.

The term, "sons of God," in Hebrew, is *bene elohim*. It is used five times in the Old Testament (twice in Genesis 6, and once each in Job 1:6, 2:1, 38:7, Authorized Version). In the passages outside of Genesis, it is always clearly used of angels. Some claim that a similar term is used in Hosea 1:10, but it is not exactly the same description because it refers specifically to the children of Israel being "sons of the living God." One should not resort to exceptions unless there is a good reason, but in this case there is no scriptural reason to do so. The angels are described as sons (*bene*) of God because He directly created them. Contrast this to the description of the "daughters of men." The Hebrew used here is *benoth adam*. If the sons of God were mortal human beings being born of humans, then the expression used should have been *bene adam*. The text itself draws a clear distinction between the offspring of humans and those directly created by God. In the New Testament, Adam, the first man, is called "the son of god" because God also supernaturally created him. The New Testament also describes Christian believers on numerous occasions as "sons of God" (Rom. 8:14; Gal. 3:26), but this makes sense because they have been "born again" and are a "new creation" in Christ (2 Cor. 5:17).[3] There are similar expressions in the Old Testament. In Daniel 3:25, the term "son of the gods" or "like the Son of God" (*bar elohim*) is used, which describes either an angel or a theophany that appeared with the three men in the "fiery furnace." (A theophany is where God appears as an angel or in human form.) The expression "sons of the mighty" (*bene elim*) is also used to describe angels in Psalms 29:1 and 89:6.

The fallen-angel view is a common view held by the translators of the Septuagint (the Greek translation of the Old Testament around 250 B.C.), ancient Jewish interpreters, the historian Josephus, the earliest Christian writers, and by many modern notable Christian apologists today.

The biggest objection to this view is the belief that it is impossible for angels to have sexual relations with humans because they are spirit beings. But as we have already seen in the UFO/abduction phenomenon, as well as in other parts of Scripture, they can also exist and manifest at a physical level.

This objection is often based on a passage in Mark 12:24–25 (repeated in Matt. 22:29–30). Here, Jesus was being questioned about a hypothetical woman who, according to Jewish law, should marry the brother of her dead husband. If there were seven brothers and they all eventually died, she would eventually have married all of them. Who would be her husband at the resurrection of the dead? Jesus replied:

> Are you not in error because you do not know the Scriptures or the power of God? When the dead rise, they will neither marry nor be given in marriage; they will be like the angels in heaven.

Some use this passage to claim that angels are incapable of having sex or procreating, but this is not what the Scripture says. It does say specifically that the angels *in heaven,* or those angels who *obey* God, do not engage in this practice. In a parallel passage in Luke 20:34–36 the context is made clear:

> Jesus replied, "The people of this age marry and are given in marriage. But those who are considered worthy of taking part in that age and in the resurrection from the dead will neither marry nor be given in marriage, and they can no longer die; for they are like the angels. They are God's children, since they are children of the resurrection."

He answered the question primarily to affirm the reality of the resurrection and the eternal life it will bring believers (like that of the angels), contradicting the beliefs of the Sadducees, who did not believe in the resurrection of the dead and who were trying to trick Jesus.

In every biblical account where angels are sent by God and manifest in physical form, the Bible records them as appearing as males, therefore with gender (e.g., Gabriel, Michael). If masquerading angels are appearing as aliens, then the experiences of abductees suggest that fallen angels, at least, can manifest as female, too. An unwarranted extrapolation of the above text is used to suggest that because believers will not be married in the resurrection life, they will also be genderless (supposedly like the angels). Once again, the passage tells us only that people won't be married in heaven, although they do marry now. God's ordained purpose for marriage was for procreation to populate the earth. Each of the angels was supernaturally created, so there was no need for procreation, and in this way we will be "like" them. Christians will not marry each other in the new heavens and Earth. They (the church) will be "married" to Christ, as His bride, throughout eternity. This expression is applied figuratively; Christ has redeemed His followers by His death and resurrection. Human beings have an individual identity, which they will never lose, and even angels are identified as individuals. It would seem strange that we would not retain our identities, of which being male or female is an integral part, in the resurrection life.

The fallen-angel view of the sons of God is a provocative concept, and thus it remains an unacceptable explanation to many. Some argue vehemently against it and have tried to explain the passage in other ways. Around the fifth century A.D. the fallen-angel view came increasingly under attack. Some theologians claimed that it was impossible for angels to father children by human women.[4] Proponents of the fallen-angel view have often pointed out, however, that angels appeared in physical bodies, such as the three visitors to Abraham who sat, ate, and spoke with him (Gen. 18:1–15). In another example, angels appeared to the inhabitants of Sodom in such a form that the depraved Sodomites wanted them for homosexual relations (this is where the word *sodomy* comes from).

2. The Sethite view

The adherents to the Sethite view believe that the "sons of God" were a hereditary line descended from Seth, and that this was a God-fearing lineage. The scriptural support for this idea comes from Genesis 4:25–26, which describes the birth of Seth to his father Adam. It says:

> Adam lay with his wife again, and she gave birth to a son and named him Seth, saying, "God has granted me another child in place of Abel, since Cain killed him." Seth also had a son, and he named him Enosh. At that time men began to call on the name of the LORD.

It was assumed to be a godly line because the passage says that men began to call out to God. However, some Christian apologists, citing ancient biblical historians, claim that "call" has been mistranslated and should actually read "profane."[5] In any case, it doesn't really matter. There were many generations after Enosh, and family heritage is not an automatic producer of piety.

This view also holds that the daughters of men were descended from the evil Cain (who murdered his brother Abel). If this were the case, however, one wonders why the Scripture did not say "sons of Seth" and "daughters of Cain."[6] There does not appear to be any textual basis for applying exclusivity to Seth's or Cain's lineage. If there is any distinctive human line at all, *benoth Adam* means the daughters of Adam, which ultimately means all women anyway. There is nothing to suggest that Seth's line was any more pious than anyone else on the face of the earth, and conversely, there is no implication that any daughters of Cain would have been more sinful than anyone else. According to 1 John 3:12, Cain belonged to "the wicked one" because he murdered his brother Abel, but this passage does not refer to his offspring. If the remaining descendants of Seth were so "godly," why were they not spared the judgment on sin that everyone received, except Noah and his family? Some have also claimed that when it says the sons of God "took" (Hebrew *laqach*) wives for themselves, the Hebrew implies a more violent "taking" than one usually associates with the normal process of betrothal. But to "take a wife" is a common term in Hebrew as well as in English. *Strong's Concordance* says that the Hebrew verb can mean "to take, get, fetch, lay hold of, seize, receive, acquire, buy, bring, marry, take a wife, snatch or to take away" — such a range of meanings does not provide a strong argument to support the claim that this was a violent "taking."

3. Kings and rulers

While it is true that many ancient rulers (and some modern ones, for that matter) have declared themselves to be gods, once again, it is hard to see any scriptural support for this claim. The text does not imply this; it is an outside idea. The term "mighty men" is often used to suggest that they may have been kings or leaders, but as we shall see, this is not what the term means.

Also, the Nephilim are always referred to in the masculine gender. Surely the offspring of human parents would occasionally produce female children as well.

4. Demons

The view that fallen angels, or demons (are they the same? — see later), possessed, or inhabited, the bodies of men, and perhaps women, is entirely possible, and we see this phenomenon throughout Scripture.

The practices of channeling, automatic writing, and perhaps even the abduction experience itself are forms of demonic possession. This then begs the question of who are the Nephilim and why are they expressly mentioned as the offspring of this union? Nowhere else in Scripture are the offspring of demon-possessed people, or anybody else, for that matter, singled out and then automatically classified as "fallen."

The offspring — "as in the days of Noah"

The word *Nephilim* was actually left untranslated by the English translators. In some earlier versions the word was rendered as "giants." It is entirely possible that these beings were indeed very large, so in one sense this translation could be correct. But its literal meaning is "fallen ones," from the Hebrew root word *naphal*, meaning "to fall or to be cast down." Why were these offspring, if they were the progeny of human parents (whether kings, ungodly, or demonically possessed) automatically condemned by God and regarded as fallen? Being born into an ungodly family by unbelieving parents does not mean that one is excluded from the promises of God that arise from faith in Him.

Some have suggested that the Nephilim were condemned because they were not fully human. This comes from the view that the sons of God were angels that cohabited with women to produce half-angelic/half-human beings — a hybrid offspring. Another often-quoted Scripture to support the angel view is Jude 6–7:

> And the angels who did not keep their positions of authority but abandoned their own home — these he has kept in darkness, bound with everlasting chains for judgment on the great Day. *In a similar way*, Sodom and Gomorrah and the surrounding towns gave themselves up to sexual immorality and perversion. They serve as an example of those who suffer the punishment of eternal fire [emphasis added].

The passage clearly links the perverted sexual practices of Sodom and Gomorrah with fallen angels who have not "kept their place." But what are the "everlasting chains for judgment?" The next passage describes angels who have been "locked up" awaiting their eternal and final punishment. Moreover, the word "hell" in this next passage is the Greek word *tartarus*, which occurs nowhere else in Scripture. The most common occurrence of the word *hell* is a translation from *sheol* in the Old Testament and *hades* in the New Testament, which describes a place of departed spirits. This distinctive treatment of fallen angels is also completely different to any other account in the Bible, because we know that even Satan himself and his minions are still allowed to roam about the earth. The aforementioned passages, read in isolation, are hard to understand, but they make sense when read with the view that the sons of God in Genesis 6 were possibly fallen angels.

> For if God did not spare angels when they sinned, but sent them to hell *[tartarus]*, putting them into gloomy dungeons to be held for judgment; if he did not spare the ancient world when he brought the flood on its ungodly people, but protected Noah, a preacher of righteousness, and seven others; if he condemned the cities of Sodom and Gomorrah by burning them to ashes, and made them an example of what is going to happen to the ungodly. . . (2 Pet. 2:4–5).

But why was this group of miscreant angels kept in chains? In the aforementioned passage, once again, specific angels are juxtaposed to the time of Noah and the sinful practices of Sodom and Gomorrah. This is the second specific reference to angels being imprisoned at the time of Noah. One can only presume that these particular angels did not "play by the rules" and that they stepped outside the boundaries of normal "warfare" engagement. In a sense, they had committed war crimes or acts of atrocity upon human beings. If these demonic angels had possessed human beings, why were they singled out for harsher treatment, since demonic possession occurred after that time and is apparently still occurring today? Some commentators also refer to 1 Peter 3:18–20, which says:

> For Christ died for sins once for all, the righteous for the unrighteous, to bring you to God. He was put to death in the body but made alive by the Spirit, through whom also he went and *preached to the spirits in prison who disobeyed long ago when God waited patiently in the days of Noah* while the ark was being built. In it only a few people, eight in all, were saved through water [emphasis added].

This could possibly be a third mention of the fallen angels of Noah's time. Although the word *spirit(s)* is used of angels, it can refer to man's spirit also. However, the text does specify a "prison," which fits with the idea of "chains" previously mentioned in relation to *tartarus*.

The whole concept of a certain group of angels participating in perverse acts is very thought-provoking because Jesus was asked about the signs that would precede His second coming. He said in Luke 17:26:

> Just as it was in the days of Noah, so also will it be in the days of the Son of Man.

Of course, Jesus was warning His listeners that the people of Noah's day did not expect the catastrophe that befell them. But Genesis 6:11–13 also tells us that the world at that time was violent and corrupt.

Some suggest the intriguing possibility that Jesus' warning may have also referred to angelic sexual interference with humans. They also believe that this prophecy is being fulfilled today with "alien" abductions and their alleged associated sexual practices. In addition, some also believe that the modern hybrid alien/humans are "real" living offspring, similar to the Nephilim of Genesis 6. However, the difficulty with this view is that the original group of angels who procreated (as opposed to some who might just have engaged in sexual activity — if that is possible) were apparently locked up in *tartarus* to await judgment at the end of time. If the angels in Noah's day were imprisoned for this sort of behavior, why wouldn't all angels who partake in these practices today automatically be "locked up" by God as well? Unless, perhaps, it is a prelude to the "end times" ("just as in the days of Noah") when literally "all hell breaks loose" before God finally deals with these matters on Judgment Day. At least this line of thought has some interesting parallels to our study.

A few apologists suggest that fallen angels are distinctly different from demons, based on the view that wherever demons are mentioned in Scripture, they seem to require embodiment in a biological creature, whereas angels do not. These apologists believe that demons are the disembodied spirits of the Nephilim destroyed in the Flood. Interestingly, the apocryphal (non-canonical) book of Enoch also describes the spirits of the Nephilim as evil spirits roaming about the earth. An account that would seem to support this idea is found in the Gospel of Mark, chapter 5. After Jesus crossed the lake in a boat, the chapter says:

> When Jesus got out of the boat, a man with an evil spirit came from the tombs to meet him. . . . When he saw Jesus

from a distance, he ran and fell on his knees in front of him. He shouted at the top of his voice, "What do you want with me, Jesus, Son of the Most High God? Swear to God that you won't torture me!" For Jesus had said to him, "Come out of this man, you evil spirit!"

Then Jesus asked him, "What is your name?"

"My name is Legion," he replied, "for we are many." And he begged Jesus again and again not to send them out of the area.

A large herd of pigs was feeding on the nearby hillside. The demons begged Jesus, "Send us among the pigs; allow us to go into them." He gave them permission, and the evil spirits came out and went into the pigs (Mark 5:2–13).

Note how the demons requested permission to possess the pigs. The view that the disembodied spirits of the Nephilim are "demons" is a radical view, but it does have some scriptural support.

The Nephilim

As mentioned previously, some claim there was another reason for God invoking the Great Flood upon the whole earth. It served the purpose of destroying the Nephilim.

A popular view is that these half-human/half-angel beings retained some of the supernatural characteristics of their fathers. This made them effectively superhuman, and they thus wielded undue influence over human affairs with their superior knowledge and strength. This view arose because of the description of the Nephilim as the "mighty men of old" and "men of renown" in Genesis 6:4. God had already said that He was going to shorten the days of mankind because He could not tolerate their wickedness any longer. It has also been suggested that the angels created the Nephilim in order to infiltrate the human gene pool. Satan had been warned in the Garden of Eden that enmity or hostility would exist between *his offspring* and the *offspring* of the first woman (and obviously the first man, Adam). In Genesis 3:15, Satan is described as having offspring in the same context as that of the woman. Satan heard from God that the woman's offspring was going to crush his head. This "offspring" may be understood generically as all humans, but more likely it is a specific reference to Christ, who, although God, was born of a woman. Interestingly, a deeper look at the expression "offspring" reveals that most translations render the word as "seed," as in a child born in the normal manner — it can also literally refer to semen.

Is it possible that these "sons of God" were trying to corrupt the human line (through the daughters of Adam/men) from which the Messiah was to come, and that this was another reason that Noah and his family was spared? As well as their being God-fearing, does the Scripture also suggest that they were untainted genetically by any angelic influence? Genesis 6:9 also says that Noah was perfect in his generations:

> These are the generations of Noah: Noah was a just man and perfect in his generations, and Noah walked with God (Authorized Version).

The first mention of the "generations" of Noah in this passage refers to his family line (Hebrew *toledoth*). The subsequent "perfect in his generations" means that he was without spot or blemish (*tamiym*) in his time or in the generation (*dowr*) in which he lived. The Hebrew word *tamiym* refers to physical, or bodily, perfection, and is the same word that was used for animals of sacrificial purity throughout the Old Testament. Perhaps it was not exclusively referring to Noah's spiritual or moral perfection.[7]

Satan has conspired on several occasions to circumvent God's plan of salvation. At the time of the birth of Christ, Satan tried, through the evil king Herod, to kill all the male babies who were born at the predicted time and city of the birth of Christ. Satan, knowing the Old Testament prophecy in Micah 5:2, knew the time and place (Bethlehem) of the birth of Jesus. Moreover, on several occasions in history, attempts have been made to exterminate the Jewish race.

Taking this view a little further, Hebrews 2:16 (Authorized Version) talks about the act of saving grace of Jesus Christ and reminds us that this did not involve Jesus taking on the form of angels, but human form — as a physical descendant of Abraham:

> For verily he took not on him the nature of angels; but he took on him the seed of Abraham.

There is no salvation for angels once they have rejected God and their heavenly abode. Only the physical descendants of the first Adam can be saved via the death and resurrection of the "last Adam." Some adherents to the angelic view believe that once the human race had been genetically corrupted by angelic seed, they would have fallen outside of God's plan of salvation for the human race (note *Nephilim* = "fallen ones"), since we need to be the literal descendants of Adam (1 Cor. 15:21–22), the first human who brought sin into the world.

If God sent the Flood and destroyed the world because of the extreme wickedness of man *and* because angels raised the intensity of the battle a notch or two, is it possible that fallen angels have "crossed the line" again? Some think that the enormous and increasing UFO/abduction activity we are seeing today is a manifestation of what Jesus foretold — "just as it was in the days of Noah." However, it may just refer to a time when fallen angels increase their deceptive practices upon mankind. The people of Noah's day ignored the warning and perished. They missed the way of escape through the ark of salvation that God provided. Today, God has provided another ark (figuratively) — that is Jesus Christ — for those who believe in His act of saving grace. Times similar to Noah's, Christ said, would be a prelude to His return.

And "after that," the land of the giants

The Authorized Version of Genesis 6:4 gives an important, but puzzling, description of Nephilim and other events before the Flood. The text says "and after that" (some translations say "afterwards"), but what is the order of events?

> There were giants [Nephilim] in the earth in those days; and also after that, when the sons of God came in unto the daughters of men, and they bare children to them, the same became mighty men which were of old, men of renown.

"Afterwards" is often presumed to mean after the Flood and include the mentioning of the Nephilim when the Hebrew nation was about to enter the Promised Land after 400 years of slavery in Egypt (Num. 13:33). This interpretation would be a major blow to the view that God used the Flood to destroy the Nephilim.

Genesis 6:1 refers to a time "when men began to increase in number upon the earth." According to rabbinical (Orthodox Jewish) interpretations of Genesis 6, the Nephilim were so named because they were fallen and caused the world to fall.[8] It gives the impression that these events occurred at a time early in the earth's history when mankind was starting to increase in number, and at this time the sons of God took for themselves *any* women that they wanted.

It should be clearly noted that the Nephilim in this passage *cannot* refer to any people group or human beings who survived the Flood in addition to Noah and his family. Those on the ark were the only human survivors. The term "after that" simply contrasts to an initial time when the sons of God took women and then *had children* by them. The text says so — "and also after that, when . . . they bare children to them. . . ." Simply put, Genesis 6 describes how the sons of God started to take women, and after that, they had children by them.

The fact that only the Noahic line survived the Flood means that the Nephilim in Numbers 13 cannot be descended from a pre-Flood group. But a closer look might reveal why they are mentioned in this passage. Moses, who authored Genesis, was writing for the Jewish nation as it was preparing to enter the Promised Land (the land of Caanan). Prior to entering and doing battle with its inhabitants, Moses sent 12 spies, one from each of the 12 tribes of Israel, on a reconnaissance mission. On their return, in verses 28 and 29, the spies commented that:

> . . . the people be strong that dwell in the land, and the cities are walled, and very great: and moreover we saw the children of Anak there. The Amalekites live in the Negev; the Hittites, Jebusites and Amorites live in the hill country; and the Canaanites live near the sea and along the Jordan (Authorized Version).

And later a fuller explanation is given:

> And they brought up an *evil report* of the land which they had searched unto the children of Israel, saying, "The land, through which we have gone to search it, is a land that eateth up the inhabitants thereof; and all the people that we saw in it are men of a great stature. And there we saw the giants, the sons of Anak, which come of the giants [Nephilim]: and we were in our own sight as grasshoppers, and so we were in their sight" (Num. 13:32–33, Authorized Version, emphasis added).

Most modern translations have replaced the word "giants" and have reverted back to the original "Nephilim" because the expression "giants" is based on tradition or beliefs rather than a literal meaning of the text (see later).

The descendants of Anak (the Anakim/Anakites) were obviously a group of large people. However, in verse 28 the spies also reported that many of the other people in the land were "strong." There are several other passages that refer to the Anakim as a powerful group of people (Deut. 9:2, for example), but verse 33 in Numbers 13 is the only passage that suggests any Anakite relationship to the Nephilim. Once again, it should be remembered that these Anakim were descendants of post-Flood people. They could not be descended from the pre-Flood Nephilim. Chapter 10 of Genesis records the "Table of Nations"; that is, the descendants of Noah's sons, and there is no mention of Anak or the Nephilim, post-Flood.

It should be noted that the spies brought back a bad, or "evil" (Hebrew *dibbah,* "to slander, whisper, or defame") report. That report included a parenthetic insertion that the large people known as the sons of Anak were descended from the Nephilim. The NIV simply puts it as:

> We saw the Nephilim there (the descendants of Anak come from the Nephilim) . . . (Num. 13:33).

At first reading, this may seem like a factual account, but it is part of the quoted false report of the spies. Of the 12 spies, only Joshua and Caleb, trusting God, were keen to enter and take possession of the land; the other 10 did not want to. Because of the false report, the whole nation was too terrified to enter the Promised Land, and they turned against Moses for bringing them there. God responded:

> The LORD said to Moses, "How long will these people treat me with contempt? . . . I will strike them down with a plague and destroy them" (Num. 14:11).

How can we be sure that it was a false report? To start with, God intended to strike down all of the people with a plague for their unbelief, but Moses interceded on their behalf. However, there were some that were not going to escape God's justice. Why? Because they brought back an untruthful report. Numbers 14:36–37 says:

> Now the men whom Moses sent to spy out the land, who returned and made all the congregation complain against him by bringing a bad report of the land, those very men who brought the evil report about the land, died by the plague before the LORD (New King James Version).

Some Christians have actually added to the (false) account of the Nephilim in the Promised Land. They say that during the time that the children of Israel wandered in the desert (38 years), fallen angels were once again cohabiting with women to produce more Nephilim as part of a satanic strategy to prevent the Hebrews entering the land. This is unlikely because, although they encountered the Anakim, they defeated them, as well as many other inhabiting tribes. When they eventually entered the land of Canaan, there was no mention of the Nephilim or encounters with them. Surely, among the descriptions of all the battles that ensued, encounters with Nephilim would have been mentioned if they occurred. And it should be remembered, according to the fallen-angel view, the original angels who stepped out of line in this manner were now in chains in *tartarus*. There is no account of these supposedly post-Flood Nephilim having been destroyed, so where are they today?

The "giant" legend

It seems likely that the real Nephilim of Genesis 6 were given iconic status, in a sense, endorsing the "superhuman" view. In the "evil report," it would appear that the spies gave the descendants of Anak an unwarranted embellishment as to their power by suggesting they were descended from the Nephilim. If the Nephilim were "super beings," as traditional Jewish beliefs subscribe to,[9] it is no wonder that the people were too scared to enter (some claim that the Nephilim "beliefs" are imaginary Jewish legends only).

The expression "the mighty men" in Hebrew is *HaGibborim,* and the rendering in English is a correct analogy of the Hebrew term. The same expression is used for the mighty ruler and hunter Nimrod in Genesis 10, who built the great city of Nineveh, among others. Nimrod is commonly believed to have been the instigator behind the Tower of Babel, and possibly one of the worst offenders in the worship of false deities. The tower was an enormous structure, planned to reach into the sky (or "unto the sky," as many similar structures of ancient Babylon were used as astrological observatories to foster the demonically inspired worship of the stars). Its builders intended it to symbolically usurp God's authority, to be a focal point for humanity's flouting of God's command to disperse across the earth. So God punished the society with a confusion of languages, causing them to disperse anyway. Nimrod's fame was legendary, and he is mentioned elsewhere in Scripture (1 Chron. 1:10). The term "men of renown" comes from the

Hebrew *shem,* which describes men of reputation, well known, famous, or even infamous. So we can glean that the Nephilim were similarly well known by reputation for their deeds. Whoever or whatever they were, they had an influence, and created an impact, on the world.

For example, some Bible versions render the term *Nephilim* as "giants" because some of the words are derived from Greek translations of the Hebrew texts. In this case, the Greek word *gigentes* has been translated into English as giants. But this is not entirely accurate because *gigentes* is the Greek word for "Titans." In Greek legend, the Titans were well known as the giant offspring of Uranus (heaven) and Gaea (Earth), and were regarded as half-human and half-god. The most famous of the Titans was Cronus (whose name is interestingly linked with Nimrod in some legends), who, legend has it, led the Titans in a war against Zeus, the most powerful of all the Olympians and the supreme ruler of all of the gods. Zeus defeated and punished the Titans by banishing them to *tartarus.*

The mention of *tartarus* is noteworthy, and these types of stories are not limited to Jewish and Greek cultures. The Romans had very similar legends — they knew Cronus as Saturn, linked to the planet which bears that name today. (We saw in chapter 8 that various false deities worshiped in the Old Testament were also associated with this planet.) Egyptian and Indian legends abound with similar stories, and different cultures of the world all have tales of god-like visitors coming down and intermarrying with humans. In the same way, stories of the great flood of Noah's time can be found in practically every culture, although distorted from the original.

Some historical evidence?

There are other ancient texts that were not included in the common Protestant Bible, or the Canon of Scripture, as it is known, but were included in the Catholic Bible. These are collectively known as the Apocrypha.[10] Although many in the early church had high regard for these apocryphal books, one of the reasons they were not included in the Bible[11] is that no council of the entire early church favored them. Jesus Christ never once quoted from, or referred to, any of these books, although some of the Bible's authors did. This does not mean that they are not of historical value, though. In a similar way, we can compare, for example, the writings of the historian Josephus, which have been useful for gleaning some extra information about historical events that were contemporary with biblical ones, while at the same time recognizing that they are not "inspired" Scripture ("God-breathed," as Paul described it in 2 Tim. 3:16).

One book of this type is the book of Enoch. Protestants do not regard it as part of the Apocrypha as such (Roman Catholics do), but as belonging to the "wider Apocrypha."[12] Noah's great-grandfather was a man called Enoch. We are told that he was a righteous man who enjoyed a close relationship with God. Genesis 5:24 says:

> Enoch walked with God; then he was no more, because God took him away.

Enoch did not see death because he was raptured or "snatched away" into God's presence. The only explanation from the Scriptures is that "he walked with God" and therefore presumably found special favor with Him.

Although there are no early manuscripts to confirm the historicity of the book of Enoch, in the 18th century, fragments were found in the Dead Sea region dated to around the second century B.C., which predated any known texts of Enoch. This confirms at least that it was not a modern fraud. Despite this, the book of Enoch is regarded as pseudepigraphical, along with the other books of the wider Apocrypha. This means that, although it holds his name, it is thought that Enoch did not write it, though it may contain quotations from him or fragments of his writing. However, it does serve as an example of the beliefs that were held at the time. Interestingly, the Book of Jude (most likely the brother of Jesus) in the New Testament also refers to the book of Enoch. Jude 14–15 says:

> And Enoch also, the seventh from Adam, prophesied of these, saying, Behold, the Lord cometh with ten thousands of his saints, to execute judgment upon all, and to convince all that are ungodly among them of all their ungodly deeds which they have ungodly committed, and of all their hard speeches which ungodly sinners have spoken against him.

This following is a portion of the book of Enoch, chapter 1:9:

> And behold! He cometh with ten thousands of His holy ones to execute judgment upon all, and to destroy all the ungodly: and to convict all flesh of all the works of their ungodliness

which they have ungodly committed, and of all the hard things which ungodly sinners have spoken against Him.

This is an exact rendering of the book of Enoch by Jude, which also demonstrates that it must have been around at the time of the early church, which obviously believed in its historicity, although not its inspiration by God. In the light of this, let's look at the following passages because it will be easy to see why traditional Jewish beliefs included the fallen-angel view of the sons of God of Genesis 6, and why the Nephilim were indeed men of (awful) renown. The book of Enoch is also a prophetic book that closely parallels the biblical texts on many occasions, particularly with regard to the predictions of the flood of Noah's time, and to the "end times" of Revelation. Enoch 6–7 says:

> And it came to pass when the children of men had multiplied that in those days were born unto them beautiful and comely daughters. And the angels, the children of the heaven, saw and lusted after them, and said to one another: "Come, let us choose us wives from among the children of men and beget us children." And Semjaza, who was their leader, said unto them: "I fear ye will not indeed agree to do this deed, and I alone shall have to pay the penalty of a great sin." And they all answered him and said: "Let us all swear an oath, and all bind ourselves by mutual imprecations not to abandon this plan but to do this thing." Then sware they all together and bound themselves by mutual imprecations upon it. And they were in all two hundred; who descended in the days of Jared on the summit of Mount Hermon, and they called it Mount Hermon, because they had sworn and bound themselves by mutual imprecations upon it. And these are the names of their leaders: Samlazaz, their leader, Araklba, Rameel, Kokablel, Tamlel, Ramlel, Danel, Ezeqeel, Baraqijal, Asael, Armaros, Batarel, Ananel, Zaqlel, Samsapeel, Satarel, Turel, Jomjael, Sariel. These are their chiefs of tens.
>
> And all the others together with them took unto themselves wives, and each chose for himself one, and they began to go in unto them and to defile themselves with them, and they taught them charms and enchantments, and the cutting of roots, and made them acquainted with plants. And they became pregnant, and they bare great giants, whose height

was three thousand ells: Who consumed all the acquisitions of men. And when men could no longer sustain them, the giants turned against them and devoured mankind. And they began to sin against birds, and beasts, and reptiles, and fish, and to devour one another's flesh, and drink the blood. Then the earth laid accusation against the lawless ones.

In graphic detail, this describes what the author says was occurring on the earth prior to the time of Noah. It supposedly shows that the Nephilim were ravaging the human race in more ways than one.

It also names more fallen angels than we previously knew of. We have seen the biblically similar name of "Ashtar" appearing as an alien visitor today. Interestingly, the name Semjaza in the book of Enoch is almost identical to Semjase, the alien entity who regularly visited the "ultra famous" Billy Meier over many years. Semjase provided Meier with a "substitute theology" to the Bible. If this is only a brazen allusion, one wonders why Meier would have chosen a name from this little-known religious text. Semjase/Semjaza features abundantly in other UFO literature including the writings of the well-known Steigers.[13]

Also, the evil angels are described as descending from a mountain, in a context similar to the Greek mythological description. Elsewhere in this book, the fallen angels are credited with providing humans with greater technology than they possessed at the time, as well as enchantments (magic spells), which are reminiscent of the occult and paranormal activities that fallen angels today, masquerading as space brothers, teach.

Similarly, the lost book of Jasher (there are no early manuscripts — only later copies), which is referred to in Joshua 10:13 and 2 Samuel 1:18, also describes events like those in the book of Enoch. It also states that the animal kingdom was being defiled by the mixing of animals with one another "to provoke the Lord," and that:

> God saw the whole earth and it was corrupt, for all flesh had corrupted its ways upon earth, all men and all animals (Jasher 4:18).

There are genetic limitations to the natural crossbreeding of different kinds of animals, so I am unsure how this could occur. However, modern technology is overcoming these "natural" boundaries through genetic implantation and enhancement, and these "extra books" suggest that many forms of ungodly practices were being taught to men. We can be sure that the state of the earth was so bad that God found it necessary to destroy it.

We have presented four common views of the identity of the sons of God in Genesis 6, and have investigated the "Nephilim question" with the evidence available. With some, there is little accompanying evidence to support the claims. Other evidence invokes much more discussion and can challenge our rational and traditional thought. Much more could be written, but the conclusion is the same: a long tradition of documents indicates that fallen angels have been deceiving mankind since the beginning of creation.

WHO MADE GOD?

As we discussed in earlier chapters, the evidence of a Creator is all around us. An ordered universe and the complexity of design in living things speaks of an intelligent designer. If one were to find a stone tool in the ground, it could be reasoned that it didn't make itself. It would be evidence of a toolmaker — or intelligence behind its construction. Once again, Romans 1:20 reminds us:

> For since the creation of the world God's invisible quali-
> ties — his eternal power and divine nature — have been clear-
> ly seen, being understood from what has been made, so that
> men are without excuse.

We have discussed the concept of God the Creator in varying sections of this book. But how many people ask, "If God created the universe, then who made God?" In our common experience, everything must have had a beginning. The first law of thermodynamics tells us that the total amount of mass-energy in the universe is constant and hence limited. The second law states that the amount of energy available for work is running out. This is also known as the law of entropy or decay. Most can understand this principle because, like a clock that was wound up at the beginning, the universe is slowly expending all of its available energy and therefore winding down. Genesis 1:1 states:

> In the beginning God created the heavens and the earth.

The universe is now in decay (winding down) so we can under-stand that it had a beginning and hence, a cause. This is an undeniable principle. Every known event or object has a beginning and so has a cause. All science and history rests upon this principle.

1. Everything which has a beginning has a cause.

2. The universe has a beginning.

3. Therefore the universe has a cause.

Einstein's theory of general relativity, which is generally well ac-cepted and has much experimental support, has shown that time is linked to matter and space. Time (as we know it) began with the cre-ation of matter and space. Since God is the Creator of the universe, He is the Creator of time also, meaning that He is not limited by the dimension of time that He created.[14] Therefore, He has no beginning in time and no end in time. Without a beginning, He does not need a cause. The Bible tells us that God inhabits eternity (Isa. 57:15). God simply "is." He is self–existing, and therefore He doesn't have a cause. He describes himself as "I AM THAT I AM" (Exod. 3:14). As finite beings linked to the dimension of our existing time and space, we find this difficult to understand (see later).

But put it this way: before the beginning of the universe — there was God. Well-known Christian apologist Ken Ham writes:

> By definition, an infinite, eternal being has always existed — no one created God. He is the self-existing one — the great "I am" of the Bible. He is outside of time — in fact, He cre-ated time.
>
> You might say, "But that means I have to accept this by faith, as I can't understand it."
>
> We read in the Book of Hebrews, "But without faith it is impossible to please him: for he that cometh to God must believe that he is, and that he is a rewarder of them that dili-gently seek him" (Heb. 11:6).
>
> But this is not blind faith, as some think. In fact, evolu-tionists who deny God have a blind faith — they have to be-lieve in something that is against real experimental observable science — namely, that information can arise from disorder by chance.[15]

AN INTERDIMENSIONAL CREATOR?

In trying to understand God, who is outside of our time and space, but can interact within them, let us try to imagine a land of two dimensions called Flatland (represented by ABCD in figure 1). It has length and breadth but no height. It is inhabited by intelligent beings shown as triangles inside circles. These beings are also two-dimensional.

One day the Flatlanders awoke to discover that someone unknown had drawn a line across their land which effectively divided their country in two. Because they lacked the dimension of height, no one could jump over or go under the line. It became an event horizon for them because their existence would be limited by the new line or boundary. They would be unable to communicate with beings on the other side.

Then the next day a footprint appeared in the area ABFE (figure 2) spontaneously and without cause (as far as the Flatlanders were concerned). Then the shape disappeared. So the next time it appeared the Flatlanders drew a circle around it to secure it (figure 3). Because they were two-dimensional beings, they created an event horizon around the footprint, thinking that nothing could get in or out. However, when they removed the circle, the footprint had disappeared. The Flatlanders had a threefold situation to deal with.

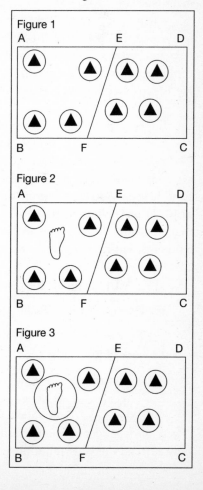

Figure 1

Figure 2

Figure 3

1. The shape seemed to appear and disappear without cause.

2. The shape was not limited to, or impeded by, an event horizon.

3. The same event horizon completely blocked the Flatlanders.

The solution to their problem was provided by a character called Dr. Zweisteinus. He explained to the Flatlanders that they were limited in their understanding due to their materialistic experience of the two dimensions in which they existed. He went on to explain to them that Flatland was not the only reality and there were other truths — a third dimension besides the two that they knew of. This third dimension was called "depth or height."

The three-dimensional being that made the foot shape could enter and exit the two-dimensional prison (or event horizon) at will and without even being observed by the Flatlanders. This is because it was not limited to the same barriers as the two-dimensional Flatlanders.[16] Two dimensions cannot accommodate anything possessing three dimensions.[17]

When God created, he had the ability (and power) to pass information for the creation of the universe across the "event horizon" that separates space-time from eternity. Similarly, the resurrected Christ could appear to His disciples in the locked room and disappear again. He is capable of crossing the "event horizon" that prevents us from performing the same action.

This concept has vast implications for our study into the UFO phenomenon, as we have correctly identified these beings as creations of God existing in another dimension but occasionally entering into ours.

One should be careful, though, about extending the concept of extra dimensions too far. Some use this "Flatland" idea to invoke as many as 10, 11 or 12 dimensions in such hypotheses as "string theories," and that somehow this confirms the Bible. There is no biblical (and very tenuous scientific) support for these concepts.

WHY IS THE UNIVERSE SO BIG?

The Psalmist wrote in Psalm 19:1:

> The heavens declare the glory of God; the skies proclaim the work of his hands.

There was a time when most people would look at the sky and find it difficult to believe there *wasn't* a God. Even with the naked eye from the earth, the night sky is an awesome sight. It can have a profound effect, as we ponder our puny existence in this universe. Yet we can see only a fraction of what is out there.

In demonstration of his awesomeness, God spoke to Abraham, the father of the Jewish people.

> He took him outside and said, "Look up at the heavens and count the stars — if indeed you can count them." Then he said to him, "So shall your offspring be" (Gen. 15:5).

God made a promise to Abraham about his descendants. They would be great in number, but how great?[18] It is doubtful that Abraham would have ever taken the time to count the number of stars in the sky — who has? It is estimated that the number of stars visible to the naked eye from Earth is around 10,000. But God said to Abraham, "If indeed you can count them." Later, God repeats his promise and adds more information:

> I will surely bless you and make your descendants as numerous as the stars in the sky and as the sand on the seashore (Gen. 22:17).

With this illustration, Abraham could really appreciate what the Creator was talking about. God was equating the number of stars with the grains of sand on the seashore. In other words, the number of stars was so vast as to be virtually countless.

When talking to the prophet Jeremiah, God made the same point, very clearly:

> I will make the descendants of David my servant and the Levites who minister before me as countless as the stars of the sky and as measureless as the sand on the seashore (Jer. 33:22).

Jeremiah must have been baffled by what God was saying. In his day, prior to the advent of the telescope, the stars could certainly be counted. Recent astronomical discoveries have confirmed that indeed the number of stars in the universe is effectively countless, and can well be equated with the innumerable grains of sand on the world's seashores.

Such discoveries not only confirm the accuracy of the Bible, they serve to increase our awe and wonder at this enormous and incredible universe. There are literally dozens of Bible verses that refer to the heavens and the stars, and which claim that these give glory to God their Creator. Sadly, modern evolutionary cosmology has sought to rob God of the credit that is His due.

Right there in that ancient book — the Bible — God, who is eternal, all knowing, and all powerful, is the "super-intelligence" that relayed information to the mortal authors. This information did not come from advanced aliens. How could any supposed extraterrestrials predict the future? God's promises to Abraham were about the future and Abraham's descendants, all of which are true and are still being fulfilled today.

In man's naturalistic thinking, the bigger the universe seems to be, the less likely it is that God may have created it. However, what is the "right size" in man's thinking, particularly when we haven't even traveled outside of our own solar system? How would we know? If we are honest, we know very little about the universe at all. In fact, the more we seem to discover, the stranger it appears to be. If the universe was a much smaller size — something that man could comprehend — then, conversely, man would likely say, "God's not that great, is He?"

Many people question why the universe is so big. Why are there so many billions of galaxies, containing countless stars, and most of them we cannot even see? But shouldn't that serve to increase our awe and wonder at God's creative power, the more we discover? And although the universe is incomprehensibly and impressively large, nothing is big to Him. In fact, stars are rather simple structures — they have been described as glowing balls of gas. In a thousand galaxies, each containing thousands of stars, there is less structural complexity than in the DNA of a simple organism. For example, it would require more creative input to create the organic structure of even a dead fish than it would to create countless quasars. This is exactly what Jesus did when He miraculously fed five thousand people with a few loaves and fishes, thus demonstrating His creative power. This was miraculous in Jesus' day, but it seems even more incredible today due to our modern discoveries and understanding of DNA.

Christian theologian John Whitcomb wrote:

> It must be recognized that . . . it required no more exertion of energy for God to create a trillion galaxies than to create one planet.[19]

Isaiah 40:28 says:

> Do you not know? Have you not heard? The Lord is the everlasting God, the Creator of the ends of the earth. He will

not grow tired or weary, and his understanding no one can fathom.

God tells us over and over in the Bible that He created an enormous universe through analogous expressions like the ones he made to Abraham earlier about stars. As human beings we often try to judge the size and the reasons behind the universe with our own limited understanding. However, we are inhibited by our understanding of the time and space in which we exist — that is, the universe which God actually created. This is our only frame of reference. For example, how big is God? Before the universe was created there was no physical realm; no matter (atoms) or space to measure anything by. God was, and is, outside of this realm but He has created it. Size is only relative to us as inhabitants of this universe. Size is not an issue for God. He exists in eternity where there is no time and space. The universe is not big for, or compared to, God— it is, in fact, futile to try to compare the two, as they are incomparable.

God put stars in the heavens, not only for His glory, but, incredibly, for mankind whom He loves. Genesis 1:14 states:

> And God said, Let there be lights in the firmament of the heaven to divide the day from the night; and let them be for signs, and for seasons, and for days, and years. . . .

For hundreds of years, the reliable signs in the sky have proved invaluable for man. In all of his awesome wonder, God loves His creation; fallen though it is and ruined by sin, He loves you and me. He knows all of the stars by name, and yours and mine, too!

> He determines the number of the stars and calls them each by name (Ps. 147:4).

The Scriptures say:

> When I consider your heavens, the work of your fingers, the moon and the stars, which you have set in place, what is man that you are mindful of him, the son of man that you care for him? You made him a little lower than the heavenly beings and crowned him with glory and honor. You made him ruler over the works of your hands; you put everything under his feet: all flocks and herds, and the beasts of the field, the birds of the air, and the fish of the sea, all that swim the paths of the

seas. O Lord, our Lord, how majestic is your name in all the earth! (Ps. 8:3–9).

Endnotes

1 Professor of natural philosophy in the Australian Centre for Astrobiology at Macquarie University, Sydney, Australia.

2 Radio interview cited in R. Stannard, *Science and Wonders: Conversations About Science and Belief* (London: Faber & Faber Limited, 2002), p. 45, cited in *TJ* 16(2):52, 2002.

3 Based on a study by Messianic Jewish writer Bill Bockleman, "Who are the 'sons of God' of Genesis 6?" April 2000.

4 Henry Morris, *The Genesis Record* (Grand Rapids, MI: Baker Book House, 1988), p. 164–175.

5 So say Targum of Onkelos, Targum of Jonathan Ben Uzziel, Kimchi, Rashi, Jerome, Maimonides and the Commentary on the Mishnah according to "Return of the Aliens? As the Days of Noah Were," <www.khouse.org/article.phtml?article_code=43>, December 10, 2002.

6 "Mischievous Angels or Sethites?" <www.khouse.org.article.phtml?article_code=110>, December 10, 2002.

7 "The Sons of God," <www.aristotle.net/~bhuie/gen6sons.htm>, September 30, 2003.

8 Based on Bockleman, "Who are the 'sons of God' of Genesis 6?"

9 For example, Josephus, *The Antiquities of the Jews*, book 1, ch.3; Philo of Alexandria (1st century A.D.), *The Works of Philo*, p. 152; *The Book of Jubilees*, ch.5, vs. 1; *The Ante-Nicene Fathers "Justin Martyr — 2nd Century,"* vol.1, p. 363, *"The Instructions of Commodianus — 3rd Century,"* vol. 4, p. 435.

10 A collection of 14 books written after the last book of the Hebrew Scriptures (Old Testament) and before the first book of the Christian Scriptures (New Testament). It is accepted by the Roman Catholic Church as part of the inspired canon of the Bible, but is rejected by most Protestant denominations. Source: <www.religioustolerance.org/gl_a1.htm>, November 8, 2003.

11 They were included in the Bible of the early church — the Vulgate. Protestants removed them at the Reformation on the grounds that they were not in the Hebrew Canon, only in the Greek Septuagint.

12 Norman L. Geisler and William E. Nix, *A General Introduction to the Bible* (Chicago, IL: Moody Press, 1986).

13 William T. Alnor, *UFOs in the New Age* (Grand Rapids, MI: Baker Book House, 1992), p. 29–30.

14 "If God Created the Universe, Then Who Created God?" <www.answersingenesis.org/docs/3791.asp>, September 15, 2003.

15 "How Would You Answer?" <www.answersingenesis.org/docs/3270.asp#r16>, March 13, 2003.

16 "The Gospel in Time and Space," <www.answersingenesis.org/creation/v21/i2/gospel.asp?Vprint=1>, November 18, 2003.

17 The concepts of Flatland, event horizons, and extra dimensions come from a 1987 book, *The Scientific Alternative to Neo-Darwinian Theory*, by the brilliant creation scientist, the late professor, Dr. A.E. Wilder-Smith. He had three earned doctorates and was a master of seven languages. The notion of Flatland was first promoted in an 1884 book by Edwin Abbott, called *Flatland: A Romance of Many Dimensions*.

18 God later sent Jesus Christ (the Creator made flesh, one of Abraham's lineage) as atonement for sin, to rescue those of the human race who would accept this sacrifice by faith.

19 John Whitcomb, *The Bible and Astronomy* (Winona Lake, IN: BMH Books, 1984), p. 28.

Recommended Resources

STARS AND THEIR PURPOSE
Dr. Werner Gitt

This book deals with questions such as:

- What are the origins of the universe?
- How big is it?
- Is its existence a coincidence or does it have predestined design?
- What are stars and why do they exist?
- What about our own solar system and its planets?

(Bielefield, Germany: Christliche Literatur-Verbreitung, 1996)
(high school–adult) 217 pages

THE PUZZLE OF ANCIENT MAN
Dr. Donald E. Chittick

- What about amazing technologies from past cultures?
- Was ancient man primitive according to the popular view, or did he have outside help?
- What does the evidence left behind from past cultures tell us?

Dr. Chittick examines what the facts say about ancient man — facts that have long gone unnoticed by today's secular media.

(Newberg, OR: Creation Compass, 1998)
(high school–adult) 80 pages

STARLIGHT AND TIME
Dr. Russell Humphreys

Using Einstein's principles of general relativity in discussing the theoretical models of how our universe came to be, this book offers a fresh scientific solution to the problem of how we can see stars that are billions of light-years away in a young universe.

(Green Forest, AR: Master Books, 1994)
(high school–adult) 133 pages

THE (UPDATED & EXPANDED) ANSWERS BOOK
Dr. Don Batten, Ken Ham, Dr. Jonathan Sarfati, and Dr. Carl Wieland

Answers 20 commonly asked questions:

- Does God exist?
- Did God really take six days?
- What about carbon-14 dating?
- How can we see distant starlight in a young universe?
- How did bad things come about?
- Who was Cain's wife?
- Who were the "sons of God" and the "nephilim" . . . extra-terrestrials?
- Was Noah's flood global?
- What about continental drift?
- How could all the animals fit on Noah's ark?
- Where are all the human fossils?
- Were there really ice ages?
- How did the different races arise?
- What happened to the dinosaurs?

(Green Forest, AR: Master Books, 2000)
(high school–adult) 265 pages

THE GENESIS FILES
Dr. Carl Wieland, editor

Meet 25 modern-day Ph.D. scientists — specialists in their fields from a wide range of disciplines — who give their reasons for believing in a six-day recent creation. Includes many photos in full color.

(Green Forest, AR: Master Books, 2004)
(high school–adult) 105 pages

REFUTING EVOLUTION
Dr. Jonathan Sarfati

Refuting Evolution is a hard-hitting critique of the most up-to-date arguments for evolution, to challenge educators, students, and parents. It is a powerful yet concise summary of the arguments in the evolution/creation debate. It will stimulate much discussion and help students and teachers think more critically about origins. This top-selling book has over 350,000 copies in print.

(Green Forest, AR: Master Books, 1999)
(high school–adult) 176 pages

REFUTING COMPROMISE
Dr. Jonathan Sarfati

Can Genesis be taken literally? Is it scientifically valid? With his usual brilliant clarity, Jonathan Sarfati, author of the best-selling *Refuting Evolution* (Vol. 1 and 2), has produced a comprehensive and detailed account of "conflicts" between science and the Bible's account of origins. The most powerful defense of a straightforward scientific view of Genesis creation ever written.

(Green Forest, AR: Master Books, 2004)
(high school–adult) 425 pages

IN THE BEGINNING WAS INFORMATION
Dr. Werner Gitt

All life is built upon the information written on the DNA molecule of all living organisms. But how did it get there? This book discusses the origin of life and its complexity from the viewpoint of information science.

(Bielefield, Germany: Christliche Literatur-Verbreitung, 1997)
(high school–adult) 256 pages

For more information, contact one of the Answers in Genesis ministries below. Answers in Genesis ministries are evangelical, Christ-centered, non-denominational, and non-profit.

Answers in Genesis
P.O. Box 6330
Florence, KY 41022
USA

Answers in Genesis
P.O. Box 6302
Acacia Ridge DC
QLD 4110
Australia

Answers in Genesis
5-420 Erb St. West
Suite 213
Waterloo, Ontario
Canada N2L 6K6

Answers in Genesis
P.O. Box 39005
Howick, Auckland
New Zealand

Answers in Genesis
P.O. Box 5262
Leicester LE2 3XU
United Kingdom

Answers in Genesis
Attn: Nao Hanada
3317-23 Nagaoka, Ibaraki-machi
Higashi-ibaraki-gun
Ibaraki-ken 311-3116
Japan

In addition, you may contact:

Institute for Creation Research
P.O. Box 2667
El Cajon, CA 92021